TAKING SIDES

Clashing Views
on Controversial Issues
in American History

Volume II
Reconstruction to the Present

4th edition

Clashing Views
on Controversial Issues
in American History
Volume II
Reconstruction to the Present

4th edition

Edited, Selected, and with Introductions by

Larry Madaras
Howard Community College

and

James M. SoRelle
Baylor University

The Dushkin Publishing Group, Inc.

To Eugene Kuzirian (1939–1987),
coeditor of the first two editions of
Taking Sides: Clashing Views on
Controversial Issues in American
History, *whose devotion to good*
teaching and critical thinking still
permeates this text

Library of Congress Catalog Card Number:
90-84857
Manufactured in the United States of America
Fourth Edition, First Printing
ISBN: 0-87967-935-2

 Printed on Recycled Paper

The Dushkin Publishing Group, Inc.
Sluice Dock, Guilford, CT 06437

PREFACE

The success of the past three editions of *Taking Sides: Clashing Views on Controversial Issues in American History* has encouraged us to remain faithful to its original objectives, methods, and format. Our aim has been to create an effective instrument to enhance classroom learning and to foster critical thinking. Historical facts presented in a vacuum are of little value to the educational process. For students, whose search for historical truth often concentrates on *when* something happened rather than on *why*, and on specific events rather than on the *significance* of those events, *Taking Sides* is designed to offer an interesting and valuable departure. The understanding that the reader arrives at based on the evidence that emerges from the clash of views encourages the reader to view history as an *interpretive* discipline, not one of rote memorization.

As in previous editions, the issues are arranged in chronological order and can be easily incorporated into any American history survey course. Each issue has an issue *introduction*, which sets the stage for the debate that follows in the pro and con selections and provides historical and methodological background to the problem that the issue examines. Each issue concludes with a *postscript*, which ties the readings together, briefly mentions alternative interpretations, and supplies detailed *suggestions for further reading* for the student who wishes to pursue the topics raised in the issue.

Changes to this edition In this edition we have continued our efforts to move beyond the traditionally ethnocentric and male-oriented focus of American history, both in terms of the issues and the authors selected to represent the clashing viewpoints. This edition depicts a society that benefited from the presence of Native Americans, African Americans, and women of various racial and ethnic origins. In this edition there are five entirely new issues: *Reconstruction: Could It Have Given Blacks Full Equality?* (Issue 1); *Were Nineteenth-Century Entrepreneurs Robber Barons?* (Issue 2); *Did Booker T. Washington's Philosophy and Actions Betray the Interests of African Americans?* (Issue 7); *Was Early Twentieth-Century American Foreign Policy in the Caribbean Basin Dominated by Economic Concerns?* (Issue 9); and *Was It Necessary to Drop the Atomic Bomb to End World War II?* (Issue 13). In addition, in the issues on Populists (Issue 5) and on the New Deal (Issue 12), one reading was changed to retain a fresh perspective. In all, there are 11 new readings included in this edition.

Supplements An *Instructor's Manual with Test Questions* (multiple-choice and essay) is available through the publisher for the instructor using *Taking Sides* in the classroom. And a general guidebook, which discusses methods and techniques for integrating the pro-con approach into any classroom setting, is also available.

i

Acknowledgments Many individuals have contributed to the successful completion of this edition. We appreciate the evaluations submitted to the Dushkin Publishing Group by those who have used *Taking Sides* in the classroom. Special thanks to those who responded with specific suggestions for this fourth edition:

William Dionisio
Sacramento City College

Nancy Zens
Central Oregon Community
    College

James H. Hitchman
Western Washington University

Jack Devine
Stockton State College

We particularly are indebted to Maggie Cullen, Cindy SoRelle, Barry A. Crouch, Virginia Kirk, Helen Mitchell, and Jean Soto, who shared their ideas for changes, pointed us toward potentially useful historical works, and provided significant editorial assistance. Finally, Lynnette Geary (Baylor University) and Marsha Madigan (Howard Community College) performed the indispensable typing duties connected with this project.

James M. SoRelle
Baylor University

Larry Madaras
Howard Community College

CONTENTS IN BRIEF

CONTENTS

Professor of history Eric Foner believes that, although Reconstruction was nonrevolutionary and conservative, it was a splendid failure because it offered blacks a temporary vision of a free society. Professor of history C. Vann Woodward argues that there was very little hope that African Americans would receive their basic freedoms when we compare our Reconstruction with the treatment accorded slaves in other societies, as well as the failure of our own land distribution policies toward poor whites and Native Americans.

Professor of history John Tipple characterizes big businessmen of the late nineteenth century as destructive forces whose power and greed undermined the nation's traditional institutions and values. Professor of business history Alfred D. Chandler, Jr., concludes that American entrepreneurs were organizational and marketing innovators whose creation of great industrial corporations strengthened the country's economy by sparking the growth of a national urban market.

Associate professor of history Leon Fink, though stopping short of a frontal attack on capitalism, argues that the Knights of Labor envisioned a kind of workingman's democracy that would ensure minimal standards of health and safety at the industrial workplace. Professor of history Carl N. Degler maintains that the American labor movement accepted capitalism and reacted conservatively to the radical organizational changes brought about in the economic system by big business.

Pulitzer Prize-winning historian Oscar Handlin argues that the immigrants were alienated from their Old World cultures as they adjusted to an unfamiliar and hostile environment. Associate professor of history John Bodnar maintains that various immigrant groups retained, modified, and transformed their Old World cultures in response to urban/industrial America in the years between 1880 and 1920.

Professor of history Norman Pollack views Populism as a genuinely radical movement that intended to establish industrial democracy in the United States through the promotion of human rights. Professor of history Richard Hofstadter focuses upon the nostalgic, reactionary nature of the Populists, whose attitudes revealed a desire to create a rural utopia by using the early nineteenth-century United States as their model.

Professor of political science and political economy Ernest S. Griffith focuses upon illegal and unethical operations of the political machine and concludes that the governments controlled by the bosses represented a betrayal of the public trust. Professor of history Jon C. Teaford argues that scholars traditionally have overlooked the remarkable success municipal governments in the late nineteenth century achieved in dealing with the challenges presented by rapid urbanization.

W. E. B. Du Bois, a founding member of the National Organization for the Advancement of Colored People, argues that Booker T. Washington became an apologist for racial injustice in America by failing to articulate the legitimate demands of African Americans for full civil and political rights. Professor of history Louis R. Harlan portrays Washington as a political realist who had the same long-range goals of progress toward equality as his black critics and whose policies and actions were designed to benefit black society as a whole.

Professor of history Richard M. Abrams maintains that progressivism was a failure because it tried to impose a uniform set of values upon a culturally diverse people and never seriously confronted the inequalities which still exist in American society. Professors of history Arthur S. Link and Richard L. McCormick argue that the progressives were a diverse group of reformers who confronted and ameliorated the worst abuses that emerged in urban industrial America during the early 1900s.

Professor of history Walter LaFeber argues that the United States developed a foreign policy which deliberately made the Caribbean nations its economic dependents from the early nineteenth century on. Professor of history David Healy maintains that the two basic goals of American foreign policy in the Caribbean were to provide security against the German threat and to develop the economies of the Latin American nations, whose peoples were considered to be racially inferior.

Former diplomat and historian George F. Kennan believes that former president Wilson was an impractical idealist who led America into the right war for the wrong reasons. Historian D. F. Trask argues that Wilson developed realistic and clearly articulated war goals and coordinated his larger diplomatic aims with the use of force better than any other wartime American president.

Professor of history Lois W. Banner concludes that, following the ratification of the Nineteenth Amendment, antifeminist trends and a lack of unity among women's organizations combined to hinder further progress on women's issues in the 1920s. Professor of history Ann Firor Scott insists that the suffrage victory produced a heightened interest in further social and political reform, which inspired Southern women to pursue these goals throughout the 1920s.

Professor of history William E. Leuchtenburg contends that the New Deal extended the power of the national government in order to humanize the worst features of American capitalism. N. V. Sivachev, former director of the Department of Modern and Contemporary History at Moscow State University, criticizes the Roosevelt administration for adopting bourgeois socioeconomic policies that benefited industrial and agricultural capitalists ("state monopolism") while stifling legitimate social protest.

Professor of history McGeorge Bundy maintains that President Truman wisely dropped the atomic bomb in order to end the war as quickly as possible. Professor of history Martin J. Sherwin argues that American policy makers ruled out other options and dropped the atomic bomb, an understandable but unnecessary act.

Professor of history Stephen E. Ambrose maintains that Eisenhower was a greater president than his predecessors and successors because he balanced the budget, stopped inflation, and kept the peace. Professor of the humanities Arthur M. Schlesinger, Jr., argues that Eisenhower failed as a president because he refused to tackle the moral and environmental issues at home and because he established a foreign policy which relied on covert CIA activities and threats of nuclear arms.

Professor of political science Guenter Lewy believes that the South Vietnamese government might not have lost the war if the United States had followed "a strategy of surprise and massed strength at decisive points" against North Vietnam. Professor of history George C. Herring argues that the policy makers exaggerated the strategic importance of Vietnam and deluded themselves about America's power.

Professor of history August Meier depicts King as a "conservative militant" whose ability to communicate black aspirations to whites and to serve as a bridge between the radical and conservative wings of the civil rights movement made him the critical link in the chain of nonviolent direct action campaigns of the 1960s. Associate professor of history Clayborne Carson concludes that the civil rights struggle would have followed a similar course of development even had King never lived because its successes depended upon mass activism, not the actions of a single leader.

Professor of history Paul Kennedy believes that the United States, like other great nations before it, has declined in power because of its excessive military commitments, its huge federal deficit, and its decreasing share of global production. Professor of internal relations Susan Strange maintains that the United States still possesses the structural power to reshape the global political economy through its military strength, financial clout, control over world knowledge, and production of goods and services.

INTRODUCTION

The Study of History

James M. SoRelle
Larry Madaras

In a pluralistic society such as ours, the study of history is bound to be a complex process. How an event is interpreted depends not only on the existing evidence but also on the perspective of the interpretor. Consequently, understanding history presupposes the evaluation of information, a task that often leads to conflicting conclusions. An understanding of history, then, requires the acceptance of historical relativism. Relativism means that redefinition of our past is always possible and desirable. History shifts, changes, and grows with new and different evidence and interpretations. As is the case with the law and even medicine, beliefs that were unquestioned one or two hundred years ago have been discredited or discarded since.

Relativism, then, encourages revisionism. There is a maxim that "the past must remain useful to the present." Historian Carl Becker argued that every generation should examine history for itself, thus assuring constant scrutiny of our collective experience through new perspectives. History, consequently, does not remain static, in part because historians cannot avoid being influenced by the times in which they live. Almost all historians commit themselves to revising the views of other historians, synthesizing theories into macrointerpretations, or revising the revisionists.

SCHOOLS OF THOUGHT

Four predominant schools of thought have emerged in American history since the first graduate seminars in history were given at The Johns Hopkins University in Baltimore in the 1870s. The *progressive* school dominated the professional field in the first half of the twentieth century. Influenced by the reform currents of Populism, Progressivism, and the New Deal, these historians explored the social and economic forces that energized America. The progressive scholars tended to view the past in terms of conflicts between groups, and they sympathized with the underdog.

The post–World War II period witnessed the emergence of a new group of historians who viewed the conflict thesis as overly simplistic. Writing against the backdrop of the Cold War, these *neoconservative* or *consensus* historians argued that Americans possess a shared set of values and that the areas of agreement within our nation's basic democratic and capitalistic framework were more important than the areas of disagreement.

In the 1960s, however, the civil rights movement, women's liberation, and the student rebellion (with its condemnation of the war in Vietnam) fragmented the consensus of values upon which historians and social scientists of the 1950s centered their interpretations. This turmoil set the stage for the emergence of another group of scholars. *New Left* historians began to reinterpret the past once again. They emphasized the significance of conflict in American history and they resurrected interest in those groups ignored by the consensus school. In addition, New Left scholars critiqued the expansionist policies of the United States and emphasized the difficulties confronted by Native Americans, African Americans, women, and urban workers in gaining full citizenship status.

Progressive, consensus, and New Left history is still being written. The most recent generation of scholars, however, focuses upon social history. Their primary concern is to discover what the lives of "ordinary Americans" were really like. These new social historians employ previously overlooked court and church documents, house deeds and tax records, letters and diaries, photographs, and census data to reconstruct the everyday lives of average Americans. Some employ new methodologies such as quantification (enhanced by advancing computer technology) and oral history, while others borrow from the disciplines of political science, economics, sociology, anthropology, and psychology for their historical investigations.

The proliferation of historical approaches, which are reflected in the issues debated in this book, has had mixed results. On the one hand, historians have become so specialized in their respective time periods and methodological styles that it is difficult to synthesize the recent scholarship into a comprehensive text for the general reader. On the other hand, historians know more about the American past than at any other time in history. They dare to ask new questions or ones that previously were considered to be germane only to scholars in other social sciences. Although there is little agreement about the answers to these questions, the methods employed and issues explored make the "new history" a very exciting field to study.

The topics that follow represent a variety of perspectives and approaches. Each of these controversial issues can be studied for its individual importance to American history. Taken as a group, they interact with one another to illustrate larger historical themes. When grouped thematically, the issues reveal continuing motifs in the development of American history.

ECONOMIC QUESTIONS

Issues 2, 3, and 17 explore the dynamics of the modern American economy through investigations of the nineteenth-century entrepreneurs, labor organizations, and the status of modern American capitalism, respectively. Issue 2 evaluates the contributions of post–Civil War entrepreneurial giants. Were these industrial leaders "robber barons," as portrayed by contemporary critics and many history texts? John Tipple believes that industrialists like Cornelius Vanderbilt and John D. Rockefeller undermined American institutions and individualistic values by rendering them impotent in face of their pursuit of wealth. In contrast, Alfred D. Chandler, Jr., characterizes those businessmen as organizational and marketing innovators who created huge corporations that stimulated the rise of a national urban economy.

The majority of modern-day historians argue that the American labor movement traditionally has been more conservative than its European counterpart. According to Carl N. Degler in Issue 3, American workers accepted capitalism and reacted conservatively to changes in the nation's economic system that were brought about by the rise of big business. Leon Fink disagrees. Through an examination of the Knights of Labor, Fink argues that this union envisioned a kind of workingman's democracy that would bring about minimal standards of health and safety in the industrial workplace.

POLITICAL REFORMS AND THE STATUS QUO

Populism, progressivism, and the New Deal represent the three major reform currents of the past one hundred years. In Issue 5, Richard Hofstadter evaluates the Populist movement in a negative light by portraying the farmers as reactionaries and bigots whose protest stemmed from their inability to cope with their loss of status in a rapidly industrializing society. Much more sympathetic to the farmers' movement is Norman Pollack, who sees Populism as a genuinely radical movement which sought to institute industrial democracy in the United States.

Issue 6 assesses the nature of urban government in the late nineteenth century. Ernest S. Griffith views these governments as conspicuous failures because they were unable to cope effectively with the numerous problems associated with the evolution of the industrial city. Jon C. Teaford takes a more positive look at the late nineteenth-century city.

In the view of Arthur S. Link and Richard L. McCormick, "progressivism was the way in which a whole generation of Americans defined themselves politically." In Issue 8, they revive a sympathetic interpretation of the Progressive Era by concluding that a diverse group of reformers confronted and ameliorated the worst of the abuses that emerged in urban America during the early 1900s. In contrast, Richard M. Abrams believes that progressivism accomplished little of value.

The Great Depression of the 1930s remains one of the most traumatic events in U.S. history. The characteristics of that decade are deeply etched in American folk memory, but the remedies that were applied to these social and economic ills—known collectively as the New Deal—are not easy to evaluate. In Issue 12, William E. Leuchtenburg contends that the New Deal extended the power of the national government in order to humanize the worst features of American capitalism. N. V. Sivachev believes that, although the masses forced the Roosevelt administration to enact some welfare measures, a business-oriented system of state socialism controlled the government and produced little of benefit in the face of the economic crisis.

The perspective gained by the passage of time often causes us to reevaluate the achievements and failures of a given individual. Such is the case with Dwight David Eisenhower, president of the United States from 1953 to 1961. In Issue 14, Stephen E. Ambrose maintains that Eisenhower was a greater president than his predecessors and successors because he balanced the budget, stopped inflation, and kept the peace. Arthur M. Schlesinger, Jr., however, argues that Eisenhower failed as a president in terms of both domestic and foreign policy.

THE OUTSIDERS: BLACKS, IMMIGRANTS, AND WOMEN

Perhaps no period of American history has been subjected to more myths than the Reconstruction Era. It has been only within the past 25 years that the older, pro-Southern interpretation has been revised in high school and college texts. This view began to change during the 1960s when, in the midst of the civil rights struggle, scholars significantly revised the negative portrayal of Reconstruction. In Issue 1, Eric Foner takes a more optimistic view than many of the postrevisionist writings of the 1980s. Although it was nonrevolutionary and conservative, says Foner, Reconstruction was a splendid failure because it offered blacks at least a temporary vision of a free society. But C. Vann Woodward, the dean of Southern historians, believes that there was little hope that Reconstruction could have succeeded.

One of the most controversial figures in American history was the early twentieth-century African American leader Booker T. Washington. Was Washington an "Uncle Tom" whose acceptance of political disfranchisement and social segregation took away the basic freedoms that African Americans earned after their emancipation from slavery? In Issue 7, W. E. B. Du Bois, the most important black intellectual and social critic of the twentieth century, argues the case against Washington, but Louis R. Harlan maintains that there were two Washingtons. Harlan argues that Booker T. Washington, while publicly assuring whites that he accepted segregation, fought active and bitter battles behind the scenes to advance the political, economic, and educational opportunities for African Americans. Washington, then, was a political realist whose long-range goals of progress toward equality was a practical response to the climate of the times in which he lived.

Issue 16 discusses the role of Martin Luther King, Jr., in the civil rights struggles of the 1950s and 1960s. Did the civil rights movement depend on King's leadership for its success? In a penetrating analysis first published in 1965, August Meier describes King as the crucial figure in the nonviolent direct action campaigns of the 1960s. Clayborne Carson, on the other hand, reflects the views of many younger black scholars who themselves were participants in the battle for black equality. Carson argues that the successes in this struggle depended upon mass activism, not the actions of a single leader.

Massive immigration to the United States in the late nineteenth and early twentieth centuries introduced widespread changes in American society.

Moreover, the presence of increasing numbers of immigrants from southern and eastern Europe, many of them Catholics and Jews, seemed to threaten native-born citizens, most of whom were Protestant and of northern and western European ancestry. Asian immigrants, mainly from China or Japan, added to nativist fears. In Issue 4, Oscar Handlin argues that the immigrants were alienated from their Old World cultures as they adjusted to an unfamiliar and often hostile environment. John Bodnar, on the other hand, shows how various immigrant groups from southern and eastern Europe retained, modified, and at times transformed their Old World cultures in response to the urban and industrial setting of the United States.

In the past two decades, scholars have devoted considerable attention to the field of women's history. Issue 11 asks the very important question *Did the Women's Movement Die in the 1920s?* In the first selection, Lois W. Banner answers "yes." Women focused so much of their energy on obtaining the vote, says Banner, that they were unable to agree on the next objective. Anne Firor Scott reaches a different conclusion in her study of Southern women in the "Jazz Age."

THE UNITED STATES AND THE WORLD

Modern American foreign policy has undergone dramatic, if not revolutionary, changes during the past half-century. Most students probably are not aware of how militant U.S. policy toward Central America was in the early 1900s. In Issue 9, David Healy argues that the two goals of American policy in the Caribbean were to provide security against the German threat and to develop the economies of the racially inferior Latin Americans. Writing from a New Left viewpoint, Professor Walter LaFeber excoriates the American foreign policy, which deliberately transformed the Caribbean nations into the economic dependents of the United States.

American intervention in World War I raises two significant questions in Issue 10. Why did America intervene on the side of Great Britain and France? Did President Woodrow Wilson use sound judgment in expanding his powers as commander in chief? George F. Kennan indicts U.S. foreign policy in general and Wilson's actions in particular. Wilson, says Kennan, was an impractical idealist who led America into the right war for the wrong reasons. In contrast, D. F. Trask argues that Wilson developed realistic and clearly articulated war goals and coordinated his larger diplomatic aims with the use of force better than any other wartime American president.

The decision to drop the atomic bomb, the subject of Issue 13, demonstrates how history affects one of the most important foreign policy decisions in the twentieth century. Could we have avoided the use of nuclear weapons? McGeorge Bundy argues that President Truman dropped the A-bomb to end the war as quickly as possible. Use of the bomb, continues Bundy, shortened the war because it brought the Russians into the Pacific a week ahead of schedule and gave the Japanese emperor leverage to pressure the Japanese military to surrender. Martin J. Sherwin understands why the bomb was dropped but concludes that it was unnecessary. Other options such as awaiting a Russian declaration of war, continuing conventional air bombings and naval blockades, or modifying the policy of unconditional surrender were ruled out because the atomic bomb seemed the simplest solution.

No discussion of American foreign policy is complete without some consideration of the Vietnam War. Issue 15 considers whether or not the United States could have prevented the fall of South Vietnam to the communists. Guenter Lewy justifies the attempt to help the South Vietnamese government repel the Vietcong insurgents. The policy would have worked, says Lewy, "if the generals, Washington bureaucrats, and the peaceniks hadn't got in the way" of the development of a consistent military policy of strength and a political policy of reform in Southeast Asia. George C. Herring, however, believes that American policymakers exaggerated the strategic importance of Vietnam for over a decade and deluded themselves about the invincibility of America's power.

Every generation has its soothsayers who predict the demise of a nation's civilization. Has America entered a period of historical decline? Paul Kennedy answers affirmatively in Issue 17, but Susan Strange denies that the United States has lost its influence.

CONCLUSION

The process of historical study should rely more on thinking than on memorizing data. Once the basics of who, what, when, and where are determined, historical thinking shifts to a higher gear. Analysis, comparison and contrast, evaluation, and explanation take command. These skills not only increase our knowledge of the past but they also provide general tools for the comprehension of all the topics about which human beings think.

The diversity of a pluralistic society, however, creates some obstacles to comprehending the past. The spectrum of differing opinions on any particular subject eliminates the possibility of quick and easy answers. In the final analysis, conclusions often are built through a synthesis of several different interpretations, but even then, they may be partial and tentative.

The study of history in a pluralistic society allows each citizen the opportunity to reach independent conclusions about the past. Since most, if not all, historical issues affect the present and future, understanding the past becomes necessary if society is to progress. Many of today's problems have a direct connection with the past. Additionally, other contemporary issues may lack obvious direct antecedents, but historical investigation can provide illuminating analogies. At first, it may appear confusing to read and to think about opposing historical views, but the survival of our democratic society depends on such critical thinking by acute and discerning minds.

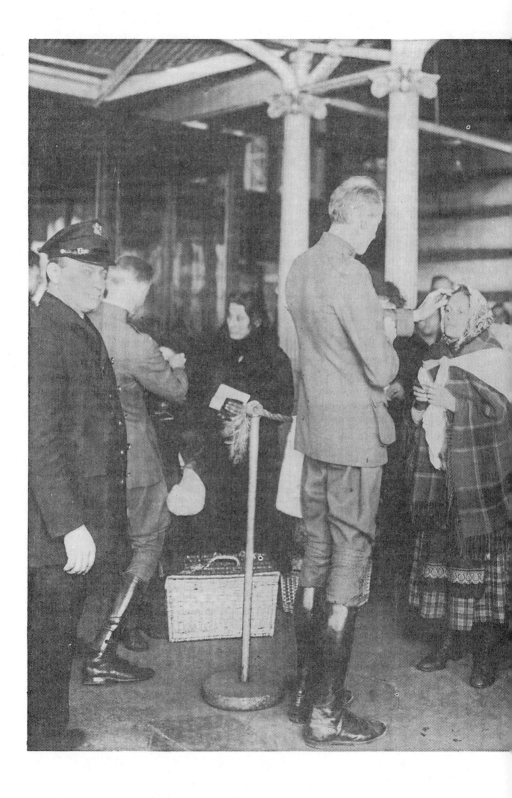

PART 1

Reconstruction, Immigration, and the Industrial Revolution

Deep and bitter wounds were left in the American nation as a result of the Civil War. Reconstruction was a period of further turmoil as the political institutions of the South were redesigned.

Economic expansion and the seemingly unlimited resources available in postbellum America offered great opportunity and created new political, social, and economic challenges. Political freedom and economic opportunity provided incentives for immigration to America. The need for cheap labor to run the machinery of the industrial revolution created an atmosphere for potential exploitation that was intensified by the concentration of capital in the hands of a few wealthy capitalists. The labor movement took root, with some elements calling for an overthrow of the capitalist system, while others sought to establish political power within the existing system. Strains began to develop between immigrant and native-born workers as well as between workers and owners.

Reconstruction: Could It Have Given Blacks Full Equality?

Were Nineteenth-Century Entrepreneurs Robber Barons?

Was the American Labor Movement Radical?

Were the Immigrants' Old World Cultures Destroyed as They Adjusted to American Life?

ISSUE 1

Reconstruction: Could It Have Given Blacks Full Equality?

YES: Eric Foner, from "The New View of Reconstruction," *American Heritage* (October/November 1983)

NO: C. Vann Woodward, from *The Future of the Past* (Oxford University Press, 1988)

ISSUE SUMMARY

YES: Professor of history Eric Foner believes that, although Reconstruction was nonrevolutionary and conservative, it was a splendid failure because it offered blacks a temporary vision of a free society.

NO: Professor of history C. Vann Woodward argues that there was very little hope that African Americans would receive their basic freedoms under Reconstruction. Taking a comparative approach and examining the treatment of freedmen in other societies, as well as the failure of U.S. land distribution policies toward poor whites and Native Americans, Woodward is skeptical about the promises of Reconstruction.

The Reconstruction era (1865–1877) contains a mythological history which has been impossible for professional historians to dislodge. While the Civil War has been portrayed as a heroic era for both sides, Reconstruction has been categorized as a tragedy for all Americans—Northerners, Southerners, whites, and blacks. According to the mythology, a vengeful Congress, dominated by radical Republicans, imposed military rule upon the Southern states. Carpetbaggers from the North, along with traitorous white scalawags and their ignorant black accomplices, rewrote the state constitutions, disenfranchised former Confederate whites, controlled the legislature, passed laws which enabled them to raise taxes, looted the government treasuries, and stole the possessions of the good white Northerners. This farce came to an end in 1877 when a deal was struck to allow Rutherford B. Hayes to assume the presidency. Hayes received 15 disputed electoral college votes (which enabled him to defeat his opponent Samuel J. Tilden by one vote). In return, Hayes agreed to end Reconstruction by withdrawing federal troops from the Southern states.

Between the years 1890 and 1930, this portrait of Reconstruction dominated the historical profession. The reasons for this are obvious. White

Southerners who wrote about this period made two basic assumptions: (1) that the South was capable of solving its own problems without federal government interference, and (2) that African Americans were intellectually inferior to whites and incapable of running a government (much less one in which whites would be their subordinates).

The traditional interpretation of Reconstruction has been under attack by professional white historians since the 1930s, but three decades earlier the brilliant African American historian W. E. B. Du Bois established many of the basic arguments used by the revisionists against the standard view of Reconstruction. In *The Souls of Black Folk* (1903, Reprint, Fawcett Publications, 1961) and "Reconstruction and Its Benefits," *American Historical Review* (July 1910), Du Bois presented treatments which placed the role of the black voter and the corruption of the Southern state governments in their proper historical context.

In response to the critics of Reconstruction, revisionists have argued that, although there was a great deal of corruption in the Republican governments of the South, the looting of state treasuries also took place in the Northern states and in Washington, D.C. While taxes increased in the Southern states, this looting was necessary because the pre–Civil War tax structure was regressive and public monies were necessary to rebuild roads and finance new systems of railroads and public schools.

Revisionist historians sharply attacked the notion that African Americans dominated the politics of the Reconstruction South. They pointed out that there were no black governors, only 2 black senators, and 15 black congressmen during this period. In no Southern state did blacks control both houses of the legislature. Black politicians were usually better educated than their constituents and, contrary to legend, generally followed moderate policies favoring black equality.

In brief, revisionist historians have painted a more positive picture of Reconstruction. New state constitutions were written during this era that outlasted the politicians who wrote them, improvements were made in local administrations, the court systems were revised, and state-supported public schools were established for both whites and blacks.

In the 1980s a third group of historians, the postrevisionist writers, have given a gloomier and more conservative portrait of the era. The first selection by Eric Foner, for example, summarizes the earlier writings on the period and at the same time searches for a new synthesis which moves beyond the negative postrevisionist studies. Foner concedes that Reconstruction was not very radical and much less revolutionary. Nevertheless, it was a "splendid failure" because it offered blacks a vision of how a free society could look. C. Vann Woodward, however, offers an ironic counterfactual analysis and argues that there was little hope for African Americans to secure equality. In addition, he thinks the idea of redistributing land confiscated from former white planters to former slaves was unrealistic.

YES

Eric Foner

THE NEW VIEW OF RECONSTRUCTION

In the past twenty years, no period of American history has been the subject of a more thoroughgoing reevaluation than Reconstruction—the violent, dramatic, and still controversial era following the Civil War. Race relations, politics, social life, and economic change during Reconstruction have all been reinterpreted in the light of changed attitudes toward the place of blacks within American society. If historians have not yet forged a fully satisfying portrait of Reconstruction as a whole, the traditional interpretation that dominated historical writing for much of this century has irrevocably been laid to rest.

Anyone who attended high school before 1960 learned that Reconstruction was an era of unrelieved sordidness in American political and social life. The martyred Lincoln, according to this view, had planned a quick and painless readmission of the Southern states as equal members of the national family. President Andrew Johnson, his successor, attempted to carry out Lincoln's policies but was foiled by the Radical Republicans (also known as Vindictives or Jacobins). Motivated by an irrational hatred of Rebels or by ties with Northern capitalists out to plunder the South, the Radicals swept aside Johnson's lenient program and fastened black supremacy upon the defeated Confederacy. An orgy of corruption followed, presided over by unscrupulous carpetbaggers (Northerners who ventured south to reap the spoils of office), traitorous scalawags (Southern whites who cooperated with the new governments for personal gain), and the ignorant and childlike freedmen, who were incapable of properly exercising the political power that had been thrust upon them. After much needless suffering, the white community of the South banded together to overthrow these "black" governments and restore home rule (their euphemism for white supremacy). All told, Reconstruction was just about the darkest page in the American saga.

Originating in Anti-Reconstruction propaganda of Southern Democrats during the 1870s, this traditional interpretation achieved scholarly legitimacy around the turn of the century through the work of William Dunning and his

From Eric Foner, "The New View of Reconstruction," *American Heritage*, vol. 34, no. 6 (October/November 1983). Copyright © 1983 by American Heritage, a division of Forbes, Inc. Reprinted by permission.

students at Columbia University. It reached the larger public through films like *Birth of a Nation* and *Gone With the Wind* and that best-selling work of myth-making masquerading as history, *The Tragic Era* by Claude G. Bowers. In language as exaggerated as it was colorful, Bowers told how Andrew Johnson "fought the bravest battle for constitutional liberty and for the preservation of our institutions ever waged by an Executive" but was overwhelmed by the "poisonous propaganda" of the Radicals. Southern whites, as a result, "literally were put to the torture" by "emissaries of hate" who manipulated the "simple-minded" freedmen, "inflaming the negroes' egotism" and even inspiring "lustful assaults" by blacks upon white womanhood.

In a discipline that sometimes seems to pride itself on the rapid rise and fall of historical interpretations, this traditional portrait of Reconstruction enjoyed remarkable staying power. The long reign of the old interpretation is not difficult to explain. It presented a set of easily identifiable heroes and villains. It enjoyed the imprimatur of the nation's leading scholars. And it accorded with the political and social realities of the first half of the century. This image of Reconstruction helped freeze the mind of the white South in unalterable opposition to any movement for breaching the ascendancy of the Democratic party, eliminating segregation, or readmitting disfranchised blacks to the vote.

Nevertheless, the demise of the traditional interpretation was inevitable, for it ignored the testimony of the central participant in the drama of Reconstruction—the black freedman. Furthermore, it was grounded in the conviction that blacks were unfit to share in political power. As Dunning's Columbia colleague John W.

Burgess put it, "A black skin means membership in a race of men which has never of itself succeeded in subjecting passion to reason, has never, therefore, created any civilization of any kind." Once objective scholarship and modern experience rendered that assumption untenable, the entire edifice was bound to fall.

The work of "revising" the history of Reconstruction began with the writings of a handful of survivors of the era, such as John R. Lynch, who had served as a black congressman from Mississippi after the Civil War. In the 1930s white scholars like Francis Simkins and Robert Woody carried the task forward. Then, in 1935, the black historian and activist W. E. B. Du Bois produced *Black Reconstruction in America*, a monumental reevaluation that closed with an irrefutable indictment of a historical profession that had sacrificed scholarly objectivity on the altar of racial bias. "One fact and one alone," he wrote, "explains the attitude of most recent writers toward Reconstruction; they cannot conceive of Negroes as men." Du Bois's work, however, was ignored by most historians.

It was not until the 1960s that the full force of the revisionist wave broke over the field. Then, in rapid succession, virtually every assumption of the traditional viewpoint was systematically dismantled. A drastically different portrait emerged to take its place. President Lincoln did not have a coherent "plan" for Reconstruction, but at the time of his assassination he had been cautiously contemplating black suffrage. Andrew Johnson was a stubborn, racist politician who lacked the ability to compromise. By isolating himself from the broad currents of public opinion that had nourished Lincoln's career, Johnson created an impasse with

Congress that Lincoln would certainly have avoided, thus throwing away his political power and destroying his own plans for reconstructing the South.

The Radicals in Congress were acquitted of both vindictive motives and the charge of serving as the stalking-horses of Northern capitalism. They emerged instead as idealists in the best nineteenth-century reform tradition. Radical leaders like Charles Sumner and Thaddeus Stevens had worked for the rights of blacks long before any conceivable political advantage flowed from such a commitment. Stevens refused to sign the Pennsylvania Constitution of 1838 because it disfranchised the state's black citizens; Sumner led a fight in the 1850s to integrate Boston's public schools. Their Reconstruction policies were based on principle, not petty political advantage, for the central issue dividing Johnson and these Radical Republicans was the civil rights of freedmen. Studies of congressional policy-making, such as Eric L. McKitrick's *Andrew Johnson and Reconstruction*, also revealed that Reconstruction legislation, ranging from the Civil Rights Act of 1866 to the Fourteenth and Fifteenth Amendments, enjoyed broad support from moderate and conservative Republicans. It was not simply the work of a narrow radical faction.

Even more startling was the revised portrait of Reconstruction in the South itself. Imbued with the spirit of the civil rights movement and rejecting entirely the racial assumptions that had underpinned the traditional interpretation, these historians evaluated Reconstruction from the black point of view. Works like Joel Williamson's *After Slavery* portrayed the period as a time of extraordinary political, social, and economic progress for blacks. The establishment of public school systems, the granting of equal citizenship to blacks, the effort to restore the devastated Southern economy, the attempt to construct an interracial political democracy from the ashes of slavery, all these were commendable achievements, not the elements of Bower's "tragic era."

Unlike earlier writers, the revisionists stressed the active role of the freedmen in shaping Reconstruction. Black initiative established as many schools as did Northern religious societies and the Freedmen's Bureau. The right to vote was not simply thrust upon them by meddling outsiders, since blacks began agitating for the suffrage as soon as they were freed. In 1865 black conventions throughout the South issued eloquent, though unheeded, appeals for equal civil and political rights.

With the advent of Radical Reconstruction in 1867, the freedmen did enjoy a real measure of political power. But black supremacy never existed. In most states blacks held only a small fraction of political offices, and even in South Carolina, where they comprised a majority of the state legislature's lower house, effective power remained in white hands. As for corruption, moral standards in both government and private enterprise were at low ebb throughout the nation in the postwar years—the era of Boss Tweed, the Credit Mobilier scandal, and the Whiskey Ring. Southern corruption could hardly be blamed on former slaves.

Other actors in the Reconstruction drama also came in for reevaluation. Most carpetbaggers were former Union soldiers seeking economic opportunity in the postwar South, not unscrupulous adventurers. Their motives, a typically American amalgam of humanitarianism and the pursuit of profit, were no more insidious than those of Western pioneers. Scalawags, previously seen as traitors to the white race, now emerged as "Old Line" Whig Unionists who had opposed secession in the first place or as poor whites who had long resented planters' domination of Southern life and who saw in Reconstruction a chance to recast Southern society along more democratic lines. Strongholds of Southern white Republicanism like east Tennessee and western North Carolina had been the scene of resistance to Confederate rule throughout the Civil War; now, as one scalawag newspaper put it, the choice was "between salvation at the hand of the Negro or destruction at the hand of the rebels."

At the same time, the Ku Klux Klan and kindred groups, whose campaign of violence against black and white Republicans had been minimized or excused in older writings, were portrayed as they really were. Earlier scholars had conveyed the impression that the Klan intimidated blacks mainly by dressing as ghosts and playing on the freedmen's superstitions. In fact, black fears were all too real: the Klan was a terrorist organization that beat and killed its political opponents to deprive blacks of their newly won rights. The complicity of the Democratic party and the silence of prominent whites in the face of such outrages stood as an indictment of the moral code the South had inherited from the days of slavery.

By the end of the 1960s, then, the old interpretation had been completely reversed. Southern freedmen were the heroes, the "Redeemers" who overthrew Reconstruction were the villains, and if the era was "tragic," it was because change did not go far enough. Reconstruction had been a time of real progress and its failure a lost opportunity for the South and the nation. But the legacy of Reconstruction—the Fourteenth and Fifteenth Amendments—endured to inspire future efforts for civil rights. As Kenneth Stampp wrote in *The Era of Reconstruction*, a superb summary of revisionist findings published in 1965, "If it was worth four years of civil war to save the Union, it was worth a few years of radical reconstruction to give the American Negro the ultimate promise of equal civil and political rights."

As Stampp's statement suggests, the reevaluation of the first Reconstruction was inspired in large measure by the impact of the second—the modern civil rights movement. And with the waning of that movement in recent years, writing on Reconstruction has undergone still another transformation. Instead of seeing the Civil War and its aftermath as a second American Revolution (as Charles Beard had), a regression into barbarism (as Bowers argued), or a golden opportunity squandered (as the revisionists saw it), recent writers argue that Radical Reconstruction was not really very radical. Since land was not distributed to the former slaves, they remained economically dependent upon their former owners. The planter class survived both the war and Reconstruction with its property (apart from slaves) and prestige more or less intact.

Not only changing times but also the changing concerns of historians have contributed to this latest reassessment of Reconstruction. The hallmark of the past decade's historical writing has been an emphasis upon "social history"—the evocation of the past lives of ordinary Americans—and the downplaying of strictly political events. When applied to Reconstruction, this concern with the "social" suggested that black suffrage and officeholding, once seen as the most radical departures of the Reconstruction era, were relatively insignificant.

Recent historians have focused their investigations not upon the politics of Reconstruction but upon the social and economic aspects of the transition from slavery to freedom. Herbert Gutman's influential study of the black family during and after slavery found little change in family structure or relations between men and women resulting from emancipation. Under slavery most blacks had lived in nuclear family units, although they faced the constant threat of separation from loved ones by sale. Reconstruction provided the opportunity for blacks to solidify their preexisting family ties. Conflicts over whether black women should work in the cotton fields (planters said yes, many black families said no) and over white attempts to "apprentice" black children revealed that the autonomy of family life was a major preoccupation of the freedmen. Indeed, whether manifested in their withdrawal from churches controlled by whites, in the blossoming of black fraternal, benevolent, and self-improvement organizations, or in the demise of the slave quarters and their replacement by small tenant farms occupied by individual families, the quest for independence from white authority and control over their own day-to-day lives shaped the black response to emancipation.

In the post-Civil War South the surest guarantee of economic autonomy, blacks believed, was land. To the freedmen the justice of a claim to land based on their years of unrequited labor appeared self-evident. As an Alabama black convention put it, "The property which they [the planters] hold was nearly all earned by the sweat of our brows." As Leon Litwack showed in *Been in the Storm So Long*, a Pulitzer-Prize-winning account of the black response to emancipation, many freedmen in 1865 and 1866 refused to sign labor contracts, expecting the federal government to give them land. In some localities, as one Alabama overseer reported, they "set up claims to the plantation and all on it."

In the end, of course, the vast majority of Southern blacks remained propertyless and poor. But exactly why the South, and especially its black population, suffered from dire poverty and economic retardation in the decades following the Civil War is a matter of much dispute. In *One Kind of Freedom*, economists Roger Ransom and Richard Sutch indicted country merchants for monopolizing credit and charging usurious interest rates, forcing black tenants into debt and locking the South into a dependence on cotton production that impoverished the entire region. But Jonathan Wiener, in his study of postwar Alabama, argued that planters used their political power to compel blacks to remain on the plantations. Planters succeeded in stabilizing the plantation system, but only by blocking the growth of alternative enterprises, like factories, that might draw off black laborers, thus locking the region into a pattern of economic backwardness.

If the thrust of recent writing has emphasized the social and economic aspects of Reconstruction, politics has not been entirely neglected. But political studies have also reflected the postrevisionist mood summarized by C. Vann Woodward when he observed "how essentially nonrevolutionary and conservative Reconstruction really was." Recent writers, unlike their revisionist predecessors, have found little to praise in federal policy toward the emancipated blacks.

A new sensitivity to the strength of prejudice and laissez-faire ideas in the nineteenth-century North has led many historians to doubt whether the Republican party ever made a genuine commitment to racial justice in the South. The granting of black suffrage was an alternative to a long-term federal responsibility for protecting the rights of the former slaves. Once enfranchised, blacks could be left to fend for themselves. With the exception of a few Radicals like Thaddeus Stevens, nearly all Northern policymakers and educators are criticized today for assuming that, so long as the unfettered operations of the marketplace afforded blacks the opportunity to advance through diligent labor, federal efforts to assist them in acquiring land were unnecessary.

Probably the most innovative recent writing on Reconstruction politics has centered on a broad reassessment of black Republicanism, largely undertaken by a new generation of black historians. Scholars like Thomas Holt and Nell Painter insist that Reconstruction was not simply a matter of black and white. Conflicts within the black community, no less than divisions among whites, shaped Reconstruction politics. Where revisionist scholars, both black and white, had celebrated the accomplishments of black political leaders, Holt, Painter, and others charge that they failed to address the economic plight of the black masses. Painter criticized "representative colored men," as national black leaders were called, for failing to provide ordinary freedmen with effective political leadership. Holt found that black officeholders in South Carolina mostly emerged from the old free mulatto class of Charleston,

which shared many assumptions with prominent whites. "Basically bourgeois in their origins and orientation," he wrote, they "failed to act in the interest of black peasants."

In emphasizing the persistence from slavery of divisions between free blacks and slaves, these writers reflect the increasing concern with continuity and conservatism in Reconstruction. Their work reflects a startling extension of revisionist premises. If, as has been argued for the past twenty years, blacks were active agents rather than mere victims of manipulation, then they could not be absolved of blame for the ultimate failure of Reconstruction.

Despite the excellence of recent writing and the continual expansion of our knowledge of the period, historians of Reconstruction today face a unique dilemma. An old interpretation has been overthrown, but a coherent new synthesis has yet to take its place. The revisionists of the 1960s effectively established a series of negative points: the Reconstruction governments were not as bad as had been portrayed, black supremacy was a myth, the Radicals were not cynical manipulators of the freedmen. Yet no convincing overall portrait of the quality of political and social life emerged from their writings. More recent historians have rightly pointed to elements of continuity that spanned the nineteenth-century Southern experience, especially the survival, in modified form, of the plantation system. Nevertheless, by denying the real changes that did occur, they have failed to provide a convincing portrait of an era characterized above all by drama, turmoil, and social change.

Building upon the findings of the past twenty years of scholarship, a new portrait of Reconstruction ought to begin by viewing it not as a specific time period, bounded by the years 1865 and 1877, but as an episode in a prolonged historical process—American society's adjustment to the consequences of the Civil War and emancipation. The Civil War, of course, raised the decisive questions of America's national existence: the relations between local and national authority, the definition of citizenship, the balance between force and consent in generating obedience to authority. The war and Reconstruction, as Allan Nevins observed over fifty years ago, marked the "emergence of modern America." This was the era of the completion of the national railroad network, the creation of the modern steel industry, the conquest of the West and final subduing of the Indians, and the expansion of the mining frontier. Lincoln's America—the world of the small farm and artisan shop—gave way to a rapidly industrializing economy. The issues that galvanized postwar Northern politics—from the question of the greenback currency to the mode of paying holders of the national debt—arose from the economic changes unleashed by the Civil War.

Above all, the war irrevocably abolished slavery. Since 1619, when "twenty negars" disembarked from a Dutch ship in Virginia, racial injustice had haunted American life, mocking its professed ideals even as tobacco and cotton, the products of slave labor, helped finance the nation's economic development. Now the implications of the black presence could no longer be ignored. The Civil War resolved the problem of slavery but, as the Philadelphia diarist Sydney George Fisher observed in June 1865, it opened an even more intractable problem: "What shall we do with the Negro?" Indeed, he went on, this was a problem *"incapable* of

any solution that will satisfy both North and South."

As Fisher realized, the focal point of Reconstruction was the social revolution known as emancipation. Plantation slavery was simultaneously a system of labor, a form of racial domination, and the foundation upon which arose a distinctive ruling class within the South. Its demise threw open the most fundamental questions of economy, society, and politics. A new system of labor, social, racial, and political relations had to be created to replace slavery.

The United States was not the only nation to experience emancipation in the nineteenth century. Neither plantation slavery nor abolition were unique to the United States. But Reconstruction was. In a comparative perspective Radical Reconstruction stands as a remarkable experiment, the only effort of a society experiencing abolition to bring the former slaves within the umbrella of equal citizenship. Because the Radicals did not achieve everything they wanted, historians have lately tended to play down the stunning departure represented by black suffrage and officeholding. Former slaves, most fewer than two years removed from bondage, debated the fundamental questions of the polity: What is a republican form of government? Should the state provide equal education for all? How could political equality be reconciled with a society in which property was so unequally distributed? There was something inspiring in the way such men met the challenge of Reconstruction. "I knew nothing more than to obey my master," James K. Greene, an Alabama black politician later recalled. "But the tocsin of freedom sounded and knocked at the door and we walked out like free men and we met the exigencies as they grew up, and shouldered the responsibilities."

"You never saw a people more excited on the subject of politics than are the negroes of the South," one planter observed in 1867. And there were more than a few Southern whites as well who in these years shook off the prejudices of the past to embrace the vision of a new South dedicated to the principles of equal citizenship and social justice. One ordinary South Carolinian expressed the new sense of possibility in 1868 to the Republican governor of the state: "I am sorry that I cannot write an elegant stiled letter to your excellency. But I rejoice to think that God almighty has given to the poor of S.C. a Gov. to hear to feel to protect the humble poor without distinction to race or color. . . . I am a native borned S.C. a poor man never owned a Negro in my life nor my father before me. . . . Remember the true and loyal are the poor of the whites and blacks outside of these you can find none loyal."

Few modern scholars believe the Reconstruction governments established in the South in 1867 and 1868 fulfilled the aspirations of their humble constituents. While their achievements in such realms as education, civil rights, and the economic rebuilding of the South are now widely appreciated, historians today believe they failed to affect either the economic plight of the emancipated slave or the ongoing transformation of independent white farmers into cotton tenants. Yet their opponents did perceive the Reconstruction governments in precisely this way—as representatives of a revolution that had put the bottom rail, both racial and economic, on top. This perception helps explain the ferocity of the attacks leveled against them and the pervasiveness of violence in the postemancipation South.

The spectacle of black men voting and holding office was anathema to large numbers of Southern whites. Even more disturbing, at least in the view of those who still controlled the plantation regions of the South, was the emergence of local officials, black and white, who sympathized with the plight of the black laborer. Alabama's vagrancy law was a "dead letter" in 1870, "because those who are charged with its enforcement are indebted to the vagrant vote for their offices and emoluments." Political debates over the level and incidence of taxation, the control of crops, and the resolution of contract disputes revealed that a primary issue of Reconstruction was the role of government in a plantation society. During presidential Reconstruction, and after "Redemption," with planters and their allies in control of politics, the law emerged as a means of stabilizing and promoting the plantation system. If Radical Reconstruction failed to redistribute the land of the South, the ouster of the planter class from control of politics at least ensured that the sanctions of the criminal law would not be employed to discipline the black labor force.

An understanding of this fundamental conflict over the relation between government and society helps explain the pervasive complaints concerning corruption and "extravagance" during Radical Reconstruction. Corruption there was aplenty; tax rates did rise sharply. More significant than the rate of taxation, however, was the change in its incidence. For the first time, planters and white farmers had to pay a significant portion of their income to the government, while propertyless blacks often escaped scot-free.

Several states, moreover, enacted heavy taxes on uncultivated land to discourage land speculation and force land onto the market, benefiting, it was hoped, the freedmen.

As time passed, complaints about the "extravagance" and corruption of Southern governments found a sympathetic audience among influential Northerners. The Democratic charge that universal suffrage in the South was responsible for high taxes and governmental extravagance coincided with a rising conviction among the urban middle classes of the North that city government had to be taken out of the hands of the immigrant poor and returned to the "best men"— the educated, professional, financially independent citizens unable to exert much political influence at a time of mass parties and machine politics. Increasingly the "respectable" middle classes began to retreat from the very notion of universal suffrage. The poor were no longer perceived as honest producers, the backbone of the social order; now they became the "dangerous classes," the "mob." As the historian Francis Parkman put it, too much power rested with "masses of imported ignorance and hereditary ineptitude." To Parkman the Irish of the Northern cities and the blacks of the South were equally incapable of utilizing the ballot: "Witness the municipal corruptions of New York, and the monstrosities of Negro rule in South Carolina." Such attitudes helped to justify Northern inaction as, one by one, the Reconstruction regimes of the South were overthrown by political violence.

In the end, then, neither the abolition of slavery nor Reconstruction succeeded in resolving the debate over the meaning of freedom in American life. Twenty years before the American Civil War,

writing about the prospect of abolition in France's colonies, Alexis de Tocqueville had written, "If the Negroes have the right to become free, the [planters] have the incontestable right not to be ruined by the Negroes' freedom." And in the United States, as in nearly every plantation society that experienced the end of slavery, a rigid social and political dichotomy between former master and former slave, an ideology of racism, and a dependent labor force with limited economic opportunities all survived abolition. Unless one means by freedom the simple fact of not being a slave, emancipation thrust blacks into a kind of no-man's land, a partial freedom that made a mockery of the American ideal of equal citizenship.

Yet by the same token the ultimate outcome underscores the uniqueness of Reconstruction itself. Alone among the societies that abolished slavery in the nineteenth century, the United States, for a moment, offered the freedmen a measure of political control over their own destinies. However brief its sway, Reconstruction allowed scope for a remarkable political and social mobilization of the black community. It opened doors of opportunity that could never be completely closed. Reconstruction transformed the lives of Southern blacks in ways unmeasurable by statistics and unreachable by law. It raised their expectations and aspirations, redefined their status in relation to the larger society, and allowed space for the creation of institutions that enabled them to survive the repression that followed. And it established constitutional principles of civil and political equality that, while flagrantly violated after Redemption, planted the seeds of future struggle.

Certainly, in terms of the sense of possibility with which it opened, Reconstruction failed. But as Du Bois observed, it was a "splendid failure." For its animating vision—a society in which social advancement would be open to all on the basis of individual merit, not inherited caste distinctions—is as old as America itself and remains relevant to a nation still grappling with the unresolved legacy of emancipation.

NO

C. Vann Woodward

RECONSTRUCTION:
A COUNTERFACTUAL PLAYBACK

The ruins of two great failures dominate the landscape of American history. They stand close together in the middle distance, back to back, but separate and distinct. One is the ruins of the Confederacy, the South's failure to gain independence. The other is the ruins of Reconstruction, the North's failure to solve the problem of the black people's place in American life. The South's failure was the North's success and vice versa. Each can be and, of course, has been described by its opponents as simply the wreckage wrought in preventing acknowledged wrong. But from the standpoint of their supporters and champions there can be no doubt that each of these ruins represents a great American failure. . . .

The achievements of the revisionists are impressive. But as a contribution to explaining the failure of Reconstruction they tend rather to complicate than to solve the enigma. For if, as they have demonstrated, the statesmanship of the Radicals was all that inspired and their motivation all that pure, if the freedmen were so responsive and capably led, if government by the Scalawag-Carpetbagger-freedmen coalition was all that constructive, and if the opposition were indeed headed by a misfit in the White House who was out of touch with the electorate, then success would seem more indicated than failure. The paradox reminds me of the first historical problem I confronted as a boy. It went something like this: If Marse Robert was all that noble and intrepid, if Stonewall was all that indomitable and fast on his feet, if Jeb Stuart was all that gallant and dashing, and if God was on our side, then why the hell did we *lose* that war?

This is not to write off the accomplishments of the revisionists. I hope the record is clear that I have aided and abetted and egged them on, presumed to teach some of them, read many of their manuscripts and all their monographs, praised what I could and encouraged when I could. What they did in the main much needed doing. I do believe that they have produced many works with better prospects of durability than the school of the 1900s or that of the 1930s.

I am more interested in what comes next and what problems remain unsolved. This brings me back to the old problem of failure. As I have remarked earlier, Americans have rather a thing about failure—about confronting it, confessing it, and accepting it, as well as about explaining it. It is noteworthy that the great bulk of work done by the revisionists has been on Andrew Johnson's administration, not on the two Grant administrations, that is, on the period where, paradoxically, the ephemeral successes and triumphs multiplied, not the period of twice that length when the failures piled up or became unavoidably conspicuous. This may be mere coincidence, but my guess is that it is more than that. Another tendency might be called the deferred success approach, the justification (or dismissal) of failure in the First Reconstruction on the ground that it prepared the way for success in the Second Reconstruction, or maybe a Third yet to come. Thus one historian writes that the failures of the First Reconstruction diminish to insignificance in comparison with successes of the Second in advancing equal civil and political rights for blacks and promise of further progress to come. This is a generational shift of the burden of responsibility. But it must be recognized as essentially another strategy of evasion.

One habit of mind that has complicated American ways of dealing with failure, apart from a relative unfamiliarity with the experience, has been the isolation of American history from comparative reference. Comparisons have indeed been used with regard to Reconstruction, but they have been inter-nalized. Lacking foreign comparisons, or indifferent to them, Americans have turned inward to compare professed ideals with actual practice. This has encouraged a strong moralistic tendency in our historical writing and controversy. Since the nation has advertised a commitment to some very lofty ideals and principles, the contrast between performance and principle has always been painful, and the application of absolute and abstract standards of judgment often sets up moral disturbance that clouds issues and distorts perspectives.

For more realistic perspective on the American experience of Reconstruction we need to turn to comparison with foreign experiences, including but not limited to those of the other twenty-odd slave societies in the New World that went through the post-emancipation ordeal. To avoid repetition, since I have sampled those comparisons before, I must be content with summarizing conclusions of the best informed authorities. The most important finding is that wherever slavery was widespread, emancipation was invariably followed by resort to drastic measures, including use of force, to put the freedmen back to work. The old masters of the American South were by no means alone in resorting to black codes and chain gangs. Old masters everywhere—West Indies, Latin America, Africa, Asia—took forceable steps to drive the freedmen back to work.

Furthermore, in those lands undergoing emancipation where the process of reconstruction was subject to outside control or supervision, whether from the crown, the mother country, an imperial or metropolitan administration, or as in the South the federal government under Northern control, such authorities proved quite ineffective in protecting the lives and rights of the emancipated. The universality of failure by authorities and oppression by old masters does not excuse or justify either the governments or the masters anywhere—especially not a government that had just fought a bloody civil war in the name of freedom. Reconstruction left a lasting blot on the American conscience and national history and continues to breed moral recrimination between regions and races. But at least the comparative context removes the stigma of uniqueness and places moral issues in a broader setting. That, I believe, is a legitimate use of history—not only to recover the past but to enable us to live with it.

Another type of comparison has often been used in interpreting Reconstruction, but not always with sufficient caution. To place a historical event in a category of events is to make a comparison. Thus, when Reconstruction is spoken of as a revolution, we are compelled to think of it in comparison with other revolutions. If we reserve the term "revolution" for the classic phenomena of England in the seventeenth century, America and France in the eighteenth century, and Russia and China in the twentieth century, then it is certainly misused when applied to the American Reconstruction of the nineteenth century. For in the last instance there were no mass executions, no class liquidations. No heads rolled. There were constitutional changes, to be sure, but they were insignificant compared with those in England, France, Russia, and China, and they were mainly effected through constitutional forms. The South's so-called Bourbons or Redeemers did not become proscribed and outlawed émigrés. They remained at home, retained their estates, took over from the ephemeral radical governments,

and after their so-called counter-revolution they did not find it necessary to make very drastic changes in the system left them by the so-called revolution. All things considered, it would be better to abandon both the concept of revolution and that of counter-revolution in writing of Reconstruction as it *was*.

But in writing of what it *might* have been, what many hoped it would be, and of why Reconstruction failed, the concept of revolution seems indispensable. It should be fairly obvious that in order to succeed with the professed aims of full civil rights, equality, and justice for the freedmen, Reconstruction would have had to go much further in the way of revolutionary measures than it ever did. Even then it might have failed, for revolutions are not invariably successful nor are their innovations always lasting. It is not very helpful to prescribe revolution in the abstract without specifying the revolutionary program. Nor is it very realistic to imagine a revolutionary program without regard to the nature of the party and the people who would carry it out and the historical context in which they would have worked. Only by that means can we test the hypothesis that the failure of Reconstruction is to be explained by the lack of revolutionary measures.

One revolutionary measure, a favorite for the speculation over a century, is the confiscation of rebel estates and redistribution of them among the freedmen. This deserves serious consideration for a number of reasons. In the first place such a proposal was seriously made and had an able and powerful advocate in Thaddeus Stevens. The Stevens plan called for the confiscation of all rebel estates over $10,000 or over 200 acres. He estimated that this would result in the taking over of some 394 million out of 465 million acres in the rebel states. The redistribution would give 40 acres to each adult male freedman. This would take 40 million acres, and the remaining 254 million would be sold to the highest bidder and the proceeds allocated to pensions for Union veterans, damages and reparations, and enough left to retire three-quarters of the national debt. The plan was defeated, of course, but it has had advocates such as W. E. B. Du Bois and various other Marxists.

Americans need no Marxist precedents, however, for there was ample precedent for the wholesale confiscation of the estates of disloyal elements of the population in the treatment of Tories during the American Revolution, and there was a spectacular contemporary example abroad in the distribution of some of the confiscated lands to emancipated serfs by the Czar of All the Russias in 1861. The American freedmen surely had as great a moral claim on the land on which they had toiled for 250 years. Furthermore if the federal government could overcome the legal and constitutional problems of confiscating the slave property of the planters, it surely could have justified confiscating their landed property as well. The planters would have objected strenuously, of course, but they would have been powerless to prevent the action had Congress been determined. Let us assume, then, that the Stevens Land Confiscation Bill actually passed, that President Ben Wade signed it in the White House after President Johnson's removal by successful impeachment, and that the Fortieth Congress then brought to bear all its experience and wisdom in refining the legislation and President Wade marshalled the best talents for administering the land act. What would have been the consequences

for the outcome of Reconstruction? Would this have converted a failure into a reasonable success?

No one can possibly say for sure, of course. What one *can* describe with some assurance, however, is the record of the same federal government, the same Congresses under the control of the same party in administering and distributing public lands elsewhere. Again we resort to the comparative approach, though this time the comparisons are drawn from domestic rather than foreign instances. The Reconstruction period coincided with the great era of public land distribution by the federal government according to the provisions of the Homestead Act of 1862 and other federal land laws placed on the books between 1862 and 1878. The public domain available for distribution under the Homestead and subsequent acts amounted to some 1,048,000,000 acres, more than half the total area of the nation and more than two and a half times the 394 million acres of confiscated rebel estates that would have been added to the public domain by the Stevens Act. This fabulous opportunity, without precedent in history, appeared to be the fruition of the American dream, the most cherished dream of reformers—free land for those who tilled the land.

What came of that dream in the administration of the Homestead Act is a matter of public record. We know that as things turned out the homesteaders got short shrift and proved to be the least favored of the various groups attracted to the western lands. The land-grant railroads alone got four times as much land as the homesteaders in the first four decades of the Homestead Act. In that period 84 percent of the new farms brought under cultivation were purchased or subdivided from larger holdings. Of the patents actually granted to homesteaders a great number were handed to pawns of speculators and monopolists, so that in all probability little more than one-tenth of the new farms were free in the homestead sense. Furthermore, the bona fide homesteader was typically shunted off into the poorest land and least desirable tracts, while the speculators pre-empted tracts closest to settlement and transportation and held them for resale at prices beyond the means of the class the Homestead Act was presumably designed to help. It is the opinion of Fred Shannon that, "In its operation the Homestead Act could hardly have defeated the hopes of the [land-reform] enthusiasts . . . more completely if the makers had drafted it with that purpose uppermost in mind."

While many of the same people who drafted and administered the Homestead Act for the West would in all probability have drafted and administered the Stevens Act for the South, it is only fair to remember that the Western land problem was complicated by variables absent from the Southern picture—granting that the latter had its own complications. But at least the South lay within the humid, forested longitudes, conditions that were far more familiar to Eastern lawmakers than Walter Webb's Great Plains, and also the rebel estates provided a larger proportion of arable land, much more conveniently located in relation to the prospective homesteaders. Because of these advantages and the idealism said to have motivated Radicals in their dealings with freedmen (however inoperative it was in the same men's dealings with Western homesteaders) it is possible that the Stevens Act would have had a happier history than the Homestead Act and that the black freedmen would have

actually entered into the promised land, peacefully and cheerfully, each one secure in the possession of his forty acres. And let us throw in an army mule apiece for good measure.

That outcome is conceivable and one would hope even probable. But in calculating the degree of probability one is forced to take into account certain other conditioning and relevant factors in addition to the western homestead experience. For one thing the Stevens Act as detailed by the Pennsylvania Radical set aside nine-tenths of the 394 million acres of confiscated rebel land for sale to the highest bidder—an open invitation to the speculator and monopolist. It is possible that these types might have behaved toward the black homesteaders of the South in much the same way they behaved toward the white homesteader in the West. If so the probability of success for the philanthropic part of the Stevens Act is appreciably diminished.

Prospects of success for the Stevens Act are also illuminated by the history of a Southern Homestead Act that actually *was* adopted by Congress. There were 47,700,000 acres of public land in five of the Confederate states in 1861, more than the amount of rebel estates set aside for freedmen by the hypothetical Stevens Act. In 1866 the Radicals pushed through a drastic bill applying exclusively to these lands, reserving them to homesteaders at 80 acres per holding, and favoring freedmen by excluding ex-Confederates from homesteading privileges. These lands were generally less accessible and less desirable than those of confiscated estates might have been, and as in the case of the Western act no provision was made for furnishing credit and transportation to homesteaders. These conditions probably explain why extremely few blacks seized upon this opportunity to double the elusive 40 acres. In that respect the act was a failure and, at any rate, Congress reversed the policy in 1876 and threw open this rich Southern empire to unrestricted speculation. There ensued a scramble of monopolists that matched any land rush of the Wild West, and the freedmen were thrust aside and forgotten. Admittedly this episode offers further discouragement for the chances of the revolutionary Stevens Act.

Determined revolutionists are not disheartened by reverses, however. They merely press forward with more heroic measures. Perhaps Thaddeus Stevens was not revolutionary enough. There is the problem of the rebel resistance to Radical Reconstruction and federal authority in the defeated states. My own researches have impressed me deeply with the seriousness of this resistance. It was often open, defiant, organized, and effective. White Southerners repeatedly insulted, persecuted, and sometimes murdered federal officials, army officers included. They scoffed at the law and ridiculed the courts. They did everything to black citizens the law forbade their doing and invented mistreatments that law never thought of. How any self-respecting government put up with such defiance unless, indeed, it was at least subliminally sympathetic with the resistance, it is difficult to understand. With overwhelming power in his hands, even an ordinary respectable non-revolutionary government could have done better than this.

Let me remind you, however, that this is a revolutionary program that we are pursuing. Here Thad Stevens lets us down. He raises the question whether any Republican, Senator Charles Sumner included, really deserved the name "Radical." It is true that his rhetoric against the "proud, bloated, and defiant rebels" was violent enough, that he promised to "startle feeble minds and shake weak nerves," that he ridiculed "the prim conservatives, the snobs, and the male waiting maids in Congress," that he asked, "How can republican institutions, free schools, free churches . . . exist in a mingled community of nabobs and serfs," and that he thundered the promise to "drive her nobility into exile," or worse. But when it came right down to it he confessed that he "never desired bloody punishments to any extent." This admission of bourgeois softness proves that Stevens has exhausted his usefulness as a guide to revolutionary solutions.

It is becoming a bit tiresome (and it is entirely unnecessary) to be flanked on the left in speculative audacity. Armchair bloodbaths can be conducted with impunity by anyone, even a professor emeritus. Let us then pursue the logic of the revolutionary process on past Stevens and Sumner, past the Old Left and the New Left, and out to the wild blue—or rather infra-red—yonder. Let us embrace in our revolutionary program, along with the Stevens Act, an act for the liquidation of the enemy class. There is ample precedent for this in the history of revolutions. Even the American Revolution drove the Tories into exile. Mass deportation, considering the merchant marine's state of total disrepair in 1865, is unfortunately not a practicable option. That leaves available only the messier alternatives. It is true that the Alaska purchase from Russia made providentially available an American Siberia in 1867, but that would take care of relatively few, and again there is the tedious problem of transportation. The numbers are formidable, for the counter-revolutionary resistance extended beyond the planter class through a very large percentage of Southern whites. A few hundred thousand Northern Copperheads can be handled in concentration camps, but in Dixie harsher measures are indicated. Let no true revolutionary blanch at the implications. Remember that we must be cruel in order to be kind, that we are the social engineers of the future, that we are forestalling future bloodbaths, race riots, and relieving our Northern metropolitan friends of problems that trouble their thoughts and for a time threatened to destroy their cities. If our work is bloody our conscience is clear, and we do all that we do—compassionately.

Having liquidated the white resistance down to the last unregenerate lord of the lash and the last bed-sheeted Ku Kluxer, let us proceed unencumbered to build the true Radical Reconstruction. We will find it expedient to import managerial talent in large numbers to replace the liquidated white resistance, and place them in charge of agriculture, industry, railroads, and mines. They will doubtless come from the same states the carpetbaggers hailed from, but they must be carefully screened to eliminate the more objectionable types and certified as nonracists and non-Copperheads. We will also establish a permanent Freedmen's Bureau, perhaps modeled on the Indian Bureau, and place in command of it the very finest talent. If not General O. O. Howard, perhaps we can get the nomination of Frederick Douglass through a miraculously radicalized U.S. Senate, after a radicalized U. S. Grant had executed a Pride's Purge of half the members.

After these Draconian, Cromwellian, Stalinist measures had removed all resistance and interference from Southern and Northern racists and Kluxers and nightriders, silenced all Confederate orators, and shut down the last obstructionist press, the revolutionists should have had a perfectly free hand. What then would have been the consequences for fulfillment of Reconstruction purposes? Would these additional measures have converted failure into success? One would surely hope so after paying such a bloody price.

But again, no one can say for sure. And again we turn to the comparative method for possible illumination. I hope that I am sufficiently alert to the dangers of these comparisons. I realize that no analogy is complete, that no two historical events are identical, and that the risks of drawing conclusions by such reasoning are most formidable. I have tried to guard against such risks and to be very tentative about drawing conclusions, but I suspect I have already outraged respected historians by mentioning Grant in the same breath with Cromwell or Stalin. Nevertheless I shall take heart and venture one last excursion into the treacherous field of comparative or counterfactual history.

Once again the comparison is close to home and contemporaneous with the Reconstruction period. Moreover, the same electorates, the same congressmen, the identical presidents and judiciary, the same editorial chorus and clerical censors are involved in the one as in the other—one cast for two dramas. The second drama also has as its plot the story of reformers using the federal government to bring justice and rights and decent lives to men of color. This time the theater is in the West instead of the South and the colored minority is red instead of black. Since we have "controlled the variable" (as the quantifiers say) of Confederate slave owners' resistance in the South—with a regrettable amount of bloodshed to be sure—the two theaters are more readily comparable. For while the reformers in the West had their own problems, they were not encumbered by die-hard Confederate reactionaries, former owners and masters of the red people, and not dogged at every step by determined and desperate nightriders. In these respects they had a relatively free hand.

The personnel and policies of the white guardians of the blacks and the white guardians of the reds were often interchangeable. General W. T. Sherman moved from command of the Southern District to command of the Western District in 1867, from the final arbiter of the black freedman's destiny to final arbiter of the redskin's fate. Many other military officers including General O. O. Howard moved back and forth from South to West. While General Howard, who had been head of the Freedmen's Bureau, was serving as president of an all-black Howard University in 1872 he was dispatched by Grant to conclude a treaty with the Apaches; in 1874 he was placed in command of the Department of Columbia, and in 1877 he led a punitive expedition against the Nez Perce Indians. Black regiments served in West and South under the same white officers. In the educational field Samuel Armstrong of Hampton Institute, Booker Washington's mentor and model, took Richard Henry Pratt, the great Indian educator, as disciple and assistant, and the two of them integrated and taught black and red students at Hampton. Later Pratt took the Armstrong-Booker Washington gospel to Indian schools. The same missionaries, preachers, editors, and reformers often concerned themselves with the problems and destinies of both colored minorities.

What can be said, in view of the relatively free hand they had in the West, of the performance of the American reformers toward the Indian, as compared with their performance toward the Negro, when they did not have the free hand I have imagined for them? Was it any better? As a matter of fact the two problems were solved in much the same way. The red man like the black man was given to understand that the white man's will was supreme, that he had few rights the white man was bound to respect. He was promised land and the land was taken away. He was promised integration and then segregated, even more completely than the black man. He was degraded, exploited, humiliated, and because he offered more resistance he was cut down ruthlessly by military force or vigilante action. Idealists like Richard Henry Pratt who operated in both South and West were as frustrated in their efforts for red man as they were with the black man. White supremacy forces were as triumphant over Eastern "Indian lovers" in Arizona and Colorado as they were over Northern "nigger lovers" in Mississippi and Alabama.

But this comparison is an outrage against established compartmentalizations of historical thought, a preposterous violation of respected conventions. Everyone knows what a "good Indian" was. And what but confusion of the undergraduate mind can possibly come from comparing Colorado and Alabama? I apologize for this travesty against sound canons of the profession. Nevertheless, I confess that these irresponsible speculations have raised such doubts in the mind of one dedicated revolutionary arm-chair ultra-radical as to palsy his hand and sickly over with the pale cast of thought the native hue of resolution. Almost am I persuaded to countermand belatedly the order for the Confederate liquidation.

I owe further apologies. Having invited you to consider the causes of the failure of Reconstruction, I have produced nothing but negative results. While applauding the revisionists for their excellent work, I have questioned the emphasis on the idealism and sincerity of the Radicals and their ephemeral triumphs as an adequate indication of their ultimate failure. In the second place, I have raised doubts about moralistic and uniquely American explanations for post-emancipation failure in the protection of freedmen on the ground that much the same pattern of forced labor occurred everywhere in the world as a sequel to abolition. Thirdly, having embraced the Stevens policy of rebel land confiscation and redistribution, I am forced to admit that contemporaneous experience with federal administration of public lands discourages optimism about the freedman's chances. And finally, after eliminating Confederate resistance with bloody measures I am overcome with doubts, caused by belated reflections on the fate of the poor red man, that even these drastic steps would ensure success. With the candor I have urged upon other historians I am obliged to confess a failure of my own, the failure to find a satisfactory explanation for the failure of Reconstruction.

The problem remains unsolved. The assignment still goes begging. It deserves high priority among the unfinished tasks of American historiography. Those who next undertake the task will not, I hope, rely too uncritically on the received ideas, the shared moral convictions and political values of their own time to sanction their premises. They should give scrupulous attention to uniquely American conditions, but remember that the post-emancipation problem they attack was not unique to America. They may well profit from consideration of allegedly idyllic race relations on happy islands in the Caribbean sun, but remember that their home problem was environed by Protestant Anglo-American institutions of a temperate zone unblessed by Pope or tropical sun. They should give due weight to constitutional issues without fruitlessly pining for an English-type constitution to deal with states' rights, a Russian-type Czar to distribute land among the emancipated, or a Soviet-type commissar of security to liquidate mass resistance.

I hope those who accept this challenge will not take these reflections as the counsel of despair, or as intimation that Reconstruction was doomed to failure, or that our ancestors might not have done better by their experiment than they actually did. Nor should other historians be discouraged from revolutionary speculations by the inconclusive results of my own. Let them be as far-out left as is currently fashionable. But in the transports of revolutionary imaginings, armchair edicts, and dreams of glory, they would do well to keep in mind the human materials and the historic context of their problem. If they do this, they will face up to the fact that nineteenth-century Americans (and some in the twentieth century as well) were fatefully stuck with a perverse mystique of squatter sovereignty. The tenets of this perversion of the democratic dogma, this squatter sovereignty, were that whatever the law or the Constitution or the Supreme Court or world opinion or moral codes said to the contrary notwithstanding, the will of the dominant white majority would prevail. And where whites were not in the majority it would prevail anyway. How it was, and how early, we got stuck with a commitment to this caricature of democracy is a long story, a very long story, and the story did not begin in 1865, and the commitment was not confined to the South.

POSTSCRIPT

Reconstruction: Could It Have Given Blacks Full Equality?

Both the traditional and revisionist writers of Reconstruction history have treated African Americans in a passive manner. Traditionalists like J. G. Randall and E. Merton Coulter, who assumed that African Americans were intellectually inferior to whites, argued that African American politicians were the junior partners of the white carpetbaggers and scalawags in robbing the Reconstruction governments. Revisionists like Kenneth M. Stampp, who believed in the biological equality of all human races, maintained that the African American politicians did not constitute a majority in the Reconstruction governments, were not totally corrupt, and did not want to disenfranchise whites. African Americans, he insisted, only desired their civil and political constitutional rights. Writing at the peak of the civil rights movement in 1965, Stampp was trying to assure his readers that African Americans only wanted to become good Americans and obtain (in this "second Reconstruction") what had been denied them a century earlier.

Foner's conclusions are more upbeat than those of most postrevisionists. "However brief," he argues, "the United States was the only society which offered the freedman a measure of political control over their own destinies. It transformed their lives in ways not measurable by statistics. It raised their expectations and aspirations . . . and established constitutional principles of civil and political equality that . . . planted the seeds of future struggle."

In *Nothing But Freedom: Emancipation and Its Legacy* (Louisiana State University Press, 1984), Foner advances his interpretation by comparing the treatment of American ex-slaves with those newly emancipated in Haiti and the British West Indies. Only in America, he claims, were the freedmen given voting and economic rights. Although these rights had been stripped away from the majority of black Southerners by 1900, Reconstruction had, nevertheless, created a legacy of freedom which inspired succeeding generations of African Americans.

C. Vann Woodward is more pessimistic about the outcome of Reconstruction than Foner. For all the successes listed by the revisionists, he claims that the experiment failed. Woodward makes clever use of both counterfactual ("what if") history and comparative history to destroy the optimistic assumption of some of the earlier revisionists that, if the national government had engaged in extensive land reforms and enforced laws protecting the civil rights of African Americans, Reconstruction would have worked. In contrast to Foner, Woodward argues that former slaves were as poorly treated in the United States as they were in other countries. He also believes that the confiscation of former plantations and the redistribution of land to the former slaves would have failed in the same way that the Homestead Act of 1862 failed to generate equal distribution of government lands to poor white settlers. Finally, Woodward claims that the reformers who worked with African Americans during Reconstruction and with Native Americans a decade or two later were often the same people who failed in both instances because their goals were out of touch with the realities of the late nineteenth century.

Much research still remains to be done on the Reconstruction period. State and local studies which employ modern social science frameworks yield new perspectives. Thomas Holt's *Black Over White* (Illinois, 1977) is a sophisticated study of African American political leadership in South Carolina during Reconstruction. Combining traditional sources, such as old letters, military service records, and newspapers, with sophisticated quantitative analyses of voting records, Holt gives a complex picture of that reconstructed state. Reconstruction failed in South Carolina, says Holt, not because of corruption but because African American leaders failed to develop a clear and unifying ideology to challenge whites who wanted to restore white supremacy.

Willie Lee Rose's *Rehearsal for Reconstruction: The Port Royal Experiment* (Bobbs Merrill, 1964) is an earlier study by a former Woodward student that describes the difficulties of enacting a land reform policy. Ten thousand slaves in the South Carolina sea islands took over lands abandoned by their owners in 1861 and ran them as self-sufficient farmers. When the national government sold off most of the lands to Northern speculators and cotton companies, the former slaves were forced to sign labor contracts or leave the lands.

Foner has provided us with a major postrevisionist summary in *Reconstruction: America's Unfinished Revolution, 1863–1867* (Harper & Row, 1988), a 600-page text which contains the most extensive bibliography on the subject. Before tackling Foner, students should read Michael Perman's *Emancipation and Reconstruction, 1862–1879* (Harlan Davidson, 1987), or earlier summaries of revisionism by John Hope Franklin, *Reconstruction* (University of Chicago, 1961), and Kenneth M. Stampp, *The Era of Reconstruction, 1865–1877* (Knopf, 1965). Traditional accounts of Reconstruction can be sampled in William Archibald Dunning's biased classic *Reconstruction: Political and Economic* (Harper & Row, 1907); the 1937 edition of J. G. Randall's *The Civil War and Reconstruction* (D. C. Heath); and E. Merton Coulter, *The South During Reconstruction, 1865–1877* (LSU Press, 1947), the last major work written from the Dunning (or traditional) point of view. A scathing critique of Coulter's work can be found in John Hope Franklin's "Whither Reconstruction Historiography," which is conveniently reprinted along with a number of other articles that deserve attention, in *Race and History: Selected Essays, 1938–1988* (LSU Press, 1989). Finally, Staughton Lynd's *Reconstruction* (Harper & Row, 1967) is an older but valuable edited collection of the main viewpoints on Reconstruction.

ISSUE 2

Were Nineteenth-Century Entrepreneurs Robber Barons?

YES: John Tipple, from "Big Businessmen and a New Economy," in H. Wayne Morgan, ed., *The Gilded Age*, rev. and enlarged ed. (Syracuse University Press, 1970)

NO: Alfred D. Chandler, Jr., from "The Beginnings of 'Big Business' in American Industry," *Business History Review* (Spring 1959)

ISSUE SUMMARY

YES: Professor of history John Tipple characterizes big businessmen of the late nineteenth century as destructive forces whose power and greed undermined the nation's traditional institutions and values.

NO: Professor of business history Alfred D. Chandler, Jr., concludes that American entrepreneurs were organizational and marketing innovators whose creation of great industrial corporations strengthened the country's economy by sparking the growth of a national urban market.

Between 1860 and 1914 the United States was transformed from a country of farms, small towns, and modest manufacturing concerns to a modern nation dominated by large cities and factories. During those years, the population tripled, and the nation experienced astounding urban growth. A new proletariat emerged to provide the necessary labor for the country's developing factory system. Between the Civil War and World War I, the value of manufactured goods in the United States increased twelvefold, and the capital invested in industrial pursuits multiplied 22 times. In addition, the application of new machinery and scientific methods to agriculture produced abundant yields of wheat, corn, and other foodstuffs, despite the decline in the number of farmers.

Why did this industrial revolution occur in the United States during the last quarter of the nineteenth century? What factors contributed to the rapid pace of American industrialization? In answering these questions, historians often point to the first half of the 1800s and the significance of the "transportation revolution," which produced better roads, canals, and railroads to move people and goods more efficiently and cheaply from one point to another. Technological improvements such as the Bessemer process, refrigeration, electricity, and the telephone also made their mark in the nation's "Machine Age." Government cooperation with business, large-scale immigration from Europe and Asia, and the availability of foreign capital for industrial investments provided still other underpinnings for this industrial growth. Finally, American industrialization depended upon a number of individuals in the United States who were willing to organize and finance the nation's industrial base for the sake of anticipated profits. These, of course, were the entrepreneurs.

American public attitudes have reflected a schizophrenic quality as regards to the activities of the industrial leaders of the late nineteenth century. Were these entrepreneurs "robber barons" who employed any means necessary to enrich themselves at the expense of their competitors? Or were they "captains of industry" whose shrewd and innovative leadership brought order out of industrial chaos and generated great fortunes that enriched the public welfare through the workings of various philanthropic agencies that these leaders established? Although the "robber baron" stereotype emerged as early as the 1870s, it probably gained its widest acceptance in the 1930s. In the midst of the Great Depression, as many critics were proclaiming the apparent failure of American capitalism, Matthew Josephson published *The Robber Barons* (1934), in which he bitterly condemned the ruthless and occasionally violent methods of industrialists such as John D. Rockefeller and Jay Gould. Since the 1930s, however, some historians, including Allan Nevins, Alfred D. Chandler, Jr., and Maury Klein, have sought to revise the negative assessments offered by earlier generations of scholars. In the hands of these "business historians," the late nineteenth-century businessmen have become "industrial statesmen" who skillfully oversaw the process of raising the United States to a prominent position among the nations of the world. The following essays reveal the divergence of scholarly opinion as it applies to these American entrepreneurs.

John Tipple points out that the public antipathy expressed toward big businessmen like Rockefeller or Andrew Carnegie stemmed from their association with huge corporations whose existence challenged traditional American values. This adverse public opinion was well deserved, says Tipple, because the business magnates frequently behaved recklessly and unethically (if not illegally) in order to amass their great fortunes.

Alfred D. Chandler, Jr., on the other hand, sees the operations of the entrepreneurs as essential to the economic expansion of the country. These business executives, he concludes, developed innovative organizational and marketing strategies that promoted the growth of the nation's urban market economy.

YES

John Tipple

BIG BUSINESSMEN
AND A NEW ECONOMY

It is more than coincidence that the beginning of the Robber Baron legend, the portrayal of the big businessman as a warlike brigand cheating and plundering his way to millions, was contemporaneous with the inauguration of the corporation as the major instrument of business control in the United States. After the Civil War, the large corporation began to dominate the American economic scene. In those same years, Charles Francis Adams, Jr., launched his first assault against the "Erie robbers," and his brother, Henry Adams, warned of the day when great corporations, "swaying power such as has never in the world's history been trusted in the hands of mere private citizens," would be controlled by one man or combinations of men who would use these new leviathans to become masters of the nation.

Such dangerous potentialities were not recognizable prior to the Civil War because the majority of businesses operated as local enterprises, usually as individual proprietorships, partnerships, or as small closed corporations in which ownership and control were almost invariably synonymous. Under most circumstances, the power and influence of the businessman were limited to the immediate environs of operation and seldom extended beyond state boundaries. Equally important, there existed among most businessmen of prewar days a nearly universal desire and a practical necessity for community esteem. This governed their conduct, kept their ventures well within the limits of individual liability, and tended to restrain irresponsible profiteering. Antebellum criticisms of the businessman therefore were few and sporadic. Disapproval usually focused on the speculator or stock gambler, and was often inspired by an agrarian distrust of big-city ways.

The bloody struggles of the Civil War helped bring about revolutionary changes in economic and political life. War needs created almost insatiable demands for goods—arms, munitions, clothing—and offered some manufacturers unsurpassed opportunities to make fortunes. More important, the stimulus of massive military demands alerted entrepreneurs to new concepts of the power and possibilities of large-scale enterprise: "The great operations of war, the handling of large masses of men, the influence of discipline, the lavish expenditure of unprecedented sums of money, the immense financial operations, the possibilities of effective cooperation, were lessons not likely to be lost on men quick to receive and apply all new ideas." Though the war prevented general economic expansion, the news ideas were profitably applied to the peacetime economy.

With the rich resources of the trans-Mississippi West open to private exploitation, the businessman had singular opportunities to become wealthy. Before him spread an immense untapped continent whose riches were his virtually for the taking; new means to turn these resources to profitable account were at hand. A host of new inventions and discoveries, the application of science to industry, and improved methods of transportation and communication were ready to assist the businessman. But all these aids would have been valueless without effective means to put them to work. The practical agency to meet these unprecedented entrepreneurial demands on capital and management proved to be the corporation. The stockholding system provided immense capital beyond the reach of any individual, and the corporate hierarchy presented a feasible solution to the greatly augmented problems of management.

The corporation was no novelty. It had served political as well as economic purposes in seventeenth-century America; as an instrumentality of business its use antedated the discovery of this continent. Seldom before in American history, however, had the corporation been used on such a large scale. From a relatively passive creature of legalistic capitalism, it was transformed by fusion with techniques into a dynamic system spearheading economic expansion.

The impact of the newborn corporation on American society was almost cataclysmic. In the first few decades of its existence the modern corporate system enabled the nation to develop more wealth more rapidly than in any period since the discovery. But it also menaced hallowed economic theories and usages, threatening to ride like a great tidal wave over the traditional democratic social and political beliefs. Its size alone was sufficient to change fundamental social and economic relationships. Of the newly formed United States Steel Corporation an awed commentator wrote at the turn of the century: "It receives and expends more money every year than any but the very greatest of the world's national governments; its debt is larger than that of many of the lesser nations of Europe; it absolutely controls the destinies of a population nearly as large as that of Maryland or Nebraska, and indirectly influences twice that number." Moreover, this concentrated economic power normally gravitated into the hands of a few, raising up a corporate ruling class with great economic authority. . . .

The dedicated businessman could make money on an unprecedented scale. Though John D. Rockefeller never quite became a billionaire, his fortune in 1892 reportedly amounted to $815,647,796.89. Andrew Carnegie did nearly as well. The profits from his industrial empire in the decade 1889 to 1899 averaged about $7,500,000 a year and, in 1900 alone, amounted to $40,000,000. In the following year he sold out his interest for several hundred million dollars. Such fortunes, exceptional even for those days, emphasized the wealth available to the big businessman. In 1892, two New York newspapers engaged in a heated contest to count the number of American millionaires, the *World* uncovering 3,045 and the *Tribune* raising it to 4,047. Regardless of the exact total, millionaires were becoming fairly common. By 1900, for instance, the Senate alone counted twenty-five millionaires among its members, most of them the well-paid agents of big business—a notorious fact that led some suspicious folk to dub that august body the "Rich Man's Club" and the "House of Dollars."

This sudden leap of big businessmen into new positions of wealth and power caught the public eye. To Americans accustomed to thinking primarily of individuals, the big businessman stood out as the conspicuous symbol of corporate power—his popular image encompassing not only his personal attributes and failings but combining also the more amorphous and impersonal aspects of the business organization by which he had climbed to fortune. Just as the diminutive Andrew Carnegie came to represent the entire steel-making complex of men and decisions which bore his name, so the lean, ascetic John D. Rockefeller personified Standard Oil, and the prominent nose and rotund figure of J. P. Morgan signified the whole of Wall Street with its thousands of operators, its ethical flaws, and its business virtues.

Big businessmen were usually attacked not for personal failings, though they had them as well as the lion's share of wealth, but as the recognizable heads of large corporations. When Carnegie and Rockefeller gave up business careers and became private citizens, the rancor against them almost ceased. Instead of being censured for past actions, which had been widely and vehemently criticized, they were praised as benefactors and good citizens. Public castigation of the steel trust was shifted from "Little Andy" to the broader shoulders of Charles Schwab. The odium of monopoly which had surrounded his father was inherited by John D. Rockefeller, Jr. Only as the active and directive heads of great corporations, and not as subordinates or members of a business elite, were big businessmen branded "Robber Barons" and indicted for alleged crimes against society.

If the big businessman was not resented as an individual but as a power symbol wielding the might of the great corporation, the provocative question arises of why there was such resentment against the corporation. The answer is that the large industrial corporation was an anomaly in nineteenth-century America. There was no place for it among existing institutions and no sanction for it in traditional American values. . . .

What was to be done with such a monster? Either the corporation had to be made to conform to American institutions and principles or those institutions and principles had to be changed to accommodate the corporation. This was the dilemma first seriously confronted by Americans during the Gilded Age, and the issue that set off the great movement of introspection and reform which activated the American people for the next fifty years.

Most flagrantly apparent was the destructive effect of the large corporation upon free competition and equal opportunity. According to the accepted theory, which was a projection of the doctrines of liberal democracy into the economic sphere, the ideal economy—the only one, in fact, sanctioned by nature—was made up of freely competing individuals operating in a market unrestricted by man but fairly ruled by the inexorable forces of natural law. The ideal polity was achieved by bargaining among free and equal individuals under the benevolent eye of nature. It was assumed that, in economic affairs, impartial rivalry between individual entrepreneurs and free competition would automatically serve the best interests of society by preventing anyone from getting more than his fair share of the wealth.

In early nineteenth-century America, this self-regulating mechanism seemed to work. Where businesses and factories were small, prices and output, wages and profits, rose and fell according to supply and demand. Every man appeared to have equal opportunity to compete with every other man. Even after the war, the individual businessman was forced, in the interests of self-preservation, to observe the common rules of competition. Ordinarily his share of the market was too small to permit any attempt at price control unless he joined with others in a pool, a trade association, or another rudimentary price-fixing agreement. The average businessman eschewed trade agreements, not out of theoretical considerations, but for the practical reason that such coalitions did not work very well, often suffering from mutual distrust and the pursuit of centrifugal aims.

But what was true in a world of individual proprietors and workers was not necessarily correct for the corporation. It possessed greater unity of control and a larger share of the market and could either dictate prices or combine successfully with other corporations in monopolistic schemes. By bringing to bear superior economic force which to a great extent invalidated the tenets of the free market, the large organization put the big businessman in the favored position of operating in an economy dedicated to the idea of freely competing individuals, yet left him unhampered by the ordinary restrictions. Under such auspicious circumstances, he soon outdistanced unorganized rivals in the race for wealth.

This unfair advantage did not go unchallenged. As the earliest of the large corporations in the United States, the railroads were the first to come under concentrated attack. The immense extension of railways after 1865, and the crucial nature of their operations as common carriers, exposed their activities to public scrutiny and subjected their mistakes or misdeeds to considerable publicity. Popular resentment against the railroads in the early 1870's grew hottest in the farming states of the Midwest, but indignant reports from all over the country accused railroads of using monopoly power against equal opportunity.

A most frequent criticism, common to both East and West, was that railway superintendents and managers showed unreasonable favoritism by discriminating between persons and places, offering rate concessions to large shippers, charging more for short than long hauls, and giving preferential treatment to large corporations in the form of secret rebates and drawbacks. That these preferential rates might sometimes have been forced upon the railroads by pressure from business made little difference. The popular consensus was that this elaborate system of special rates denied the little man equal opportunity with the rich and influential, breaking the connection between individual merit and success. The ultimate effect extended further monopoly by preventing free competition among businesses where railway transportation was an important factor.

The Standard Oil Company seemed to be the outstanding example of a monopoly propagated in this manner, the charge being that the determining factor behind Rockefeller's spectacular conquest of the oil business had been this railway practice of secrecy and favoritism which had aided his company and ruined others. By collecting rebates on their own shipments and drawbacks on those of competitors, Standard had gained virtual control of oil transportation. It then could regulate the prices of crude oil, with the detrimental result, so Henry Demarest Lloyd charged, that by 1881, though the company produced only one-fiftieth of the nation's petroleum, Standard refined nine-tenths of the oil produced in the United States and dictated the price of all of it.

As the whipping boy among trusts, Standard undoubtedly got more than its share of criticism, yet by contemporary standards of competition, the corporation was fairly adjudged a monopoly. Through the testimony of H. H. Rogers, an executive of the company, The Hepburn Committee in 1879 was able to establish that 90 to 95 percent of all the refiners in the country acted in harmony with Standard Oil. In 1886, the monopolistic proclivities of the oil trust were attested to by the Cullom Committee:

It is well understood in commercial circles that the Standard Oil Company brooks no competition; that its settled policy and firm determination is to crush out all who may be rash enough to enter the field against it; that it hesitates at nothing in the accomplishment of this purpose, in which it has been remarkably successful, and that it fitly represents the acme and perfection of corporate greed in its fullest development.

Similar convictions were expressed by a New York senate committee before which Rockefeller and other executives testified in 1888. Four years later, in 1892, the Supreme Court of Ohio declared that the object of the Standard Oil Company was "to establish a virtual monopoly of the business of producing petroleum, and of manufacturing, refining and dealing in it and all its products, throughout the entire country, and by which it might not merely control the production, but the price, at its pleasure."

These findings were reaffirmed by new investigations. In 1902, the United States Industrial Commission reported that Standard, through its control of pipe lines, practically fixed the price of crude oil. In 1907, the commissioner of corporations supported and amplified this conclusion. The company might fall short of an absolute monopoly, the commissioner pointed out, but its intentions were monopolistic. In 1911, the United States Supreme Court confirmed this allegation, observing that "no disinterested mind" could survey the history of the Standard Oil combination from 1870 onward "without being irresistibly driven to the conclusion that the very genius for commercial development and organization . . . soon begot an intent and purpose . . . to drive others from the field and to exclude them from their right to trade and thus accomplish the mastery which was the end in view."

Far from regarding the intricate system of business combination he had developed as a monster to be cured or destroyed, a big businessman such as Rockefeller looked proudly upon his creation as a marvel of beneficence, an extraordinary and distinctive expression of American genius. And Carnegie contended "not evil, but good" had come from the phenomenal development of the corporation. He and others pointed out that the world obtained goods and commodities of excellent quality at pries which earlier generations would have considered incredibly cheap. The poor enjoyed what the richest could never before have afforded.

The big businessman supported his actions as being entirely in keeping with the business requisites of the day. Rather than engaging in a conscious conspiracy to undermine equal opportunity, he had sought only the immediate and practical rewards of successful enterprise, rationalizing business conduct on the pragmatic level of profit and loss.

Instead of deliberately blocking free competition, big businessmen maintained that their actions were only natural responses to immutable law. Charles E. Perkins, president of the Chicago, Burlington and Quincy Railroad Company, denied deliberate misuses of power in establishing rates, and claimed that the price of railroad transportation, like all other prices, adjusted itself. Discriminatory practices were viewed as part of an inevitable conflict between buyer and seller, a necessary result of competition. The payment of rebates and drawbacks was simply one method of meeting the market. In answer to the accusation that the railroads had made "important discriminations" in favor of Standard Oil, an executive of that company replied: "It may be frankly stated at the outset that the Standard Oil Company has at all times within the limits of fairness and with due regard for the law ought to secure the most advantageous freight rates and routes possible." Rockefeller went on record as saying that Standard had received rebates from the railroads prior to 1880, because it was simply the railroads' way of doing business. Each shipper made the best bargain he could, hoping to outdo his competitor.

Furthermore, Rockefeller claimed this traffic was more profitable to the railroads than to the Standard Oil Company, stating that whatever advantage the oil company gained was passed on in lower costs to the consumer. Just as his company later justified certain alleged misdemeanors as being typical of the sharp practices prevailing in the oil fields in the early days, so Rockefeller exonerated the whole system of rebates and drawbacks on the grounds that everybody was doing it, concluding cynically that those who objected on principle did so only because they were not benefiting from it.

Yet despite his public rationalizations, the big businessman's attitude toward competition was ambivalent. He lauded it as economic theory, but denied it in practical actions. Theoretically, there was no such thing as an absolute monopoly; there was always the threat of latent competition. Whenever a trust exacted too much, competitors would automatically appear. Competition as a natural law would survive the trusts. "It is here; we cannot evade it," declaimed Carnegie. "And while the law may be sometimes hard for the individual, it is best for the race, because it insures the survival of the fittest in every department."

In practical matters, however, the big businessman acted as if the law had long since become outmoded, if not extinct. Progressive opinion in the business world heralded the growing monopolistic trend as a sign of economic maturity. Increased concentration in capital and industry was defended as necessary and inevitable. Monopolistic practices in general were upheld in business circles on the grounds that they prevented disastrous competition. In the long run they benefited, rather than plundered, the public by maintaining reasonable rates and prices. "There seems to be a great readiness in the public mind to take alarm at these phenomena of growth, there might rather seem to be reason for public congratulation," announced Professor William Graham Sumner of Yale. "We want to be provided with things abundantly and cheaply; that means that we want increased economic power. All these enterprises are efforts to satisfy that want, and they promise to do it." Many big businessmen believed that, practically at least, the trust proved the superiority of combination over competition. . . .

In condemning trusts as "dangerous to Republican institutions" and in branding corporate leaders as Robber Barons "opposed to free institutions and free commerce between the states as were the feudal barons of the middle ages," aroused Americans of the Gilded Age had clearly seized upon the major issue. They had somehow recognized that American society with its individualistic traditions was engaged in a life-and-death struggle with the organized forces of dissolution.

The once-welcome business and industrial concentration threatened the foundations of the nation. There was more individual power than ever, but those who wielded it were few and formidable. Charles Francis Adams, Jr., denounced these "modern potentates for the autocratic misuse of that power":

The system of corporate life and corporate power, as applied to industrial development, is yet in its infancy. . . . It is a new power, for which our language contains no name. We know what aristocracy, autocracy, democracy are; but we have no word to express government by monied corporations. . . . It remains to be seen what the next phase in this process of gradual development will be. History never quite repeats itself, and . . . the old familiar enemies may even now confront us, though arrayed in such a modern garb that no suspicion is excited. . . . As the Erie ring represents the combination of the corporation and the hired proletariat of a great city; as Vanderbilt embodies the autocratic power of Caesarism introduced into corporate life, and neither alone can obtain complete control of the government of the State, it, perhaps, only remains for the coming man to carry the combination of elements one step in advance, and put Caesarism at once in control of the corporation and of the proletariat, to bring our vaunted institutions within the rule of all historic precedent.

Yet the public already sensed that something had gone wrong with American institutions and values. With less understanding than Adams, they felt that somehow the old rules had been broken. Behind their growing animosity to the big businessman was the feeling that in some way he cheated his countrymen. The belief was becoming fairly common that extreme wealth was incompatible with honesty. "The great cities," Walt Whitman wrote in 1871, "reek with respectable as much as non-respectable robbery and scoundrelism." There were undoubtedly moral men of wealth, but many Americans agreed with Thomas A. Bland, who in *How to Grow Rich* suggested: "In all history, ancient and modern, the examples of men of honest lives and generous hearts who have become rich . . . is so rare as to be exceedingly exceptional, and even these have invariably profited largely . . . by the labor of others."

Very revealing in this regard was the portrayal of the big businessman in contemporary fiction. Socialist writers naturally depicted him as a "criminal of greed" or an "economic monster" who with other "business animals" preyed upon the life of the nation. Oddly enough, however, in an age when the corporation made unprecedented achievements in production and organization to the enrichment of countless people, when material success was widely favored as a legitimate goal, scarcely a single major novelist presented the big businessman as a hero or even in a favorable light. Except at the hands of a few hack writers, the business or industrial leader was consistently portrayed as powerful and capable, but nonetheless an enemy of American society. This may have reflected the bias of the aesthetic or creative temperament against the pragmatic money-maker, but the big businessman was in disfavor with most of American society.

In the popular mind, the vices of lying and stealing were legendarily associated with Wall Street. The big businessmen who dominated "the street" were regarded by some as the ethical counterparts of the pirate and buccaneer. By the simple devices of "stock-watering" or the issuance of fictitious securities not backed by capital assets, speculators were generally believed to have stolen millions of dollars from the American people. In the opinion of the more jaundiced, the men of Wall Street had barely escaped prison bars. "If the details of the great reorganization and trustification deals put through since 1885 could be laid bare," contended Thomas W. Lawson, a financier turned critic, "eight out of ten of our most successful stock-jobbing financiers would be in a fair way to get into State or federal prisons."

The iniquity of Wall Street was not merely legendary, but had firm basis in fact. Though not all speculators were swindlers nor all speculation gambling, only a small number of the stock exchange transactions were unquestionably of an investment character. The vast majority were virtually gambling. Many corporations, although offering huge blocks of stock to the public, issued only the vaguest and most ambiguous summary of assets and liabilities. While this was not iniquitous in itself, secrecy too often cloaked fraud.

The men at the top who had used the corporate device to make millions did not see it this way at all. They justified their millions on the ground that they had fairly earned it. Cornelius Vanderbilt, at the age of eighty-one, boasted that he had made a million dollars for every year of his life, but added that it had been worth "three times that to the people of the United States." Others shared his belief. In *The Railroad and the Farmer,* Edward Atkinson made practically the same statement, asserting that the gigantic fortune of the older Vanderbilt was but a small fraction of what the country gained from the development of the railway system under his genius. The Reverend Julian M. Sturtevant of Illinois College also envisioned the Vanderbilts and Astors of the world as "laborers of gigantic strength, and they must have their reward and compensation for the use of their capital." Carnegie maintained that great riches were no crime. "Under our present conditions the millionaire who toils on is the cheapest article which the community secures at the price it pays for him, namely, his shelter, clothing, and food."

Most Americans, however, did not so readily accept this evaluation. Some recognized that the big businessman in pursuing private ends had served national prosperity—the majority felt that he had taken extravagant profits entirely out of proportion to the economic services he had rendered. Rockefeller's millions were thought to be typical of the fortunes made by Robber Barons, representing "the relentless, aggressive, irresistible seizure of a particular opportunity, the magnitude of which . . . was due simply to the magnitude of the country and the immensity of the stream of its prosperous industrial life." The feeling was general that the great fortunes of all the big business magnates— Vanderbilt, Gould, Harriman, Stanford, Carnegie, Morgan, and the rest—represented special privilege which had enabled them to turn the abundant natural resources and multitudinous advantages offered by a growing nation into a private preserve for their own profit.

The public at large was not clearly aware of it, but the chief instrument of special privilege was the corporation. Though public franchises and political favoritism played a large part in the aggrandizement of the Robber Barons, in the money-making world of late nineteenth-century America special privilege invariably meant corporate privilege. The corporation enabled Vanderbilt to unify his railroads while making large speculative profits on the side. The same device made it possible for men like Rockefeller to create and combine private enterprises embodying new technological and financial techniques while diverting enormous profits to themselves. The corporation was the constructive power behind the building of the cross-country railroads, but it was also the destructive instrument used by Jay Gould, Tom Scott, Collis P. Huntington, and others to convert them into quick money-making

machines with no regard for their obligations as public carriers.

The problem remained of establishing the relationship of big businessmen to the corporation. Judging by their conduct, they were not fully cognizant of the tremendous power placed in their hands by the corporation with single men controlling "thousands of men, tens of millions of revenue, and hundreds of millions of capital." Or they wilfully exerted this prodigious force for private benefit regardless of consequences to the nation or ideals. Unhappily, most of those labeled Robber Baron by their contemporaries fell into the latter category. Cornelius Vanderbilt held the law in contempt. Except where his own interests were involved, he had little regard for the consequences of his actions, manipulating and watering every corporate property he captured. One year after he took over the New York Central railroad, he increased the capitalization by $23,000,000, almost every cent of which represented inside profits for himself and friends. When admonished that some of his transactions were forbidden by law, he supposedly roared, "Law! What do I care about the law? Hain't I got the power?" He confirmed this attitude in testimony before the committee on railroads of the New York State Assembly in 1869. But Vanderbilt's methods were in no way exceptional. Most of the biggest businessmen made their millions in similar fashion. Twenty-four who because of notoriety and conspicuous power might be regarded as "typical" Robber Barons combined the role of promoter with that of entrepreneur. Stock manipulation along with corporate consolidation was probably the easiest way to wealth that ever existed in the United States. The exuberance with which promoters threw themselves into it proved that they were well aware of its golden possibilities.

As a consequence of these reckless corporate maneuverings, however, public opinion turned against the big businessman. While from a corporate point of view the conduct of the money-makers was often legal, although ethically dubious, the public often felt cheated. Puzzled and disenchanted by the way things had turned out, they questioned the way every millionaire got his money, and were quite ready to believe that a crime was behind every great fortune. While its exact nature escaped them, they felt they had been robbed. The classic statement of this feeling of outrage appeared in the Populist platform of 1892: "The fruits of the toil of millions are boldly stolen to build up colossal fortunes for a few, unprecedented in the history of mankind; and the possessors of these, in turn, despise the Republic and endanger liberty."

The inchoate charges were basically accurate: too much wealth was being selfishly appropriated by a few. By the irresponsible use of the corporation, essentially a supralegal abstraction above the traditional laws of the land, they were undermining individualistic institutions and values. Big businessmen like John D. Rockefeller were attacked as Robber Barons because they were correctly identified as destroyers, the insurgent vanguard of the corporate revolution.

NO
Alfred D. Chandler, Jr.

THE BEGINNINGS OF "BIG BUSINESS" IN AMERICAN INDUSTRY

Between the depression of the 1870's and the beginning of the twentieth century, American industry underwent a significant transformation. In the 1870's, the major industries serviced an agrarian economy. Except for a few companies equipping the rapidly expanding railroad network, the leading industrial firms processed agricultural products and provided farmers with food and clothing. These firms tended to be small, and bought their raw materials and sold their finished goods locally. Where they manufactured for a market more than a few miles away from the factory, they bought and sold through commissioned agents who handled the business of several other similar firms.

By the beginning of the twentieth century, many more companies were making producers' goods, to be used in industry rather than on the farm or by the ultimate consumer. Most of the major industries had become dominated by a few large enterprises. These great industrial corporations no longer purchased and sold through agents, but had their own nation-wide buying and marketing organizations. Many, primarily those in the extractive industries, had come to control their own raw materials. In other words, the business economy had become industrial. Major industries were dominated by a few firms that had become great, vertically integrated, centralized enterprises.

In the terms of the economist and sociologist a significant sector of American industry had become bureaucratic, in the sense that business decisions were made within large hierarchical structures. Externally, oligopoly was prevalent, the decision-makers being as much concerned with the actions of the few other large firms in the industry as with over-all changes in markets, sources of supplies, and technological improvements.

These basic changes came only after the railroads had created a national market. The railroad network, in turn, had grown swiftly primarily because of the near desperate requirements for efficient transportation created by the movement of population westward after 1815. Except for the Atlantic seaboard between Boston and Washington, the construction of the American railroads was stimulated almost wholly by the demand for better transportation to move crops, to bring farmers supplies, and to open up new territories to commercial agriculture.

By greatly expanding the scope of the agrarian economy, the railroads quickened the growth of the older commercial centers, such as New York, Philadelphia, Cincinnati, Cleveland, and St. Louis, and helped create new cities like Chicago, Indianapolis, Atlanta, Kansas City, Dallas, and the Twin Cities. This rapid urban expansion intensified the demand for the products of the older consumer goods industries—particularly those which processed the crops of the farmer and planter into food, stimulants, and clothing.

At the same time, railroad construction developed the first large market in this country for producers' goods. Except for the making of relatively few textile machines, steamboat engines, and ordnance, the iron and nonferrous manufacturers had before 1850 concentrated on providing metals and simple tools for merchants and farmers. Even textile machinery was usually made by the cloth manufacturers themselves. However, by 1860, only a decade after beginning America's first major railroad construction boom, railroad companies had already replaced the blacksmiths as the primary market for iron products, and had become far and away the most important market for the heavy engineering industries. By then, too, the locomotive was competing with the Connecticut brass industry as a major consumer of copper. More than this, the railroads, with their huge capital outlay, their fixed operating costs, the large size of their labor and management force, and the technical complexity of their operations, pioneered in the new ways of oligopolistic competition and large-scale, professionalized, bureaucratized management.

The new nation-wide market created by the construction of the railroad network became an increasingly urban one. From 1850 on, if not before, urban areas were growing more rapidly than rural ones. In the four decades from 1840 to 1880 the proportion of urban population rose from 11 per cent to 28 per cent of the total population, or about 4 per cent a decade. In the two decades from 1880 to 1900 it grew from 28 per cent to 40 per cent or an increase of 6 per cent a decade. Was this new urban and national market, then, the primary stimulant for business innovation and change, and for the coming of big business to American industry?

CHANGES IN THE CONSUMERS' GOODS INDUSTRIES

The industries first to become dominated by great business enterprises were those making consumer goods, the majority of which were processed from products grown on the farm and sold in the urban markets. Consolidation and centralization in the consumers' goods industries were well under way by 1893. The unit that appeared was one which integrated within a single business organization the major economic processes: production or purchasing of raw materials, manufacturing, distribution, and finance.

Such vertically integrated organizations came in two quite different ways. Where the product tended to be somewhat new in kind and especially fitted for the urban market, its makers created their businesses by first building large marketing and then purchasing organizations. This technique appears to have been true of the manufacturers or distributors of fresh meat, cigarettes, high-grade flour, bananas, harvesters, sewing machines, and typewriters. Where the products were established staple items, horizontal combination tended to precede vertical integration. In the sugar, salt, leather, whiskey, glucose, starch, biscuit, kerosene, fertilizer, and rubber industries a large number of small manufacturers first combined into large business units and then created their marketing and buying organizations. For a number of reasons the makers of the newer types of products found the older outlets less satisfactory and felt more of a need for direct marketing than did the manufacturers of the long-established goods.

Integration via the Creation of Marketing Organization

The story of the changes and the possible reasons behind them can be more clearly understood by examining briefly the experience of a few innovating firms. First, consider the experience of companies that grew large through the creation of a nation-wide marketing and distributing organization. Here the story of Gustavus F. Swift and his brother Edwin is a significant one. Gustavus F. Swift, an Easterner, came relatively late to the Chicago meat-packing business. Possibly because he was from Massachusetts, he appreciated the potential market for fresh western meat in the eastern cities. For after the Civil War, Boston, New York, Philadelphia, and other cities were rapidly outrunning their local meat supply. At the same time, great herds of cattle were gathering on the western plains. Swift saw the possibilities of connecting the new market with the new source of sup-ply by the use of the refrigerated railroad car. In 1878, shortly after his first experimental shipment of refrigerated meat, he formed a partnership with his younger brother, Edwin, to market fresh western meat in the eastern cities.

For the next decade, Swift struggled hard to carry out his plans, the essence of which was the creation, during the 1880's, of the nation-wide distributing and marketing organization built around a network of branch houses. Each "house" had its storage plant and its own marketing organization. The latter included outlets in major towns and cities, often managed by Swift's own salaried representatives. In marketing the product, Swift had to break down, through advertising and other means, the prejudices against eating meat killed more than a thousand miles away and many weeks earlier. At the same time he had to combat boycotts of local butchers and the concerted efforts of the National Butchers' Protective Association to prevent the sale of his meat in the urban markets.

To make effective use of the branch house network, the company soon began to market products other than beef. The "full line" soon came to include lamb, mutton, pork, and, some time later, poultry, eggs, and dairy products. The growing distributing organization soon demanded an increase in supply. So between 1888 and 1892, the Swifts set up meat-packing establishments in Kansas City, Omaha, and St. Louis, and, after the depression of the 1890's, three more in St. Joseph, St. Paul, and Ft. Worth. At the same time, the company systematized the buying of its cattle and other products at the stockyards. In the 1890's, too, Swift began a concerted effort to make more profitable use of by-products.

Before the end of the 1890's, then, Swift had effectively fashioned a great, vertically integrated organization. The major departments—marketing, processing, purchasing, and accounting—were all tightly controlled from the central office in Chicago. A report of the Commissioner of Corporations published in 1905 makes clear the reason for such control:

> Differences in quality of animals and of their products are so great that the closest supervision of the Central Office is necessary to enforce the exercise of skill and sound judgement on the part of the agents who buy the stock, and the agents who sell the meat. With this object, the branches of the Selling and Accounting Department of those packing companies which have charge of the purchasing, killing, and dressing and selling of fresh meat, are organized in the most extensive and thorough manner. The Central Office is in constant telegraphic correspondence with the distributing houses, with a view to adjusting the supply of meat and the price as nearly as possible to the demand.

As this statement suggests, the other meat packers followed Swift's example. To compete effectively, Armour, Morris, Cudahy, and Schwarzschild & Sulzberger had to build up similar integrated organizations. Those that did not follow the Swift model were destined to remain small local companies. Thus by the middle of the 1890's, the meat-packing industry, with the rapid growth of these great vertically integrated firms had become oligopolistic (the "Big Five" had the major share of the market) and bureaucratic; each of the five had its many departments and several levels of management.

This story has parallels in other industries processing agricultural products. In tobacco, James B. Duke was the first to appreciate the growing market for the cigarette, a new product which was sold almost wholly in the cities. However, after he had applied machinery to the manufacture of cigarettes, production soon outran supply. Duke then concentrated on expanding the market through extensive advertising and the creation of a national and then world-wide selling organization. In 1884, he left Durham, North Carolina, for New York City, where he set up factories, sales, and administrative offices. New York was closer to his major urban markets, and was the more logical place to manage an international advertising campaign than Durham. While he was building his marketing department, Duke was also creating the network of warehouses and buyers in the tobacco-growing areas of the country.

In 1890, he merged his company with five smaller competitors in the cigarette business to form the American Tobacco Company. By 1895 the activities of these firms had been consolidated into the manufacturing, marketing, purchasing, and finance departments of the single operating structure Duke had earlier fashioned. Duke next undertook development of a full line by handling all types of smoking and chewing tobacco. By the end of the century, his company completely dominated the tobacco business. Only two other firms, R. J. Reynolds & Company and P. Lorillard & Company had been able to build up comparable vertically integrated organizations. When they merged with American Tobacco they continued to retain their separate operating organizations. When the 1911 antitrust decree split these and other units off from the American company, the tobacco industry had become, like the meat-packing business, oligopolistic, and its dominant firms bureaucratic.

What Duke and Swift did for their industries, James S. Bell of the Washburn-Crosby Company did during these same years in the making and selling of high-grade flour to the urban bakeries and housewives, and Andrew J. Preston achieved in growing, transporting, and selling another new product for the urban market, the banana. Like Swift and Duke, both these men made their major innovations in marketing, and then went on to create large-scale, departmentalized, vertically integrated structures.

The innovators in new consumer durables followed much the same pattern. Both Cyrus McCormick, pioneer harvester manufacturer, and William Clark, the business brains of the Singer Sewing Machine Company, first sold through commissioned agents. Clark soon discovered that salaried men, working out of branch offices, could more effectively and at less cost display, demonstrate, and service sewing machines than could the agents. Just as important, the branch offices were able to provide the customer with essential credit. McCormick, while retaining the dealer to handle the final sales, came to appreciate the need for a strong selling and distributing organization, with warehouses, servicing facilities, and a large salaried force, to stand behind the dealer. So in the years following the Civil War, both McCormick and Singer Sewing Machine Company concentrated on building up national and then world-wide marketing departments. As they purchased their raw materials from a few industrial companies rather than from a mass of farmers, their purchasing departments were smaller, and required less attention than those in the firms processing farmers' products. But

the net result was the creation of a very similar type of organization.

Integration via Horizontal Combination

In those industries making more standard goods, the creation of marketing organizations usually followed large-scale combinations of a number of small manufacturing firms. For these small firms, the coming of the railroad had in many cases enlarged their markets but simultaneously brought them for the first time into competition with many other companies. Most of these firms appear to have expanded production in order to take advantage of the new markets. As a result, their industries became plagued with overproduction and excess capacity; that is, continued production at full capacity threatened to drop prices below the cost of production. So in the 1880's and early 1890's, many small manufacturers in the leather, sugar, salt, distilling and other corn products, linseed and cotton oil, biscuit, petroleum, fertilizer and rubber boot and glove industries, joined in large horizontal combinations.

In most of these industries, combination was followed by consolidation and vertical integration, and the pattern was comparatively consistent. First, the new combinations concentrated their manufacturing activities in locations more advantageously situated to meet the new growing urban demands. Next they systematized and standardized their manufacturing processes. Then, except in the case of sugar and corn products (glucose and starch), the combinations began to build large distributing and smaller purchasing departments. In so doing, many dropped their initial efforts to buy out competitors or to drive them out of business by price-cutting. Instead they concentrated on the creation of a more efficient flow from the producers of their raw materials to the ultimate consumer, and of the development and maintenance of markets through brand names and advertising. Since the large majority of these combinations began as regional groupings, most industries came to have more than one great firm. Only oil, sugar, and corn products remained long dominated by a single company. By World War I, partly because of the dissolutions under the Sherman Act, these industries had also become oligopolistic, and their leading firms vertically integrated.

Specific illustrations help to make these generalizations more precise. The best-known is the story of the oil industry. but equally illustrative is the experience of the leading distilling, baking, and rubber companies.

The first permanent combination in the whiskey industry came in 1887 when a large number of Midwestern distillers, operating more than 80 small plants, formed the Distillers' and Cattle Feeders' Trust. Like other trusts, it adopted the more satisfactory legal form of a holding company shortly after New Jersey in 1889 passed the general incorporation law for holding companies. The major efforts of the Distillers Company were, first, to concentrate production in a relatively few plants. By 1895 only 21 were operating. The managers maintained that the large volume per plant permitted by such concentration would mean lower costs, and also that the location of few plants more advantageously in relation to supply and marketing would still reduce expenses further. However, the company kept the price of whiskey up, and since the cost of setting up a distillery was small, it soon had competition

from small local plants. The company's answer was to purchase the new competitors and to cut prices. This strategy proved so expensive that the enterprise was unable to survive the depression of the 1890's.

Shortly before going into receivership in 1896, the Distillers Company had begun to think more about marketing. In 1895, it had planned to spend a million dollars to build up a distributing and selling organization in the Urban East—the company's largest market. In 1898, through the purchase of the Standard Distilling & Distributing Company and the Spirits Distributing Company, it did acquire a marketing organization based in New York City. In 1903, the marketing and manufacturing units were combined into a single operating organization under the direction of the Distillers Securities Company. At the same time, the company's president announced plans to concentrate on the development of brand names and specialties, particularly through advertising and packaging. By the early years of the twentieth century, then, the Distillers Company had become a vertically integrated, departmentalized, centralized operating organization, competing in the modern manner, more through advertising and product differentiation than price.

The experience of the biscuit industry is even more explicit. The National Biscuit Company came into being in 1898 as a merger of three regional combinations: The New York Biscuit Company formed in 1890, the American Biscuit and Manufacturing Company, and the United States Biscuit Company founded a little later. Its initial objective was to control price and production, but as in the case of the Distillers Company, this strategy proved too expensive. The Annual Report for 1901 suggests why National Biscuit shifted its basic policies:

> This Company is four years old and it may be of interest to shortly review its history. . . . When the company started, it was an aggregation of plants. It is now an organized business. When we look back over the four years, we find that a radical change has been wrought in our methods of business. In the past, the managers of large merchandising corporations have found it necessary, for success, to control or limit competition. So when this company started, it was thought that we must control competition, and that to do this we must either fight competition or buy it. The first meant a ruinous war of prices, and a great loss of profit; the second, a constantly increasing capitalization. Experience soon proved to us that, instead of bringing success, either of those courses, if persevered in, must bring disaster. This led us to reflect whether it was necessary to control competition. . . . we soon satisfied ourselves that within the Company itself we must look for success.

> We turned our attention and bent our energies to improving the internal management of our business, to getting full benefit from purchasing our raw materials in large quantities, to economizing the expenses of manufacture, to systematizing and rendering more effective our selling department; and above all things and before all things to improve the quality of our goods and the condition in which they should reach the customer.

> It became the settled policy of this Company to buy out no competition. . . .

In concentrating on distribution, the company first changed its policy from selling in bulk to wholesalers to marketing small packages to retailers. It developed the various "Uneeda Biscuit" brands, which immediately became popular. "The next point," the same Annual Report continued, "was to reach the customer. Thinking we had something that the customer wanted, we had to advise the customer of its existence. We did this by extensive advertising." This new packaging and advertising not only quickly created a profitable business, but also required the building of a sizable marketing organization. Since flour could be quickly and easily purchased in quantity from large milling firms, the purchasing requirements were less complex, and so the company needed a smaller purchasing organization. On the other hand, it spent much energy after 1901 in improving plant layout and manufacturing processes in order to cut production costs and to improve and standardize quality. Throughout the first decade of its history, National Biscuit continued the policy of "centralizing" manufacturing operations, particularly in its great New York and Chicago plants.

In the rubber boot, shoe, and glove industries, the story is much the same. Expansion of manufacturing facilities and increasing competition as early as 1874, led to the formation, by several leading firms, of the Associated Rubber Shoe Companies—an organization for setting price and production schedules through its board of directors. This company continued until 1886. Its successor, the Rubber Boot and Shoe Company, which lasted only a year, attempted, besides controlling prices and production, to handle marketing, which had always been done by commissioned agents. After five years of uncontrolled competition, four of the five firms that had organized the selling company again combined, this time with the assistance of a large rubber importer, Charles A. Flint. The resulting United States Rubber Company came, by 1898, to control 75 per cent of the nation's rubber boot, shoe, and glove output.

At first the new company remained a decentralized holding company. Each constituent company retained its corporate identity with much freedom of action, including the purchasing of raw materials and the selling of finished products, which was done, as before, through jobbers. The central office's concern was primarily with controlling price and production schedules. Very soon, however, the company began, in the words of the 1896 Annual Report, a policy of "perfecting consolidation of purchasing, selling, and manufacturing." This was to be accomplished in four ways. First, as the 1895 Annual Report had pointed out, the managers agreed "so far as practicable, to consolidate the purchasing of all supplies of raw materials for the various manufacturies into one single buying agency, believing that the purchase of large quantities of goods can be made at more advantageous figures than the buying of small isolated lots." The second new "general policy" was "to undertake to reduce the number of brands of goods manufactured, and to consolidate the manufacturing of the remaining brands in those factories which have demonstrated superior facilities for production or advantageous labor conditions. This course was for the purpose of utilizing the most efficient instruments of production and closing those that were inefficient and unprofitable." The third policy was to consolidate sales through the formation of a "Selling Department," which was to handle all goods made by the constituent companies in order to achieve "economy in the distribution expense." Selling was now to be handled by a central office in the New York City headquarters, with branch offices throughout the United States and Europe. Of the three great new departments, actually manufacturing was the slowest to be fully consolidated and centralized. Finally, the treasurer's office at headquarters began to obtain accurate data on profit and loss through the institution of uniform, centralized cost accounting.

Thus United States Rubber, National Biscuit, and the Distillers Securities Company soon came to have organizational structures paralleling those of Swift and American Tobacco. By the first decade of the twentieth century, the leading firms in many consumers' goods industries had become departmentalized and centralized. This was the organizational concomitant to vertical integration. Each major function, manufacturing, sales, purchasing, and finance, became managed by a single and separate department head, usually a vice president, who, assisted by a director or a manager, had full authority and responsibility for the activities of his unit. These departmental chiefs, with the president, coordinated and evaluated the work of the different functional units, and made policy for the company as a whole. In coordinating, appraising, and policy-making, the president and the vice presidents in charge of departments came to rely more and more on the accounting and statistical information, usually provided by the finance department, on costs, output, purchases, and sales. . . .

CONCLUSION: THE BASIC INNOVATIONS

The middle of the first decade of the new

century might be said to mark the end of an era. By 1903, the great merger movement was almost over, and by then the metals industries and those processing agricultural products had developed patterns of internal organization and external competition which were to remain. In those years, too, leading chemical, electrical, rubber, power machinery and implement companies had initiated their "full line" policy, and had instituted the earliest formal research and development departments created in this country. In this decade also, electricity was becoming for the first time a significant source of industrial power, and the automobile was just beginning to revolutionize American transportation. From 1903 on, the new generators of power and the new technologies appear to have become the dominant stimuli to innovation in American industry, and such innovations were primarily those which created new products and processes. Changes in organizational methods and marketing techniques were largely responses to technological advances.

This seems much less true of the changes during the 20 to 25 years before 1903. In that period, the basic innovations were more in the creation of new forms of organization and new ways of marketing. The great modern corporation, carrying on the major industrial processes, namely, purchasing, and often production of materials and parts, manufacturing, marketing, and finance —all within the same organizational structure—had its beginnings in that period. Such organizations hardly existed, outside of the railroads, before the 1880's. By 1900 they had become the basic business unit in American industry.

Each of these major processes became managed by a corporate department, and all were coordinated and supervised from a central office. Of the departments, marketing was the most significant. The creation of nation-wide distributing and selling organizations was the initial step in the growth of many larger consumer goods companies. Mergers in both the consumer and producer goods industries were almost always followed by the formation of a centralized sales department.

The consolidation of plants under a single manufacturing department usually accompanied or followed the formation of a national marketing organization. The creation of such a manufacturing department normally meant the concentration of production in fewer and larger plants, and such consolidation probably lowered unit costs and increased output per worker. The creation of such a department in turn led to the setting up of central traffic, purchasing, and often engineering organizations. Large-scale buying, more rational routing of raw materials and finished products, more systematic plant lay-out, and plant location in relation to materials and markets probably lowered costs still further. Certainly the creators of these organizations believed that it did. In the extractive and machinery industries integration went one step further. Here the motives for controlling raw materials or parts and components were defensive as well as designed to cut costs through providing a more efficient flow of materials from mine to market.

These great national industrial organizations required a large market to provide the volume necessary to support the increased overhead costs. Also, to be profitable, they needed careful coordination between the different functional departments. This coordination required a steady flow of accurate data on costs, sales, and on all purchasing, manufacturing, and marketing activities. As a result, the comptroller's office became an increasingly important department. In fact, one of the first moves after a combination by merger or purchase was to institute more effective and detailed accounting procedures. Also, the leading entrepreneurs of the period, men like Rockefeller, Carnegie, Swift, Duke, Preston, Clark, and the DuPonts, had to become, as had the railroad executives of an earlier generation, experts in reading and interpreting business statistics.

Consolidation and departmentalization meant that the leading industrial corporations became operating rather than holding companies, in the sense that the officers and managers of the companies were directly concerned with operating activities. In fact, of the 50 companies with the largest assets in 1909, only United States Steel, Amalgamated Copper, and one or two other copper companies remained purely holding companies. In most others, the central office included the heads of the major functional departments, usually the president, vice presidents, and sometimes a chairman of the board and one or two representatives of financial interests. These men made major policy and administrative decisions and evaluated the performance of the departments and the corporation as a whole. In the extractive industries a few companies, like Standard Oil (N.J.) and some of the metals companies, were partly holding and partly operating companies. At Standard Oil nearly all important decisions were made in the central headquarters, at 26 Broadway, which housed not only the presidents of the subsidiaries but the powerful policy formulating and coordinating committees. But in some of the metals companies, the subsidiaries producing and transporting raw materials retained a large degree of autonomy.

The coming of the large vertically integrated, centralized, functionally departmentalized industrial organization altered the internal and external situations in which and about which business decisions were made. Information about markets, supplies, and operating performance as well as suggestions for action often had to come up through the several levels of the departmental hierarchies, while decisions and suggestions based on this data had to be transmitted down the same ladder for implementation. Executives on each level became increasingly specialists in one function—in sales, production, purchasing, or finance—and most remained in one department and so handled one function only for the major part of their business careers. Only he who climbed to the very top of the departmental ladder had a chance to see his own company as a single operating unit. Where a company's markets, sources of raw materials, and manufacturing processes remained relatively stable, as was true in the metals industries and in those processing agricultural goods, the nature of the business executive's work became increasingly routine and administrative.

When the internal situation had become bureaucratic, the external one tended to be oligopolistic. Vertical integration by one manufacturer forced others to follow. Thus, in a very short time, many American industries became dominated by a few large firms, with the smaller ones handling local and more specialized aspects of the business. Occasionally industries like oil, tobacco, and sugar, came to be controlled by one company, but in most cases legal action by the federal government in the years after 1900 turned monopolistic industries into oligopolistic ones.

Costs, rather than interfirm competition, began to determine prices. With better information on costs, supplies, and market conditions, the companies were able to determine price quite accurately on the basis of the desired return on investment. The managers of the different major companies had little to gain by cutting prices below an acceptable profit margin. On the other hand, if one firm set its prices excessively high, the other firms could increase their share of the market by selling at a lower price and still maintain a profit. They would, however, rarely cut to the point where this margin was eliminated. As a result, after 1900, price leadership, price umbrellas, and other evidences of oligopolistic competition became common in many American industries. To increase their share of the market and to improve their profit position, the large corporations therefore concerned themselves less with price and concentrated more on obtaining new customers by advertising, brand names, and product differentiations; on cutting costs through further improvement and integration of the manufacturing, marketing, and buying processes; and on developing more diversified lines of products.

The coming of the large vertically integrated corporation changed more than just the practices of American industrialists and their industries. The effect on the merchant, particularly the wholesaler, and on the financier, especially the investment banker, has been suggested here. The relation between the growth of these great industrial units and the rise of labor unions has often been pointed out. Certainly the regulation of the large corporation became one of the major political issues of these years, and the devices created to carry out such a regulation were significant innovations in American constitutional, legal, and political institutions. But an examination of such effects is beyond the scope of this paper.

Reasons for the Basic Innovations

One question remains to be reviewed. Why did the vertically integrated corporation come when it did, and in the way it did? The creation by nearly all the large firms of nation-wide selling and distributing organizations indicates the importance of the national market. It was necessary that the market be an increasingly urban one. The city took the largest share of the goods manufactured by the processors of agricultural products. The city, too, with its demands for construction materials, lighting, heating and many other facilities, provided the major market for the metals and other producers' goods industries after railroad construction slowed. Without the rapidly growing urban market there would have been little need and little opportunity for the coming of big business in American industry. And such a market could hardly have existed before the completion of a nation-wide railroad network.

What other reasons might there have been for the swift growth of the great industrial corporation? What about foreign markets? In some industries, particularly oil, the overseas trade may have been an important factor. However, in most businesses the domestic customers took the lion's share of the output, and in nearly all of them the move abroad appears to have come after the creation of the large corporation, and after such corporations had fashioned their domestic marketing organization.

What about the investor looking for profitable investments, and the promoter seeking new promotions? Financiers and promoters certainly had an impact on the changes after 1897, but again they seem primarily to have taken advantage of what had already proved successful. The industrialists themselves, rather than the financiers, initiated most of the major changes in business organization. Availability of capital and cooperation with the financier figured much less prominently in these industrial combinations and consolidations than had been the case with the earlier construction of the railroads and with the financing of the Civil War.

What about technological changes? Actually, except for electricity, the major innovations in the metals industries seem to have come before or after the years under study here. Most of the technological improvements in the agricultural processing industries appear to have been made to meet the demands of the new urban market. The great technological innovations that accompanied the development of electricity, the internal combustion engine, and industrial chemistry did have their beginning in these years, and were, indeed, to have a fundamental impact on the American business economy. Yet this impact was not to be really felt until after 1900.

What about the entrepreneurial talent? Certainly the best-known entrepreneurs of this period were those who helped to create the large industrial corporation. If, as Joseph A. Schumpeter suggests, "The defining characteristic [of the entrepreneur and his function] is simply the doing of new things, and doing things that are already done, in a new way (innovation)," Rockefeller, Carnegie, Frick, Swift, Duke, McCormick, the DuPonts, the Guggenheims, Coffin of General Electric, Preston of United Fruit, and Clark of Singer Sewing Machine were all major innovators of their time. And their innovations were not in technology, but rather in organization and in marketing. "Doing a new thing," is, to Schumpeter a "creative response" to a new situation, and the situation to which these innovators responded appears to have been the rise of the national urban market.

POSTSCRIPT

Were Nineteenth-Century Entrepreneurs Robber Barons?

Regardless of whether American entrepreneurs are regarded as "captains of industry" or "robber barons," there is no doubt that they constituted a powerful elite and were responsible for defining the character of society in the Gilded Age. For many Americans, these businessmen represented the logical culmination of the country's attachment to laissez-faire economics and rugged individualism. In fact, it was not unusual at all for the nation's leading industrialists to be depicted as the real-life models for the "rags-to-riches" theme epitomized in the self-help novels of Horatio Alger. Closer examination of the lives of most of these entrepreneurs, however, reveals the mythical dimensions of this American ideal. Simply put, the typical business executive of the late nineteenth century did not rise up from humble circumstances, a product of the American rural tradition or the immigrant experience, as frequently claimed. Rather, most of these big businessmen (Andrew Carnegie may have been an exception) were of Anglo-Saxon origin and reared in a city by middle-class parents. On Sundays, they attended an Episcopal or Congregational Protestant Church. According to one survey, over half the leaders had attended college at a time when even the pursuit of a high school education was considered unusual. In other words, instead of having to pull themselves up by their own bootstraps from the bottom of the social heap, these individuals usually started their climb to success at the middle of the ladder or higher.

The reader may be surprised to learn that in spite of the massive influx of immigrants from Asia and southern and eastern Europe in the years 1880 to 1924, today's leaders are remarkably similar in their social and economic backgrounds to their nineteenth-century counterparts. A 1972 study by Thomas Dye listing the top 4,000 decisionmakers in corporate, governmental, and public-interest sectors of American life revealed that 90 percent were affluent, white, Anglo-Saxon males. There were only two African Americans in the whole group; there were no Native Americans, Hispanics, or Japanese Americans, and very few recognizable Irish, Italians, or Jews.

A useful contextual framework for examining the role of the American entrepreneur can be found in Thomas C. Cochran and William Miller, *The Age of Enterprise: A Social History of Industrial America*, rev. ed. (Harper & Row, 1961), and in Glenn Porter, *The Rise of Big Business, 1860–1910* (Harlan Davidson, 1973). Peter d'A. Jones, ed., *The Robber Barons Revisited* (D. C. Heath, 1968), has assembled an excellent collection of the major viewpoints on the "robber baron" thesis. For efforts to present the actions of the late nineteenth-century businessmen in a favorable light, see Allan Nevins, *A*

Study in Power: John D. Rockefeller, Industrialist and Philanthropist, 2 vols. (Scribner's, 1953); Harold Livesay, *Andrew Carnegie and the Rise of Big Business* (Little, Brown, 1975); and Maury Klein, *The Life and Legend of Jay Gould* (Johns Hopkins Press, 1986). Robert Sobel's *The Entrepreneurs: Explorations Within the American Business Tradition* (Weybright and Talley, 1974) presents sympathetic sketches of the builders of often neglected industries of the nineteenth and twentieth centuries. For a critique of Matthew Josephson, one of the architects of the "robber baron" thesis, see Maury Klein, "A Robber Historian," *Forbes* (October 26, 1987).

The works of Alfred D. Chandler, Jr., are vital to the understanding of American industrialization. Chandler almost singlehandedly reshaped the way in which historians write about American corporations. Instead of arguing about the morality of nineteenth-century businessmen, he employed organizational theories of decision-making borrowed from the sociologists and applied them to case studies of corporate America. See *Strategy and Structure: Chapters in the History of the American Industrial Enterprise* (MIT Press, 1962); *The Visible Hand: The Managerial Revolution in American Business* (Harvard, 1977); and *Scale and Scope: The Dynamics of Industrial Capitalism* (Harvard, 1990). Chandler's most important essays are collected in Thomas K. McCraw, ed., *The Essential Alfred Chandler: Essays Toward a Historical Theory of Big Business* (Harvard Business School Press, 1988). For an assessment of Chandler's approach and contributions, see Louis Galambos's, "The Emerging Organizational Synthesis in Modern American History," *Business History Review* (Autumn 1970) and Thomas K. McCraw's, "The Challenge of Alfred D. Chandler, Jr.: Retrospect and Prospect," *Reviews in American History* (March 1987).

ISSUE 3

Was the American Labor Movement Radical?

YES: Leon Fink, from *Workingmen's Democracy: The Knights of Labor and American Politics* (University of Illinois Press, 1983)

NO: Carl N. Degler, from *Out of Our Past: The Forces That Shaped Modern America,* 3d ed. (Harper & Row, 1984)

ISSUE SUMMARY

YES: Associate professor of history Leon Fink, though stopping short of a frontal attack on capitalism, argues that the Knights of Labor envisioned a kind of workingman's democracy that would ensure minimal standards of health and safety at the industrial workplace.
NO: Professor of history Carl N. Degler maintains that the American labor movement accepted capitalism and reacted conservatively to the radical organizational changes brought about in the economic system by big business.

The two major labor unions that developed in the late nineteenth century were the Knights of Labor and the American Federation of Labor. Because of the hostility toward labor unions, the Knights of Labor functioned for a dozen years as a secret organization. Between 1879 and 1886 the Knights grew from 10,000 to 700,000 members. Idealistic in many of its aims, the union supported social reforms such as equal pay for men and women, prohibition of alcoholic liquor, and the abolition of convict and child labor. Economic reforms included the development of workers' cooperatives, public ownership of utilities, and a more moderate, eight-hour workday. The Knights declined after 1886 for several reasons. Though opposed to strikes, the union received a black eye, as did the whole labor movement, when it was blamed for the bombs thrown at the police during the Haymarket Square riot in Chicago. According to most historians, other reasons usually associated with the decline of the Knights include the failure of some cooperative businesses, conflict between skilled and unskilled workers, and, most importantly, competition from the American Federation of Labor. By 1890 the Knights membership had dropped to 100,000. It died in 1917.

A number of skilled unions got together in 1886 and formed the American Federation of Labor. Samuel Gompers was elected its first president and his philosophy permeated the AFL during his 37 years in office. He pushed for practical reforms—better hours, wages, and working conditions. Unlike the Knights, the AFL avoided associations with political parties, workers' cooperatives, unskilled workers, immigrants, and women. Decision-making power was in the hands of the locals rather than the central board. Gompers was heavily criticized by his contemporaries, and later by historians, for his narrow craft unionism. But membership increased in spite of the depression of the 1890s from 190,000 to 500,000 by 1900, to 1,500,000 in 1904, and 2,000,000 by the eve of World War I.

Gomper's cautiousness is best understood in the context of his times. The national and local governments were in the hands of men sympathetic to the rise of big business and hostile to the attempts of labor to organize. Whether it was the Railroad Strike of 1877, the Homestead steel strike of 1892, or the Pullman car strike of 1894, the pattern of repression was always the same. Companies would cut wages, workers would go out on strike, scab workers would be brought in, fights would break out, companies would get court injunctions, and the police and state and federal militia would beat up the unionized workers. After a strike was broken, workers would lose their jobs or would accept pay cuts and longer workdays.

On the national level, Theodore Roosevelt became the first president to show any sympathy for the workers. As a police commissioner in New York City and later as governor of New York, Roosevelt observed firsthand the deplorable occupational and living conditions of the workers. Although he avoided recognition of the collective bargaining rights of labor unions, Roosevelt forced the anthracite coal owners in Pennsylvania to mediate before an arbitration board for an equitable settlement of a strike with the mine workers.

In 1905 a coalition of socialists and industrial unionists formed America's most radical labor union—the Industrial Workers of the World (IWW). There were frequent splits within this union and much talk of violence. But in practice the IWW was more interested in organizing workers into industrial unions, like the earlier Knights of Labor and the later Congress of Industrial Organizations, than in fighting. Strikes were encouraged to improve the daily conditions of the workers through long-range goals, which included reducing the power of the capitalists by increasing the power of the workers.

In the following selections, Leon Fink argues that the Knights of Labor envisioned a kind of workingman's democracy which would bring about minimal standards of health and safety in the industrial workplace. Although the Knights did not espouse socialism, the union did search for alternatives to the hourly wage system, which had become a standard feature in the new assembly line factories. Carl N. Degler believes that American workers accepted capitalism and, like business unionist Samuel Gompers, were interested in obtaining better hours, wages, and working conditions. Socialism was rejected, he argues, because workers believed they were achieving economic and social mobility under capitalism.

YES   Leon Fink

WORKINGMEN'S DEMOCRACY

Two well-traveled routes into the Gilded Age are likely to leave the present-day visitor with the same puzzled and unsatisfied feeling. One itinerary pursuing the political history of the era begins in 1876 with the official end of Reconstruction and winds through the election of William McKinley in 1896. The other route, this one taking a social prospectus, departs with the great railroad strikes of 1877 and picks its way through the drama and debris of an industrializing society. The problem is that the two paths never seem to meet. Compartmentalization of subject matter in most textbooks into "politics," "economic change," "social movements," and so on only papers over the obvious unanswered question—what impact did an industrial revolution of unprecedented magnitude have on the world's most democratic nation?

The question, or course, permits no simple answer. By most accounts the political era inaugurated in 1876 appears, except for the Populist outburst of the mid-1890s, as a conservative, comparatively uneventful time sandwiched between the end of Radical Reconstruction and the new complexities of the twentieth century. With the Civil War's financial and social settlement out of the way, a society desperately wanting to believe that it had removed its last barriers to social harmony by and large lapsed into a period of ideological torpor and narrow-minded partisanship. Political contests, while still the national pastime (national elections regularly drew 80 percent, state and local elections 60–80 percent of eligible voters, 1876–96), seem to have dwelt less on major social issues than on simple party fealty. Fierce rivalries engendered by the sectional, ethnocultural, and economic interest group divisions among the American people increasingly were presided over and manipulated by party professionals. To be sure, genuine policy differences—e.g., over how best to encourage both industry and trade, the degree of danger posed by the saloon, honesty in government—fueled a venomous political rhetoric. As echoed by both national parties from the late 1870s through the early 1890s, however, a complacent political consensus had emerged, stressing individual opportunity, rights in property, and economic freedom from constraints. The welfare of the American Dream, in the minds of both Democrats and Republicans, required no significant governmental tinkering or popular mobilization. Acknowledging the parties' avoidance of changing social and economic realities, a most compelling recent commentary on the late nineteenth-century polity suggests that the "distinct, social need" of the time was in part filled by heightened partisanship and the act of political participation itself.

In contrast to the ritualistic quality of politics, the contemporary social world seems positively explosive. Consolidation of America's industrial revolution touched off an era of unexampled change and turmoil. As work shifted decisively away from agriculture between 1870 and 1890, the manufacturing sector, with a spectacular increase in the amount of capital invested, the monetary value of product, and the number employed, sparked a great economic leap forward. By 1880 Carroll D. Wright, U.S. Commissioner of Labor Statistics, found that the application of steam and water power to production had so expanded that "at least four-fifths" of the "nearly 3 millions of people employed in the mechanical industries of this country" were working under the factory system. It was not just the places of production but the people working within them that represented a dramatic departure from preindustrial America. While only 13 percent of the total population was classified as foreign-born in 1880, 42 percent of those engaged in manufacturing and extractive industries were immigrants. If one adds to this figure workers of foreign parentage and of Afro-American descent, the resulting nonnative/nonwhite population clearly encompassed the great majority of America's industrial work force. Not only, therefore, had the industrial revolution turned a small minority in America's towns and cities into the direct employers of their fellow citizens, but the owners of industry also differed from their employees in national and cultural background. This sudden transformation of American communities, accompanied as it was by a period of intense price competition and unregulated swings in the business cycle, provided plentiful ingredients for social unrest, first manifest on a national scale in the railroad strike of 1877.

The quintessential expression of the labor movement in the Gilded Age was the Noble and Holy Order of the Knights of Labor, the first mass organization of the American working class. Launched as one of several secret societies among Philadelphia artisans in the late 1860s, the Knights grew in spurts by the accretion of miners (1874–79) and skilled urban tradesmen (1879–85). While the movement formally concentrated on moral and political education, cooperative enterprise, and land settlement, members found it a convenient vehicle for trade union action, particularly in the auspicious economic climate following the depression of the 1870s. Beginning in 1883, local skirmishes escalated into highly publicized confrontations with railroad financier Jay Gould, a national symbol of new corporate power. Strikes by Knights of Labor telegraphers and railroad shopmen touched off an unprecedented wave of strikes and boycotts that carried on into the renewed depression in 1884–85 and spread to thousands of previously unorganized semiskilled and unskilled laborers, both urban and rural. The Southwest Strike on Gould's Missouri and Texas-Pacific railroad lines together with massive urban eight-hour campaigns in 1886 swelled a tide of unrest that has become known as the "Great Upheaval." The turbulence aided the efforts of organized labor, and the Knights exploded in size, reaching more than three-quarters of a million members. Although membership dropped off drastically in the late 1880s, the Knights remained a powerful force in many areas through the mid-1890s. Not until the Congress of Industrial Organizations revival of the 1930s would the organized labor movement again lay claim to such influence within the working population.

At its zenith the movement around the Knights helped to sustain a national debate over the social implications of industrial capitalism. Newspaper editors, lecturers, and clergymen everywhere addressed the Social Question. John Swinton, the leading labor journalist of the day, counted Karl Marx, Hawaii's King Kalakaua, and the Republican party's chief orator, Robert G. Ingersoll, among the enlightened commentators on the subject. Even the U.S. Senate in 1883 formally investigated "Relations between Labor and Capital." Nor was the debate conducted only from on high. In laboring communities across the nation the local press as well as private correspondence bore witness to no shortage of eloquence from the so-called inarticulate. One of the busiest terminals of communications was the Philadelphia office of Terence Vincent Powderly, General Master Workman of the Knights of Labor. Unsolicited personal letters expressing the private hopes and desperations of ordinary American citizens daily poured in upon the labor leader: an indigent southern mother prayed that her four young girls would grow up to find an honorable living, an unemployed New York cakemaker applied for a charter as an organizer, a Cheyenne chief sought protection for his people's land, an inventor offered to share a new idea for the cotton gin on condition that it be used cooperatively.

Amidst spreading agitation, massed strength, and growing public awareness, the labor issues ultimately took tangible political form. Wherever the Knights of Labor had organized by the mid-1880s, it seemed, contests over power and rights at the workplace evolved into a community-wide fissure over control of public policy as well. Indeed, in some 200 towns and cities from 1885 to 1888 the labor movement actively fielded its own political slates. Adopting "Workingmen's," "United Labor," "Union Labor," "People's Party," and "Independent" labels for their tickets, or alternatively taking over one of the standing two-party organizations in town, those local political efforts revealed deep divisions within the contemporary political culture and evoked sharp reactions from traditional centers of power. Even as manufacturer's associations met labor's challenge at the industrial level, business response at the political level was felt in the dissolution of party structures, creation of antilabor citizens' coalitions, new restrictive legislation, and extralegal law and order leagues. In their ensemble, therefore, the political confrontations of the 1880s offer a most dramatic point of convergence between the world leading out of 1876 and that stretching from 1877. As a phenomenon simultaneously entwined in the political and industrial history of the Gilded Age the subject offers an opportunity to redefine the main issues of the period. . . .

WORKING-CLASS RADICALISM IN THE GILDED AGE: DEFINING A POLITICAL CULTURE

The Labor Movement of the Gilded Age, not unlike its nineteenth-century British counterpart, spoke a "language of class" that was "as much political as economic." In important ways an eighteenth-century republican political inheritance still provided the basic vocabulary. The emphasis within the movement on equal rights, on the identity of work and self-worth, and on secure, family-centered households had informed American political radicalism for decades. A republican outlook lay at the heart of the protests of journeymen-mechanics and women millworkers during the Jacksonian period; it likewise inspired abolitionist and the women's suffrage and temperance movements and even contributed to the common school crusade. Within the nineteenth-century political mainstream this tradition reached its height of influence in the free labor assault of the Radical Republicans against slavery. The fracture of the Radical Republican bloc, as David Montgomery has demonstrated, signaled a break in the tradition itself. The more conspicuous and politically dominant side of the schism reflected the growing ideological conservatism of America's industrialists and their steady merger into older socioeconomic elites. A less complacent message, however, also percolated through the age of Hayes, Harrison, and Hanna. Taking place largely outside the party system, this renewed radicalism found a home within an invigorated labor movement.

Working-class radicalism in the Gilded Age derived its principles—as grouped around economic, national-political, and cultural themes—from the period of the early revolutionary-democratic bourgeoisie. Implicitly, labor radicals embraced a unifying conception of work and culture that Norman Birnbaum has labeled the *Homo faber* ideal: "an artisanal conception of activity, a visible, limited, and directed relationship to nature." The

Homo faber ethic found its political embodiment in Enlightenment liberalism. "From that source," notes Trygve R. Tholfson in a recent commentary on mid-Victorian English labor radicalism, "came a trenchant rationalism, a vision of human emancipation, the expectation of progress based on reason, and an inclination to take the action necessary to bring society into conformity with rationally demonstrable principles." In the late nineteenth century Enlightenment liberalism was harnessed to a historical understanding of American nationalism, confirmed by both the American Revolution and the Civil War. Together these political, economic, and moral conceptions coalesced around a twin commitment to the citizen-as-producer and the producer-as-citizen. For nearly a century Americans had been proud that their country, more than anywhere else in the world, made republican principles real. In this respect the bloody war over slavery served only to confirm the ultimate power of the ideal.

Certain tendencies of the Gilded Age, however, heralded for some an alarming social regression. The permanency of wage labor, the physical and mental exhaustion inflicted by the factory system, and the arrogant exercise of power by the owners of capital threatened the rational and progressive march of history. "Republican institutions," the preamble to the constitution of the Knights of Labor declared simply, "are not safe under such conditions." "We have openly arrayed against us," a Chicago radical despaired in 1883, "the powers of the world, most of the intelligence, all the wealth, and even law itself." . . .

In response the labor movement in the Gilded Age turned the plowshares of a consensual political past into a sword of class conflict. "We declare," went the Knights' manifesto, "an inevitable and irresistible conflict between the wage-system of labor and republican system of government." To some extent older demons seemed simply to have reappeared in new garb, and, as such, older struggles beckoned with renewed urgency. A Greenback editor in Rochester, New Hampshire, thus proclaimed that "patriots" who overturn the "lords of labor" would be remembered next to "the immortal heroes of the revolution and emancipation." . . .

To many other outside observers in the 1880s, the American working class—in terms of organization, militancy, and collective self-consciousness—appeared more advanced than its European counterparts. A leader of the French Union des Chambres Syndicales Ouvrières compared the self-regarding, individualist instincts of the French workers to those of the Americans enrolled in the Knights of Labor (Ordre des Chevaliers du Travail):

Unfortunately, the French worker, erratic as he is enthusiastic, of an almost discouraging indolence when it is a question of his own interests, does not much lend himself to organization into a great order like yours. He understands nevertheless their usefulness, even cites them as an example each time that he has the occasion to prove the possibility of the solidarity of workers; but when it comes to passing from the domain of theory to that of practice, he retreats or disappears. Thirsty for freedom he is always afraid of alienating any one party while contracting commitments toward a collectivity; mistrustful, he is afraid of affiliating with a group whose positions might not correspond exactly to those inscribed on his own flag; undisciplined, he conforms with difficulty to

rules which he has given to himself. . . . He wants to play it safe and especially will not consent to any sacrifice without having first calculated the advantages it will bring to him.

Eleanor Marx and Edward Aveling returned from an 1886 American tour with a glowing assessment of the workers' mood. Friedrich Engels, too, in the aftermath of the eight-hour strikes and the Henry George campaign, attached a special preface to the 1887 American edition of *The Condition of the Working Class in England in 1844*:

In European countries, it took the working class years and years before they fully realized the fact that they formed a distinct and, under the existing social conditions, a permanent class of modern society; and it took years again until this class-consciousness led them to form themselves into a distinct political party, independent of, and opposed to, all the old political parties, formed by the various sections of the ruling classes. On the more favored soil of America, where no medieval ruins bar the way, where history begins with the elements of the modern bourgeois society as evolved in the seventeenth century, the working class passed through these two stages of its development within ten months.

Nor was it in the eyes of eager well-wishers that the developments of the 1880s seemed to take on a larger significance. Surveying the map of labor upheaval, the conservative Richmond *Whig* wrote in 1886 of "socialistic and agrarian elements" threatening "the genius of our free institutions." The Chicago *Times* went so far in its fear of impending revolution as to counsel the use of hand grenades against strikers.

Revolutionary anticipations, pro or con, proved premature. That was true at least partly because both the movement's distant boosters as well as its domestic detractors sometimes misrepresented its intentions. Gilded Age labor radicals did not self-consciously place themselves in opposition to a prevailing economic system but displayed a sincere ideological ambivalence toward the capitalist marketplace. On the one hand, they frequently invoked a call for the "abolition of the wage system." On the other hand, like the classical economists, they sometimes spoke of the operation of "natural law" in the marketplace, acknowledged the need for a "fair return" on invested capital, and did not oppose profit per se. Employing a distinctly pre-Marxist economic critique that lacked a theory of capital accumulation or of surplus value, labor leaders from Ira Steward to Terence Powderly tried nevertheless to update and sharpen the force of received wisdom. The Knights thus modified an earlier radical interpretation of the labor-cost theory of value, wherein labor, being the source of all wealth, should individually be vested with the value of its product, and demanded for workers only an intentionally vague "proper share of the wealth they create." In so doing they were able to shift the weight of the analysis (not unlike Marx) to the general, collective plight of the laboring classes. In their eyes aggregation of capital together with cutthroat price competition had destroyed any semblance of marketplace balance between employer and employee. Under the prevailing economic calculus labor had been demoted into just another factor of production whose remuneration was determined not by custom or human character but by market price. In such a situation they concluded, as Samuel Walker has noted, that "the contract was not and could not be entered into

freely. . . . The process of wage determination was a moral affront because it degraded the personal dignity of the workingman." This subservient position to the iron law of the market constituted "wage slavery," and like other forms of involuntary servitude it had to be "abolished."

Labor's emancipation did not, ipso facto, imply the overthrow of capitalism, a system of productive relations that the Knights in any case never defined. To escape wage slavery workers needed the strength to redefine the social balance of power with employers and their allies—and the will and intelligence to use that strength. One after another the Knights harnessed the various means at their disposal—education, organization, cooperation, economic sanction, and political influence—to this broad end: "To secure to the workers the full enjoyment [note, not the full return] of the wealth they create, sufficient leisure in which to develop their intellectual, moral and social faculties, all of the benefits of recreation, and pleasures of association; in a word to enable them to share in the gains and honors of advancing civilization."

A wide range of strategic options was represented within the counsels of the labor movement. One tendency sought to check the rampant concentration of wealth and power with specific correctives on the operation of the free market. Radical Greenbackism (with roots in Kelloggism and related monetary theories), Henry George's single tax, and land nationalization, each of which commanded considerable influence among the Knights of Labor, fit this category. Another important tendency, cooperation, offered a more self-reliant strategy of alternative institution-building, or, as one advocate put it, "the organization of production without the intervention of the capitalist." Socialism, generally understood at the time as a system of state as opposed to private ownership of production, offered a third alternative to wage slavery. Except for a few influential worker-intellectuals and strong pockets of support among German-Americans, however, Socialism . . . carried comparatively little influence in the 1880s. The argument of veteran abolitionist and labor reformer Joseph Labadie—"To say that state socialism is the rival of co-operation is to say that Jesus Christ was opposed to Christianity"—met a generally skeptical reception. Particularly in the far West, self-identified anarchists also agitated from within the ranks of the Order.

If Gilded Age labor representatives tended to stop short of a frontal rejection of the political-economic order, there was nevertheless no mistaking their philosophic radicalism. Notwithstanding differences in emphasis, the labor movement's political sentiments encompassed both a sharp critique of social inequality and a broad-based prescription for a more humane future. Indeed, the labor representative who shrugged off larger philosophical and political commitments in favor of a narrow incrementalism was likely to meet with incredulity. One of the first, and most classic, enunciations of business unionism, for example, received just this response from the Senate Committee on Labor and Capital in 1883. After taking testimony from workers and labor reformers across the country for six months, the committee, chaired by New Hampshire Senator Henry Blair, interviewed Adolph Strasser, president of the cigar-makers' union. Following a disquisition on the stimulating impact of shorter working hours on workers' consumption patterns, Strasser was asked if

he did not contemplate a future beyond the contemporary exigencies of panic and overproduction, "some time [when] every man is to be an intelligent man and an enlightened man?" When Strasser did not reply, Senator Blair interceded to elaborate the question. Still, Strasser rebuffed the queries, "Well, our organization does not consist of idealists . . . we do [not] control the production of the world. That is controlled by employers, and that is a matter for them." Senator Blair was taken aback.

> Blair. I was only asking you in regard to your ultimate ends.
> Witness. We have no ultimate ends. We are going on from day to day. We are fighting only for immediate objects—objects that can be realized in a few years. . . .
> Blair. I see that you are a little sensitive lest it should be thought that you are a mere theorizer. I do not look upon you in that light at all.
> Witness. Well, we say in our constitution that we are opposed to theorists, and I have to represent the organization here. We are all practical men.
> Blair. Have you not a theory upon which you have organized?
> Witness. Yes, sir: our theory is the experience of the past in the United States and in Great Britain. That is our theory, based upon actual facts. . . .
> Blair. In other words you have arrived at the theory which you are trying to apply?
> Witness. We have arrived at a practical result.
> Blair. But a practical result is the application of a theory is it not?

On a cultural level, labor's critique of American society bore the same relation to Victorian respectability that its political radicalism bore to contemporary liberalism. In both cases the middle-class and working-class radical variants derived from a set of common assumptions but drew from them quite different, even opposing, implications. No contemporary, for example, took more seriously than the Knights of Labor the cultural imperatives toward productive work, civic responsibility, education, a wholesome family life, temperance, and self-improvement. The intellectual and moral development of the individual, they would have agreed with almost every early nineteenth-century lyceum lecturer, was a precondition for the advancement of democratic civilization. In the day of Benjamin Franklin such values may well have knit together master craftsmen, journeymen, and apprentices. In the age of the factory system, however, the gulf between employer and employee had so widened that the lived meanings of the words were no longer the same. . . .

For the Knights the concept of the producing classes indicated an ultimate social division that they perceived in the world around them. Only those associated with idleness (bankers, speculators), corruption (lawyers, liquor dealers, gamblers), or social parasitism (all of the above) were categorically excluded membership in the Order. Other social strata such as local merchants and manufacturers were judged by their individual acts, not by any inherent structural antagonism to the worker's movement. Those who showed respect for the dignity of labor (i.e., who sold union-made goods or employed union workers at union conditions) were welcomed into the Order. Those who denigrated the laborer or his product laid themselves open to the righteous wrath of the boycott or strike. Powderly characteristically chastised one ruthless West Virginia coal owner, "Don't die, even if you do smell bad. We'll need you in a few years as a sample to show how *mean* men used to be."

This rather elastic notion of class boundaries on the part of the labor movement was reciprocated in the not inconsequential number of shopkeepers and small manufacturers who expressed sympathy and support for the labor movement. . . .

Idealization of hearth and home, a mainstay of familial sentimentality in the Gilded Age, also enjoyed special status within the labor movement. For here, as clearly as anywhere in the radicals' world view, conventional assumptions had a critical, albeit ambivalent, edge in the context of changing social circumstances. Defense of an idealized family life as both moral and material mainstay of society served as one basis of criticism of capitalist industry. Machinist John Morrison argued before the Senate investigating committee that the insecurities of the unskilled labor market were so threatening family life as to make the house "more like a dull prison instead of a home." A self-educated Scottish-born leader of the type-founders, Edward King, associated trade union morality with the domestic "sentiments of sympathy and humanity" against the "business principles" of the age. Almost unanimously, the vision of the good life for labor radicals included the home. . . .

The importance of the domestic moral order to the late nineteenth-century radical vision also translated into an unparalleled opening of the labor movement to women. As Susan Levine has recently documented, the Knights of Labor beckoned both to wage-earning women and workingmen's wives to join in construction of a "cooperative commonwealth," which, without disavowing the Victorian ideal of a separate female sphere of morality and domestic virtue, sought to make that sphere the center of an active community life.

Both their self-improving and domestic commitments converged in the working-class radicals' antipathy to excessive drinking. The Knights' oath of temperance, which became known as "the Powderly pledge," appealed in turn to intellectual development and protection of the family as well as to the collective interests of the labor movement. Like monopoly, the bottle lay waiting to fasten a new form of slavery upon the free worker. In another sense, as David Brundage has suggested, the growing capitalization of saloons together with expansion of saloon-linked variety theatre directly threatened a family-based producers' community. While most radicals stopped short of prohibition, exhortations in behalf of temperance were commonplace. In part it was a matter of practical necessity. Tension between the mores of traditional plebeian culture and the need for self-discipline by a movement striving for organization and power were apparent. . . .

In general, then, the labor movement of the late nineteenth century provided a distinct arena of articulation and practice for values that crossed class lines. Two aspects of this use of inherited values for radical ends merit reemphasis. First, to the extent that labor radicalism shared in the nineteenth century's cult of individualism, it established a social and moral framework for individual achievement. The culture of the labor movement stressed the development of individual capacity, but not competition with other individuals; while striving to elevate humanity, it ignored what S. G. Boritt has identified as the essence of the Lincoln-sanctified American Dream—the individual's "right to rise." The necessary reliance by the labor movement upon collective strength and community sanction militated against the possessive individualism that anchored the world of the workers' better-off neighbors. By its very nature, the labor movement set limits to the individual accumulation of wealth extracted from others' efforts and represented, in Edward King's words, "the graduated elimination of the personal selfishness of man."

Second, in an age of evolutionary, sometimes even revolutionary, faith in progress and the future (a faith generally shared by labor radicals), the movement made striking use of the past. Without renouncing the potential of industrialism for both human liberty and material progress, radicals dipped selectively into a popular storehouse of memory and myth to capture alternative images of human possibility. The choice of the name "Knights of Labor" itself presented images of chivalry and nobility fighting the unfeeling capitalist marketplace. Appeals to the "nobility of toil" and to the worker's "independence" conjured up the proud village smithy—not the degradation of labor in the factory system. Finally, celebrations of historic moments of human liberation and political advancement challenged a political- economic orthodoxy beholden to notions of unchanging, universal laws of development. Indeed, so conspicuously sentimental were the celebrations of Independence Day and Memorial Day that Powderly had to defend the Order from taunts of "spread-eagleism" and Yankee doodleism."

This sketch of working-class radicalism in the Gilded Age raises one final question. Whose movement—and culture— was it? In a country as diverse as the United States, with a labor force and labor movement drawn from a heterogeneous mass of trades, races, and nationalities, any group portrait runs the risk of oversimplification. The varying contours of the late nineteenth-century working class do require specific inquiry, to which the next several chapters of this work contribute. Nevertheless, the Knights of Labor did provide a vast umbrella under which practically every variety of American worker sought protection. As such, the dynamic of the Order itself offers important clues to the general social context in which working-class radicalism as defined here flourished. . . .

This dominant stream within the labor movement included people who had enjoyed considerable control over their jobs, if not also economic autonomy, men who often retained claim to the tools as well as the knowledge of their trade. They had taken seriously the ideal of a republic of producers in which hard work would contribute not only to the individual's improved economic standing but also to the welfare of the community. So long as they could rely on their own strength as well as their neighbors' support, this skilled stratum organized in an array of craft unions showed economic and political resilience. But the spreading confrontations with national corporate power, beginning in the 1870s, indicated just how much erosion had occurred in the position of those who relied on custom, skill, and moral censure as ultimate weapons. Industrial dilution of craft skills and a direct economic and political attack on union practices provided decisive proof to these culturally conservative workingmen of both the illegitimacy and ruthlessness of the growing power of capital. It was they, according to every recent study of late nineteenth-century laboring communities,

who formed the backbone of local labor movements. The Knights were, therefore, first of all a coalition of reactivating, or already organized, trade unions. . . .

For reasons of their own masses of workers who had not lost full and equal citizenship—for they had never possessed it—joined the skilled workers within the Knights. Wherever the Order achieved political successes, it did so by linking semiskilled and unskilled industrial workers to its base of skilled workers and leaders. The special strength of the Knights, noted the Boston *Labor Leader* astutely, lay "in the fact that the whole life of the community is drawn into it, that people of all kinds are together . . . and that they all get directly the sense of each others' needs. . . .

The Knights of Labor envisioned a kind of workingmen's democracy. The organized power of labor was capable of revitalizing democratic citizenship and safeguarding the public good within a regulated marketplace economy. Through vigilant shop committees and demands such as the eight-hour day, organized workers—both men and women—would ensure minimal standards of safety and health at the industrial workplace, even as they surrounded the dominant corporate organizational model of business with cooperative models of their own. A pride in honest and useful work, rational education, and personal virtue would be nurtured through a rich associational life spread out from the workplace to meeting hall to the hearth and home. Finally, the integrity of public institutions would be vouchsafed by the workingmen in politics. Purifying government of party parasitism and corruption, cutting off the access to power that allowed antilabor employers to bring the state apparatus to their side in industrial disputes, improving and widening the scope of vital public services, and even contemplating the takeover of economic enterprises that had passed irreversibly into monopoly hands—by these means worker-citizens would lay active claim to a republican heritage.

The dream was not to be. At the workplace management seized the initiative toward the future design and control of work. A managerial revolution overcoming the tenacious defenses of the craft unions transferred autonomy over such matters as productivity and skill from custom and negotiation to the realm of corporate planning. Except for the garment trades and the mines, the national trade unions had generally retreated from the country's industrial heartland by 1920. In the local community as well, the differences, even antagonisms, among workers often stood out more than did the similarities. Segmentation of labor markets, urban ethnic and socioeconomic residential segregation, cultural as well as a protectionist economic disdain for the new immigrants, and the depoliticization of leisure time (i.e., the decline of associational life sponsored by labor organizations) all contributed toward a process of social fragmentation. In such circumstances working-class political cooperation proved impossible. The Socialist party and the Progressive slates could make little more than a dent in the hold of the two increasingly conservative national parties over the electorate. Only with the repolarization of political life beginning in 1928 and culminating in the New Deal was the relation of labor and the party system again transformed. By the late 1930s and 1940s a revived labor movement was beginning, with mixed success, to play the role of a leading interest group and reform conscience within the Democratic party.

This impressionistic overview permits one further observation of a quite general nature. One of the favorite tasks of American historians has been to explain why the United States, alone among the nations of the Western world, passed through the industrial revolution without the establishment of a class consciousness and an independent working-class political movement. Cheap land, the cult of individualism, a heterogeneous labor force, social mobility, and the federal separation of powers comprise several of the numerous explanations that have been offered. While not directly denying the importance of any of the factors listed above, this study implicitly suggests a different approach to the problem of American exceptionalism.

The answer appears to lie less in a permanent structural determinism—whether the analytic brace be political, economic, or ideological—than in a dynamic and indeed somewhat fortuitous convergence of events. To understand the vicissitudes of urban politics, we have had to keep in mind the action on at least three levels: the level of working-class social organization (i.e., the nature and strength of the labor movement), the level of business response, and the level of governmental response. During the Gilded Age each of these areas took an incendiary turn, but only briefly and irregularly and most rarely at the same moment. The 1880s, as R. Laurence Moore has recently reiterated, were the international seedtime for the strong European working-class parties of the twentieth century. In America, too, the momentum in the 1880s was great. Indeed, examined both at the level of working-class organization and industrial militancy, a European visitor might understandably have expected the most to happen here first. At the political level, as well, American workers were in certain respects relatively advanced. In the 1870s and in the 1880s they established independently organized local labor regimes well before the famous French Roubaix or English West Ham labor-Socialist town councils of the 1890s. Then, a combination of forces in the United States shifted radically away from the possibilities outlined in the 1880s. The labor movement fragmented, business reorganized, and the political parties helped to pick up the pieces. The initiatives from without directed at the American working class from the mid-1890s through the mid-1920s—part repression, part reform, part assimilation, and part recruitment of a new labor

force—at an internationally critical period in the gestation of working-class movements may mark the most telling exceptionalism about American developments.

It would in any case be years before the necessary conditions again converged and labor rose from the discredited icons of pre-Depression America with a new and powerful political message. Workplace, community, and ballot box would all once again be harnessed to a great social movement. But no two actors are ever in quite the same space at the same time. The choices open to the CIO, it is fair to say, were undoubtedly influenced both by the achievement and failure of their counterparts a half-century earlier.

NO

Carl N. Degler

OUT OF OUR PAST

THE WORKERS' RESPONSE

To say that the labor movement was affected by the industrialization of the postwar years is an understatement; the fact is, industrial capitalism created the labor movement. Not deliberately, to be sure, but in the same way that a blister is the consequence of a rubbing shoe. Unions were labor's protection against the forces of industrialization as the blister is the body's against the irritation of the shoe. The factory and all it implied confronted the working-man with a challenge to his existence as a man, and the worker's response was the labor union.

There were labor unions in America before 1865, but, as industry was only emerging in those years, so the organizations of workers were correspondingly weak. In the course of years after Appomattox, however, when industry began to hit a new and giant stride, the tempo of unionization also stepped up. It was in these decades, after many years of false starts and utopian ambitions, that the American labor movement assumed its modern shape.

Perhaps the outstanding and enduring characteristic of organized labor in the United States has been its elemental conservatism, the fantasies of some employers to the contrary notwithstanding. Indeed, it might be said that all labor unions, at bottom, are conservative by virtue of their being essentially reactions against a developing capitalism. Though an established capitalist society views itself as anything but subversive, in the days of its becoming and seen against the perspective of the previous age, capitalism as an ideology is radically subversive, undermining and destroying many of the cherished institutions of the functioning society. This dissolving process of capitalism is seen more clearly in Europe than in America because there the time span is greater. But, as will appear later, organized labor in the United States was as much a conservative response to the challenge of capitalism as was the European trade union movement.

Viewed very broadly, the history of modern capitalism might be summarized as the freeing of the three factors of production—land, labor, and capital—from the web of tradition in which medieval society held them. If capitalism was to function, it was necessary that this liberating process take place. Only when these basic factors are free to be bought and sold according to the dictates of the profit motive can the immense production which capitalism promises be realized. An employer, for example, had to be free to dismiss labor when the balance sheet required it, without being compelled to retain workers because society or custom demanded it. Serfdom, with its requirement that the peasant could not be taken from the land, was an anachronistic institution if capitalism was to become the economic ideology of society. Conversely, an employer needed to be unrestricted in his freedom to hire labor or else production could not expand in accordance with the market. Guild restrictions which limited apprenticeships were therefore obstacles to the achievement of a free capitalism.

The alienability of the three factors of production was achieved slowly and unevenly after the close of the Middle Ages. By the nineteenth century in most nations of the West, land had become absolutely alienable—it could be bought and sold at will. With the growth of banking, the development of trustworthy monetary standards, and finally the gold standard in the nineteenth century, money or capital also became freely exchangeable. Gradually, over the span of some two centuries, the innovating demands of capitalism stripped from labor the social controls in which medieval and mercantilistic government had clothed it. Serfdom as an obstacle to the free movement of labor was gradually done away with; statutes of laborers and apprenticeships which fixed wages, hours, and terms of employment also fell into disuse or suffered outright repeal. To avoid government interference in the setting of wage rates, the English Poor Law of 1834 made it clear that the dole to the unemployed was always to be lower than the going rate for unskilled labor. Thus supply and demand would be the determinant of wage levels. Both the common law and the Combination Acts in the early nineteenth century in England sought to ensure the operation of a free market in labor by declaring trade unions to be restraints on trade.

Like land and capital, then, labor was being reduced to a commodity, freely accessible, freely alienable, free to flow where demand was high. The classical economists of the nineteenth century analyzed this long historical process, neatly put it together, and called it the natural laws of economics.

To a large extent, this historical development constituted an improvement in the worker's status, since medieval and mercantilist controls over labor had been more onerous than protective. Nevertheless, something was lost by the dissolution of the ancient social ties which fitted the worker into a larger social matrix. Under the old relationship, the worker belonged in society; he enjoyed a definite if not a high status; he had a place. Now he was an individual, alone; his status was up to him to establish; his urge for community with society at large had no definite avenue of expression. Society and labor alike had been atomized in pursuit of an individualist economy. Herein lay the radical character of the capitalist ideology.

That the workingman sensed the radical change and objected to it is evident from what some American labor leaders said about their unions. Without rejecting the new freedom which labor enjoyed, John Mitchell, of the Mine Workers, pointed out that the union "stands for fraternity, complete and absolute." Samuel Gompers' eulogy of the social microcosm which was the trade union has the same ring. "A hundred times we have said it," he wrote, "and we say it again, that trade unionism contains within itself the potentialities of working class regeneration." The union is a training ground for democracy and provides "daily object lessons in ideal justice; it breathes into the working classes the spirit of unity"; but above all, it affords that needed sense of community. The labor union "provides a field for noble comradeship, for deeds of loyalty, for self-sacrifice beneficial to one's fellow-workers." In the trade union, in short, the workers could obtain another variety of that sense of community, of comradeship, as Gompers put it, which the acid of individualistic capitalism had dissolved.

And there was another objection to the transformation of labor into an exchangeable commodity. The theoretical justification for the conversion of the factors of production into commodities is that the maximum amount of goods can be produced under such a regime. The increased production is deemed desirable because it would insure greater amounts of goods for human consumption and therefore a better life for all. Unfortunately for the theory, however, labor cannot be separated from the men who provide it. To make labor a commodity is to make the men who provide labor commodities also. Thus one is left with the absurdity of turning men into commodities in order to give men a better life! . . .

Seen in this light, the trade union movement stands out as a truly conservative force. Almost instinctively, the workers joined labor unions in order to preserve their humanity and social character against the excessively individualistic doctrines of industrial capitalism. Eventually, the workers' organizations succeeded in halting the drive to the atomized society which capitalism demanded, and in doing so, far from destroying the system, compelled it to be humane as well as productive.

The essential conservatism of the labor movement is to be seen in particular as well as in general. The organizations of American labor that triumphed or at least survived in the course of industrialization were conspicuous for their acceptance of the private property, profit-oriented society. They evinced little of the radical, anticapitalist ideology and rhetoric so common among European trade unions. Part of the reason for this was the simple fact that all Americans—including workers—were incipient capitalists waiting for "the break." But at bottom it would seem that the conservatism of American labor in this sense is the result of the same forces which inhibited the growth of socialism and other radical anticapitalist ideologies. This question will be dealt with at some length at the end of this chapter.

"The overshadowing problem of the American labor movement," an eminent labor historian has written, "has always been the problem of staying organized. No other labor movement has ever had to contend with the fragility so characteristic of American labor organizations." So true has this been that even today the United States ranks below Italy and Austria in percentage of workers organized (about 25 per cent as compared, for instance, with Sweden's 90 per cent). In such an atmosphere, the history of organized labor in America has been both painful and conservative. Of the two major national organizations of workers which developed in the latter half of the nineteenth century, only the cautious, restrictive, pragmatic American Federation of Labor lived into the twentieth century. The other, the Knights of Labor, once the more powerful and promising, as well as the less accommodating in goals and aspirations, succumbed to Selig Perlman's disease of fragility.

Founded in 1869, the Noble Order of the Knights of Labor recorded its greatest successes in the 1880's, when its membership rolls carried 700,000 names. As the A.F. of L. was later to define the term for Americans, the Knights did not seem to constitute a legitimate trade union at all. Anyone who worked, except liquor dealers, bankers, lawyers, and physicians, could join, and some thousands of women workers and Negroes were members in good standing of this brotherhood of toilers. But the crucial deviation of the Knights from the more orthodox approach to labor organization was its belief in worker-owned producers' co-operatives, which were intended to make each worker his own employer. In this way, the order felt, the degrading dependence of the worker upon the employer would be eliminated. "There is no good reason," Terence V. Powderly, Grand Master Workman of the order, told his followers, "why labor cannot, through co-operation, own and operate mines, factories and railroads."

In this respect the order repudiated the direction in which the America of its time was moving. It expressed the small-shopkeeper mentality which dominated the thinking of many American workers, despite the obvious trend in the economy toward the big and the impersonal. As the General Assembly of 1884 put it, "our Order contemplates a radical change, while Trades' Unions . . . accept the industrial system as it is, and endeavor to adapt themselves to it. The attitude of our Order to the existing industrial system is necessarily one of war." Though the order called this attitude "radical," a more accurate term, in view of the times, would have been "conservative" or "reactionary."

In practice, however, the Knights presented no more of a threat to capitalism than any other trade union. Indeed, their avowed opposition to the strike meant that labor's most potent weapon was only reluctantly drawn from the scabbard. The Constitution of 1884 said, "Strikes at best afford only temporary relief"; members should learn to depend on education, co-operation, and political action to attain "the abolition of the wage system."

Though the order officially joined in political activity and Grand Master Workman Powderly was at one time mayor of Scranton, its forays into politics accomplished little. The experience was not lost on shrewd Samuel Gompers, whose American Federation of Labor studiously eschewed any alignments with political parties, practicing instead the more neutral course of "rewarding friends and punishing enemies."

In a farewell letter in 1893, Powderly realistically diagnosed the ills of his moribund order, but offered no cure: "Teacher of important and much-needed reforms, she has been obliged to practice differently from her teachings. Advocating arbitration and conciliation as first steps in labor disputes she has been forced to take upon her shoulders the responsibilities of the aggressor first and, when hope of arbitrating and conciliation failed, to beg of the opposing side to do what we should have applied for in the first instance. Advising against strikes we have been in the midst of them. While not a political party we have been forced into the attitude of taking political action."

For all its fumblings, ineptitude, and excessive idealism, the Knights did organize more workers on a national scale than had ever been done before. At once premature and reactionary, it nonetheless planted the seeds of industrial unionism which, while temporarily overshadowed by the successful craft organization of the A.F. of L., ultimately bore fruit in the C.I.O. Moreover, its idealism, symbolized in its admission of Negroes and women, and more in tune with the midtwentieth century than the late nineteenth, signified its commitment to the ideals of the democratic tradition. For these reasons the Knights were a transitional type of unionism, somewhere between the utopianism of the 1830's and the pragmatism of the A.F. of L. It seemed to take time for labor institutions to fit the American temper.

In the course of his long leadership of the American Federation of Labor, Samuel Gompers welcomed many opportunities to define the purposes of his beloved organization. . . .

"The trade unions are the business organizations of the wage-earners," Gompers explained in 1906, "to attend to the business of the wage-earners." Later he expressed it more tersely: "The trade union is not a Sunday school. It is an organization of wage-earners, dealing with economic, social, political and moral questions." As Gompers' crossing of swords with Hillquit demonstrated, there was no need or place for theories. "I saw," the labor leader wrote years later, in looking back on his early life in the labor movement, "the danger of entangling alliances with intellectuals who did not understand that to experiment with the labor movement was to experiment with human life. . . . I saw that the betterment of workingmen must come primarily through workingmen."

In an age of big business, Samuel Gompers made trade unionism a business, and his reward was the survival of his Federation. In a country with a heterogeneous population of unskilled immigrants, reviled and feared Negroes, and native workers, he cautiously confined his fragile organization to the more skilled workers and the more acceptable elements in the population. The result was a narrow but lasting structure.

Though never ceasing to ask for "more," the A.F. of L. presented no threat to capitalism. "Labor Unions are *for* the workingman, but against no one," John Mitchell of the United Mine Workers pointed out. "They are not hostile to employers, not inimical to the interests of the general public. . . . There is no necessary hostility between labor and capital," he concluded. Remorselessly pressed by Morris Hillquit as Gompers was, he still refused to admit that the labor movement was, as Hillquit put it, "conducted against the interests of the employing people." Rather, Gompers insisted, "It is conducted for the interests of the employing people." And the rapid expansion of the American economy bore witness to the fact that the Federation was a friend and not an enemy of industrial capitalism. Its very adaptability to the American scene—its conservative ideology, if it was an ideology at all—as Selig Perlman has observed, contained the key to its success. "The unionism of the American Federation of Labor 'fitted' . . . because it recognized the virtually inalterable conservatism of the American community as regards private property and private initiative in economic life."

This narrow conception of the proper character of trade unionism—job consciousness, craft unionism, lack of interest in organizing the unskilled, the eschewing of political activity—which Gompers and his Federation worked out for the American worker continued to dominate organized labor until the earthquake of the depression cracked the mold and the Committee for Industrial Organization issued forth.

NOBODY HERE BUT US CAPITALISTS

"By any simple interpretation of the Marxist formula," commented Socialist Norman Thomas in 1950, "the United States, by all odds the greatest industrial nation and that in which capitalism is most advanced, should have had long ere this is a very strong socialist movement if not a socialist revolution. Actually," he correctly observed, "in no advanced western nation is organized socialism so weak." Nor was this the first time Socialists had wondered about this. Over eighty years ago, in the high noon of European socialism, Marxist theoretician Werner Sombart impatiently put a similar question: *"Warum gibt es in den Vereinigten Staaten keinen Sozialismus?"*

The failure of the American working class to become seriously interested in socialism in this period or later is one of the prominent signs of the political and economic conservatism of American labor and, by extension, of the American

people as a whole. This failure is especially noteworthy when one recalls that in industrialized countries the world over—Japan, Italy, Germany, Belgium, to mention only a few—a Socialist movement has been a "normal" concomitant of industrialization. Even newly opened countries like Australia and New Zealand have Labour parties. Rather than ask, as Americans are wont to do, why these countries have nurtured such frank repudiators of traditional capitalism, it is the American deviation from the general pattern which demands explanation.

In large part, the explanation lies in the relative weakness of class consciousness among Americans. Historically, socialism is the gospel of the *class-conscious* working class, of the workingmen who feel themselves bound to their status for life and their children after them. It is not accidental, therefore, that the major successes of modern socialism are in Europe, where class lines have been clearly and tightly drawn since time immemorial, and where the possibility of upward social movement has been severely restricted in practice if not in law. Americans may from time to time have exhibited class consciousness and even class hatred, but such attitudes have not persisted, nor have they been typical. As Matthew Arnold observed in 1888, "it is indubitable that rich men are regarded" in America "with less envy and hatred than rich men in Europe." A labor leader like Terence Powderly was convinced that America was without classes. "No matter how much we may say about classes and class distinction, there are no classes in the United States. . . . I have always refused to admit that we have classes in our country just as I have refused to admit that the labor of a man's hand or brain is a commodity." And there was a long line of commentators on American society, running back at least to Crèvecoeur, to illustrate the prevalence of Powderly's belief.

The weakness of American class consciousness is doubtless to be attributed, at least in part, to the fluidity of the social structure. Matthew Arnold, for example, accounted for the relative absence of class hatred on such grounds, as did such very different foreign observers as Werner Sombart and Lord Bryce. The British union officials of the Mosely Commission, it will be recalled, were convinced of the superior opportunities for success enjoyed by American workers. Stephan Thernstrom in his study of Newburyport gave some measure of the opportunities for economic improvement among the working class when he reported that all but 5 per cent of those unskilled workers who persisted from 1850 to 1900 ended the period with either property or an improvement in occupational status.

Men who are hoping to move upward on the social scale, and for whom there is some chance that they can do so, do not identify themselves with their present class. "In worn-out, king-ridden Europe, men stay where they are born," immigrant Charles O'Conor, who became an ornament of the New York bar, contended in 1869. "But in America a man is accounted a failure, and certainly ought to be, who has not risen about his father's station in life." So long as Horatio Alger means anything to Americans, Karl Marx will be just another German philosopher.

The political history of the United States also contributed to the failure of socialism. In Europe, because the franchise came slowly and late to the worker, he often found himself first an industrial worker and only later a voter. It was perfectly natural, in such a context, for him to vote according to his economic interests and to join a political party avowedly dedicated to those class interests. The situation was quite different in American, however, for political democracy came to America prior to the Industrial Revolution. By the time the industrial transformation was getting under way after 1865, all adult males could vote and, for the most part, they had already chosen their political affiliations without reference to their economic class; they were Republicans or Democrats first and workers only second—a separation between politics and economics which has become traditional in America. "In the main," wrote Lord Bryce about the United States of the 1880's, "political questions proper have held the first place in a voter's mind and questions affecting his class second." Thus, when it came to voting, workers registered their convictions as citizens, not as workingmen. (In our own day, there have been several notable failures of labor leaders to swing their labor vote, such as John L. Lewis' attempt in 1940 and the C.I.O.'s in 1950 against Senator Taft and the inability of union leaders to be sure they could hold their members to support Hubert Humphrey in the Presidential election of 1968.) To most workers, the Socialist party appeared as merely a third party in a country where such parties are political last resorts.

Nor did socialism in America gain much support from the great influx of immigration. It is true that many Germans came to this country as convinced Socialists and thus swelled the party's numbers, but they also served to pin the stigma of "alien" upon the movement. Even more important was the fact that the very heterogeneity of the labor force, as a result of immigration, often made animosities between ethnic groups more important to the worker than class antagonism. It must have seemed to many workers that socialism, with its central concern for class and its denial of ethnic antagonism, was not dealing with the realities of economic life.

In the final reckoning, however, the failure of socialism in America is to be attributed to the success of capitalism. The expanding economy provided opportunities for all, no matter how meager they might appear or actually be at times. Though the rich certainly seemed to get richer at a prodigious rate, the poor, at least, did not get poorer—and often got richer. Studies of real wages between 1865 and 1900 bear this out. Though prices rose, wages generally rose faster, so that there was a net gain in average income for workers during the last decades of the century. The increase in real wages in the first fifteen years of the twentieth century was negligible—but, significantly, there was no decline. The high wages and relatively good standard of living of the American worker were patent as far as the twenty-three British labor leaders of the Mosely Commission were concerned. The American is a "better educated, better housed, better clothed and more energetic man than his British brother," concluded the sponsor, Alfred Mosely, a businessman himself.

But America challenged socialism on other grounds than mere material things. Some years ago an obscure Socialist, Leon Samson, undertook to account for the failure of socialism to win the allegiance of the American working class; his psychological explanation merits attention because it illuminates the influence exercised by the American Dream. Americanism, Samson observes, is not so much a tradition as it is a doctrine; it is "what socialism is to a socialist." Americanism to the American is a body of ideas like "democracy, liberty, opportunity, to all of which the American adheres rationalistically much as a socialist adheres to his socialism—because it does him good, because it gives him work, because, so he thinks, it guarantees him happiness. America has thus served as a substitute for socialism."

Socialism has been unable to make headway with Americans, Samson goes on, because "every concept in socialism has its substitutive counterconcept in Americanism." As Marxism holds out the prospect of a classless society, so does Americanism. The opportunities for talent and the better material life which socialism promised for the future were already available in America and constituted the image in which America was beheld throughout the world. The freedom and equality which the oppressed proletariat of Europe craved were a reality in America—or at least sufficiently so to blunt the cutting edge of the Socialist appeal. Even the sense of mission, of being in step with the processes of history, which unquestionably was one of the appeals of socialism, was also a part of the American Dream. Have not all Americans cherished their country as a model for the world? Was not this the "last, best hope of earth"? Was not God on the side of America, as history, according to Marx, was on the side of socialism and the proletariat?

Over a century ago, Alexis de Tocqueville predicted a mighty struggle for the minds of men between two giants of Russia and the United States. In the ideologies of socialism and the American Dream, his forecast has been unexpectedly fulfilled.

POSTSCRIPT

Was the American Labor Movement Radical?

Fink presents a very sophisticated analysis of how the Knights of Labor traced its values back to the republican ideology of the late eighteenth-century enlightenment thinkers. The Knights embraced a unified conception of work and culture which extolled the virtues of individual hard work, love of family, and love of country. All members of the producing classes were invited to join, including businessmen. According to Fink, excluded were "only those associated with idleness (bankers, speculators) and corruption (lawyers, liquor dealers, gamblers)."

During the 1880s the Knights employed a "pre-Marxist economic critique" of the industrial system. There were discussions about the "abolition of the wage system" and the analysis shifted away from the problems of the individual workers to the "general, collective, plight of labor." Yet Fink admits that the Knights never made a frontal attack on capitalism.

Degler takes a different approach to this issue. In his view the real radicals were the industrialists who created a more mature system of capitalism. Labor was merely fashioning a conservative response to the radical changes brought about by big business. The inability of the Knights of Labor to accept the changes in the industrial system led to its demise. Its place was taken by the American Federation of Labor whose long-time leader Samuel Gompers was famous for his acceptance of the wage system and American capitalism. The American Federation of Labor adopted practical goals. It strove to improve the lot of the worker by negotiating for better hours, wages, and working conditions.

Degler is also more concrete in the reasons he lists for the failure of socialism in America. He argues that Americans lacked a working-class consciousness because they believed in real mobility. Also, a labor party failed to emerge because Americans developed their commitment to the two-party system before the issues of the Industrial Revolution came to the forefront. The influx of immigration from a variety of countries created a heterogeneous labor force, and animosities between rival ethnic groups appeared more real than class antagonisms.

For the past two decades historians have begun to study the social and cultural environment of the American working class. The approach is modeled after E. P. Thompson's highly influential and sophisticated Marxist analysis, *The Making of the English Working Class* (1963), a work which is the capstone of an earlier generation of British and French social historians. The father of the "new labor history" in the United States is the late Herbert G. Gutman, whose articles collected in *Work, Culture, and Society* (Knopf, 1976) and *Power and Culture: Essays On the American Working Class* (Pantheon, 1987) are the starting point for every student of the period. It was Gutman who first discussed American workers as a group separate from the organized union movement. Gutman's distinction between preindustrial and industrial values laid the groundwork for a whole generation of scholars who have engaged in case studies of both union and nonunion workers in both urban and rural areas of America. Such works have proliferated in recent years but should be sampled first in the following collections of articles: Daniel J. Lieb, ed., *The Labor History Reader* (University of Illinois, 1985); Michael H. Frisch and Daniel J. Walkowitz, eds., *Working Class America: Essays on Labor, Community and American Society* (University of Illinois, 1983); Charles Stephenson and Robert Asher, eds., *Life and Labor: Dimensions of American Working Class History* (State University of New York Press, 1986); and Milton Cantor, ed., *American Working Class Culture: Explorations in American Labor and Social History* (Greenwood Press, 1979).

Students who wish to sample the latest scholarship on the American workers should consult "A Round Table: Labor, Historical Pessimism, and Hegemony," *Journal of American History* (June 1988), in which five historians respond to Fink's assessment of the new labor history and the case of the Knights of Labor.

The question of why the United States never developed a major socialist movement or labor party has been the subject of much speculation. A good starting point is John H. Laslett and Seymour Martin Lipset, eds., *Failure of a Dream: Essays in the History of American Socialism* (Anchor Press/Doubleday, 1974), a collection of articles which generally reinforces Degler's arguments. Political scientist Theodore J. Lowi argues that our political system of federalism is the primary reason in "Why Is There No Socialism in the United States?" *Society* (January/February 1985). Finally, historian Eric Foner tears down all explanations and asks "Why Has There Been No Socialist Transformation in Any Advanced Capitalist Society?" *History Workshop* (Spring 1984).

ISSUE 4

Were the Immigrants' Old World Cultures Destroyed as They Adjusted to American Life?

YES: Oscar Handlin, from *The Uprooted: The Epic Story of the Great Migrations That Made the American People,* 2d ed. (Little, Brown, 1973)

NO: John Bodnar, from *The Transplanted: A History of Immigrants in Urban America* (Indiana, 1985)

ISSUE SUMMARY

YES: Pulitzer Prize–winning historian Oscar Handlin argues that the immigrants were alienated from their Old World cultures as they adjusted to an unfamiliar and hostile environment.
NO: Associate professor of history John Bodnar maintains that various immigrant groups retained, modified, and transformed their Old World cultures in response to urban/industrial America in the years between 1880 and 1920.

Historians of immigration like to divide the forces that encouraged voluntary migrations from one country to another into push and pull factors. The major reason why people left their native countries was the breakdown of feudalism and the subsequent rise of a commercially oriented economy. Peasants were pushed off the feudal estates of which they had been a part for generations. In addition, religious and political persecution for dissenting groups and lack of economic opportunities for many middle-class emigrés also contributed to the migrations from Europe to the New World.

The American continent was attractive to settlers long before the American Revolution took place. While the United States may not have been completely devoid of feudal tradition, immigrants perceived the United States as a country with a fluid social structure where opportunities abounded for everyone. There was some truth to this assessment. By the middle of the nineteenth century, the Industrial Revolution had provided opportunities for jobs in a nation that experienced a chronic labor shortage.

There were four major periods of migration to the United States: 1607–1830, 1830–1890, 1890–1925, and 1968 to the present. In the seventeenth and eighteenth centuries, the white settlers came primarily, though not entirely, from the British Isles. They were joined by millions of African slaves. Both groups lived next to several hundred thousand Native Americans. In those years the cultural values of Americans were a combination of what history professor Gary Nash has referred to as "Red, White, and Black." In the 30 years before the Civil War, a second phase began when immigrants came from other countries in northern and western Europe as well as China. Two European groups dominated. Large numbers of Irish-Catholics emigrated in the 1850s as a result of the potato famine. Religious and political factors were as instrumental as economic factors in pushing the Germans to America. Chinese immigrants were also encouraged to come during the middle and later decades of the nineteenth century in order to help build the western portion of America's first transcontinental railroad and to work in low-paying service industries like laundries and restaurants.

By 1890 a third period of immigration began. Attracted by the unskilled jobs provided by the Industrial Revolution and the cheap transportation costs of fast-traveling, steam-powered ocean vessels, immigrants poured in at a rate of close to a million a year from Italy, Greece, Russia, and other countries of southern and eastern Europe. This flood continued until the early 1920s when fears of a foreign takeover led Congress to pass legislation restricting the number of immigrants into the country to 150,000 per year.

For the next 40 years America was ethnically frozen. In the 1880s the Chinese were excluded. Laws passed in the 1920s that barred Japanese and were biased against southern and eastern Europeans. When the restrictions against Asians and Africans were lifted by the Immigration Reform Act of 1965, a fourth wave of immigration began. In contrast to earlier migrations, the newest groups have poured in from Latin America and Asia. Ethnic enclaves have been reestablished in American cities and are similar to those in the first two decades of the twentieth century. In addition, the illegal immigration from Mexico and other Latin American and Central American countries has become a major issue for states in the Sunbelt.

How well did the immigrants assimilate into the Anglo-Saxon core culture that constituted the major value system of American life by the mid-nineteenth century? How many traditions and customs were maintained by the first- and second-generation immigrants? Was America a melting pot or a salad bowl?

In the following readings, Oscar Handlin argues that the immigrants were uprooted from their Old World cultures as they adjusted to an unfamiliar and often hostile environment. John Bodnar substantially modifies Handlin's view, explaining that, while immigrants in the years between 1880 and 1920 were sucked into an economic system dominated by the worldwide industrial revolution, they maintained a substantial amount of their Old World cultures via tight-knit family systems.

YES

Oscar Handlin

THE UPROOTED

In this work, I wished to regard the subject [of immigration] from an altogether different point of view. Immigration altered America. But it also altered the immigrants. And it is the effect upon the newcomers of their arduous transplantation that I have tried to study.

My theme is emigration as the central experience of a great many human beings. I shall touch upon broken homes, interruptions of a familiar life, separation from known surroundings, then becoming a foreigner and ceasing to belong. These are the aspects of alienation; and seen from the perspective of the individual received rather than of the receiving society, the history of immigration is a history of alienation and its consequences.

I have tried historically to trace the impact of separation, of the disruption in the lives and work of people who left one world to adjust to a new. These are the bleaker pages of our history. For the effect of the transfer was harsher upon the people than upon the society they entered.

The experience of these men on the move was more complex than that of eighteenth-century Negroes or of seventeenth-century Englishmen or of eleventh-century Normans. The participants in the earlier mass migrations had either wandered to unoccupied places, where they had only to adjust to new conditions of the physical environment, or they had gone under the well-defined conditions of conquering invader or imported slave.

It was the unique quality of the nineteenth-century immigration that the people who moved entered the life of the United States at a status equal to that of the older residents. So far as law and the formal institutions of the nation were concerned, the newcomers were one with those long settled in the New World. The immigrants could not impose their own ways upon society; but neither were they constrained to conform to those already established. To a significant degree, the newest Americans had a wide realm of choice.

Therein lay the broader meaning of their experience. Emigration took these people out of traditional, accustomed environments and replanted them in strange ground, among strangers, where strange manners prevailed. The customary modes of behavior were no longer adequate, for the problems of life were new and different. With old ties snapped, men faced the enormous compulsion of working out new relationships, new meanings to their lives, often under harsh and hostile circumstances.

The responses of these folk could not be easy, automatic, for emigration had stripped away the veneer that in more stable situations concealed the underlying nature of the social structure. Without the whole complex of institutions and social patterns which formerly guided their actions, these people became incapable of masking or evading decisions.

Under such circumstances, every act was crucial, the product of conscious weighing of alternatives, never simple conformity to a habitual pattern. No man could escape choices that involved, day after day, an evaluation of his goals, of the meaning of his existence, and of the purpose of the social forms and institutions that surrounded him.

The immigrants lived in crisis because they were uprooted. In transplantation, while the old roots were sundered, before the new were established, the immigrants existed in an extreme situation. The shock, and the effects of the shock, persisted for many years; and their influence reached down to generations which themselves never paid the cost of crossing.

No one moves without sampling something of the immigrants' experience—mountaineers to Detroit, Okies to California, even men fixed in space but alienated from their culture by unpopular ideas or tastes. But the immigrants' alienation was more complete, more continuous, and more persistent. Understanding of their reactions in that exposed state may throw light on the problems of all those whom the modern world somehow uproots. . . .

NEW WORLDS, NEW VISIONS

Often, they would try to understand. They would think about it in the pauses of their work, speculate sometimes as their minds wandered, tired, at the close of a long day.

What had cut short the continuous past, severed it from the unrelated present? Immigration had transformed the entire economic world within which the peasants had formerly lived. From surface forms to inmost functionings, the change was complete. A new setting, new activities, and new meanings forced the newcomers into radically new roles as producers and consumers of goods. In the process, they became, in their own eyes, less worthy as men. They felt a sense of degradation that raised a most insistent question: Why had this happened?

More troubling, the change was not confined to economic matters. The whole American universe was different. Strangers, the immigrants could not locate themselves; they had lost the polestar that gave them their bearings. They would not regain an awareness of direction until they could visualize themselves in their new context, see a picture of the world as it appeared from this perspective. At home, in the wide frame of the village, their eyes had taken in the whole of life, had brought to their perceptions a clearly defined view of the universe. Here the frame narrowed down, seemed to reveal only fragmentary distorted glimpses that were hardly reminiscent of the old outlines. . . .

These were the contents with which the hearts and minds of the peasants were laden as they came to the New World. This was the stock of ideas on which they drew when they came to account for their situation in America, once they had arrived and were at work and the work they did seemed not fit work for a man. Now there would be new questions. Would the old answers do when these people tried to explain what had happened to them?

They found it difficult, of course, to reconstruct a coherent record out of the excess of their experience since they had left the village. Many impressions remained fragmentary, unrelated to any whole adjustment.

This they knew, though, and could not mistake it: they were lonely. In the midst of teeming cities, in the crowded tenements and the factories full of bustling men, they were lonely.

Their loneliness had more than one dimension. It had the breadth of unfamiliarity. Strange people walked about them; strange sounds assailed their inattentive ears. Hard pavements cut them off from nature in all its accustomed manifestations. Look how far they could, at the end of no street was a familiar horizon. Hemmed in by the tall buildings, they were fenced off from the realm of growing things. They had lost the world they knew of beasts and birds, of blades of grass, of sprays of idle flowers. They had acquired instead surroundings of a most outlandish aspect. That unfamiliarity was one aspect of their loneliness.

Loneliness had also the painful depth of isolation. The man who once had been surrounded with individual beings was here cast adrift in a life empty of all but impersonal things. In the Old Country, this house in this village, these fields by these trees, had had a character and identity of their own. They had testified to the peasant's I, had fixed his place in the visible universe. The church, the shrine, the graveyard and the generations that inhabited it had also had their

personality, had also testified to the peasant's I, and had fixed his place in a larger invisible universe.

In the new country, all these were gone; that was hard enough. Harder still was the fact that nothing replaced them. In America, the peasant was a transient without meaningful connections in time and space. He lived now with inanimate objects, cut off from his surroundings. His dwelling and his place of work had no relationship to him as a man. The scores of established routines that went with a life of the soil had disappeared and with them the sense of being one of a company. Therefore the peasant felt isolated and isolation added to his loneliness.

Strangeness and isolation oppressed even those who returned to the soil. They too were lonely. Everywhere, great wastes of empty land dissevered the single farm from the rest of the world. Wrapped up in the unfamiliar landscapes of prairie distance or forest solitude, the peasants found nowhere an equivalent of the village, nowhere the basis for reestablishing the solidarity of the old communal life. Therefore they were each alone, in city and in country, for that of which they had been a part was no longer about them.

The shattering loneliness disrupted the communion of persons and places and events. This was difficult enough for those who found agriculture their calling; the change of scene upset the traditional calendar, falsified the traditional signs of nature that paced the year's activities. But that destroyed communion was more difficult still in the urban places. In the cities, the seasons lost entirely their relevance. For the worker, winter and spring were very much alike; whether he worked and how he worked had nothing to do, as it had at home, with the passing cycle of the year.

If the outward aspects were the same—the falling snow or warm summer wind—that only made more poignant the sense of lost significance. And they never were long the same; tinged with soot, the virgin snow at once acquired the pavement's gray, or the dull wind dragged the smell of city heat through confining streets. So it was with the noteworthy days. Formal observances persisted for a time; the villagers longingly went through the motions, celebrated saints' days, mourned at the time of memories. But snatched out of context these occasions had not the old flavor. Self-conscious under the gaze of strangers, the peasants could no longer find the old meanings. For all peasants, and particularly for those dominated by the mechanical monotony of factory or construction labor, their loneliness entailed also the desolating loss of the precious sense of solidarity. Without that, was there any purpose left to life?

Was it not true, did not your whole experience teach you the futility of striving? *What needs must be no man can flee!* How helpless were humans before the forces arrayed against them! Of what value were calculations? In the Old Country, at least, you could take care, do what was necessary in the proper way at the proper time, follow experience and use the knowledge of generations. Even so, your very emigration is evidence of the slight value of all precautions. Search back over your lifetime. Think: have you reason to believe that wiser decisions on your part could have stayed the famines, put off the displacements? And how much deeper is your helplessness now than then; now you cannot even recognize the proper ways.

Every element of the immigrants' experience since the day they had left home added to this awareness of their utter helplessness. All the incidents of the journey were bound up with chance. What was the road to follow, what the ship to board, what port to make? These were serious questions. But who knew which were the right answers? Whether they survived the hazards of the voyage, and in what condition, these too were decisions beyond the control of the men who participated in it. The capricious world of the crossing pointed its own conclusion as to the role of chance in the larger universe into which the immigrants plunged.

It was the same with their lives after landing. To find a job or not, to hold it or to be fired, in these matters laborers' wills were of slight importance. Inscrutable, distant persons determined matters on the basis of remote, unknown conditions. The most fortunate of immigrants, the farmers, knew well what little power they had to influence the state of the climate, the yield of the earth, or the fluctuations of the market, all the elements that determined their lot. Success or failure, incomprehensible in terms of peasant values, seemed altogether fortuitous. Time and again, the analogy occurred to them: man was helpless like the driven cog in a great machine.

Loneliness, separation from the community of the village, and despair at the insignificance of their own human abilities, these were the elements that, in America, colored the peasants' view of their world. From the depths of a dark pessimism, they looked up at a frustrating universe ruled by haphazard, capricious forces. Without the capacity to control or influence these forces men could but rarely gratify their hopes or wills. Their most passionate desires were doomed to failure; their lives were those of the feeble little birds which hawks attack, which lose strength from want of food, and which, at last surrendering to the savage blasts of the careless elements, flutter unnoticed to the waiting earth.

Sadness was the tone of life, and death and disaster no strangers. Outsiders would not understand the familiarity with death who had not daily met it in the close quarters of the steerage; nor would they comprehend the riotous Paddy funerals who had no insight of the release death brought. The end of life was an end to hopeless striving, to ceaseless pain, and to the endless succession of disappointments. There was a leaden grief for the ones who went; yet the tomb was only the final parting in a long series of separations that had started back at the village crossroads.

In this world man can only be resigned. Illness takes a child away; from the shaft they bring a father's crippled body; sudden fire eats up a block of flimsy shanties, leaves half of each family living. There is no energy for prolonged mourning. Things are as they are and must remain so. Resist not but submit to fortune and seek safety by holding on.

In this world the notion of improvement is delusive. The best hope is that matters grow not worse. Therefore it is desirable to stand against change, to keep things as they are; the risks involved in change are incomparably more formidable than those involved in stability. There is not now less poverty, less misery, less torture, less pain than formerly. Indeed, today's evils, by their nearness, are far more oppressive than yesterday's which, after all, were somehow survived. Yesterday, by its distance, acquires a happy glow. The peasants look back (they remember they lived through yesterday; who knows if they will live through today?) and their fancy rejoices in the better days that have passed, when they were on the land and the land was fertile, and they were young and strong, and virtues were fresh. And it was better yet in their fathers' days, who were wiser and stronger than they. And it was best of all in the golden past of their distant progenitors who were every one a king and did great deeds. Alas, those days are gone, that they believed existed, and now there is only the bitter present.

In this world then, as in the Old Country, the safest way was to look back to tradition as a guide. Lacking confidence in the individual's capacity for independent inquiry, the peasants preferred to rely upon the tested knowledge of the past. It was difficult of course to apply village experience to life in America, to stretch the ancient aphorisms so they would fit new conditions. Yet that strain led not to a rejection of tradition but rather to an eager quest for a reliable interpreter. Significantly, the peasants sought to acknowledge an authority that would make that interpretation for them.

Their view of the American world led these immigrants to conservatism, and to the acceptance of tradition and authority. Those traits in turn shaped the immigrants' view of society, encouraged them to retain the peasants' regard for status and the divisions of rank. In these matters too striving was futile; it was wiser to keep each to his own station in the social order, to respect the rights of others and to exact the obligations due. For most of these people that course involved the acceptance of an inferior position. But was that not altogether realistic? The wind always blew in the face of the poor; and it was in the nature of society that some should have an abundance of possessions and others only the air they breathed.

The whole configuration of the peasants' ideas in the United States strengthened the place in his life of the established religion he brought with him. It was not only an institutional reluctance to change that held him to his faith, but also the greater need that faith satisfied in the New World.

Emigration had broken the ties with nature. The old stories still evoked emotional responses in their hearers; and the housewives still uttered imprecations and blessings and magic words to guard against the evil eye. But it was hard to believe that the whole world of spirits and demons had abandoned their familiar homes and come also across the Atlantic. It was hard too to continue to think in terms of the natural cycle of growth, of birth, death, and regeneration, away from the setting in which it was every day illustrated in peasant life.

Instead these immigrants found their Christianity ever more meaningful. Here they discovered the significance of their suffering. It was true, what the priest said, that evil was everywhere present in the world; they had themselves experienced the evidence of it. It was true they were imperfect and full of sin, not worthy of a better lot. What they tried bore no results. What they touched turned to dust.

Still all this toil and trouble was not without purpose. What seemed on the surface like the rule of chance in the world was not really so, but part of a plan. The whole of it was not yet revealed, man could not see the end, only the start, because this was not an earthly plan. Rather it extended far beyond this immediate existence and would reach its culmination in an altogether different life that came after the release of death.

Fixing his vision on that life eternal which would follow this, the peasant perceived that caprice in mundane things was an element in an ordered design. If injustice now seemed to triumph, then it was only that retribution should come after. Did the evil flourish, then would they be punished. Were the good oppressed and humiliated, it was to make their rewards the richer. This he knew was the mystery and the reason for his being in the universe.

As he participated in that other mystery of the divine sacrifice that assured him salvation, all the scattered elements of his existence became whole. Let him but have faith enough in the God Who had gone to the cross, for him; Who had come over the water, with him; and he would be repaid for the loss of his home, for the miseries of the way, and for the harshness of his present life. Not indeed in this world, but in an everlasting future. For the lonely and isolated, for the meek and humble, for the strangers, there was hope of a sort, and consolation. . . .

The immigrants find their first homes in quarters the old occupants no longer desire. As business grows, the commercial center of each city begins to blight the neighboring residential districts. The well-to-do are no longer willing to live in close proximity to the bustle of warehouses and offices; yet that same proximity sets a high value on real estate. To spend money on the repair or upkeep of houses in such areas is only wasteful; for they will soon be torn down to make way for commercial buildings. The simplest, most profitable use is to divide the old mansions into tiny lodgings. The rent on each unit will be low; but the aggregate of those sums will, without substantial investment or risk, return larger dividends than any other present use of the property.

Such accommodations have additional attractions for the immigrants. They are close to the familiar region of the docks and they are within walking distance of the places where labor is hired; precious carfare will be saved by living here. In every American city some such district of first settlement receives the newcomers.

Not that much is done to welcome them. The carpenters' hammers shut connecting doors and build rude partitions up across the halls; middle-class homes thus become laborers'—only not one to a family, but shared among many. What's more, behind the original structures are grassy yards where children once had run about at play. There is to be no room for games now. Sheds and shanties, hurriedly thrown up, provide living space; and if a stable is there, so much the better: that too can be turned to account. In 1850 already in New York some seven thousand households are finding shelter in such rear buildings. By this time too ingenuity has uncovered still other resources: fifteen hundred cellars also do service as homes. . . .

There were drastic social consequences to living under these dense conditions. The immigrants had left villages which counted their populations in scores. In the Old World, a man's whole circle of acquaintances had not taken in as many individuals as lived along a single street here. By a tortuous course of adjustments, the newcomers worked out new modes of living in response to their environment. But the cost of those adjustments was paid out of the human energies of the residents and through the physical deterioration of the districts in which they lived.

The tenement flourished most extensively in New York, the greatest point of immigrant concentration. But it was also known in Boston and in the other Atlantic ports. In the interior cities it was less common; there land values were not so rigid and commercial installations not such barriers to the centrifugal spread of population. From the barracklike buildings of the area of first settlement, the immigrants could move out to smaller units where at least the problems of density were less oppressive. Little two-story cottages that held six families were characteristic of places like Buffalo. Elsewhere were wooden three- or four-floor structures that contained a dozen households. Even single homes were to be found, dilapidated shanties or jerry-built boxes low in rent. Yet internally these accommodations were not superior to those of the tenement. In one form or another, the available housing gave the districts to which the immigrants went the character of slums. . . .

The man who joined a mutual aid association, who took a newspaper or went to the theater, was adjusting thereby to the environment of the United States. These were not vestiges of any European forms, but steps in his Americanization.

Yet the same steps brought him ever deeper within a separate existence, loose within the total community in which he lived. The neighborhood and the clubs added up to a society with its own activities and its own media of communication, a society whole and coherent within the larger American society. Paradoxically, as the immigrant adapted himself to the life of the New World, he found himself more often and more completely operating inside the limits of these cultural and social enclaves.

The prevalence of highly developed group activities did not in itself make the position of the newcomers exceptional. This was the general pattern of association in the United States. Those many generations in the country as well as those recently arrived found the most important social concerns here considered the function of voluntary, autonomous combinations, free of the State and all on an equal footing. In this realm of spontaneous organization, the appearance of immigrant associations was taken as a matter of course; every aggregation of individuals acted so in America. This was the means by which all groups discovered the distinctive similarities within themselves, the distinctive differences that cut them off from the whole society.

Becoming an American meant therefore not the simple conformity to a previous pattern, but the adjustment to the needs of a new situation. In the process the immigrants became more rather than less conscious of their own peculiarities. As the immediate environment called forth the succession of fresh institutions and novel modes of behavior, the immigrants found themselves progressively separated as groups.

NO
John Bodnar

THE TRANSPLANTED: A HISTORY OF IMMIGRANTS IN URBAN AMERICA

INTRODUCTION

The people who moved to American cities and industrial towns during the first century of American capitalism have been chronicled and described by an abundant number of scholars, novelists, journalists, and other writers and have been ascribed an array of characteristics. Often their flight to America has been seen as the act of desperate individuals fleeing poverty and disorder only to be further weakened by back-breaking labor and inhospitable cities in America. Their fate was one of a life in insulated ethnic ghettos, continual struggle, and an eventual but precarious attachment to the new economy. Others have celebrated these humble newcomers as bearers of proud, long-established traditions which helped to organize their lives amidst the vagaries of the industrial city and served as a context in which they organized their transition, rather successfully, to a new land. A third school of thought has advanced the argument that these newcomers were aspiring individuals whose ties to tradition were loosened in their homelands and who moved to America eager for opportunity, advancement, and all the rewards of capitalism. In this final framework, immigrants moved from tradition-bound peasants to modern, acquisitive individuals.

Most previous descriptions of immigrants assume that the immigrant experience was a common experience shared equally by all; the transition to capitalism is either entirely difficult, conducted entirely within the confines of a traditional but apparently adaptive culture, or entirely rewarding over a given period of time. But even the most cursory glance at an immigrant community or stream will suggest that not all newcomers behaved in a similar fashion, that varying degrees of commitment to an assortment of cultures and ideologies were evident, and that not everyone faced identical experiences. Some individuals pursued modern forms of life and livelihood while others valued more traditional patterns. Workers existed who championed socialism and others died for their attachment to Catholicism. Some immigrants came to America and acquired large fortunes, and many more simply went to work every day with no appreciable gain. What they actually shared in common was a need to confront a new economic order and provide for their own welfare and that of their kin or household group. They all did this but they did so in different ways and with divergent results. . . .

In essence neither immigration nor capitalism as it emerged in the United States would have been possible without each other. Prior to the 1830s American economic growth was extremely slow as little investment in material capital took place and technology advanced slowly. A virtual absence of productivity-raising activity characterized the nation and small populations, low levels of per capita income, and primitive technologies of transportation and communications existed. By 1840, however, this picture was changing as economic growth and output per capita were showing signs of increasing. Stimulated by a growing foreign demand for American staples, the economy began to expand and offer greater incentives for investments in material capital, inventions, and acquisition of skills, and, of course, inexpensive labor. Manufacturing sectors grew and stimulated the growth of cities. Dependent upon economies of scale, manufacturers had to locate where transportation routes facilitated the acquisitions of raw materials and the presence of population concentrations could easily meet demands for larger supplies of labor. American population growth led to expanded markets which made possible the exploitation of economies of large-scale production. These economies were realized from specialization and the division of labor within firms and from increased specialization among firms as well as technological innovation. Slowly the merchant capitalism which predominated prior to the Civil War gave way to an industrial capitalism which rationalized production under the factory system and looked for an ever-increasing supply of labor to fill the growing number of simple tasks it created and keep labor costs somewhat depressed. By 1870 the United States had a manufacturing output equal to that of France and Germany combined. By 1913 American manufacturing output equaled that of France, Germany and the United Kingdom, and it was the chief producer of foodstuffs in the world. In 1870 over one-half of all workers were farmers or farm laborers. Forty years later over two-thirds were industrial toilers, many of whom had come from regions as diverse as Japan, Mexico, Ireland, Germany, and Italy.

Immigrants were quite important to the entire industrial transformation. Without European immigration to America, for instance, it has been estimated that wages in Eastern industries would have been 11 percent higher than they were in 1910. Immigrants also brought a sizable body of skills and knowledge which were absolutely indispensable for the growth of some industries, and the presence of a large pool of unskilled labor attracted further investment. Additionally, the fact that the cost of rearing and training a huge labor force was largely borne outside the United States allowed for even greater levels of investment and growth. Without immigration in the first century of American capitalism, the United States work force would have been only 70 percent of what it was by 1940.

Finally, by going beyond vague dichotomies of preindustrial immigrants and American culture and looking precisely at the specific points of contact between capitalism as both an economic system and a way of life and specific categories of newcomers, the entire scope of immigration history is rescued from a model of understanding which has dominated scholarly and popular understanding for decades. Whether immigrants were upwardly mobile achievers or dispirited peasants, they were always assumed to move in a linear progression from a premodern, holistic community to a modern, atomistic one. Such a framework presented immigration as a clash of cultures. But if the entire experience is broken down into innumerable points of contact between various categories and beliefs, what emerges is a clearer portrait of the process of social change stimulated almost incessantly by the changing imperatives of the marketplace and the diverse responses of human beings themselves. Their response, conditioned by their social station, familial status, and ideological orientation, becomes a variable itself helping to structure not only their own life path but even somewhat the all-embracing economic system. Ordinary individuals were rescued from the status of victims; they are not simply manipulated by leaders, their class standing, or their culture, but active participants in a historical drama whose outcome is anything but predictable. This view further accentuates a process hidden from sight in previous accounts. Immigrants now are no longer confronting an amorphous mass called America or modern society but specific leaders and ideologies which evoke acceptance, resistance, and divergent paths into the capitalist economy. Agents of tradition preaching ethnic culture, conservatism, and religious devotion appear alongside champions of assimilation, education, and even worker militancy. Spokesmen for what Fernand Braudel calls the "material life," the old routines handed down from time immemorial, compete against advocates of modernization and protest. Occasionally an ideology of tradition will be used in the service of social change. The point is that instead of linear progression, immigrants faced a continual dynamic between economy and society, between class and culture. It was in the swirl of this interaction and competition that ordinary individuals had to sort out options, listen to all the prophets, and arrive at decisions of their own in the best manner they could. Inevitably the results were mixed. Some fared better than others; some stayed in America and others returned home. Immigrants existed who became radicals and others worshiped the ethic of entrepreneurship. Some did not even care either way. In many cases decisions were incomplete and imprecise. These were after all neither heroes nor villains but ordinary people. Life for them as for us was never clear-cut. What was ultimately important amidst the political and economic currents of their times was not only how they adapted to it all but what if anything endured in their lives and brought it order and stability. . . .

THE CULTURE OF EVERYDAY LIFE

Immigrant people by definition related to capitalism and its attendant social order in complex and often ingenious ways which have often been misunderstood. Generally, this process of understanding and adjusting was carried on in two broad categories. In reality two immigrant Americas existed. One consisted largely of workers with menial jobs. The other, a smaller component, held essentially positions which pursued personal gain and leadership. Immigrants did not enter a common mass called America but adapted to two separate but related worlds which might be termed broadly working class and middle class.

These two components were represented everywhere. Middle-class supporters of capitalism could be found among commercial farmers in Mexico, Sicily, or Hungary, entrepreneurs within immigrant groups, or industrialists in all American cities. They wielded relatively more power than most of their contemporaries, enjoyed extensive reinforcement from loyal supporters in political and public life including government officials, educators and even reformers and placed a high value on individual freedom, personal gain, political power, and an improved future. Below them, although far more numerous, stood millions of ordinary people whose perspective was considerably more circumscribed. They were not immune to the satisfaction to be derived from personal gain or political power but could not realistically indulge in such pursuits for too long a period of time. Their power to influence public affairs and their supporters in public institutions were minimal. Tied considerably more to the concerns of family and communal welfare, they focused daily activities, in the words of folklorist Henry Glassie, "in the place where people are in control of their own destinies." These public and private spheres were not totally separate and, indeed, were part of a common system, but one was substantially more expansive, confident, and less circumscribed than the other.

Somewhere in time and space all individuals meet the larger structural realities of their existence and construct a relationship upon a system of ideas, values, and behavior which collectively gives meaning to their world and provides a foundation upon which they can act and survive. Collectively their thought and action are manifestations of a consciousness, a mentality, and ultimately a culture. Immigrants, who were after all common men and women, could not completely understand what was taking place as capitalism entered their world. They were not fully aware of the sweeping political and economic decisions and transitions which were altering the nineteenth and twentieth centuries. In lieu of a comprehensive understanding of social and historical change, they fashioned their own explanations for what they could feel and sense. To give meaning to the realities and structures which now impinged upon them, they forged a culture, a constellation of behavioral and thought patterns which would offer them explanations, order, and a prescription for how to proceed with their lives. This culture was not a simple extension of their past, an embracement of the new order of capitalism, or simply an affirmation of a desire to become an American. It was nurtured not by any one reality such as their new status as workers but was produced from whatever resources were at hand: kinship networks, folklife, religion, socialism, unions. It was a product of both men and women, believers and non-believers, workers and entrepreneurs, leaders and followers. It was creative yet limited by available options. It drew from both a past and a present and continually confronted "the limits of what was possible." The demands of economic forces, social structures, political leaders, kin, and community were real and could not be ignored. Life paths and strategies were informed by knowledge from the past and estimates about the future but largely from the specific options of the present. Immigrants were free to choose but barely.

It must be made clear, however, that this culture of everyday life, while generated at the nexus of societal structures and subjective experience, was ultimately the product of a distinct inequality in the distribution of power and resources within the system of capitalism. It would be convenient to call this a culture of the working class but it was not tied that simply to the means of production or the workplace and was not simply the prerogative of laborers. It was also tied to traditional culture, although it was certainly not entirely ethnic or premodern. Its core was a fixation upon the needs of the family-household for both laborers and entrepreneurs and the proximate community. The relative lack of resources and of a comprehensive knowledge of vast social economic change forced immigrants (and probably ordinary people in other places) to focus an inordinate amount of their lives in two areas. First, they had to devise explanations of their status in terms intelligible to themselves by drawing on folk thought, religion, ancestry, and similar devices close at hand. Second, they had to devote nearly all their attention to that portion of their world in which they actually could exert some power and influence: the family-household, the workplace, and the local neighborhood or community. They sought, in other words, a degree of meaning and control. Like peasants in the Pyrenees studied by Pierre Bourdieu, they forged a world view that allowed for

safeguarding what was considered "essential" at all times. The alternative would have been a life completely out of their hands, entirely bewildering and completely orchestrated by industrialists, public institutions, and economic forces.

The thrust of almost all previous scholarship seeking to interpret the immigrant experience in urban America around considerations of ethnic culture or class has been much too narrow and has failed to make a crucial distinction between the content and foundation of immigrant mentalities. The content which drew from ethnic traditions and present realities seemed as much cultural as it was class-based. That is to say, the newcomers acted as workers but also remained tied to selected ethnic symbols and institutions which appeared to mute solely class concerns. But the basis for this preoccupation with familiar ways, as well as with working-class realities, was to be found in the placement of these ordinary people in the larger social structure of capitalism. Even traditional family and ethnic communities were a preoccupation ultimately not because they were familiar but because they represented somewhat manageable and understandable systems to people who possessed little control or understanding of the larger society. Because they possessed relatively less material and social influence, they were preoccupied with understanding and constructing life at very immediate levels. They did this in part because they were relatively powerless to affect the sweeping currents of their times but, ironically, in doing so they actually generated a degree of power and social control of their own and transcended a status as simply victims.

This pragmatic culture of everyday life accepted the world for what it was and what it was becoming and yet ceaselessly resisted the inevitable at numerous points of contact in the workplace, the classroom, the political hall, the church, and even at home. *Mentalité* for the immigrants was an amalgam of past and present, acceptance and resistance. Ordinary people could never live a life insulated from the actions of their social superiors, nor could they ever fully retreat from their present. Peasants responded to the whims of nobles, immigrants responded to the profit-seeking activities of commercial farmers or industrial capitalists. Since they could not control the direction of either elites or capital, they placed most of their priorities and focused most of their attention on the immediate, the attainable, the portion of their world in which they could exert some influence. This was true in "material life" and life under capitalism as well. By implication the culture of everyday life, shaped primarily by social status and unequal ownership of the means of production and informed by traditions and communal needs, always aspired to modest goals and was devoid of extremely radical or liberal impulses. The extent newcomers would go in either direction depended a great deal on the ability and impact of various leaders. And still ordinary people left their mark. Leaders constantly had to modify their ideology to effectively attract immigrant support. Peasants in the homelands could do little to dissuade the upper classes from promoting the spread of commercial agriculture. They did, however, force local elites to pay more for their farm labor by deciding to emigrate. Similarly, immigrants could not make decisions where to locate plants or invest large amounts of capital, but they could force industrialists to change personnel and

wage policies by their transiency which stemmed from their private agendas. Some scholars might call this a form of class antagonism, but it also represented an effort to construct life strategies within available options.

Ultimately, then, the mentality and culture of most immigrants to urban America was a blend of past and present and centered on the immediate and the attainable. Institutions from the past such as the family-household were modified but retained; the actions of landed elites at home and industrial capitalists abroad forced them to confront a new market and social order which they accepted but somewhat on their own terms. They would move, several times, if they had to, and become wage laborers or even small entrepreneurs. They did so not because they were victimized by capitalism or embraced it but because they pursued the immediate goal of family-household welfare and industrial jobs which were very accessible. If they had the skills or capital, which some did, even a small business was not out of the question. Those that moved had eschewed any retreat into a fictitious peasant past or becoming large, commercial farmers, although many still dreamed of living on the land. Overall, however, for people in the middle, immigration made a great deal of sense. Barrington Moore, who has written about German workers in the early twentieth century, has suggested that they were consumed by practical issues, such as the possible inability of the breadwinner to earn a living. Secondary concerns did include injustice and unfair treatment at the workplace but basically their fears and hopes revolved around everyday life: getting enough to eat and having a home of one's own. They expressed hopes for a better future but were usually too busy making ends meet to do much about it. The pattern apparently transcended time and space.

Since capitalism was the central force which created these immigrants, it is still not possible to conclude they made an inevitable and smooth transition to a new way of life and a new culture. They were not one-dimensional beings rooted only to old ways of life or a new economy. They did not proceed simply from an ethnic world to a class world. Rather their consciousness and culture were continually grounded in several levels of status and culture prior to emigration and after arrival as well. It was tied simultaneously to the lower levels of tradition, household, and community as well as to the higher levels of capitalism, industrialization, and urbanization. Between the microscopic forces of daily life, often centering around ethnic communal and kinship ties, and the macroscopic world of economic change and urban growth stood the culture of everyday life. This was a culture not based exclusively on ethnicity, tradition, class, or progress. More precisely, it was a mediating culture which confronted all these factors. It was simultaneously turbulent and comforting: It looked forward and backward, although not very far in either direction. It could not hope to exert the influence on history that industrial capitalism did, but it was far from being simply reflexive. Depending on premigration experience and leadership in America, it could prepare the way for a transition to a working-class or a middle-class America but seldom did it lead to a complete embracement of any new order.

If the culture of everyday life dominated the lives of most American immigrants, it did not mean that all newcomers were alike. Even within similar ethnic aggregations, a preoccupation with the practical and the attainable did not create identical life strategies. Some manifested a sojourning orientation and planned to return home fortified in their ability to live off the land. Others came to stay and effectively exploited their skills and resources to establish careers and businesses in urban America. Still others never really made up their minds and simply worked from day to day. Divergent resources and orientations in the homeland, moreover, often led to varying rates of attainment and participation in the culture of capitalism; those who settled in higher social stations and were already further removed from "material life" prior to emigration began to move more purposefully toward the new culture of acquisitiveness and personal gain. The origins of inequality in urban America were not located solely in the industrial workplace, or the city, or even ethnic cultures. They were also rooted in the social structure of the homeland and immigrant stream. Such divisions, in fact, would fragment immigrant communities and insure that urban-ethnic enclaves and settlements would only exist temporarily. But fragmentation at the group level should not obscure the ties that most of the first generation had to the culture of everyday life and the need to take what was available and secure the welfare of those closest to them. Immigrants were generally part of the masses and the culture of the masses in the nineteenth and much of the twentieth century was not solely traditional, modern, or working class. It was a dynamic culture, constantly responding to changing needs and opportunities and grounded in a deep sense of pragmatism and mutual assistance. Fernand Braudel spoke of three levels of historic time: political, which was rapid and episodic; social, which was modulated by the slower pace of everyday life; geographical, where change was nearly imperceptible. Immigrants were closely preoccupied with social time and the realities of the immediate and the present, although the levels of time and culture were never completely separated.

The center of every life was to be found in the family-household and the proximate community. It was here that past values and present realities were reconciled, examined on an intelligible scale, evaluated, and mediated. No other institution rivaled the family-household in its ability to filter the macrocosm and microcosm of time and space. Kinship and the household, of course, are not necessarily identical concepts and family and work need not be inextricably linked. The truth of the matter, however, was that during the first century of American capitalism they inevitably were. The family-household mobilized resources and socialized people. Even though capitalism entered the peasant household in the homeland and caused a shift from subsistence to market production, the transition was essentially one of function and not form. The linking of individuals to a wage rather than a household economy did not inevitably lead to a decline of the family-household. In the first century of industrial capitalism, the family-household continued to remain effective because supporting institutions of capitalism such as the state, public education, and even federally regulated unions had not yet become strong enough to fully penetrate the confines of private space.

Because of the continued viability of the family-household, the small community or urban neighborhood, usually built upon congeries of such units, continued to function and the culture of everyday life persisted. But this did not mean that private space was immune from public ritual and activity. Repeatedly, albeit episodically, the culture of everyday life was punctuated by "political time," by the rhetoric and ambitions of competing leaders. A new society and a new economy presented opportunities for newcomers with particular skills or resources to pursue power and middle-class status, to forsake the ambiguity of the culture of everyday life for the single-minded culture of power, wealth, and personal gain. Among all groups, not just among Japanese or Jewish entrepreneurs, this process of middle-class formation and pursuit of individual power took place to one extent or another.

While leaders emerged within all immigrant communities, they did not all advocate ideas and values consistent with the new order of capitalism or with each other. Many successful entrepreneurs advocated rapid Americanization and individual achievement. These leaders, such as Carl Schurz, A. P. Giannini, and Peter Rovnianek, were usually reinforced by the larger society which supported them and shared their faith. American political parties actually subsidized part of the ethnic press and further attempted to violate the boundaries of everyday life. Opposed to these accommodationists, however, were those who exhibited a stronger defense of tradition and communal values. They included clerics and fraternal leaders, were usually less tied to the new economy than politicians and entrepreneurs, and while not opposed to Americanization, were skeptical of rapid change, growing secularism, and the dangers inherent in a pluralistic society which threatened their elevated status. Irish Catholic prelates, for instance, could allow for Americanization but not accept public education in a society dominated by other cultures and religions. Advocates of religious authority and homeland causes, while often bitterly divided, were both ultimately defenders of the "everyday culture" in which they usually held prominent positions. Because they were tied closer to the culture of the masses, they generally exerted a stronger influence than leaders attached to external cultures such as trade unionists, socialists, educational reformers, or national political figures. . . .

But not all leaders or elites were equally effective. Ideology cannot be reduced to simple strategies advanced by the prominent to further their own interests nor does it simply flow from the top to the bottom of society. The rhetoric and symbols of leaders were most effective when they reflected to some extent the feeling and thought of ordinary people themselves. Educational reformers, socialists, some political figures, and even trade unionists often failed to realize this fully. Those that did, such as unionists who recruited ethnic organizers or editors who championed the cause of the homeland, were much more successful in mobilizing portions of the immigrant population. The Irish Land League, the rise of Catholic schools, the quest for German-language instruction, the rise of the United Mine Workers, and the cause of Russian Jews even in the 1890s illustrate how private issues could effectively enter public space. Religion, the homeland, and labor matters were probably the most debated issues. These matters concerned key elements of the past and present and of everyday culture; religion and labor especially had deep implications for a well-ordered family-household.

Immigrants not only influenced their leaders in an episodic fashion but resisted intervention into the only world they could control on an ongoing basis even while adjusting to a new economic order. They were not simply duped by a hegemonic culture. Neither the prominent within their groups nor the owners of the means of production were beyond their influence. Immigrant laymen fought to maintain control of churches, Italians practiced rituals in defiance of clerical authority, religious and ethnic schools were established to resist the culture of outsiders, laborers controlled production, left jobs they did not like and struck spontaneously in colorful, communal fashion if it suited their purposes. They never tired of assisting friends and relatives to find jobs and probably had as much as managers to do with shaping the informal system of employment recruitment which dominated American industry during the century before World War II. Leaders who urged newcomers to support extended schooling or various political parties usually made little headway unless they addressed the issues relating to the family-household and community that newcomers felt strongest about: homeownership, jobs, neighborhood services, steady work, and traditional beliefs.

Immigrants lived in scattered urban-ethnic enclaves which were heavily working class. But these settlements were neither structurally nor ideologically monolithic. Newcomers were tied to no single reality. The workplace, the church, the host society, the neighborhood, the political boss, and even the homeland all competed for their minds and bodies. On a larger level, industrial capitalism could not be stopped. But on the level of everyday life, where ordinary people could inject themselves into the dynamic of history, immigrants acquiesced, resisted, hoped, despaired, and ultimately fashioned a life the best they could. Transplanted by forces beyond their control, they were indeed children of capitalism. But like children everywhere they were more than simply replicas of their parents; independence and stubborn resistance explained their lives as much as their lineage. Their lives were not entirely of their own making, but they made sure that they had something to say about it.

POSTSCRIPT

Were the Immigrants' Old World Cultures Destroyed as They Adjusted to American Life?

A prolific writer, Handlin has been recognized as the most influential scholar on immigration history since his dissertation won the Dunning prize when he was only 26. First published in 1941 by the Harvard University Press, *Boston's Immigrants: A Study in Acculturation* has been reprinted nine times in the years 1968 to 1974. Earlier writings about the immigrants were mainly descriptive or filiopietistic defenses of a particular ethnic group against the stereotypical prejudicial attitudes of mainstream Americans. *Boston's Immigrants* was the first work to integrate sociological concepts within a historical framework. Ten years later, Handlin wrote *The Uprooted*, in which he combined the interdisciplinary framework with a personal narrative of the immigrant's history. Though many historians were critical of this approach, the book earned Handlin a Pulitzer Prize.

Although Handlin and Bodnar employ different theoretical frameworks to reconstruct the immigrants' pasts, there are striking similarities in *The Uprooted* and *The Transplanted*. Both books are generalized accounts of the immigrant experience. While Handlin's work is more poetic and fully deserving of the Pulitzer Prize in its attempt to reach a wider audience, Bodnar also portrays the immigrants sympathetically. Both scholars also write interdisciplinary history and borrow concepts from the social sciences.

Handlin and Bodnar differ, however, in their perspectives about America's ethnic past. Handlin views the immigrant as a person who was uprooted from Old World cultures and assimilated into the New World's value system within two generations. In contrast, Bodnar argues that first-generation immigrants maintained a viable life-style centered around the family household and neighboring community. "Not solely traditional, modern or working class," says Bodnar, "it was a dynamic culture, constantly responding to changing needs and opportunities and grounded in a deep sense of pragmatism and mutual assistance."

The Harvard Encyclopedia of American Ethnic Groups (Harvard University Press, 1980), edited by Stephan Thernstrom and Oscar Handlin, is a collection of articles on every ethnic group in America. It also contains 29 thematic essays on such subjects as prejudice, assimilation, and folklore. Also useful and more manageable is Stephanie Bernardo, *The Ethnic Almanac* (Doubleday, 1981), whose purpose is to "amuse, inform and entertain you with facts about your heritage and that of your friends, neighbors and relatives." *Ethnic Americans: A History of Immigration and Assimilation*, 2d ed., by Leonard Dinnerstein and David Reimers (Harper & Row, 1982), is a short, but accurate, text, while Joe R. Feagan's *Racial and Ethnic Relations*, 2d ed. (Prentice Hall, 1985) is a useful sociological text that examines the major ethnic groups in a historical fashion by means of assimilationist and power-conflict models.

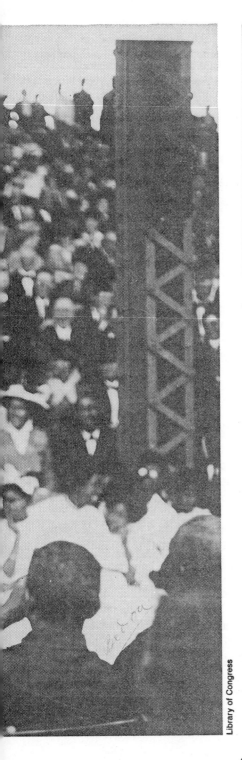

PART 2

The Response to Industrialism

The mechanization of agriculture led to a surplus production of goods in the late nineteenth century. Farmers who specialized in cotton and wheat in the South and Midwest formed cooperatives, joined the third party Populists, and pressured the state legislatures to pass laws regulating the shipping rates of the railroads. Many of the Populist attacks were directed at the bankers who controlled the nation's money supply and the middlemen who ran the grain exchange.

The cities also had problems. Improvements in water and sewage, street cleaning, housing, mass transit, and fire and crime prevention developed slowly because the incredible population growth strained municipal services and urban governments had limited powers, which often fell under the control of political bosses. The progressive reformers attempted to deal with problems of urban-industrial America in the early twentieth century. They ameliorated some of the worst problems but often created others by attempting to impose Anglo-Saxon Protestant standards on a diverse immigrant population.

Were the Populists Democratic Reformers?

Was City Government in Late Nineteenth-Century America a "Conspicuous Failure"?

Did Booker T. Washington's Philosophy and Actions Betray the Interests of African Americans?

Did the Progressives Fail?

ISSUE 5

Were the Populists Democratic Reformers?

YES: Norman Pollack, from *The Populist Response to Industrial America: Midwestern Populist Thought* (Harvard University Press, 1962)

NO: Richard Hofstadter, from *The Age of Reform: From Bryan to F.D.R.* (Knopf, 1955)

ISSUE SUMMARY

YES: Professor of history Norman Pollack views Populism as a genuinely radical movement that intended to establish industrial democracy in the United States through the promotion of human rights.

NO: Professor of history Richard Hofstadter focuses upon the nostalgic, reactionary nature of the Populists, whose attitudes revealed a desire to create a rural utopia by using the early nineteenth-century United States as their model.

Industrialism produced significant changes and affected every major group in American society. Manufacturers and laborers obviously experienced the impact of these new forces, but industrial influences were felt beyond the confines of the nation's growing cities. Industrialism also altered the lives of rural Americans who depended upon the soil for their livelihoods. Although they hoped to benefit from new markets and increased prosperity, the reality for most American farmers was greater poverty. After 1815, the independent, self-sufficient farmer began his retreat into American mythology in the wake of the relentless advance of commercial agriculture.

Between 1860 and 1900, American farmers confronted a steady downward spiral of agricultural prices, especially among major cash crops like wheat, corn, and cotton. Greater efficiency created higher production levels, which drove prices to lower levels. Meanwhile, farmers and their families had to purchase manufactured goods, many of which were artificially inflated in price by existing tariff schedules. Purchasing new land and better machinery to offset declining prices only compounded the problem and created a new one—the difficulty of repaying credit extended by the nation's banks. By 1890, many farmers were losing their lands to foreclosure and were forced into tenant farming or sharecropping; others abandoned the countryside for the city. The independent yeoman farmer, once described by Thomas Jefferson as the backbone of the nation, seemed to be losing everything.

The discontent bred by these factors led American farmers to conclude that the best solution lay in organizing. This was a momentous decision on the part of a group of citizens who for generations had expressed a commitment to individualism of the most rugged sort. But with industrialists forming managers' associations and urban workers pushing for the recognition of their unions, many farmers decided to follow suit. Initial attempts to form organizations resulted in the National Grange of the Patrons of Husbandry in the 1860s, an essentially social group, and the Alliance movement of the 1870s and 1880s. Finally, farmers attempted to organize an effective political movement in the 1890s, which culminated in the People's, or Populist, party. The Populists mounted political opposition to the forces that threatened to make beggars of agricultural and urban workers alike, but with the defeat of William Jennings Bryan in the presidential election of 1896, Populism passed quickly from the scene. Nevertheless, many of the ideas and programs advanced by the People's party subsequently were secured by reformers in the twentieth century.

What were the goals of the Populists? What kinds of changes were they seeking to introduce in the United States? Were those goals consistent with the demands of an urban, industrial nation at the turn of the century? Or were they efforts to return to a simpler, more traditional rural American dream? These are some of the questions addressed in the essays that follow.

Norman Pollack portrays the Populists as radicals who offered a penetrating critique of industrial America in the late nineteenth century. According to Pollack, the People's party accepted industrialism but believed that the age of monopolistic privilege threatened human liberty. The Populists, therefore, sought to establish an industrial democracy characterized by more humane institutions and a more equitable distribution of wealth.

Richard Hofstadter credits the Populists with releasing reform sentiments that fueled the protests of the Progressive era. He agrees with Pollack that the movement was a response to industrialism and that it was the first political movement to insist upon federal responsibility for the common good of American society. At the same time, Hofstadter claims, Populism was provincial, nativistic, nationalistic, and anti-Semitic. These characteristics reveal that the Populists were not forward-looking champions of democracy but rather bigoted seekers of a utopian rural past.

YES

Norman Pollack

THE POPULIST RESPONSE TO
INDUSTRIAL AMERICA

Populism had a peculiar notion of freedom: Man was free only when society encouraged the fullest possible development of human potentiality. Addressing the mammoth Tattersall rally, which climaxed the 1894 People's party campaign in Chicago, Henry Demarest Lloyd declared: "The people's party is more than the organized discontent of the people. It is the organized aspiration of the people for a fuller, nobler, richer, kindlier life for every man, woman, and child in the ranks of humanity." Seeking to enhance human self-fulfillment, it could not be a temporary phenomenon: "The people's party is not a passing cloud on the political sky. It is not a transient gust of popular discontent caused by bad crops or hard times." Rather, "It is an uprising of principle, and the millions who have espoused these principles will not stop until they have become incorporated into the constitution of the government and the framework of society." Thus, the goal of Populism was "the hope of realizing and incarnating in the lives of the common people the fullness of the divinity of humanity."

Here, then, was a standard for judging industrial America in the 1890's: Did it promote "the divinity of humanity," or merely produce dehumanized and impoverished men? While human rights is an abstraction admirably suited to campaign rhetoric, the theme recurs with sufficient frequency and intensity to indicate that Populists took it seriously. As Hamlin Garland stated to James B. Weaver, in the midst of the latter's 1892 presidential campaign: "Don't confine the fight to any one thing money or land. Let's make the fight for *human liberty* and for the rights of man." Ignatius Donnelly, in a circular prepared for party members in the 1896 campaign, defined the task at hand as "the preservation of humanity in the highest estate of which it is capable on earth." And Senator [William V.] Allen of Nebraska similarly held that Populism "rests on the cause of labor and the brotherhood of man."

Populists further clarified their conception of human rights by distinguishing it from property rights. Governor Lorenzo D. Lewelling of Kansas, in a major speech, reminded his Kansas City audience that "we have so much regard for the rights of property that we have forgotten the liberties of the individual." A Broken Bow, Nebraska, paper saw the conflict as that of the "rights of. man" and the "rights of capital." And one in Nelson, Nebraska, characterized it as between "the wealthy and powerful classes who want the control of the government to plunder the people" and "the people" themselves, who are "contending for equality before the law and the rights of man."

More concretely, human rights are a sham unless predicated upon an equitable distribution of wealth. An editorial in the Lincoln, Nebraska, *Farmers' Alliance* expressed the view in these words: "The people's party has sprung into existence not to make the black man free, but to emancipate all men; not to secure political freedom to a class, but to gain for all *industrial* freedom, without which there can be no political freedom; no lasting people's government." Making "industrial freedom" the precondition for political freedom, it further asserted that the People's party "stands upon the declaration that 'all men are created equal,' having equal right to live, labor and enjoy the fruits of their labor. It teaches that none should have power to enjoy without labor." On the contrary, Populism "demands equal opportunities and exact justice in business for each individual and proposes to abolish all monopolistic privileges and power." Thus, the perspective is refined still further: Monopoly poses the principal threat to human rights. Significantly, the editorial immediately added that the People's party "is the first party that has comprehended the great question of injustice and proposed an adequate remedy for the evils

of society." Its closing sentence reveals that, while opposing monopoly, Populism accepted industrialism: Populists "shall make of this nation an industrial democracy in which each citizen shall have an equal interest."

At the same Tattersall rally where Lloyd spoke, Clarence Darrow also called for a more democratic industrial system: "We of the People's party believe that the men who created our wonderful industrial system have the right to enjoy the institution which they have created." A Columbus, Nebraska, paper voiced the same sentiment: "The people do not want to tear up the railroads nor pull down the factories." Instead "they want to build up and make better everything." And social protest became necessary to secure these conditions, for "even a worm will writhe and struggle when stepped upon, and surely, if Americans cannot be anything higher, they can be a nation of worms." As the Populist organ in Wahoo, Nebraska, simply observed: "There should be no want." Thus, industrial America could, but did not, provide greater material benefits for the total society. The technological potential was present for overcoming poverty, the results otherwise. A correspondent to Lloyd summarized this feeling when he wrote: "The whole ideal of our civilization is wrong."

But privation was not inevitable; measures *could* be taken to create a more equitable distribution of wealth. Here the essential rationality of Populism becomes clear: Man could rationally control his society, particularly by harnessing the productive forces already in existence. But this could not occur under the existing form of social organization, for industrial capitalism was not responsive to human needs. Society, in a word, had to be changed. And while the means selected were moderate—working through the political system—this should not obscure the radical conception Populists maintained of politics. The same Columbus paper defined politics as the ability to control "the distribution of wealth." Politics no longer meant seeking office, still less preserving the status quo. Rather, this paper added, "Politics can cause this country to bloom and blossom like the rose; it can make our people, generally speaking, prosperous, happy and contented, or it can stagnate every kind of enterprise, reduce the masses to want and misery and cause our people to become restless, desperate and bloodthirsty."

Frank Doster, a Populist leader in Kansas, spelled out in detail this demand for political action to achieve the benefits of technology. Speaking at Topeka on Labor Day of 1894, Doster pointed out that although "steam, electricity, compressed air, are utilized to do the work of man," the expected gains failed to materialize. These productive forces, which are "the common property of all," have not benefited the total society because they "have been made the monopoly of the few." Through this monopoly structure they "have been turned aside from the beneficent ends for which designed, to serve the selfish purposes of avarice and greed." Moreover, Populism was, according to Doster, the only major political force which sought to control economic concentration in the interests of the larger society: "In the face of the power exerted by the monopolists of these tremendous engines of industry and commerce the republican and democratic parties stand paralyzed—hypnotized, as it were, unable to control it or give direction and shape for common good." Here

the traditional charge is reversed; a Populist holds that the major parties have been overwhelmed by these rapid changes. "The failure to adapt the legislation of the country to the strange conditions which this new life has forced upon us is the cause in greater part of our industrial ills." The statement suggests the attempt to confront, not retreat from, the new situation. Accordingly, Doster closed with a presentation of "two political formulae," serving as the "philosophic bases" for reliance upon governmental action: Government must "do that for the individual which he can not successfully do for himself, and which other individuals will not do for him upon just and equitable terms." And more comprehensively, "the industrial system of a nation, like its political system, should be a government of and for and by the people alone."

Stepping back momentarily to view Populist thought in a wider ideological spectrum, one immediately recognizes its challenge to what are generally considered the prevailing ideologies of the period—the success myth, social Darwinism, and laissez faire. Governor Lewelling's Kansas City speech clearly states the Populist case for paternalism: "It is the business of the Government to make it possible for me to live and sustain the life of my family." Further, "It is the duty of government to protect the weak, because the strong are able to protect themselves." This is totally at variance with the success-myth faith in individual self-help through character development, industry, and perseverance. An article in the *Farmers' Alliance* suggests why Populists could not subscribe to the success myth: It contradicted their actual experiences, denied their grievances, and led to markedly different conclusions regarding the operation of the economic system. Hence, "No effort of the people, no degree of economy, no amount of industry in their several avocations could have averted these results. The people are as powerless as though they were actually in a state of bondage." A change in the nature of society, not a reliance on individual self-help, was necessary: "While the cause exists the evils *must* and *will* remain."

But Populism rejected the success myth, and indeed laissez faire and social Darwinism, for a more basic reason. Unbridled individualism, it contended, destroyed rather than promoted the general welfare. Its own counter-formulation, simply, was that cooperation and mutual help, not competition and self-help, led to true individualism.

An editorial in the *Farmers' Alliance* stated the argument as follows: "The plutocracy of to-day is the logical result of the individual freedom which we have always considered the pride of our system." In fact, "The theory of our government has been and is that the individual should possess the very greatest degree of liberty consistent, not with the greatest good of the greatest number, but with the very least legal restraint compatible with law and order. Individual enterprise was allowed unlimited scope." Thus, individualism creates monopoly capitalism, where "the corporation has absorbed the community." Instead, the reverse must take place: "The community must now absorb the corporation— must merge itself into it. Society must enlarge itself to the breadth of humanity." The editorial closed with an unmistakable repudiation of these other value systems: "A stage must be reached in which each will be for all and all for each. The welfare of the individual must be the object and end of all effort." And three years later, this paper (under its new name, *Alliance-Independent*) succinctly noted that "a reigning plutocracy with the masses enslaved, is the natural development and end of individualism." It remained for the Topeka *Advocate* to add a final, somewhat ironic, comment: "The horror of 'paternalism' hangs like a black pall over the buried hopes of the helpless poor."

Populism was even more unsparing in its criticism of social Darwinism, especially the latter's sanction of competition and survival of the fittest. Governor Lewelling, again in the Kansas City speech, warned that unless the government exerted greater control over industrial capitalism there would be "a state of barbarism and everywhere we slay, and the slayer in turn is slain and so on the great theatre of life is one vast conspiracy all creatures from the worm to the man in turn rob their fellows." For him, social Darwinism meant "the law of natural selection the survival of the fittest—Not the survival of the fittest, but the survival of the strongest." Lewelling concluded: "It is time that man should rise above it."

George H. Gibson, in a letter to the *Alliance-Independent* (he later became its editor), expressed a similar view of competition. Arguing that the type of social reform represented by Jane Addams was futile, he observed: "Uplifting the masses is all right, but it would be much better to put a stop to the beastly struggle which crowds them down." Nor did Gibson reason abstractly; he denied the wisdom of competition by what was daily taking place in American society. "There are tens of thousands in this city [Chicago] all the time out of work, fighting for positions and the low wages which enable capitalists to rake off dividends for idle and scheming stock-holders." Writing later to Henry D. Lloyd, Gibson outlined his counter-proposal to competition: "We must put together our property, labor, economic wisdom, knowledge, varying talents, Christianizing or democratizing what we have and are . . . We feel that it is wrong to continue the selfish struggle, even with charitable or philanthropic intent, as many noble souls are doing."

Using for his standard "political and economic equality," a Walnut Grove, Minnesota, editor judged competitive society in these terms: "The calamities that have heretofore and that now are upon us—as a nation—are but the measure or indicator of the extent that this standard has been departed from in the practice of the competitive system." Nor did Populists admire those who were presumably the fittest. Ignatius Donnelly characterized them as follows: "Shallow-pated, sordid, unintellectual, they stand there, grabbing and grinning, while their brethren march past them to destruction." The Columbus, Nebraska, paper was less charitable, describing "the so-called great men" as "moral cowards and public plunderers" who have "reversed the code of morals and stand up like hypocrites of olden times and thank god they are not like other men are." And it opposed these men, again not on abstract grounds, but because it regarded competition as destroying all but the victors: "They have the power to impoverish the farmers, make millions of good men tramps; to reduce their employees to silent slaves; to ruin great cities; to plunge a happy and prosperous nation into sorrow and bankruptcy."

These criticisms do not, however, reflect a conspiracy theory of history; Populists were concerned with the con-sequences of power, not the personalities or motivations of successful men. Referring to Rockefeller, Henry D. Lloyd noted that personal questions are extraneous because "the main point is the simple issue of monopoly." Even if "they are angels," he continued, the problem remains critical so long as they "have obtained the power of controlling the markets." Lloyd argued somewhat earlier in this same fashion against Carnegie, "I have no sort of feeling" against the man, but he is nonetheless "one of the worst representatives of our mercenary system of ordering industry which is perverting it from the supply of demand and the production and distribution of the wealth in nature for the use of all men, and making it an instrument of personal aggrandisement and cannibalistic selfishness."

Nor did Populism concede the more attractive side of social Darwinism, the latter's belief that society evolved into progressively higher stages. Technological progress was one matter—its translation into material well-being quite another. "While we think, brag of it, how far we are ahead of any former civilization," wrote a Minnesota state senator to Donnelly, "I for one am disgusted of the bragging and boasting and simply believe it is not true." Surely, through improvements in communications, "we are making history a little faster than when those elements were lacking in the worlds affairs." But, he added, "I disdain to call it progress when, considering what it eventually . . . will lead to." This position is exceedingly interesting, for it starts from the recognition that technology provides the means for the liberation of man: "I have heard it asserted that the printing Press, telegraph, etc. have educated the masses, that the direful relapse will not come again as in the past." Yet, he then reaches a decidedly unexpected conclusion. While it can serve man, technology can also be used to insure a greater domination over man. In a word, progress is not only meaningless for a defective society; it actually becomes harmful by intensifying these defects. For Populism, then, progress was not an unmixed blessing: "Bosh, our would be masters have a corner on the whole outfit of the inventions, and they are now just as much employed to the destruction of human rights as formerly in the absence of those inventions the peoples ignorance was used as a means."

Yet, Populism denied not the idea of progress but its realization in existing society. Optimistic in reforming zeal, Populism was still essentially pessimistic in its awareness of the ensuing obstacles. Not surprisingly, the result was an ambivalence with pessimism the overriding factor. A letter to Bryan after the 1896 election stated that an "appeal to reason may elevate the human race to a point we dream not of." But the same letter tempered this optimistic outburst with a sobering reminder: "A social system which permits puny children to toil in grimy factories and foul sweatshops while brawny men walk the streets vainly begging for work . . . is damnable!" How, then, could the net balance be otherwise than on the pessimistic side when Populists continually asked themselves such questions as this: "And for what object has this tremendous slaughter of the human family and this unparalleled suffering of the living been inflicted upon mankind?"

Thus, Populism did not subscribe to the ideologies of individualism, competition, and progress. But its response, far from being negative, was to redefine en-

tirely the relation between society and the individual. Contrary to Populism, the other three ideologies held the individual alone responsible for his plight; perseverance, ruthlessness, or industry determined one's position in the social structure. Populism reversed this: society itself was blamed for human impoverishment. The way was therefore cleared for social protest. No longer was man thrown back upon his imagined inadequacies; self-recrimination and additional frenetic activity were rejected as guides to improving one's life-situation. Atomized man gave way to social man, individual responsibility to social responsibility. Society, not the individual, had to be changed. Indeed. Populism was the major radical alternative of this period.

NO

Richard Hofstadter

THE FOLKLORE OF POPULISM

THE TWO NATIONS

For a generation after the Civil War, a time of great economic exploitation and waste, grave social corruption and ugliness, the dominant note in American political life was complacency. Although dissenting minorities were always present, they were submerged by the overwhelming realities of industrial growth and continental settlement. The agitation of the Populists, which brought back to American public life a capacity for effective political indignation, marks the beginning of the end of this epoch. In the short run the Populists did not get what they wanted, but they released the flow of protest and criticism that swept through American political affairs from the 1890's to the beginning of the first World War.

Where contemporary intellectuals gave the Populists a perfunctory and disdainful hearing, later historians have freely recognized their achievements and frequently overlooked their limitations. . . .

There is indeed much that is good and usable in our Populist past. While the Populist tradition had defects that have been too much neglected, it does not follow that the virtues claimed for it are all fictitious. Populism was the first modern political movement of practical importance in the United States to insist that the federal government has some responsibility for the common weal; indeed, it was the first such movement to attack seriously the problems created by industrialism. The complaints and demands and prophetic denunciations of the Populists stirred the latent liberalism in many Americans and startled many conservatives into a new flexibility. Most of the "radical" reforms in the Populist program proved in later years to be either harmless or useful. In at least one important area of American life a few Populist leaders in the South attempted something profoundly radical and humane—to build a popular movement that would cut across the old barriers of race—until persistent use of the Negro bogy distracted their following. To discuss the broad ideology of the Populists does them some injustice, for it was in their

From Richard Hofstadter, *The Age of Reform: From Bryan to F.D.R.* (Alfred A. Knopf, 1955). Copyright © 1955 by Richard Hofstadter. Reprinted by permission of Alfred A. Knopf, Inc.

concrete programs that they added most constructively to our political life, and in their more general picture of the world that they were most credulous and vulnerable. Moreover, any account of the fallibility of Populist thinking that does not acknowledge the stress and suffering out of which that thinking emerged will be seriously remiss. But anyone who enlarges our portrait of the Populist tradition is likely to bring out some unseen blemishes. In the books that have been written about the Populist movement, only passing mention has been made of its significant provincialism; little has been said of its relations with nativism and nationalism; nothing has been said of its tincture of anti-Semitism. . . .

The utopia of the Populists was in the past, not the future. According to the agrarian myth, the health of the state was proportionate to the degree to which it was dominated by the agricultural class, and this assumption pointed to the superiority of an earlier age. The Populists looked backward with longing to the lost agrarian Eden, to the republican America of the early years of the nineteenth century in which there were few millionaires and, as they saw it, no beggars, when the laborer had excellent prospects and the farmer had abundance, when statement still responded to the mood of the people and there was no such thing as the money power. What they meant—though they did not express themselves in such terms—was that they would like to restore the conditions prevailing before the development of industrialism and the commercialization of agriculture. It should not be surprising that they inherited the traditions of Jacksonian democracy, that they revived the old Jacksonian cry: "Equal Rights for All, Special Privileges for None," or that most of the slogans of 1896 echoed the battle cries of 1836. General James B. Weaver, the Populist candidate for the presidency in 1892, was an old Democrat and Free-Soiler, born during the days of Jackson's battle with the United States Bank, who drifted into the Greenback movement after a short spell as a Republican, and from there to Populism. His book, A Call to Action, published in 1892, drew up an indictment of the business corporation which reads like a Jacksonian polemic. Even in those hopeful early days of the People's Party, Weaver projected no grandiose plans for the future, but lamented the course of recent history, the growth of economic oppression, and the emergence of great contrasts of wealth and poverty, and called upon his readers to do "All in [their] power to arrest the alarming tendencies of our times." . . .

. . . As opposed to the idea that society consists of a number of different and frequently clashing interests—the social pluralism expressed, for instance, by Madison in the Federalist—the Populists adhered, less formally to be sure, but quite persistently, to a kind of social dualism: although they knew perfectly well that society was composed of a number of classes, for all practical purposes only one simple division need be considered. There were two nations. "It is a struggle," said Sockless Jerry Simpson, "between the robbers and the robbed." "There are but two sides in the conflict that is being waged in this country today," declared a Populist manifesto. "On the one side are the allied hosts of monopolies, the money power, great trusts and railroad corporations, who seek the enactment of laws to benefit them and impoverish the people. On the other are the farmers, laborers, merchants and all other people who produce wealth and bear the burdens of taxation. . . . Between these two there is no middle ground." "On the one side," said Bryan in his famous speech against the repeal of the Sherman Silver Purchase Act, "stand the corporate interests of the United States, the moneyed interests, aggregated wealth and capital, imperious, arrogant, compassionless. . . . On the other side stand an unnumbered throng, those who gave to the Democratic party a name and for whom it has assumed to speak." The people versus the interests, the public versus the plutocrats, the toiling multitude versus the money power—in various phrases this central antagonism was expressed. From this simple social classification it seemed to follow that once the techniques of misleading the people were exposed, victory over the money power ought to be easily accomplished, for in sheer numbers the people were overwhelming. "There is no power on earth that can defeat us," said General Weaver during the optimistic days of the campaign of 1892. "It is a fight between labor and capital, and labor is in the vast majority." . . .

HISTORY AS CONSPIRACY

There was something about the Populist imagination that loved the secret plot and the conspiratorial meeting. There was in fact a widespread Populist idea that all American history since the Civil War could be understood as a sustained conspiracy of the international money power. . . .

. . . Wherever one turns in the Populist literature of the nineties one can find this conspiracy theory expressed. It is in the Populist newspapers, the proceed-ings of the silver conventions, the immense pamphlet literature broadcast by the American Bimetallic League, the Congressional debates over money; it is elaborated in such popular books as Mrs. S. E. V. Emery's *Seven Financial Conspiracies which have Enslaved the American People* or Gordon Clark's *Shylock: as Banker, Bondholder, Corruptionist, Conspirator.*

Mrs. Emery's book, first published in 1887, and dedicated to "the enslaved people of a dying republic," achieved great circulation, especially among the Kansas Populists. According to Mrs. Emery, the United States had been an economic Garden of Eden in the period before the Civil War. The fall of man had dated from the war itself, when "the money kings of Wall Street" determined that they could take advantage of the wartime necessities of their fellow men by manipulating the currency. "Controlling it, they could inflate or depress the business of the country at pleasure, they could send the warm life current through the channels of trade, dispensing peace, happiness, and prosperity, or they could check its flow, and completely paralyze the industries of the country." With this great power for good in their hands, the Wall Street men preferred to do evil. Lincoln's war policy of issuing greenbacks presented them with the dire threat of an adequate supply of currency. So the Shylocks gathered in convention and "perfected" an conspiracy to create a demand for their gold. The remainder of the book was a recital of a series of seven measures passed between 1862 and 1875 which were alleged to be a part of this continuing conspiracy, the total effect of which was to contract the currency of the country further and further until finally it squeezed the industry of the country like a hoop of steel.

Mrs. Emery's rhetoric left no doubt of the sustained purposefulness of this scheme—described as "villainous robbery," and as having been "secured through the most soulless strategy." She was most explicit about the so-called "crime of 1873," the demonetization of silver, giving a fairly full statement of the standard greenback-silverite myth concerning that event. As they had it, an agent of the Bank of England, Ernest Seyd by name, had come to the United States in 1872 with $500,000 with which he had bought enough support in Congress to secure the passage of the demonetization measure. This measure was supposed to have greatly increased the value of American four per cent bonds held by British capitalists by making it necessary to pay them in gold only. To it Mrs. Emery attributed the panic of 1873, its bankruptcies, and its train of human disasters: "Murder, insanity, suicide, divorce, drunkenness and all forms of immorality and crime have increased from that day to this in the most appalling ratio."

"Coin" Harvey, the author of the most popular single document of the whole currency controversy, *Coin's Financial School*, also published a novel, *A Tale of Two Nations*, in which the conspiracy theory of history was incorporated into a melodramatic tale. In this story the powerful English banker Baron Rothe plans to bring about the demonetization of silver in the United States, in part for his own aggrandizement but also to prevent the power of the United States from outstripping that of England. He persuades an American Senator (probably John Sherman, the *bete noire* of the silverites) to co-operate in using British gold in a campaign against silver. To be sure that the work is successful, he also sends to the United States a relative and ally, one Rogasner, who stalks through the story like the villains in the plays of Dion Boucicault, muttering to himself such remarks as "I am here to destroy the United States—Cornwallis could not have done more. For the wrongs and insults, for the glory of my own country, I will bury the knife deep into the heart of this nation." Against the plausibly drawn background of the corruption of the Grant administration, Rogasner proceeds to buy up the American Congress and suborn American professors of economics to testify for gold. He also falls in love with a proud American beauty, but his designs on her are foiled because she loves a handsome young silver Congressman from Nebraska who bears a striking resemblance to William Jennings Bryan!

One feature of the Populist conspiracy theory that has been generally overlooked is its frequent link with a kind of rhetorical anti-Semitism. The slight current of anti-Semitism that existed in the United States before the 1890's had been associated with problems of money and credit. During the closing years of the century it grew noticeably. While the jocose and rather heavy-handed anti-Semitism that can be found in Henry Adam's letters of the 1890's shows that this prejudice existed outside Populist literature, it was chiefly Populist writers who expressed that identification of the Jew with the usurer and the "international gold ring" which was the central theme of the American anti-Semitism of the age. The omnipresent symbol of Shylock can hardly be taken in itself as evidence of anti-Semitism, but the frequent references to the House of Rothschild make it clear that for many silverites the Jew was an organic part of the conspiracy theory of history. Coin Harvey's

Baron Rothe was clearly meant to be Rothschild; his Rogasner (Ernest Seyd?) was a dark figure out of the coarsest anti-Semitic tradition. "You are very wise in your way," Rogasner is told at the climax of the tale, "the commercial way, inbred through generations. The politic, scheming, devious way, inbred through generations also." One of the cartoons in the effectively illustrated *Coin's Financial School* showed a map of the world dominated by the tentacles of an octopus at the site of the British Isles, labeled: "Rothschilds." In Populist demonology, anti-Semitism and Anglophobia went hand in hand.

The note of anti-Semitism was often sounded openly in the campaign for silver. A representative of the New Jersey Grange, for instance, did not hesitate to warn the members of the Second National Silver Convention of 1892 to watch out for political candidates who represented "Wall Street, and the Jews of Europe." Mary E. Lease described Grover Cleveland as "the agent of Jewish bankers and British gold." Donnelly represented the leader of the governing Council of plutocrats in *Caesar's Column*, one Prince Cabano, as a powerful Jew, born Jacob Isaacs; one of the triumvirate who lead the Brotherhood of Destruction is also an exiled Russian Jew, who flees from the apocalyptic carnage with a hundred million dollars which he intends to use to "revive the ancient splendors of the Jewish race, in the midst of the ruins of the world." One of the more elaborate documents of the conspiracy school traced the power of the Rothschilds over America to a transaction between Hugh McCulloch, Secretary of the Treasury under Lincoln and Johnson, and Baron James Rothschild. "The most direful part of this business between Rothschild and the United States Treasury was not the loss

of money, even by hundreds of millions. It was the resignation of the country itself INTO THE HANDS OF ENGLAND, as England had long been resigned into the hands of HER JEWS."

Such rhetoric, which became common currency in the movement, later passed beyond Populism into the larger stream of political protest. By the time the campaign of 1896 arrived, an Associated Press reporter noticed as "one of the striking things" about the Populist convention at St. Louis "the extraordinary hatred of the Jewish race. It is not possible to go into any hotel in the city without hearing the most bitter denunciation of the Jews as a class and of the particular Jews who happen to have prospered in the world." This report may have been somewhat overdone, but the identification of the silver cause with anti-Semitism did become close enough for Bryan to have to pause in the midst of his campaign to explain to the Jewish Democrats of Chicago that in denouncing the policies of the Rothschilds he and his silver friends were "not attacking a race; we are attacking greed and avarice which know no race or religion."

It would be easy to misstate the character of Populist anti-Semitism or to exaggerate its intensity. For Populist anti-Semitism was entirely verbal. It was a mode of expression, a rhetorical style, not a tactic or a program. It did not lead to exclusion laws, much less to riots or pogroms. There were, after all, relatively few Jews in the United States in the late 1880's and early 1890's, most of them remote from the areas of Populist strength. It is one thing, however, to say that this prejudice did not go beyond a certain symbolic usage, quite another to say that a people's choice of symbols is of no significance. Populist anti-Semitism does have its importance—chiefly as a symptom of a certain ominous credulity in the Populist mind. It is not too much to say that the Greenback-Populist tradition activated most of what we have of modern popular anti-Semitism in the United States. From Thaddeus Stevens and Coin Harvey to Father Coughlin, and from Brooks and Henry Adams to Ezra Pound, there has been a curiously persistent linkage between anti-Semitism and money and credit obsessions. A full history of modern anti-Semitism in the United States would reveal, I believe, its substantial Populist lineage, but it may be sufficient to point out here that neither the informal connection between Bryan and the Klan in the twenties nor Thomas E. Watson's conduct in the Leo Frank case were altogether fortuitous. And Henry Ford's notorious anti-Semitism of the 1920's, along with his hatred of "Wall Street," were the foibles of a Michigan farm boy who had been liberally exposed to Populist notions.

THE SPIRIT MILITANT

The conspiratorial theory and the associated Anglophobic and Judophobic feelings were part of a larger complex of fear and suspicion of the stranger that haunted, and still tragically haunts, the nativist American mind. This feeling, though hardly confined to Populists and Bryanites, was none the less exhibited by them in a particularly virulent form. Everyone remote and alien was distrusted and hated—even Americans, if they happened to be city people. The old agrarian conception of the city as the home of moral corruption reached a new pitch. Chicago was bad; New York, which housed the Wall Street bankers, was still farther away and still, worse; London was still father away

and still worse. This traditional distrust grew stronger as the cities grew larger, and as they were filled with immigrant aliens. As early as 1885 the Kansas preacher Josiah Strong had published *Our Country,* a book widely read in the West, in which the cities were discussed as a great problem of the future, much as though they were some kind of monstrous malignant growths on the body politic. Hamlin Garland recalled that when he first visited Chicago in the late 1880's, having never seen a town larger than Rockford, Illinois, he naturally assumed that it swarmed with thieves. "If the city is miles across," he wondered, "how am I to get from the railway station to my hotel without being assaulted?" While such extreme fears could be quieted by some contact with the city, others were actually confirmed—especially when the farmers were confronted with city prices. Nativist prejudices were equally aroused by immigration, for which urban manufacturers, with their insatiable demand for labor were blamed. "We have become the world's melting pot," wrote Thomas E. Watson. "The scum of creation has been dumped on us. Some of our principal cities are more foreign than American. The most dangerous and corrupting hordes of the Old World have invaded us. The vice and crime which they have planted in our midst are sickening and terrifying. What brought these Goths and Vandals to our shores? The manufacturers are mainly to blame. They wanted cheap labor: and they didn't care a curse how much harm to our future might be the consequence of their heartless policy." . . .

As we review these aspects of Populist emotion, an odd parallel obtrudes itself. Where else in American thought during this period do we find this militancy and nationalism, these apocalyptic forebodings and drafts of world-political strategies, this hatred of big businessmen, bankers, and trusts, these fears of immigrants and urban workmen, even this occasional toying with anti-Semitic rhetoric? We find them, curiously enough, most conspicuous among a group of men who are in all obvious respects the antithesis of the Populists. During the late 1880's and the '90's there emerged in the eastern United States a small imperialist elite representing, in general, the same type that had once been Mugwumps, whose spokesmen were such solid and respectable gentlemen as Henry and Brooks Adams, Theodore Roosevelt, Henry Cabot Lodge, John Hay, and Albert J. Beveridge. While the silverites were raging openly and earnestly against the bankers and the Jews, Brooks and Henry Adams were expressing in their sardonic and morosely cynical private correspondence the same feelings, and acknowledging with bemused irony their kinship at this point with the mob. While Populist Congressmen and newspapers called for war with England or Spain, Roosevelt and Lodge did the same, and while Mrs. Lease projected her grandiose schemes of world partition and tropical colonization, men like Roosevelt, Lodge, Beveridge, and Mahan projected more realistic plans for the conquest of markets and the annexation of territory. While Populist readers were pondering over Donnelly's apocalyptic fantasies, Brooks and Henry Adams were also bemoaning the approaching end of their type of civilization, and even the characteristically optimistic T. R. could share at moments in "Brooks Adams' gloomiest anticipations of our gold-ridden, capitalist-bestridden, usurer-mastered future." Not long after Mrs. Lease wrote that "we

need a Napoleon in the industrial world who, by agitation and education, will lead the people to a realizing sense of their condition and the remedies," Roosevelt and Brooks Adams talked about the threat of the eight-hour movement and the danger that the country would be "enslaved" by the organizers of the trusts, and played with the idea that Roosevelt might eventually lead "some great outburst of the emotional classes which should at least temporarily crush the Economic Man."

Not only were the gentlemen of this imperialist elite better read and better fed than the Populists, but they despised them. This strange convergence of unlike social elements on similar ideas has its explanation, I believe, in this: both the imperialist elite and the Populists had been bypassed and humiliated by the advance of industrialism, and both were rebelling against the domination of the country by industrial and financial capitalists. The gentlemen wanted the power and status they felt due them, which had been taken away from their class and type by the *arriviste* manufacturers and railroaders and the all-too-potent banking houses. The Populists wanted a restoration of agrarian profits and popular government. Both elements found themselves impotent and deprived in an industrial culture and balked by a common enemy. On innumerable matters they disagreed, but both were strongly nationalistic, and amid the despairs and anxieties of the nineties both became ready for war if that would unseat or even embarrass the moneyed powers, or better still if it would topple the established political structure and open new opportunities for the leaders of disinherited farmers or for ambitious gentlemen. But if there seems to be in this situation any suggestion of a forerunner or analogue of modern authoritarian movements, it should by no means be exaggerated. The age was more innocent and more fortunate than ours, and by comparison with the grimmer realities of the twentieth century many of the events of the nineties take on a comic-opera quality. What came in the end was only a small war and a quick victory; when the farmers and the gentlemen finally did coalesce in politics, they produced only the genial reforms of Progressivism; and the man on the white horse turned out to be just a graduate of the Harvard boxing squad, equipped with an immense bag of platitudes, and quite willing to play the democratic game.

POSTSCRIPT

Were the Populists Democratic Reformers?

The thesis advanced by Richard Hofstadter represented the first major challenge to the favorable interpretation of the Populists presented in John D. Hicks, *The Populist Revolt: A History of the Farmers' Alliance and the People's Party* (University of Minnesota Press, 1931). This critique was extended, however, by Victor C. Ferkiss, a political scientist, whose "Populist Influences in American Fascism," *Western Political Quarterly* (June 1957) argued that the Populist movement was not based upon egalitarian goals of human freedom. In fact, Ferkiss concluded, the Populists, by encouraging majority rule over governmental institutions, committed themselves to a "plebiscitary democracy" very similar to that proposed for Germany by Adolf Hitler. A rejoinder to Ferkiss' argument appears in Walter T. K. Nugent, *The Tolerant Populists: Kansas Populism and Nativism* (University of Chicago Press, 1963). In this effort to rehabilitate the Populist image, Nugent concluded that in Kansas, agrarian reformers were neither xenophobic, anti-Semitic, nor paranoid over a conspiracy of the "money interests."

Agricultural History (April 1965) published the results of a symposium on Populism in the form of essays written by several revisionists and their critics. Two historiographical collections that are also valuable are Raymond J. Cunningham, ed., *The Populists in Historical Perspective* (D. C. Heath, 1968) and Theodore Saloutos, ed., *Populism: Reaction or Reform?* (Holt, Rinehart & Winston, 1968). Norman Pollack, *The Just Polity: Populism, Law, and Human Welfare* (University of Illinois Press, 1987), approaches the farmers' revolt from a different direction than his earlier work but continues to take a positive view of Populism. Lawrence Goodwyn's *Democratic Promise: The Populist Moment in America* (Oxford University Press, 1976) is a sensitive portrait that depicts Populism as a cooperative "people's movement" whose supporters espoused true egalitarianism. Robert C. McMath, Jr., *Populist Vanguard: A History of the Southern Farmers' Alliance* (University of North

Carolina Press, 1975), and Stephen Hahn, *The Roots of Southern Populism: Yeoman Farmers and the Transformation of the Georgia Upcountry, 1850–1890* (Oxford University Press, 1983), examine the origins of Populism in Texas and Georgia, respectively. Bruce Palmer, *"Man Over Money": The Southern Populist Critique of American Capitalism* (University of North Carolina Press, 1980), offers divergent views of some of the themes developed by Lawrence Goodwyn. Gerald H. Gaither, *Blacks and the Populist Revolt: Ballots and Bigotry in the "New South"* (University of Alabama Press, 1977), explores the issue of race relations, while Robert F. Durden's, *The Climax of Populism: The Election of 1896* (University of Kentucky Press, 1966) is a competent study of the Populists' electoral defeat. Not to be overlooked is C. Vann Woodward's *Tom Watson: Agrarian Rebel* (Oxford University Press, 1938). Finally, for an intriguing argument, see Henry M. Littlefield, "The Wizard of Oz: Parable of Populism," *American Quarterly* (Spring 1964).

ISSUE 6

Was City Government in Late Nineteenth-Century America a "Conspicuous Failure"?

YES: Ernest S. Griffith, from *A History of American City Government: The Conspicuous Failure, 1870–1900* (Praeger, 1974)

NO: Jon C. Teaford, from *The Unheralded Triumph: City Government in America, 1860–1900* (Johns Hopkins University Press, 1984)

ISSUE SUMMARY

YES: Professor of political science and political economy Ernest S. Griffith focuses upon illegal and unethical operations of the political machine and concludes that the governments controlled by the bosses represented a betrayal of the public trust.

NO: Professor of history Jon C. Teaford argues that scholars traditionally have overlooked the remarkable success municipal governments in the late nineteenth century achieved in dealing with the challenges presented by rapid urbanization.

During the late nineteenth century, American farmers based their grievances on revolutionary changes that had occurred in the post–Civil War United States. Specifically, they saw themselves as victims of an industrial wave that had swept over the nation and submerged their rural, agricultural world in the undertow. Indeed, the values, attitudes, and interests of all Americans were affected dramatically by the rapid urbanization that accompanied industrial growth. The result was the creation of the modern city with its coordinated network of economic development, which emphasized mass production and mass consumption.

In the years from 1860 to 1920, the number of urban residents in the United States increased much more rapidly than the national population as a whole. For example, the Census Bureau reported in 1920 that the United States housed 105,711,000 people, three times the number living in the country on the eve of the Civil War. Urban dwellers, however, increased ninefold during the same period. The number of "urban" places (incorporated towns with 2,500 or more residents, or unincorporated areas with at least 2,500 people per square mile) increased from 392 in 1860 to 2,722 by 1920. Cities with populations in excess of 100,000 increased from 9 in 1860 to 68 in 1920.

Reflecting many of the characteristics of "modern" America, these industrial cities produced a number of problems for the people who lived in them—problems associated with fire and police protection, sanitation, utilities, and a wide range of social services. These coincided with increased concerns over employment opportunities and demands for transportation and housing improvements. Typically, municipal government became the clearinghouse for such demands. What was the nature of city government in the late nineteenth-century United States? How effectively were American cities governed? To what extent did municipal leaders listen to and redress the grievances of urban dwellers? In light of James Lord Bryce's blunt statement in 1888 that city government in the United States was a "conspicuous failure," it is worthwhile to explore scholarly assessments of Bryce's conclusion.

Ernest S. Griffith surveys the nature of municipal government in the last three decades of the nineteenth century and concludes that city politics was consumed by a "cancer of corruption" which predominated in the years from 1880 to 1893. He identifies numerous factors that contributed to this unethical environment, as well as the disreputable and illegal lengths gone to that perpetuated the power of the bosses but prevented city government from operating in the true interest of the people.

Jon C. Teaford, on the other hand, complains that scholars like Griffith are too eager to condemn the activities of late nineteenth-century municipal governments without recognizing their accomplishments. While admitting numerous shortcomings, Teaford argues that American city dwellers enjoyed a higher standard of public services than any other urban residents in the world. Also, in contrast to the portrait of boss dominance presented by Griffith and others, Teaford claims that authority was widely distributed among various groups, which peacefully coexisted with one another. For Teaford, nineteenth-century cities failed to develop a political image but succeeded to a remarkable degree in meeting the needs of those dependent upon them.

YES

Ernest S. Griffith

THE CANCER OF CORRUPTION

INTRODUCTION

Corruption may be defined as personal profit at the expense of the public—stealing and use of office for private gain, including the giving and taking of bribes outside of the law. More broadly defined, it is any antisocial conduct that uses government as an instrument. Its twilight zone is never the same from age to age, from community to community, or even from person to person. . . .

Historically, the motivations of the electorate, the uses to which tax money and campaign contributions were put, the pressures of reward and punishment to which candidates and officeholders were subjected, were never very far from the gray zone in which the line between the corrupt and the ethical—or even the legal—had somehow to be drawn. Votes were "coin of the realm" in a democracy; office holding or power-wielding was secured by votes. They might be freely and intelligently given; they might be the result of propaganda, friendship, or pressure; they might be purchased by money or otherwise; they might be manufactured out of election frauds. Those who were members of the government, visible or invisible, were ultimately dependent on the voters for their opportunity to serve, for their livelihood, for the chance to steal or betray. These conditions existed in the late nineteenth century; with differing emphases they still exist today.

What, then, determined whether a late-nineteenth-century city government was corrupt or ethical, or something in between? Ethically speaking, the nadir of American city government was probably reached in the years between 1880 and 1893. Why and how? There was obviously no one answer. The time has long since passed when municipal reformers, not to mention historians, believed there was a single answer. There was present a highly complex situation—a *Gestalt*, or pattern—never identical in any two places, but bearing a family resemblance in most respects. The path to better municipal governance was long and difficult because of this very complexity.

From Ernest S. Griffith, *A History of American City Government: The Conspicuous Failure, 1870–1900* (National Civic League Press, 1974). Copyright © 1974 by the National Municipal League. Reprinted by permission.

The story of the 1890's and of the Progressive Era of the first twelve or fifteen years of the twentieth century was the story of a thousand battles on a thousand fronts—the unraveling of a refractory network of unsuitable charters and procedures, of a human nature that at times led to despair, of an economic order that put a premium on greed, of a social order of class and ethnic divisions reflected often in incompatible value systems—all infinitely complicated by rapidity of growth and population mobility. . . .

PATRONAGE

[H]ow are we to account for the corrupt machine in the first place, and for what came to be its endemic character in American cities for two or three decades? This is part of a broader analysis, and will be undertaken presently. As always, in the end the legacy of a corrupt and corrupting regime was a malaise of suspicion, discouragement, and blunted ideals in society as a whole.

In examining the fact of corruption, it was obvious that the city—any city, good or bad—provided livelihood for scores, hundreds, even thousands of people directly employed. They would fight if their livelihood were threatened. There were also large numbers dependent upon the city for contracts, privileges, and immunities. Not as sharply defined, and often overlapping one or both of these categories, were persons who served as organizers, brokers, or instruments of these other two groups, and whose livelihoods therefore also depended upon the city. They, too, would fight to attain, keep, or augment this livelihood, and probably the sense of power (and occasionally the constructive achievements) that their positions carried with them. They were the "machine," the "ring," the "boss," the professional politician, the political lawyer. This is to say, for many people (as regards the city) employment, power, and access to those with power were matters of economic life or death for themselves and their families—and, if these same people were wholly self-seeking, to them the end justified the means.

First, consider the municipal employees. "To the victors belong the spoils"—the party faction and machine rewarded their own and punished the others. In 1889 the mayor of Los Angeles appointed all of his six sons to the police force, but this helped to defeat him in the next election. In the smaller cities, and in the larger ones before skills seemed essential, a change of administration or party was the signal for wholesale dismissals and wholesale patronage. This fact created the strongest incentive for those currently employed to work for the retention in power of those influential in their employment; that they had so worked constituted a logical basis for their dismissal; given the success of the opposing candidates. That the city might suffer in both processes was unimportant to those whose livelihood was at stake in the outcome of the struggle. Those involved, in many instances, would not even respect the position of school teacher, and could usually find ways and means to subvert the civil service laws when they emerged, in intent if not in formal ritual. In Brooklyn, for example, during the Daniel Whitney administration of 1885, only favored candidates were informed of the dates of the examinations in time to apply. Examinations were then leniently graded, to put it mildly. One illiterate received a grade of 97.5 per cent on a written test. About 1890, each member of the Boston city council received a certain number of tickets corresponding to his quota of men employed by the city. No one was eligible without such a ticket, and existing employees were discharged to make room if necessary.

SALE OF PRIVILEGES AND IMMUNITIES

As regards the sale for cash of privileges and immunities, many politicians and officials did not stop with the twilight zone of liquor violations, gambling, and prostitution, but went on to exploit what would be regarded as crime in any language or society. Denver (incidentally, at least until the 1960's) was one of the worst. From the late 1880's until 1922, Lou Blonger, king of the city's underworld, held the police department in his grasp. For many of these years he had a direct line to the chief of police, and his orders were "law." Criminals were never molested if they operated outside the city limits, and often not within the limits, either. He contributed liberally to the campaign funds of both parties, those of the district attorneys being especially favored. Blonger was sent to jail in 1922 by Philip Van Cise, a district attorney who had refused his conditional campaign contribution of $25,000.

Yet, it was the insatiable appetite of men for liquor, sex, and the excitement and eternal hope of gambling that proved by all the odds the most refractory and the most corrupting day-to-day element. . . .

The police of most cities, and the politicians and officials, took graft or campaign contributions from the liquor interests so that they would overlook violations of the law. Judging from extant material of the period, corruption by the liquor trade occurred more frequently than any other. Over and over again the question of enforcement of whatever laws existed was an issue at the polls. The fact was that, at this time, the trade did not want *any* regulation and resented all but the most nominal license fee, unless the license in effect granted a neighborhood semimonopoly, and increased profitability accordingly. It was prepared to fight and pay for its privileges. Council membership was literally jammed with saloon keepers, and Buffalo (1880) was not too exceptional in having a brewer as mayor. Apparently in one instance (in Nebraska), the liquor interests resorted to assassination of the clerk of the U.S. Federal Circuit Court in revenge for his part in the fight against them.

More clearly illegal, because here it was not a question of hours of sale but of its right to exist, was commercial gambling. State laws and even municipal ordinances were fairly usual in prohibiting it, but these laws were sustained neither by enforcement nor by public opinion. If the public opinion calling for enforcement was present, the requisite ethical standard was not there that would preclude the offering and accepting of the bribes that made the continuance of gambling possible—except for an occasional spasm of raids and reform.

Oklahoma City will serve as a case study. At one point gambling houses regularly paid one fine a month. Four-fifths of the businessmen refused to answer whether they would favor closing such joints; going on record either way would hurt their business. Citing District Attorney William T. Jerome's views of attempts to secure enforcement of this type of law, one writer commented: "The corrupt politician welcomes the puritan as an ally. He sees in laws that cannot and will not be permanently enforced a yearly revenue in money and in power."

The situation regarding commercialized vice was similar. Laws and ordinances forbidding brothels were on the statute books. Brothels existed in every large city and most of the smaller ones. Especially in the Western cities where men greatly outnumbered women, they appeared in large numbers, and the same might be said of the commercial centers and the seaport towns. A boss like Boies Penrose of Philadelphia patronized them. So, in fact, did a number of presumably otherwise respectable citizens. Many of this last group also drew rent from the brothels.

What this meant to the city government of a place like Seattle may be illustrated by an episode in 1892:

> The police department thought it had a vested property right in the collections from prostitutes and gamblers. The new mayor, Ronald was waited on almost immediately by a group of high ranking police officers who asked him how much of a cut he wanted out of the monthly "pay off" for gambling and prostitution. "Not a cent! Moreover, there isn't going to be any collection or places that pay protection money," he said as he pounded the table. The committee patiently explained that it was "unofficial licensing," a very effective way to control crime. The mayor exploded again and one of the captains took out a revolver and dropped it on the table. "Somebody is going to get hurt—maybe." The mayor tried as hard as ever anyone could to clean up, but found it impossible. He was powerless because he had no real support. He resigned in less than a year.

For the depths of degradation into which the combination of lust and greed can sink a city government, one can only cite the example of Kansas City, where girls at the municipal farm were sold by the politicians (who of course pocketed the money) and sent to brothels in New Orleans. . . .

Each city, as the pressures of urban living forced regulation, found itself under conflicting demands. The people as a whole probably wanted "nuisances" cleared up—unsanitary dwellings, cattle in the streets, sign encroachments, garbage left around, and a hundred other annoying matters—the counterpart in today's world of illegal parking. But to the particular person involved, there was an interest in leaving things as they were— an interest for which he was prepared to pay by a tip or a vote. Compulsory education laws ran up against parents who regarded them as a violation of their God-given right to employ their children as they wished. Political revenge might well await the enforcer—the truant officer, health officer, inspector of meat, dairies, or housing, or policeman. Political and often pecuniary rewards awaited those who would overlook matters of this type. There were other favors, tips on the location of a proposed public improvement or on the location of a road or a park relevant to real estate value. These were advantageous to the official and his friends to know and to control for their own personal profit. Real estate profit through advance notice or an actual share in the decision on a municipal improvement or purchase was one of the most lucrative perquisites of councilors or the "ring" members. A special instance of this was the desire of many members of Congress for seats on the low-status District of Columbia Committee so as to secure advance information as to what would be profitable real estate purchases in the District. In general, these examples came under the heading of "honest graft" in those days, as not necessarily costing the city treasury an undue amount. The term was invented by George W. Plunkett of Tammany as a rationalization.

GRAFT FROM CONTRACTS AND FRANCHISES

Quite otherwise were the profits, direct and indirect, from lucrative city contracts. Probably in the majority of cities there was a tacit understanding that a favored contractor would "kick back" a substantial amount (10 per cent or more being quite usual) either to party campaign funds for which accounting was rare, as fees to a "political lawyer," with the ultimate distribution uncertain, or as out-and-out bribes to those with the power to make the decisions. There were always any number of devices to evade the intent of the law, even in situations where the law called for competitive bidding. Pittsburgh for years found that William Flinn, one of its two bosses, was always the lowest "responsible" bidder for contracts. In other instances, specifications were such that only the favored one could meet them. In New Orleans, around 1890, in spite of the protests of the property owners, almost all paving was with rosetta gravel (in which one man had a monopoly). In other cases, the lowest bid was accepted, but there would be advance assurance (private and arranged) that the inspectors would not insist that the contractor meet the specifications. Contractors in Portland (Oregon) in 1893 whose men voted "right" were laxly supervised. In still other instances, the bidders themselves formed rings, bid high, and arranged for distribution of the contracts among them-

selves. This practice seems to have been a particular bent among paving contractors. William Gabriel of Cleveland, high in Republican circles, will serve as an example. This was not incompatible with generous bribes to municipal officials or rings as well. Graft in contracts extended to the schools—to their construction and to the textbooks purchased. Things were probably not so flagrant in Cleveland, where campaign contributions and not bribes were the favored means of business.

Franchises and privileges for the railroads and the various utilities came to be special sources of demoralization, particularly for the councils that usually had the responsibility for granting them. Initially, a community welcomed the railroad and even subsidized its coming. With growing urbanization, it looked forward to waterworks, lighting (gas or electricity), street cars (horse or cable), and eventually electricity and the telephone. The earliest of the franchises were likely to be most liberal with respect to rate allowed, duration, and service rendered. The cities wanted the utilities and often urged their coming. Later, as the latter proved enormously profitable, the stakes grew high, and betrayal of the public interest probably took place in the majority of cases. Power to grant franchises greatly increased the desirability of membership on the council. Hazen Pingree, mayor of Detroit in the early 1890's wrote:

My experiences in fighting monopolistic corporations as mayor of Detroit, and in endeavoring to save to the people some of their right as against their greed, have further convinced me that they, the corporations, are responsible for nearly all the thieving and boodling with which cities are made to suffer from their servants. They seek almost uniformly to secure what they want by means of bribes, and in this way they corrupt our councils and commissions.

Providence, in the 1890's allowed only property owners to vote. They elected businessmen to the city council. This council then awarded Nelson Aldrich, the state boss, a perpetual franchise, which he sold out at an enormous profit. He went to the Senate through wholesale bribery of rural voters, with money contributed by the sugar magnates for whom as congressman he had arranged a protective tariff. The city of Pawtucket, which sought to block a franchise, was overridden by the rurally dominated state legislature.

It was Lincoln Steffens who later dramatized beyond any forgetting the unholy link between the protected underworld, the city governments, and the portion of the business community in search of contracts and franchises—a link found in city after city. The story of his exposures belongs to the Progressive Era. At the time, these betrayals of the public interest were either not known or, if known, were enjoyed and shared, shrugged off and rationalized, or endured in futile fury.

Two or three further examples of documented franchise bribery might be cited. In 1884, in New York City, the Broadway Surface Railroad paid $25,000 to each of eighteen alderman and received the franchise. The rival company had offered the *city* $1 million. Another corporation set aside $100,000 to buy the council. The street-car companies of Indianapolis contributed to both political parties. So it went in city after city.

Some other examples of business corruption might be cited. Governor John P. Altgeld of Illinois sent a message (1895) to the state legislature, calling attention to the fantastically low rents paid by newspapers for school lands. In a most complex arrangement involving shipping companies, boarding-house keepers, "crimps" (recruiters of seamen), and the city authorities, the San Francisco waterfront instituted a reign of near-peonage, in which seamen were grossly overcharged for their lodging and shore "amenities," prevented from organized resistance, and virtually terrorized and blackmailed into signing on the ships again. In the early 1870's, local speculators of Dubuque, including two former mayors, bought up city bonds for a small amount and held out for redemption at par. Favored banks (that is, those contributing through appropriate channels to the city treasurer, the party, or the boss) received city deposits without having to pay interest thereon, or, as in Pittsburgh, paying the interest to the politicians. Finally, the employer power structure threw its weight and its funds in support of almost any administration that would protect strikebreakers, break up "radical" gatherings, and otherwise preserve the "American system" against alien ideas—this, without reference to the extent of the known corruption of the administration.

THEFT, ASSESSMENT FAVORITISM, "KICKBACKS," "RAKE-OFFS"

As might be expected, there were a number of examples of actual theft, most frequently by a city treasurer. Judges would occasionally keep fines. A certain amount of this was to be expected in an age of ruthless money-making when business ethics condoned all kinds of sharp practices in the private sector. What was more discouraging was that many of these thieves remained unpunished, as the machine with its frequent control over the courts protected its own. City officials of Spokane even stole funds contributed for relief after its great fire (1889).

How widespread was political favoritism in tax assessment would be extraordinarily difficult to determine. The practice of underassessment across the board to avoid litigation was almost universal, and in some communities it had a statutory base. Certainly many corporations were favored, in part because they were deemed an asset to the community's economic life. What was more probable was the widespread fear that, if a person were to criticize the city administration, he would find his underassessment raised. This particular form of blackmail took place in blatant fashion at one time in Jersey City. It also occurred under Park Board administration in the Bronx in 1874. From time to time, there would be exposures in the local press of assessment anomalies, but the press was itself vulnerable to punitive retaliation of this type because of its frequent underassessment.

The practice of compensating certain employees by fees instead of fixed salaries lingered on, in spite of or often because of the large amounts of money involved. Such employees were usually expected, by virtue of their election or appointment, to "kick back" a substantial portion to the party organization. Such "kickbacks" from the receiver of taxes amounted in Philadelphia to $200,000 in one of the years after 1873—divided among the small number who constituted the gas-house ring. Other compensations by the fee system were abandoned in 1873, and the employees were put on salaries. Some nominations and appointments were sold, with the receipts going, it was hoped, to the party campaign

funds, concerning the use of which there was rarely in these days any effective accounting. Political assessments of city employees probably ruled in the majority of the cities.

How much graft in fact found its way into the pockets of the city employees for their betrayal of trust or, for that matter, for services they should have rendered in any event, how much "rake-off" the ring or the boss took, will never be known. What was graft and what was "rake-off" shaded into a gray zone after a while. The amount must have been colossal in the cities—certainly enough, had it been dedicated to municipal administration, to have enhanced efficiency and service enormously, or to have cut the tax rate drastically. Utility rates would have tumbled and service improved. . . .

EXTORTION AND BLACKMAIL

Extortion and blackmail, if not standard practice, were frequent enough to call for comment. Once in a while, as in Fort Worth (1877), they were used in an intriguing and perhaps constructive fashion. It was proposed that the sale of intoxicants be forbidden at the theaters. The ordinance was tabled, with the notation that it would be passed unless one of the theater owners paid his taxes.

In Brooklyn during the Whitney administration, the head of the fire department blocked an electric franchise until he was given one-fifth of the company's stock and several other politicians had taken a cut.

The newspapers were particularly vulnerable to blackmail. A threat of loss of the city's advertising was a marvelous silencer. In Tacoma (1889), enough businessmen believed a particular gambling house was a community asset that the newspaper that had denounced its protected status as a result lost heavily in both advertising and circulation.

The gangs of Detroit seemed to be immune in the 1880's and able to bring about the promotion or dismissal of a policeman. Sailors, tugmen, longshoremen made up the bulk of their personnel. In the early 1880's in Indianapolis, citizens were arrested on trumped-up charges and fined by judges who at that time were paid by the fines.

POLICE AND THE COURTS

. . . [D]ifficulties stemmed from the key role played by the police in the electoral process, the graft from the under-world, and the desire on the part of the allegedly more respectable for immunities. In Tacoma, the mayor reprimanded the chief of police for raiding a brothel in which a umber of the city's influential men were found. All these factors meant that in city after city the police force was really regarded as an adjunct of the political party or machine. In some of the smaller cities, the patronage aspect was expressed in extreme form. For example, until 1891 each new mayor of Wilmington (Delaware) appointed a new set of policemen, usually of his own party.

Nor were the courts immune as adjuncts to corruption. The district attorney and the judges, especially the local ones, were usually elected, and by the same processes as the mayors and councils. The same network of political and corrupt immunities that pervaded the police and stemmed from the rings and other politicians was present in the courts. Four hazards to justice were thus in a sense vulnerable to pressure and purchase—the stages of arrest, prosecution, the verdicts (and delays) of the judge, and the possibilities of a packed or bribed jury. William Howard Taft commented at a later date as follows:

> [The] administration of criminal law is a disgrace to our civilization, and the prevalence of crime and fraud, which here is greatly in excess of that in European countries, is due largely to the failure of the law to bring criminals to justice.

Quite apart from overt corruption, there were numerous ways in which courts could reward the party faithful, such as by appointment as favored bondsmen, stenographers, or auctioneers.

It was not surprising that an exasperated and otherwise respectable public occasionally fought back by violent means. In Cincinnati (1884), so flagrant had been the court delays and acquittals that a mass meeting, held to protest the situation, evolved into a mob bent on direct action. They burned the courthouse and attempted to storm the jail. For days the mob ruled. Police and militia failed, and only federal troops finally restored order. There were over fifty deaths. In Dallas, in the early 1880's, the "respectable" element, despairing of action by the city government in closing some of the worst resorts, took to burning them. Acquittal of the murderers of the chief of police of New Orleans by a probably corrupted jury was followed by lynchings. . . .

SUMMARY SCENARIO

This in general was the scenario of most American cities about 1890: fitful reforms, usually not lasting; charters hopelessly tangled, with no agreement on remedies; civil service laws circumvented in the mad search for patronage opportunities; election frauds virtually normal; an underworld capitalizing on man's appetites and finding it easy to purchase allies in the police and the politician; countless opportunities for actual theft; business carrying over its disgraceful private ethics into subverting city government for its own ends, and city officials competing to obtain the opportunity to be lucratively subverted; citizens who might be expected to lead reforms generally indifferent, discouraged, frightened, and without the time necessary to give to the effort; a community with conflicting value systems into which the exploiter entered, albeit with an understanding and a sympathy denied to those from another class; ballots complicated; a nomination process seemingly built to invite control by the self-seeking; sinecures used to provide full-time workers for the party machine; state governments ready to step in to aid in the corruption if local effort proved inadequate; confusion over the claims of party loyalty; a press often intimidated and frequently venal; countless opportunities to make decisions that would favor certain real estate over other locations; a burgeoning population rapidly urbanizing and dragging in its train innumerable problems of municipal services and aspirations.

For the unraveling of this tangled mess, the reformer and the career administrator had no acceptable philosophy.

NO

Jon C. Teaford

TRUMPETED FAILURES AND UNHERALDED TRIUMPHS

In 1888 the British observer James Bryce proclaimed that "there is no denying that the government of cities is the one conspicuous failure of the United States." With this pronouncement he summed up the feelings of a host of Americans. In New York City, residents along mansion-lined Fifth Avenue, parishioners in the churches of then-sedate Brooklyn, even petty politicos at party headquarters in Tammany Hall, all perceived serious flaws in the structure of urban government. Some complained, for example, of the tyranny of upstate Republican legislators, others attacked the domination of ward bosses, and still others criticized the greed of public utility companies franchised by the municipality. Mugwump reformer Theodore Roosevelt decried government by Irish political machine hacks, the moralist Reverend Charles Henry Parkhurst lambasted the reign of rum sellers, and that pariah of good-government advocates, New York City ward boss George Washington Plunkitt, also found fault, attacking the evils of civil service. For each, the status quo in urban government was defective. For each, the structure of municipal rule needed some revision. By the close of the 1880s the litany of criticism was mounting, with one voice after another adding a shrill comment on the misrule of the cities.

During the following two decades urban reformers repeated Bryce's words with ritualistic regularity, and his observation proved one of the most-quoted lines in the history of American government. Time and again latter-day Jeremiahs damned American municipal rule of the late nineteenth century, denouncing it as a national blight, a disgrace that by its example threatened the survival of democracy throughout the world. In 1890 Andrew D. White, then-president of Cornell University, wrote that "without the slightest exaggeration . . . the city governments of the United States are the worst in Christendom—the most expensive, the most inefficient, and the most corrupt." Four years later the reform journalist Edwin Godkin claimed that "the present condition of city governments in the United States is bringing democratic institutions into contempt the world over, and imperiling some of

From Jon C. Teaford, *The Unheralded Triumph: City Government in America, 1860–1900* (The Johns Hopkins University Press, 1984). Copyright © 1984 by The Johns Hopkins University Press. Reprinted by permission.

the best things in our civilization." Such preachers as the Reverend Washington Gladden denounced the American city as the "smut of civilization," while his clerical colleague Reverend Parkhurst said of the nation's municipalities: "Virtue is at the bottom and knavery on top. The rascals are out of jail and standing guard over men who aim to be honorable and law-abiding." And in 1904 journalist Lincoln Steffens stamped American urban rule with an indelible badge of opprobrium in the corruption-sated pages of his popular muckraking exposé *The Shame of the Cities*. Books, magazines, and newspapers all recited the catalog of municipal sins.

Likewise, many twentieth-century scholars passing judgment on the development of American city government have handed down a guilty verdict and sentenced American urban rule to a place of shame in the annals of the nation. In 1933 a leading student of municipal home rule claimed that "the conduct of municipal business has almost universally been inept and inefficient" and "at its worst it has been unspeakable, almost incredible." That same year the distinguished historian Arthur Schlesinger, Sr., in his seminal study *The Rise of the City*, described the development of municipal services during the last decades of the nineteenth century and found the achievements "distinctly creditable to a generation . . . confronted with the phenomenon of a great population everywhere clotting into towns." Yet later in his study he returned to the more traditional position, recounting tales of corruption and describing municipal rule during the last two decades of the century as "the worst city government the country had ever known." Writing in the 1950s, Bessie Louise Pierce, author of

the finest biography to date of an American city, a multivolume history of Chicago, described that city's long list of municipal achievements but closed with a ritual admission of urban shortcomings, citing her approval of Bryce's condemnation. Similarly, that lifelong student of American municipal history, Ernest Griffith, subtitled his volume on late-nineteenth-century urban rule "the conspicuous failure," though he questioned whether municipal government was a greater failure than state government.

Historians such as Schlesinger and Griffith were born in the late nineteenth century, were raised during the Progressive era, and early imbibed the ideas of such critics as Bryce and White. Younger historians of the second half of the twentieth century were further removed from the scene of the supposed municipal debacle and could evaluate it more dispassionately. By the 1960s and 1970s, negative summations such as "unspeakable" and "incredible" were no longer common in accounts of nineteenth-century city government, and historians professing to the objectivity of the social sciences often refused to pronounce judgment on the quality of past rule. Yet recent general histories of urban America have continued both to describe the "deterioration" of city government during the Gilded Age and to focus on political bosses and good-government reformers who were forced to struggle with a decentralized, fragmented municipal structure supposedly unsuited to fast-growing metropolises of the 1880s and 1890s. Some chronicles of the American city have recognized the material advantages in public services during the late nineteenth century, but a number speak of the failure of the municipality to adapt to changing realities and of the shortcomings of an outmoded and ineffectual municipal framework. Sam Bass Warner, Jr., one of the leading new urban historians of the 1960s, has characterized the pattern of urban rule as one of "weak, corrupt, unimaginative municipal government." Almost one hundred years after Bryce's original declaration, the story of American city government remains at best a tale of fragmentation and confusion and at worst one of weakness and corruption.

If modern scholars have not handed down such damning verdicts as the contemporary critics of the 1880s and 1890s, they have nevertheless issued evaluations critical of the American framework of urban rule. As yet, hindsight has not cast a golden glow over the municipal institutions of the late nineteenth century, and few historians or political scientists have written noble tributes to the achievements of American municipal government. Praise for the nation's municipal officials has been rare and grudging. Though many have recognized the elitist predilections of Bryce and his American informants, the influence of Bryce's words still persists, and the image of nineteenth-century city government remains tarnished. Historians have softened the harsh stereotype of the political boss, transforming him from a venal parasite into a necessary component of a makeshift, decentralized structure. Conversely, the boss's good-government foes have fallen somewhat from historical grace and are now typified as crusaders for the supremacy of an upper-middle-class business culture. But historians continue to aim their attention at these two elements of municipal rule, to the neglect of the formal, legal structure. They write more of the boss than of the mayor, more on the civic leagues than on the sober but significant city comptroller. Moreover they continue to stage the drama of bosses and reformers against a roughly sketched backdrop of municipal disarray. The white and black hats of the players may have shaded to gray, but the setting of the historian's pageant remains a ramshackle municipal structure.

Nevertheless, certain nagging realities stand in stark contrast to the traditional tableau of municipal rule. One need not look far to discover the monuments of nineteenth-century municipal achievement that still grace the nation's cities, surviving as concrete rebuttals to Bryce's words. In 1979 the architecture critic for the *New York Times* declared Central Park and the Brooklyn Bridge as "the two greatest works of architecture in New York . . . each . . . a magnificent object in its own right; each . . . the result of a brilliant synthesis of art and engineering after which the world was never quite the same." Each was also a product of municipal enterprise, the creation of a city government said to be the worst in Christendom. Moreover, can one visit San Francisco's Golden Gate Park or enter McKim, Mead, and White's palatial Boston Public Library and pronounce these landmarks evidence of weakness or failure? Indeed, can those city fathers be deemed "unimaginative" who hired the great landscape architect Frederick Law Olmsted to design the first public park systems in human history? And were the vast nineteenth-century water and drainage schemes that still serve the cities the handiwork of bumbling incompetents unable to cope with the demands of expanding industrial metropolises? The aqueducts of Rome were among the glories of ancient civilization; the grander water systems of nineteenth-century New York City are often overlooked by those preoccupied with the more lurid aspects of city rule.

A bright side of municipal endeavor did, then, exist. American city governments could claim grand achievements, and as Arthur Schlesinger, Sr., was willing to admit in 1933, urban leaders won some creditable victories in the struggle for improved services. Certainly there were manifold shortcomings: Crime and poverty persisted; fires raged and pavements buckled; garbage and street rubbish sometimes seemed insurmountable problems. Yet no government has ever claimed total success in coping with the problems of society; to some degree all have failed to service their populations adequately. If government ever actually succeeded, political scientists would have to retool and apply themselves to more intractable problems, and political philosophers would have to turn to less contemplative pursuits. Those with a negative propensity can always find ample evidence of "bad government," and late-nineteenth-century critics such as Bryce, White, and Godkin displayed that propensity. In their writings the good side of the municipal structure was as visible as the dark side of the moon.

Thus, observers of the late-nineteenth-century American municipality have usually focused microscopic attention on its failures while overlooking its achievements. Scoundrels have won much greater coverage than conscientious officials. Volumes have appeared, for example, on that champion among municipal thieves, New York City's political boss William M. Tweed, but not one book exists on the life and work of a perhaps more significant figure in nineteenth-century city government, Ellis Chesbrough the engineer who served both Boston and Chicago and who transformed the public

works of the latter city. Only recently has an admirable group of studies begun to explore the work of such municipal technicians who were vital to the formulation and implementation of public policy. But prior to the 1970s accounts of dualistic conflicts between political bosses and good-government reformers predominated, obscuring the complexities of municipal rule and the diversity of elements actually vying for power and participating in city government. And such traditional accounts accepted as axiomatic the inadequacy of the formal municipal structure. Critics have trumpeted its failures, while its triumphs have gone unheralded.

If one recognizes some of the challenges that municipal leaders faced during the period 1870 to 1900, the magnitude of their achievements becomes clear. The leaders of the late nineteenth century inherited an urban scene of great tumult and stress and an urban population of increasing diversity and diversion. . . . The melting pot was coming to a boil, and yet throughout the 1870s, 1880s, and 1890s, waves of newcomers continued to enter the country, including more and more representatives of the alien cultures of southern and eastern Europe. To many in 1870, social and ethnic diversity seemed to endanger the very foundation of order and security in the nation, and municipal leaders faced the need to maintain a truce between Protestants and Catholics, old stock and new, the native business elite and immigrant workers.

The rush of migrants from both Europe and rural America combined with a high birth rate to produce another source of municipal problems, a soaring urban population. . . . During the last thirty years of the century, the nation's chief cities absorbed thousands of acres of new territory to accommodate this booming population, and once-compact cities sprawled outward from the urban core. This expansion sprawl produced demands for the extension of services and the construction of municipal facilities. The newly annexed peripheral wards needed sewer lines and water mains; they required fire and police protection; and residents of outlying districts expected the city to provide paved streets and lighting. Municipal governments could not simply maintain their services at existing levels; instead, they had to guarantee the extension of those services to thousands of new urban dwellers.

Improved and expanded municipal services, however, required funding, and revenue therefore posed another challenge for city rulers. . . . Inflation in the 1860s and economic depression in the 1870s exacerbated the financial problems of the city, leading to heightened cries for retrenchment. And throughout the 1880s and 1890s city governments faced the difficult problem of meeting rising expectations for services while at the same time satisfying demands for moderate taxes and fiscal conservatism. This was perhaps the toughest task confronting the late-nineteenth-century municipality.

During the last three decades of the century, American city government did, however, meet these challenges of diversity, growth, and financing with remarkable success. By century's close, American city dwellers enjoyed, on the average, as high a standard of public services as any urban residents in the world. Problems persisted, and there were ample grounds for complaint. But in America's cities, the supply of water was the most abundant, the street lights were the most brilliant, the parks the grandest, the libraries the largest, and

the public transportation the fastest of any place in the world. American city fathers rapidly adapted to advances in technology, and New York City, Chicago, and Boston were usually in the forefront of efforts to apply new inventions and engineering breakthroughs to municipal problems. Moreover, America's cities achieved this level of modern service while remaining solvent and financially sound. No major American municipality defaulted on its debts payments during the 1890s, and by the end of the century all of the leading municipalities were able to sell their bonds at premium and pay record-low interest. Any wise financier would have testified that the bonds of those purported strongholds of inefficiency and speculation, the municipal corporations, were far safer investments than were the bonds of those quintessential products of American business ingenuity: the railroad corporations.

Not only did the city governments serve their residents without suffering financial collapse, but municipal leaders also achieved an uneasy balance of the conflicting forces within the city, accommodating each through a distribution of authority. Though commentators often claimed that the "better elements" of the urban populace had surrendered municipal administration to the hands of "low-bred" Irish saloonkeepers, such observations were misleading. Similarly incorrect is the claim that the business and professional elite abandoned city government during the late nineteenth century to decentralized lower-class ward leaders. The patrician, the plutocrat, the plebeian, and the professional bureaucrat all had their place in late-nineteenth-century municipal government; each staked an informal but definite claim to a particular domain within the municipal structure.

Upper-middle-class business figures presided over the executive branch and the independent park, library, and sinking-fund commissions. Throughout the last decades of the nineteenth century the mayor's office was generally in the hands of solid businessmen or professionals who were native-born Protestants. The leading executive officers were persons of citywide reputation and prestige, and during the period 1870 to 1900 their formal authority was increasing. Meanwhile, the legislative branch—the board of aldermen or city council—became the stronghold of small neighborhood retailers, often of immigrant background, who won their aldermanic seats because of their neighborhood reputation as good fellows willing to gain favors for their constituents. In some cities men of metropolitan standing virtually abandoned the city council, and in every major city this body was the chief forum for lower-middle-class and working-class ward politicians.

At the same time, an emerging body of trained experts was also securing a barony of power within city government. Even before the effective application of formal civil service laws, mayors and commissioners deferred to the judgment and expertise of professional engineers, landscape architects, educators, physicians, and fire chiefs, and a number of such figures served decade after decade in municipal posts, despite political upheavals in the executive and legislative branches. By the close of the century these professional civil servants were securing a place of permanent authority in city government. Their loyalty was not to downtown business interests nor to ward or ethnic particularism, but to their profession and their department. And they were gradually transforming those departments into strongholds of expertise.

The municipal professional, the downtown business leader, and the neighborhood shopkeeper and small-time politico each had differing concepts of city government and differing policy priorities. They thus represented potentially conflicting interests that could serve to divide the municipal polity and render it impotent. Yet, during the period 1870 to 1900, these elements remained in a state of peaceful, if contemptuous, coexistence. Hostilities broke out, especially if any element felt the boundaries of its domain were violated. But city governments could operate effectively if the truce between these elements was respected; in other words, if ward business remained the primary concern of ward alderman, citywide policy was in the hands of the business elite, and technical questions were decided by experts relatively undisturbed by party politics. This was the informal détente that was gradually developing amid the conflict and complaints.

Such extralegal participants as political parties and civic leagues also exerted their influence over municipal government, attempting to tip the uneasy balance of forces in their direction. The political party organization with its ward-based neighborhood bosses was one lever that the immigrants and less affluent could pull to affect the course of government. Civic organizations and reform leagues, in contrast, bolstered the so-called better element in government, the respected businessmen who usually dominated the leading executive offices and the independent commissions. Emerging professional groups such as engineering clubs and medical societies often lent their support to the rising ambitions and growing authority of the expert bureaucracy and permanent civil servants. And special-interest lobbyists like the fire insurance underwriters also urged professionalism in such municipal services as the fire department. Municipal government was no simple dualistic struggle between a citywide party boss with a diamond shirt stud and malodorous cigar and a good-government reformer with a Harvard degree and kid gloves. Various forces were pushing and pulling the municipal corporations, demanding a response to petitions and seeking a larger voice in the chambers of city government.

State legislatures provided the structural flexibility to respond to these demands. The state legislatures enjoyed the sovereign authority to bestow municipal powers and to determine the municipal structure, but when considering local measures, state lawmakers generally deferred to the judgment of the legislative delegation from the affected locality. If the local delegation favored a bill solely affecting its constituents, the legislature usually ratified the bill without opposition or debate. This rule of deference to the locality no longer applied, however, if the bill became a partisan issue, as it occasionally did. But in most cases authorization for new powers or for structural reforms depended on the city's representatives in the state legislature, and each session the state assemblies and senates rubber-stamped hundreds of local bills. Thus, indulgent legislator provided the vital elasticity that allowed urban governments to expand readily to meet new challenges and assume new responsibilities. . . .

Even so, this process of perpetual adjustment resulted in a mechanism that succeeded in performing the job of city government. Municipal leaders adapted to the need for experts trained in the new technologies and hired such technicians. Moreover, downtown businessmen and ward politicos, the native-born and the immigrants, Protestants and Catholics, loosened the lid on the melting pot and reduced the boiling hostility of the mid-century to a simmer. The cities provided services; they backed off from the brink of bankruptcy; and the municipal structure guaranteed a voice to the various elements of society in both immigrant wards and elite downtown clubs.

Why, then, all the complaints? Why did so many critics of the 1880s and 1890s indulge in a rhetoric of failure, focusing on municipal shortcomings to the neglect of municipal successes? Why was municipal government so much abused? The answer lies in a fundamental irony: The late-nineteenth-century municipal structure accommodated everyone but satisfied no one. It was a system of compromise among parties discontented with compromise. It was a marriage of convenience, with the spouses providing a reasonably comfortable home for America's urban inhabitants. But it was not a happy home. The parties to the nuptials tolerated one another because they had to. Nevertheless, the businessman-mayors and plutocrat park commissioners disliked their dependence on ward politicians, whom they frequently regarded as petty grafters, and they frowned upon the power of the immigrant voters. Likewise, the emerging corps of civil servants was irked by interference from laypersons of both high and law status. And the plebeian party boss opposed efforts to extend the realm of the civil servants who had performed no partisan duties and thus merited no power. None liked their interdependence with persons they felt to be unworthy, incompetent, or hostile.

Enhancing this dissatisfaction was the cultural absolutism of the Victorian era. The late nineteenth century was an age when the business elite could refer to itself as the "best element" of society and take for granted its "God-given" superiority. It was an age when professional engineers, landscape architects, public health experts, librarians, educators, and fire fighters were first becoming aware of themselves as professionals, and with the zeal of converts they defended their newly exalted state of grace. It was also an age when most Protestants viewed Catholics as papal pawns and devotees of Italian idolatry, while most Catholics believed Protestants were little better than heathens and doomed to a quick trip to hell with no stops in purgatory. The late nineteenth century was not an age of cultural relativism but one of cultural absolutes, an age when people still definitely knew right from wrong, the correct from the erroneous. The American municipality, however, was a heterogeneous polyarchy, a network of accommodation and compromise in an era when accommodation and compromise smacked of unmanly dishonor and unprincipled pragmatism. Municipal government of the 1870s, 1880s, and 1890s rested on a system of broker politics, of bargaining and dealing. . . .

Late-nineteenth-century urban government was a failure not of structure but of image. The system proved reasonably successful in providing services, but there was no prevailing ideology to validate its operation. In fact, the beliefs of the various participants were at odds with the structure of rule that governed them. The respectable elements believed in sobriety and government by persons of character. But the system of accommodation permitted whiskey taps to flow on the Sabbath for the Irish and for Germans, just as it allowed men in shiny suits with questionable reputations to occupy seats on the city council and in the municipal party conventions. The ward-based party devotees accepted the notions of Jacksonian democracy and believed quite literally in the maxim To the victor belong the spoils. But by the 1890s they faced a growing corps of civil servants more devoted to their profession than to any party. Although new professional bureaucrats preached a gospel of expertise, they still had to compromise with party-worshiping hacks and the supposedly diabolical forces of politics. Likewise, special-interest lobbyists such as the fire insurance underwriters were forced to cajole or coerce political leaders whom they deemed ignorant and unworthy of public office. Each of these groups worked together, but only from necessity and not because they believed in such a compromise of honor. There was no ideology of heterogeneous polyarchy, no system of beliefs to bolster the existing government structure. Thus late-nineteenth-century city government survived without moral support, and to many urban dwellers it seemed a bargain with the devil.

Twentieth-century historians also had reasons for focusing on urban failure rather than urban success. Some chroniclers in the early decades accepted rhetoric as reality and simply repeated the condemnations of critics such as Bryce, White, and Godkin. By the midcentury greater skepticism prevailed, but so did serious ills. In fact, the urban crisis of the 1960s provided the impetus for a great upsurge of interest in the history of the city, inspiring a search for the historical roots of urban breakdown and collapse. Urban problems were the scholars' preoccupation. Not until the much-ballyhooed "back-to-the-city" movement of the 1970s did the city become less an object of pity or contempt and more a treasured relic. By the late 1970s a new rhetoric was developing, in which sidewalks and streets assumed a nostalgic significance formerly reserved to babbling brooks and bucolic pastures.

The 1980s, then, seem an appropriate time to reevaluate the much-maligned municipality of the late nineteenth century. Back-to-the-city euphoria, however, should not distort one's judgment of the past. Instead, it is time to understand the system of city government from 1870 to 1900 complete with blemishes and beauty marks. One should not quickly dismiss the formal mechanisms of municipal rule as inadequate and outdated, requiring the unifying grasp of party bosses. Nor should one mindlessly laud municipal rule as a triumph of urban democracy. A serious appreciation of the municipal structure is necessary.

POSTSCRIPT

Was City Government in Late Nineteenth-Century America a "Conspicuous Failure"?

The opposing viewpoints expressed by Griffith and Teaford represent a longstanding scholarly debate about the consequences of boss politics in the United States. James Bryce, *The American Commonwealth*, 2 vols. (Macmillan and Company, 1888); Moisei Ostrogorski, *Democracy and the Organization of Political Parties* (1902; Anchor Books, 1964); and Lincoln Steffens, *The Shame of the Cities* (McClure, Phillips and Company, 1904), present a litany of misdeeds associated with those who controlled municipal government. Political bosses, these authors charged, were guilty of malfeasance in office and all forms of graft and corruption.

Efforts to rehabilitate the sullied reputations of the machine politicians can be dated to the comments of one of Boss Tweed's henchmen, George Washington Plunkitt, a New York City ward heeler whose turn-of-the-century observations included a subtle distinction between "honest" and "dishonest" graft. A more scholarly effort was presented by Robert K. Merton, a political scientist, who identified numerous "latent functions" of the political machine. According to Merton, city bosses created effective political organizations that humanized the dispensation of assistance, offered valuable political privileges for businessmen, and created alternate routes of social mobility for citizens, many of them immigrants, who typically were excluded from conventional means of personal advancement.

There are several excellent urban history texts which devote space to the development of municipal government in the late nineteenth century. Among these are David R. Goldfield and Blaine A. Brownell, *Urban America: From Downtown to No Town* (Houghton Mifflin, 1979); Howard P. Chudacoff and Judith E. Smith, *The Evolution of American Urban Society*, 3d ed. (Prentice Hall, 1981); and Charles N. Glaab and A. Theodore Brown, *A History of Urban America*, 3d ed. (Macmillan, 1983). Various developments in the industrial period are discussed in Blake McKelvey, *The Urbanization of America, 1860–1915* (Rutgers University Press, 1963), and Raymond A. Mohl, *The New City: Urban America in the Industrial Age, 1860-1920* (Harlan Davidson, 1985).

Boss politics is analyzed in William L. Riordon, *Plunkitt of Tammany Hall* (E. P. Dutton, 1963); Robert K. Merton, *Social Theory and Social Structure* (Free Press, 1957); and John M. Allswang, *Bosses, Machines, and Urban Voters: An American Symbiosis* (Kennikat Press, 1977). The most famous urban boss is analyzed in Alexander B. Callow, Jr., *The Tweed Ring* (Oxford University Press, 1966), and Leo Hershkowitz, *Tweed's New York: Another Look* (Anchor Press, 1977). Scott Greer, ed., *Ethnics, Machines, and the American Future* (Harvard University Press, 1981), and Bruce M. Stave and Sondra Astor Stave, eds., *Urban Bosses, Machines, and Progressive Reformers*, 2d ed. (D. C. Heath, 1984), are excellent collections of essays on urban political machinery. Significant contributions to urban historiography are Sam Bass Warner, Jr., *Streetcar Suburbs: The Process of Growth in Boston, 1870–1900* (Harvard University Press, 1962); Stephan Thernstrom, *Poverty and Progress: Social Mobility in the Nineteenth-Century City* (Harvard University Press, 1964); Gunther Barth, *City People, The Rise of Modern City Culture in Nineteenth-Century America* (Oxford University Press, 1980); and Martin V. Melosi, *Garbage in the Cities: Refuse, Reform, and the Environment, 1880–1980* (Texas A & M University Press, 1982).

ISSUE 7

Did Booker T. Washington's Philosophy and Actions Betray the Interests of African Americans?

YES: W. E. B. Du Bois, from *The Souls of Black Folk* (1903, Reprint, Fawcett Publications, 1961)

NO: Louis R. Harlan, from "Booker T. Washington and the Politics of Accommodation," in John Hope Franklin and August Meier, eds., *Black Leaders of the Twentieth Century* (University of Illinois Press, 1982)

ISSUE SUMMARY

YES: W. E. B. Du Bois, a founding member of the National Organization for the Advancement of Colored People, argues that Booker T. Washington became an apologist for racial injustice in America by failing to articulate the legitimate demands of African Americans for full civil and political rights.
NO: Professor of history Louis R. Harlan portrays Washington as a political realist who had the same long-range goals of progress toward equality as his black critics and whose policies and actions were designed to benefit black society as a whole.

In the late nineteenth and early twentieth centuries, most black Americans' lives were characterized by increased inequality and powerlessness. Although the Thirteenth Amendment had fueled a partial social revolution by emancipating approximately four million Southern slaves, the efforts of the Fourteenth and Fifteenth Amendments to provide all African Americans with the protections and privileges of full citizenship had been undermined by the United States Supreme Court.

By 1910, seventy-five percent of all African Americans resided in rural areas. Ninety percent lived in the South, where they suffered from abuses associated with the sharecropping and crop-lien systems, political disfranchisement, and antagonistic race relations, which often boiled over into acts of violence, including race riots and lynchings. Black Southerners who moved north in the decades preceding World War I to escape the ravages of racism instead discovered a society in which the color line was drawn more rigidly to limit black opportunities. Residential segregation led to the emergence of racial ghettos. Jim Crow also affected Northern education, and competition for jobs produced frequent clashes between black and white workers. By the early twentieth century, then, most African Americans endured a second-class citizenship reinforced by segregation laws (both customary and legal) in the "age of Jim Crow."

Prior to 1895, the foremost spokesman for the nation's African American population was former slave and abolitionist Frederick Douglass, whose crusade for blacks emphasized the importance of civil rights, political power, and immediate integration. August Meier has called Douglass "the greatest living symbol of the protest tradition during the 1880s and 1890s." At the time of Douglass's death in 1895, however, this tradition was largely replaced by the emergence of Booker T. Washington. Born into slavery in Virginia in 1856, Washington became the most prominent black spokesman in the United States as a result of a speech delivered at the Cotton States Exposition in Atlanta, Georgia. Known as the "Atlanta Compromise," this address, with its conciliatory tone, found favor among whites and gave Washington, who was president of Tuskegee Institute in Alabama, a reputation as a "responsible" spokesman for black America.

What did Booker T. Washington really want for African Americans? Did his programs realistically address the difficulties confronted by blacks in a society where the doctrine of white supremacy was prominent? Is it fair to describe Washington simply as a conservative whose accommodationist philosophy betrayed his own people? Did the "Sage of Tuskegee" consistently adhere to his publicly stated philosophy of patience, self-help, and economic advancement?

One of the earliest and most outspoken critics of Washington's program was his contemporary, W. E. B. Du Bois. In a famous essay in *The Souls of Black Folk*, Du Bois levels an assault upon Washington's narrow educational philosophy for blacks and his apparent acceptance of segregation. By submitting to disfranchisement and segregation, Du Bois charges, Washington had become an apologist for racial injustice in the United States. He also claims that Washington's national prominence was bought at the expense of black interests throughout the nation.

Louis R. Harlan's appraisal of Washington, while not totally uncritical, illuminates the complexity of Washington's personality and philosophy. Washington, according to Harlan, understood the reality of Southern race relations and knew what he was capable of accomplishing without endangering his leadership position, which was largely controlled by whites. He was, then, a consummate politician—master of the art of the possible in turn-of-the-century race relations.

YES
W. E. B. Du Bois

OF MR. BOOKER T. WASHINGTON
AND OTHERS

Easily the most striking thing in the history of the American Negro since 1876 is the ascendancy of Mr. Booker T. Washington. It began at the time when war memories and ideals were rapidly passing; a day of astonishing commercial development was dawning; a sense of doubt and hesitation overtook the freedmen's sons,—then it was that his leading began. Mr. Washington came, with a single definite programme, at the psychological moment when the nation was a little ashamed of having bestowed so much sentiment on Negroes, and was concentrating its energies on Dollars. His programme of industrial education, conciliation of the South, and submission and silence as to civil and political rights, was not wholly original; . . . But Mr. Washington first indisolubly linked these things; he put enthusiasm, unlimited energy, and perfect faith into this programme, and changed it from a by-path into a veritable Way of Life. And the tale of the methods by which he did this is a fascinating study of human life.

It startled the nation to hear a Negro advocating such a programme after many decades of bitter complaint; it startled and won the applause of the South, it interested and won the admiration of the North; and after a confused murmur of protest, it silenced if it did not convert the Negroes themselves.

To gain the sympathy and coöperation of the various elements comprising the white South was Mr. Washington's first task; and this, at the time Tuskegee was founded, seemed, for a black man, well-nigh impossible. And yet ten years later it was done in the word spoken at Atlanta: "In all things purely social we can be as separate as the five fingers, and yet one as the hand in all things essential to mutual progress." This "Atlanta Compromise" is by all odds the most notable thing in Mr. Washington's career. The South interpreted it in different ways: the radicals received it as a complete surrender of the demand for civil and political equality; the conservatives, as a generously conceived working basis for mutual understanding. So both approved it, and to-day its author is certainly the most distinguished

From W. E. B. Du Bois, *The Souls of Black Folk* (1903). Reprint. Fawcett Publications, 1961.

Southerner since Jefferson Davis, and the one with the largest personal following.

Next to this achievement comes Mr. Washington's work in gaining place and consideration in the North. Others less shrewd and tactful had formerly essayed to sit on these two stools and had fallen between them; but as Mr. Washington knew the heart of the South from birth and training, so by singular insight he intuitively grasped the spirit of the age which was dominating the North. And so thoroughly did he learn the speech and thought of triumphant commercialism, and the ideals of material prosperity, that the picture of a lone black boy poring over a French grammar amid the weeds and dirt of a neglected home soon seemed to him the acme of absurdities. One wonders what Socrates and St. Francis of Assisi would say to this.

And yet this very singleness of vision and thorough oneness with his age is a mark of the successful man. It is as though Nature must needs make men narrow in order to give them force. So Mr. Washington's cult has gained unquestioning followers, his work has wonderfully prospered, his friends are legion, and his enemies are confounded. To-day he stands as the one recognized spokesman of his ten million fellows, and one of the most notable figures in a nation of seventy millions. One hesitates, therefore, to criticise a life which, beginning with so little, has done so much. And yet the time is come when one may speak in all sincerity and utter courtesy of the mistakes and shortcomings of Mr. Washington's career, as well as of his triumphs, without being thought captious or envious, and without forgetting that it is easier to do ill than well in the world.

The criticism that has hitherto met Mr. Washington has not always been of this broad character. In the South especially has he had to walk warily to avoid the harshest judgments,—and naturally so, for he is dealing with the one subject of deepest sensitiveness to that section. Twice—once when at the Chicago celebration of the Spanish-American War he alluded to the color-prejudice that is "eating away the vitals of the South," and once when he dined with President Roosevelt—has the resulting Southern criticism been violent enough to threaten seriously his popularity. In the North the feeling has several times forced itself into words, that Mr. Washington's counsels of submission overlooked certain elements of true manhood, and that his educational programme was unnecessarily narrow. Usually, however, such criticism has not found open expression, although, too, the spiritual sons of the Abolitionists have not been prepared to acknowledge that the schools founded before Tuskegee, by men of broad ideals and self-sacrificing spirit, were wholly failures or worthy of ridicule. While, then, criticism has not failed to follow Mr. Washington, yet the prevailing public opinion of the land has been but too willing to deliver the solution of a wearisome problem into his hands, and say, "If that is all you and your race ask, take it."

Among his own people, however, Mr. Washington has encountered the strongest and most lasting opposition, amounting at times to bitterness, and even to-day continuing strong and insistent even though largely silenced in outward expression by the public opinion of the nation. Some of this opposition is, of course, mere envy; the disappointment of displaced demagogues and the spite of narrow minds. But aside from this, there is among educated and thoughtful colored men in all parts of the land a feeling of deep regret, sorrow, and apprehension at the wide currency and ascendancy which some of Mr. Washington's theories have gained. These same men admire his sincerity of purpose, and are willing to forgive much to honest endeavor which is doing something worth the doing. They coöperate with Mr. Washington as far as they conscientiously can; and, indeed, it is no ordinary tribute to this man's tact and power that, steering as he must between so many diverse interests and opinions, he so largely retains the respect of all.

But the hushing of the criticism of honest opponents is a dangerous thing. It leads some of the best of the critics to unfortunate silence and paralysis of effort, and others to burst into speech so passionately and intemperately as to lose listeners. Honest and earnest criticism from those whose interests are most nearly touched,—criticism of writers by readers, of government by those governed, of leaders by those led,—this is the soul of democracy and the safeguard of modern society. If the best of the American Negroes receive by outer pressure a leader whom they had not recognized before, manifestly there is here a certain palpable gain. Yet there is also irreparable loss,—a loss of that peculiarly valuable education which a group receives when by search and criticism it finds and commissions its own leaders. The way in which this is done is at once the most elementary and the nicest problem of social growth. History is but the record of such group-leadership; and yet how infinitely changeful is its type and character! And of all types and kinds, what can be more instructive than the leadership of a group within a group?— that curious double movement where

real progress may be negative and actual advance be relative retrogression. All this is the social student's inspiration and despair.

Now in the past the American Negro has had instructive experience in the choosing of group leaders, founding thus a peculiar dynasty which in the light of present conditions is worth while studying. When sticks and stones and beasts form the sole environment of a people, their attitude is largely one of determined opposition to and conquest of natural forces. But when to earth and brute is added an environment of men and ideas, then the attitude of the imprisoned group may take three main forms,—a feeling of revolt and revenge; an attempt to adjust all thought and action to the will of the greater group; or, finally, a determined effort at self-realization and self-development despite environing opinion. The influence of all of these attitudes at various times can be traced in the history of the American Negro, and in the evolution of his successive leaders. . . .

Booker T. Washington arose as essentially the leader not of one race but of two,—a compromiser between the South, the North, and the Negro. Naturally the Negroes resented, at first bitterly, signs of compromise which surrendered their civil and political rights, even though this was to be exchanged for larger chances of economic development. The rich and dominating North, however, was not only weary of the race problem, but was investing largely in Southern enterprises, and welcomed any method of peaceful coöperation. Thus, by national opinion, the Negroes began to recognize Mr. Washington's leadership; and the voice of criticism was hushed.

Mr. Washington represents in Negro thought the old attitude of adjustment and submission; but adjustment at such a peculiar time as to make his programme unique. This is an age of unusual economic development, and Mr. Washington's programme naturally takes an economic cast, becoming a gospel of Work and Money to such an extent as apparently almost completely to overshadow the higher aims of life. Moreover, this is an age when the more advanced races are coming in closer contact with the less developed races, and the race-feeling is therefore intensified; and Mr. Washington's programme practically accepts the alleged inferiority of the Negro races. Again, in our own land, the reaction from the sentiment of war time has given impetus to race-prejudice against Negroes, and Mr. Washington withdraws many of the high demands of Negroes as men and American citizens. In other periods of intensified prejudice all the Negro's tendency to self-assertion has been called forth; at this period a policy of submission is advocated. In the history of nearly all other races and peoples the doctrine preached at such crises has been that manly self-respect is worth more than lands and houses, and that a people who voluntarily surrender such respect, or cease striving for it, are not worth civilizing.

In answer to this, it has been claimed that the Negro can survive only through submission. Mr. Washington distinctly asks that black people give up, at least for the present three things,—

First, political power,

Second, insistence on civil rights,

Third, higher education of Negro youth,—

and concentrate all their energies on industrial education, the accumulation of wealth, and the conciliation of the South. This policy has been courageously and insistently advocated for over fifteen years, and has been triumphant for perhaps ten years. As a result of this tender of the palm-branch, what has been the return? In these years there have occurred:

1. The disfranchisement of the Negro.

2. The legal creation of a distinct status of civil inferiority for the Negro.

3. The steady withdrawal of aid from institutions for the higher training of the Negro.

These movements are not, to be sure, direct results of Mr. Washington's teachings; but his propaganda has, without a shadow of doubt, helped their speedier accomplishment. The question then comes: Is it possible, and probable, that nine millions of men can make effective progress in economic lines if they are deprived of political rights, made a servile caste, and allowed only the most meagre chance for developing their exceptional men? If history and reason give any distinct answer to these questions, it is an emphatic *No*. And Mr. Washington thus faces the triple paradox of his career:

1. He is striving nobly to make Negro artisans business men and property-owners; but it is utterly impossible, under modern competitive methods, for workingmen and property-owners to defend their rights and exist without the right of suffrage.

2. He insists on thrift and self-respect, but at the same time counsels a silent submission to civic inferiority such as is bound to sap the manhood of any race in the long run.

3. He advocates common-school and industrial training, and depreciates institutions of higher learning; but neither

the Negro common-schools, nor Tusk-egee itself, could remain open a day were it not for teachers trained in Negro colleges, or trained by their graduates.

This triple paradox in Mr. Washington's position is the object of criticism by two classes of colored Americans. One class is spiritually descended from Toussaint the Savior, through Gabriel, Vesey, and Turner, and they represent the attitude of revolt and revenge; they hate the white South blindly and distrust the white race generally, and so far as they agree on definite action, think that the Negro's only hope lies in emigration beyond the borders of the United States. And yet, by the irony of fate, nothing has more effectually made this programme seem hopeless than the recent course of the United States toward weaker and darker peoples in the West Indies, Hawaii, and the Philippines,—for where in the world may we go and be safe from lying and brute force?

The other class of Negroes who cannot agree with Mr. Washington has hitherto said little aloud. They deprecate the sight of scattered counsels, of internal disagreement; and especially they dislike making their just criticism of a useful and earnest man an excuse for a general discharge of venom from small-minded opponents. Nevertheless, the questions involved are so fundamental and serious that it is difficult to see how men like the Grimkes, Kelly Miller, J. W. E. Bowen, and other representatives of this group, can much longer be silent. Such men feel in conscience bound to ask of this nation three things:

1. The right to vote.
2. Civic equality.
3. The education of youth according to ability.

They acknowledge Mr. Washington's invaluable service in counselling patience an courtesy in such demands; they do not ask that ignorant black men vote when ignorant whites are debarred, or that any reasonable restrictions in the suffrage should not be applied; they know that the low social level of the mass of the race is responsible for much discrimination against it, but they also know, and the nation knows, that relentless color-prejudice is more often a cause than a result of the Negro's degradation; they seek the abatement of this relic of barbarism, and not its systematic encouragement and pampering by all agencies of social power from the Associated Press to the Church of Christ. They advocate, with Mr. Washington, a broad system of Negro common schools supplemented by thorough industrial training; but they are surprised that a man of Mr. Washington's insight cannot see that no such educational system ever has rested or can rest on any other basis than that of the well-equipped college and university, and they insist that there is a demand for a few such institutions throughout the South to train the best of the Negro youth as teachers, professional men, and leaders.

This group of men honor Mr. Washington for his attitude of conciliation toward the white South; they accept the "Atlanta Compromise" in its broadest interpretation; they recognize, with him, many signs of promise, many men of high purpose and fair judgment, in this section; they know that no easy task has been laid upon a region already tottering under heavy burdens. But, nevertheless, they insist that the way to truth and right lies in straightforward honesty, not in indiscriminate flattery; in praising those of the South who do well and criticising uncompromisingly those who do ill; in taking advantage of the opportunities at hand and urging their fellows to do the same, but at the same time remembering that only a firm adherence to their higher ideals and aspirations will ever keep those ideals within the realm of possibility. They do not expect that the free right vote, to enjoy civic rights, and to be educated, will come in a moment; they do not expect to see the bias and prejudices of years disappear at the blast of a trumpet; but they are absolutely certain that the way for a people to gain their reasonable rights is not by voluntarily throwing them away and insisting that they do not want them; that the way for a people to gain respect is not by continually belittling and ridiculing themselves; that, on the contrary, Negroes must insist continually, in season and out of season, that voting is necessary to modern manhood, that color discrimination is barbarism, and that black boys need education as well as white boys.

In failing thus to state plainly and unequivocally the legitimate demands of their people, even at the cost of opposing an honored leader, the thinking classes of American Negroes would shirk a heavy responsibility,—a responsibility to themselves, a responsibility to the struggling masses, a responsibility to the darker races of men whose future depends so largely on this American experiment, but especially a responsibility to this nation,—this common Fatherland. It is wrong to encourage a man or a people in evil-doing; it is wrong to aid and abet a national crime simply because it is unpopular not to do so. The growing spirit of kindliness and reconciliation between the North and South after the frightful difference of a generation ago ought to be a source of deep congratula-tion to all, and especially to those whose mistreatment caused the war; but if that reconciliation is to be marked by the industrial slavery and civic death of those same black men, with permanent legislation into a position of inferiority, then those black men, if they are really men, are called upon by every considera-tion of patriotism and loyalty to oppose such a course by all civilized methods, even though such opposition involves disagreement with Mr. Booker T. Wash-ington. We have no right to sit silently by while the inevitable seeds are sown for a harvest of disaster to our children, black and white.

First, it is the duty of black men to judge the South discriminatingly. The present generation of Southerners are not responsible for the past, and they should not be blindly hated or blamed for it. Furthermore, to no class is the indiscriminate endorsement of the recent course of the South toward Negroes more nauseating than to the best thought of the South. The South is not "solid"; it is a land in the ferment of social change, wherein forces of all kinds are fighting for supremacy; and to praise the ill the South is to-day perpetrating is just as wrong as to condemn the good. Discrim-inating and broad-minded criticism is what the South needs,—needs it for the sake of her own white sons and daugh-ters, and for the insurance of robust, healthy mental and moral development.

To-day even the attitude of the South-ern whites toward the blacks is not, as so many assume, in all cases the same; the ignorant Southerner hates the Negro, the workingmen fear his competition, the money-makers wish to use him as a laborer, some of the educated see a men-ace in his upward development, while others—usually the sons of masters—

wish to help him to rise. National opinion has enabled this last class to maintain the Negro common schools, and to protect the Negro partially in property, life, and limb. Through the pressure of the money-makers, the Negro is in danger of being reduced to semi-slavery, especially in the country districts; the workingmen, and those of the educated who fear the Negro, have united to disfranchise him, and some have urged his deportation; while the passions of the ignorant are easily aroused to lynch and abuse any black man. To praise this intricate whirl of thought and prejudice is nonsense; to inveigh indiscriminately against "the South" is unjust; but to use the same breath in praising Governor [Charles B.] Aycock, exposing Senator [John T.] Morgan, arguing with Mr. Thomas Nelson Page, and denouncing Senator Ben Tillman, is not only sane, but the imperative duty of thinking black men.

It would be unjust to Mr. Washington not to acknowledge that in several instances he has opposed movements in the South which were unjust to the Negro; he sent memorials to the Louisiana and Alabama constitutional conventions, he has spoken against lynching, and in other ways has openly or silently set his influence against sinister schemes and unfortunate happenings. Notwithstanding this, it is equally true to assert that on the whole the distinct impression left by Mr. Washington's propaganda is, first, that the South is justified in its present attitude toward the Negro because of the Negro's degradation; secondly, that the prime cause of the Negro's failure to rise more quickly is his wrong education in the past; and, thirdly, that his future rise depends primarily on his own efforts. Each of these propositions is a dangerous half-truth. The supplementary truths must never be lost sight of: first, slavery and race-prejudice are potent if not sufficient causes of the Negro's position; second, industrial and common-school training were necessarily slow in planting because they had to await the black teachers trained by higher institutions,—it being extremely doubtful if any essentially different development was possible, and certainly a Tuskegee was unthinkable before 1880; and, third, while it is a great truth to say that the Negro must strive and strive mightily to help himself, it is equally true that unless his striving be not simply seconded, but rather aroused and encouraged, by the initiative of the richer and wiser environing group, he cannot hope for great success.

In his failure to realize and impress this last point, Mr. Washington is especially to be criticised. His doctrine has tended to make the whites, North and South, shift the burden of the Negro problem to the Negro's shoulders and stand aside as critical and rather pessimistic spectators; when in fact the burden belongs to the nation, and the hands of none of us are clean if we bend not our energies to righting these great wrongs.

The South ought to be led, by candid and honest criticism, to assert her better self and do her full duty to the race she has cruelly wronged and is still wronging. The North—her co-partner in guilt—cannot salve her conscience by plastering it with gold. We cannot settle this problem by diplomacy and suaveness, by "policy" alone. If worse come to worst, can the moral fibre of this country survive the slow throttling and murder of nine millions of men?

The black men of America have a duty to perform, a duty stern and delicate,—a forward movement to oppose a part of the work of their greatest leader. So far as Mr. Washington preaches Thrift, Patience, and Industrial Training for the masses, we must hold up his hands and strive with him, rejoicing in his honors and glorying in the strength of this Joshua called of God and of man to lead the headless host. But so far as Mr. Washington apologizes for injustice, North or South, does not rightly value the privilege and duty of voting, belittles the emasculating effects of caste distinctions, and opposes the higher training and ambition of our brighter minds,—so far as he, the South, or the Nation, does this,—we must unceasingly and firmly oppose them. By every civilized and peaceful method we must strive for the rights which the world accords to men, clinging unwaveringly to those great words which the sons of the Fathers would fain forget: "We hold these truths to be self-evident: That all men are created equal; that they are endowed by their Creator with certain unalienable rights; that among these are life, liberty, and the pursuit of happiness."

NO

Louis R. Harlan

BOOKER T. WASHINGTON AND THE POLITICS OF ACCOMMODATION

It is ironic that Booker T. Washington, the most powerful black American of his time and perhaps of all time, should be the black leader whose claim to the title is most often dismissed by the lay public. Blacks often question his legitimacy because of the role that favor by whites played in Washington's assumption of power, and whites often remember him only as an educator or, confusing him with George Washington Carver, as "that great Negro scientist." This irony is something that Washington will have to live with in history, for he himself deliberately created the ambiguity about his role and purposes that has haunted his image. And yet, Washington was a genuine black leader, with a substantial black following and with virtually the same long-range goals for Afro-Americans as his rivals. This presentation is concerned with Washington's social philosophy, such as it was, but it also addresses his methods of leadership, both his Delphic public utterances that meant one thing to whites and another to blacks and his adroit private movements through the brier patch of American race relations. It does not try to solve the ultimate riddle of his character.

Washington's own view of himself was that he was the Negro of the hour, whose career and racial program epitomized what blacks needed to maintain themselves against white encroachments and to make progress toward equality in America. The facts of his life certainly fitted his self-image. He was the last of the major black leaders to be born in slavery, on a small farm in western Virginia in 1856. Growing up during the Reconstruction era in West Virginia, he believed that one of the lessons he learned was that the Reconstruction experiment in racial democracy failed because it began at the wrong end, emphasizing political means and civil rights acts rather than economic means and self-determination. Washington learned this lesson not so much through experiences as a child worker in the salt works and coal

From Louis R. Harlan, "Booker T. Washington and the Politics of Accommodation," in Franklin and Meier, eds., *Black Leaders of the Twentieth Century* (University of Illinois Press, 1982). Copyright © 1982 by the University of Illinois Press. Reprinted by permission.

mines as by what he was taught as a houseboy for the leading family of Malden, West Virginia, and later as a student at Hampton Institute in Virginia. Hampton applied the missionary method to black education and made its peace with the white South.

After teaching school in his home town, Washington briefly studied in a Baptist seminary and in a lawyer's office. But he soon abandoned these alternative careers, perhaps sensing that disfranchisement and the secularization of society would weaken these occupations as bases for racial leadership. He returned to Hampton Institute as a teacher for two years and then founded Tuskegee Normal and Industrial Institute in Alabama in 1881. Over the next quarter of a century, using Hampton's methods but with greater emphasis on the skilled trades, Washington built up Tuskegee Institute to be an equal of Hampton.

Washington's bid for leadership went beyond education and institution-building, however. Symbolic of his fresh approach to black-white relations was a speech he gave in 1895 before a commercial exposition, known as the Atlanta Compromise Address, and his autobiography, *Up from Slavery* (1901). As Washington saw it, blacks were toiling upward from slavery by their own efforts into the American middle class and needed chiefly social peace to continue in this steady social evolution. Thus, in the Atlanta Compromise he sought to disarm the white South by declaring agitation of the social equality question "the merest folly" and proclaiming that in "purely social" matters "we can be as separate as the fingers, yet one as the hand in all things essential to mutual progress." These concessions came to haunt Washington as southerners used segregation

as a means of systematizing discrimination, and northerners followed suit. And they did not stop at the "purely social."

Washington's concessions to the white South, however, were only half of a bargain. In return for downgrading civil and political rights in the black list of priorities, Washington asked whites to place no barriers to black economic advancement and even to become partners of their black neighbors "in all things essential to mutual progress." Washington saw his own role as the axis between the races, the only leader who could negotiate and keep the peace by holding extremists on both sides in check. He was always conscious that his unique influence could be destroyed in an instant of self-indulgent flamboyance.

Washington sought to influence whites, but he never forgot that it was the blacks that he undertook to lead. He offered blacks not the empty promises of the demagogue but a solid program of economic and educational progress through struggle. It was less important "just now," he said, for a black person to seek admission to an opera house than to have the money for the ticket. Mediating diplomacy with whites was only half of Washington's strategy; the other half was black solidarity, mutual aid, and institution-building. He thought outspoken complaint against injustice was necessary but insufficient, and he thought factional dissent among black leaders was self-defeating and should be suppressed.

Washington brought to his role as a black leader the talents and outlook of a machine boss. He made Tuskegee Institute the largest and best-supported black educational institution of his day, and it spawned a large network of other industrial schools. Tuskegee's educational function is an important and debatable subject, of course, but the central concern here is Washington's use of the school as the base of operations of what came to be known as the Tuskegee Machine. It was an all-black school with an all-black faculty at a time when most black colleges were still run by white missionaries. Tuskegee taught self-determination. It also taught trades designed for economic independence in a region dominated by sharecrop agriculture. At the same time, by verbal juggling tricks, Washington convinced the southern whites that Tuskegee was not educating black youth away from the farms. Tuskegee also functioned as a model black community, not only by acquainting its students with a middle-class way of life, but by buying up the surrounding farmland and selling it at low rates of interest to create a community of small landowners and homeowners. The Institute became larger than the town.

Washington built a regional constituency of farmers, artisans, country teachers, and small businessmen; he expanded the Tuskegee Machine nationwide after the Atlanta Compromise seemed acceptable to blacks all over the country, even by many who later denounced it. His first northern black ally was T. Thomas Fortune, editor of the militant and influential New York *Age* and founder of the Afro-American Council, the leading forum of black thought at the time. Washington was not a member, but he usually spoke at the annual meetings, and his lieutenants so tightly controlled the council that it never passed an action or resolution not in Washington's interest. Seeking more direct allies, Washington founded in 1900 the National Negro Business League, of which he was president for life. The league was important not so much for what it did for black

business, which was little, but because the local branch of the league was a stronghold of Washington men in every substantial black population center.

Other classes of influential blacks did not agree with Washington's stated philosophy but were beholden to him for the favors he did them or offered to do for them. He was not called the Wizard for nothing. White philanthropists who approved of him for their own reasons gave him the money to help black colleges by providing for a Carnegie library here, a dormitory there. Through Washington Andrew Carnegie alone gave buildings to twenty-nine black schools. Not only college administrators owed him for favors, but so did church leaders, YMCA directors and many others. Though never much of a joiner, he became a power in the Baptist church, and he schemed through lieutenants to control the secret black fraternal orders and make his friends the high potentates of the Pythians, Odd Fellows, and so on. Like any boss, he turned every favor into a bond of obligation.

It was in politics, however, that Washington built the most elaborate tentacle of the octopus-like Tuskegee Machine. In politics as in everything else, Washington cultivated ambiguity. He downgraded politics as a solution of black problems, did not recommend politics to the ambitious young black man, and never held office. But when Theodore Roosevelt became president in 1901 and asked for Washington's advice on black and southern appointments, Washington consented with alacrity. He became the chief black adviser of both Presidents Roosevelt and William Howard Taft. He failed in his efforts to liberalize Republican policy on voting rights, lynching, and racial discrimination, however, and relations between the Republican party and black voters reached a low ebb.

In patronage politics, however, Washington found his opportunity. For a man who minimized the importance of politics, Washington devoted an inordinate amount of his time and tremendous energy to securing federal jobs for his machine lieutenants. These men played a certain role in the politics of the period, but their first obligation was to the Tuskegean. Washington advised the presidents to replace the old venal officeholding class of blacks with men who had proven themselves in the independent world of business, but in practice it took only loyalty to Washington to cleanse miraculously an old-time political hack. . . .

Washington's outright critics and enemies were called "radicals" because they challenged Washington's conservatism and bossism, though their tactics of verbal protest would seem moderate indeed to a later generation of activists. They were the college-educated blacks, engaged in professional pursuits, and proud of their membership in an elite class—what one of them called the Talented Tenth. The strongholds of the radicals were the northern cities and southern black colleges. They stood for full political and civil rights, liberal education, free expression, and aspiration. They dreamed of a better world and believed Booker T. Washington was a menace to its achievement. . . .

Washington dismissed his black critics by questioning their motives, their claim to superior wisdom, and—the politician's ultimate argument—their numbers. Washington understood, if his critics did not, that his leadership of the black community largely depended on his recognition by whites as the black leader. If he did not meet some minimal standards of sat-

isfactoriness to whites, another Washington would be created. He obviously could not lead the whites; he could not even divide the whites. He could only, in a limited way, exploit the class divisions that whites created among themselves. He could work in the cracks of their social structure, move like Brer Rabbit through the brier patch, and thus outwit the more numerous and powerful whites.

While Washington recognized the centrality of black-white relations in his efforts to lead blacks, he was severely restricted by the historical context of his leadership. It was an age of polarization of black and white. The overheated atmosphere of the South at the turn of the century resembled that of a crisis center on the eve of war. Lynching became a more than weekly occurrence; discrimination and humiliation of blacks were constant and pervasive and bred a whole literature and behavioral science of self-justification. Race riots terrorized blacks in many cities, and not only in the South. It would have required not courage but foolhardiness for Washington, standing with both feet in Alabama, to have challenged this raging white aggression openly and directly. Even unqualified verbal protest would have brought him little support from either southern blacks or white well-wishers. Du Bois took higher ground and perhaps a better vision of the future when he urged forthright protest against every white injustice, on the assumption that whites were rational beings and would respond dialectically to black protest. But few white racists of the early twentieth century cared anything for the facts. And when Du Bois in his Atlanta years undertook to implement his protest with action, he was driven to the negative means of refusing to pay his poll tax or refusing to ride segregated streetcars and elevators.

Instead of either confronting all of white America or admitting that his Faustian bargain for leadership had created a systemic weakness in his program, Washington simply met each day as it came, pragmatically, seeking what white allies he could against avowed white enemies. A serious fault of this policy was that Washington usually appealed for white support on a basis of a vaguely conceived mutual interest rather than on ideological agreement. For example, in both the South and the North Washington allied himself with the white upper class against the masses. In the South he joined with the planter class and when possible with the coal barons and railroad officials against the populists and other small white farmer groups who seemed to him to harbor the most virulent anti-black attitudes born of labor competition. Similarly, in the North, Washington admired and bargained with the big business class. The bigger the businessman, the more Washington admired him, as the avatar and arbiter of American society. At the pinnacle in his measure of men were the industrialists Carnegie, John D. Rockefeller, and Henry H. Rogers and the merchant princes Robert C. Ogden and Julius Rosenwald. To be fair to Washington, he appreciated their philanthropic generosity at least as much as he admired their worldly success, but his lips were sealed against criticism of even the more rapacious and ungenerous members of the business elite.

Washington made constructive use of his philanthropic allies to aid not only Tuskegee but black education and black society as a whole. He guided the generous impulse of a Quaker millionairess into the Anna T. Jeanes Foundation to improve the teaching in black public schools. He persuaded the Jewish philanthropist Julius Rosenwald to begin a program that lasted for decades for building more adequate black schoolhouses all over the South. Washington's influence on Carnegie, Rockefeller, Jacob Schiff, and other rich men also transcended immediate Tuskegee interests to endow other black institutions. In short, Washington did play a role in educational statesmanship. There were limits, however, to his power to advance black interests through philanthropy. When his northern benefactors became involved in the Southern Education Board to improve the southern public school systems, for example, he worked repeatedly but without success to get this board to redress the imbalance of public expenditures or even to halt the rapid increase of discrimination against black schools and black children. He had to shrug off his failure and get from these so-called philanthropists whatever they were willing to give.

Having committed himself to the business elite, Washington took a dim view of the leaders of the working class. Immigrants represented to him, as to many blacks, labor competitors; Jews were the exception here, as he held them up to ambitious blacks as models of the work-ethic and group solidarity. He claimed in his autobiography that his disillusionment with labor unions went back to his youthful membership in the Knights of Labor and stemmed from observation of their disruption of the natural laws of economics. In his heyday, however, which was also the age of Samuel Gompers, Washington's anti-union attitudes were explained by the widespread exclusion of blacks from membership in many unions and hence from employment in many trades. There is no evidence that Washington ever actively supported black strikebreaking, but his refusal to intervene in behalf of all-white unions is understandable. It was more often white employees rather than employers who excluded blacks, or so Washington believed. He worked hard to introduce black labor into the non-union, white-only cotton mills in the South, even to the extent of interesting northern capitalists in investing in black cotton mills and similar enterprises.

Washington was a conservative by just about any measure. Though he flourished in the Progressive era it was not he, but his opponents who were the men of good hope, full of reform proposals and faith in the common man. Washington's vision of the common man included the southern poor white full of rancor against blacks, the foreign-born anarchist ready to pull down the temple of American business, and the black sharecropper unqualified by education or economic freedom for the ballot. Though Washington opposed the grandfather clause and every other southern device to exclude the black man from voting solely on account of his color, Washington did not favor universal suffrage. He believed in literacy and property tests, fairly enforced. He was no democrat. And he did not believe in woman suffrage, either.

In his eagerness to establish common ground with whites, that is, with some whites, Washington overstepped his purpose in public speeches by telling chicken-thief, mule, and other dialect stories intended to appeal to white stereotypes of blacks, and he occasionally spoke of the Afro-American as "a child race." No doubt his intent was to disarm his listeners, and before mixed audiences he often alternately addressed the two groups, reassuring whites that blacks should cooperate with their white neighbors in all constructive efforts, but saying to blacks that in their cooperation there should be "no unmanly cowering or stooping." At the cost of some forcefulness of presentation, Washington did have a remarkable capacity to convince whites as well as blacks that he not only understood them but agreed with them. It is one of Washington's intangible qualities as a black leader that he could influence, if not lead, so many whites. The agreement that whites sensed in him was more in his manner than in his program or goals, which always included human rights as well as material advancement for blacks.

In his constant effort to influence public opinion, Washington relied on the uncertain instruments of the press and the public platform. A flood of books and articles appeared over his name, largely written by his private secretary and a stable of ghostwriters, because he was too busy to do much writing. His ghostwriters were able and faithful, but they could not put new words or new ideas out over his signature, so for the crucial twenty years after 1895, Washington's writings showed no fresh creativity or real response to events, only a steady flood of platitudes. Washington's speeches generally suffered from an opposite handicap, that he was the only one who could deliver them. But he was too busy making two or three speeches a day to write a new one for each occasion, so the audiences rather than the speeches changed. But everywhere he went, North, South, or West, he drew large crowds ready to hear or rehear his platitudes.

Washington did try to change his world by other means. Some forms of racial injustice, such as lynching, disfranchisement, and unequal facilities in education and transportation, Washington dealt with publicly and directly. Early in his career as a leader he tried to sidestep the lynching question by saying that, deplorable though it was, he was too busy working for the education of black youth to divide his energies by dealing with other public questions. Friends and critics alike sharply told him that if he proposed to be a leader of blacks, he was going to have to deal with this subject. So he began an annual letter on lynching that he sent to all the southern white dailies, and he made Tuskegee Institute the center of statistical and news information on lynching. He always took a moderate tone, deplored rape and crime by blacks, but always denied that the crime blacks committed was either the cause of or justification for the crime of lynching. He tried to make up for his moderation by persistence, factual accuracy, and persuasive logic. Disfranchisement of black voters swept through the South from Texas to Virginia during Washington's day. He publicly protested in letters to the constitutional conventions and legislatures in Alabama, Georgia, and Louisiana and aided similar efforts in several other states. He failed to stop lynching, to prevent the loss of voting rights, and to clean up the Jim Crow cars or bring about even minimal standards of fairness in the public schools. But he did try.

As for social segregation, Washington abided by southern customs while in the South but forthrightly declared it unreasonable for white southerners to dictate his behavior outside of the South. His celebrated dinner at the White House in 1901, therefore, though it caused consternation and protest among white southerners, was consistent with his lifetime practice. Tuskegee Institute underwent an elaborate ritual of segregation with every white visitor, but the man who came to dinner at the White House, had tea with the queen of England, and attended hundreds of banquets and private meals with whites outside the South certainly never internalized the attitudes of the segregators.

What Washington could not do publicly to achieve equal rights, he sought to accomplish secretly. He spent four years in cooperation with the Afro-American Council on a court case to test the constitutionality of the Louisiana grandfather clause, providing funds from his own pocket and from northern white liberal friends. In his own state of Alabama, Washington secretly directed the efforts of his personal lawyer to carry two grandfather-clause cases all the way to the U.S. Supreme Court, where they were lost on technicalities. He took the extra precaution of using code names in all the correspondence on the Alabama cases. Through private pressure on railroad officials and congressmen, Washington tried to bring about improvement in the Jim Crow cars and railroad waiting rooms. He had more success in the Dan Rogers case, which overturned a criminal verdict against a black man because blacks were excluded from the jury. He also secretly collaborated with two southern white attorneys to defend Alonzo Bailey, a farm laborer held in peonage for debt; the outcome here was also successful, for the Alabama peonage law was declared unconstitutional. These and other secret actions were certainly not enough to tear down the legal structure of white supremacy, but they show that Washington's role in Afro-American history was not always that of the accommodationist "heavy." He was working, at several levels and in imaginative ways, and always with vigor, toward goals similar to those of his critics. If his methods did not work, the same could be said of theirs. And he did not take these civil rights actions as a means of answering criticism, because he kept his part in the court cases a secret except to a handful of confidants, a secret not revealed until his papers were opened to historians in recent decades.

There was another, uglier side of Washington's secret behavior, however—his ruthless spying and sabotage against his leading black critics. Washington never articulated a justification for these actions, perhaps because, being secret, they did not require defense. And yet Washington and Emmett Scott left the evidence of his secret machinations undestroyed in his papers, apparently in the faith that history would vindicate him when all the facts were known. Then, too, Washington was not given to explaining himself. . . .

The Booker T. Washington who emerges into the light of history from his private papers is a complex, Faustian character quite different from the paragon of self-uplift and Christian forbearance that Washington projected in his autobiography. On the other hand, there is little evidence for and much evidence against the charge of some of his contemporaries that he was simply an accommodationist who bargained away his race's birthright for a mess of pottage. Nor does he fit some historians' single-factor explanations of his career: that he offered "education for the new slavery," that he was a proto-black-nationalist, that he was or must have been psychologically crippled by the constraints and guilt feelings of his social role.

Washington's complexity should not be overstressed, however, for the more we know about anybody the more complex that person seems. And through the complexity of Washington's life, its busyness and its multiple levels, two main themes stand out, his true belief in his program for black progress and his great skill in and appetite for politics, broadly defined, serving both his goals and his personal power.

First, let us look closely at Washington's industrial education and small business program. It may have been anachronistic preparation for the age of mass production and corporate gigantism then coming into being, but it had considerable social realism for a black population which was, until long after Washington's death, predominantly rural and southern. Furthermore, it was well attuned to the growth and changing character of black business in his day. Increasingly, the nineteenth-century black businesses catering to white clients surrendered predominance to ghetto businesses such as banks, insurance companies, undertakers, and barbers catering to black customers. These new businessmen, with a vested interest in black solidarity, were the backbone of Washington's National Negro Business League. Washington clearly found congenial the prospect of an elite class of self-made businessmen as leaders and models for the struggling masses. There was also room for the Talented Tenth of professional men in the Tuskegee Machine, however. Washington welcomed every college-educated recruit he could secure. Directly or through agents, he was the largest employer in the country of black college graduates.

Second, let us consider Washington as a powerful politician. Though he warned young men away from politics as a dead-end career, what distinguished Washington's career was not his rather conventional goals, which in public or private he shared with almost every other black spokesman, but his consummate political skill, his wheeling and dealing. . . .

Washington's program was not consensus politics, for he always sought change, and there was always vocal opposition to him on both sides that he never tried to mollify. Denounced on the one hand by the Niagara Movement and the NAACP for not protesting enough, he was also distrusted and denounced by white supremacists for bringing the wooden horse within the walls of Troy. All of the racist demagogues of his time—Benjamin Tillman, James Vardaman, Theodore Bilbo, Thomas Dixon, and J. Thomas Heflin, to name a few—called Washington their insidious enemy. One descriptive label for Washington might be centrist coalition politics. The Tuskegee Machine had the middle and undecided majority of white and black people behind it. Washington was a rallying point for the southern moderates, the northern publicists and makers of opinion, and the thousands who read his autobiography or crowded into halls to hear him. Among blacks he had the businessmen solidly behind him, and even, as August Meier has shown, a majority of the Talented Tenth of professional men, so great was his power to reward and punish, to make or break careers. He had access to the wellsprings of philanthropy, political preferment, and other white sources of black opportunity. For blacks at the bottom of the ladder, Washington's program offered education, a self-help formula, and, importantly for a group demor-alized by the white aggression of that period, a social philosophy that gave dignity and purpose to lives of daily toil.

It could be said with some justification that the Tuskegee Machine was a stationary machine, that it went nowhere. Because the machine was held together by the glue of self-interest, Washington was frequently disappointed by the inadequate response of his allies. The southern upper class did not effectively resist disfranchisement as he had hoped and never gave blacks the equal economic chance that he considered an integral part of the Atlanta Compromise. Washington's philanthropist-friends never stood up for equal opportunity in public education. Black businessmen frequently found their own vested interest in a captive market rather than a more open society. And Washington himself often took the view that whatever was good for Tuskegee and himself was good for the Negro.

To the charge that he accomplished nothing, it can only be imagined what Washington would have answered, since he did not have the years of hindsight and self-justification that some of his critics enjoyed. He would probably have stressed how much worse the southern racial reaction would have been without his coalition of moderates, his soothing syrup, and his practical message to blacks of self-improvement and progress along the lines of least resistance. Washington's power over his following, and hence his power to bring about change, have probably been exaggerated. It was the breadth rather than the depth of his coalition that was unique. Perhaps one Booker T. Washington was enough. But even today, in a very different society, Washington's autobiography is still in print. It still has some impalpable power to bridge the racial gap, to move new readers to take the first steps across the color line. Many of his ideas of self-help and racial solidarity still have currency in the black community. But he was an important leader because, like Frederick Douglass before him and Martin Luther King after him, he had the program and strategy and skill to influence the behavior of not only the Afro-American one-tenth, but the white nine-tenths of the American people. He was a political realist.

POSTSCRIPT

Did Booker T. Washington's Philosophy and Actions Betray the Interests of African Americans?

Discussions of race relations in the late nineteenth- and early twentieth-century United States invariably focus upon the ascendancy of Booker T. Washington, his apparent accommodation to existing patterns of racial segregation, and the conflicting traditions within black thought, epitomized by the clash between Washington and Du Bois. Seldom, however, is attention given to black nationalist thought in the "age of Booker T. Washington."

Black nationalism, centered on the concept of racial solidarity, has been a persistent theme in African American history and reached one of its most important stages of development between 1880 and 1920. In the late 1800s, Henry McNeal Turner and Edward Wilmot Blyden encouraged greater interest in the repatriation of black Americans to Africa, especially Liberia. This goal continued into the twentieth century and culminated in the "Back-to-Africa" program of Marcus Garvey and his Universal Negro Improvement Association. Interestingly, Booker T. Washington also exhibited nationalist sentiment by encouraging blacks to withdraw from white society, develop their own institutions and businesses, and engage in economic and moral uplift. Washington's nationalism concentrated on economic self-help and manifested itself in 1900 with the establishment of the National Negro Business League.

A thorough assessment of the protest and accommodationist views of black Americans is presented in August Meier, *Negro Thought in America, 1800-1915* (University of Michigan Press, 1963). Rayford Logan, *The Betrayal of the Negro: From Rutherford B. Hayes to Woodrow Wilson* (Macmillan, 1965), describes the last quarter of the nineteenth century as "the nadir" for black life. By far the best studies of Booker T. Washington are two volumes by Louis R. Harlan: *Booker T. Washington: The Making of a Black Leader, 1856-1901* (Oxford University Press, 1972) and *Booker T. Washington: The Wizard of Tuskegee, 1901-1915* (Oxford University Press, 1983). For assessments of two of Booker T. Washington's harshest critics, see Elliott M. Rudwick, *W. E. B. Du Bois: A Study in Minority Group Leadership* (University of Pennsylvania Press,

1960), and Stephen R. Fox, *The Guardian of Boston: William Monroe Trotter* (Atheneum, 1970). John H. Bracey, Jr., August Meier, and Elliott Rudwick, *Black Nationalism in America* (Bobbs-Merrill, 1970), provide an invaluable collection of documents pertaining to black nationalism. See also Edwin S. Redkey, *Black Exodus: Black Nationalist and Back-to-Africa Movements, 1890–1910* (Yale University Press, 1969), and Hollis R. Lynch, *Edward Wilmot Blyden: Pan-Negro Patriot, 1832–1912* (Oxford University Press, 1967). Diverse views of Marcus Garvey, who credited Booker T. Washington with inspiring him to seek a leadership role on behalf of African Americans, are found in Edmund David Cronon, *Black Moses: The Story of Marcus Garvey and the Universal Negro Improvement Association* (University of Wisconsin Press, 1955); Tony Martin, *Race First: The Ideological and Organizational Struggles of Marcus Garvey and the UNIA* (Greenwood Press, 1976); and Judith Stein, *The World of Marcus Garvey: Race and Class in Modern Society* (Louisiana State University Press, 1986).

ISSUE 8

Did the Progressives Fail?

YES: Richard M. Abrams, from "The Failure of Progressivism," in Richard Abrams and Lawrence Levine, eds., *The Shaping of the Twentieth Century*, 2d ed. (Little, Brown, 1971)

NO: Arthur S. Link and Richard L. McCormick, from *Progressivism* (Harlan Davidson, 1983)

ISSUE SUMMARY

YES: Professor of history Richard M. Abrams maintains that progressivism was a failure because it tried to impose a uniform set of values upon a culturally diverse people and never seriously confronted the inequalities which still exist in American society.
NO: Professors of history Arthur S. Link and Richard L. McCormick argue that the Progressives were a diverse group of reformers who confronted and ameliorated the worst abuses that emerged in urban industrial America during the early 1900s.

Progressivism is a word used by historians to define the reform currents in the years between the end of the Spanish-American War and America's entrance into the Great War in Europe in 1917. The so-called Progressive movement had been in operation for over a decade before the label was first used in the 1919 electoral campaigns. Former president Theodore Roosevelt ran as a third-party candidate in the 1912 election on the Progressive party ticket, but in truth the party had no real organization outside of the imposing figure of Theodore Roosevelt. Therefore, as a label, "progressivism" was rarely used as a term of self-identification for its supporters. Even after 1912, it was more frequently used by journalists and historians to distinguish the reformers of the period from socialists and old-fashioned conservatives.

The 1890s was a crucial decade for many Americans. From 1893 until almost the turn of the century, the nation went through a terrible economic depression. With the forces of industrialization, urbanization, and immigration wreaking havoc upon the traditional political, social, and economic structures of American life, changes were demanded. The reformers responded in a variety of ways. The proponents of good government believed that democracy was threatened because the cities were ruled by corrupt political machines while the state legislatures were dominated by corporate interests. The cure was to purify democracy and place government directly in the hands of the people through such devices as the initiative, referendum, recall, and the direct election of local school board officials, judges, and U.S. senators.

Social justice proponents saw the problem from a different perspective. Settlement workers moved into cities and tried to change the urban environment. They pushed for sanitation improvements, tenement house reforms, factory inspection laws, regulation of the hours and wages of women, and the abolition of child labor.

A third group of reformers considered the major problem to be the trusts. They argued for controls over the power of big business and for the preservation of the free enterprise system. Progressives disagreed whether the issue was size or conduct and whether the remedy was trust-busting or the regulation of big business. But none could deny the basic question: How was the relationship between big business and the U.S. government to be defined?

How successful was the Progressive movement? What triggered the reform impulse? Who were its leaders? How much support did it attract? More important, did the laws which resulted from the various movements fulfill the intentions of its leaders and supporters?

In the following selections, Richard M. Abrams performs a real service in distinguishing the Progressives from other reformers of the era, such as the Populists, the Socialists, the mainstream labor unions, and the corporate reorganization movement. According to Abrams, the Progressive movement failed because it tried to impose a uniform set of middle-class Protestant moral values upon a nation which was growing more culturally diverse, and because the reformers supported movements which brought about no actual changes or only superficial ones at best. The real inequalities in American society, says Abrams, were never addressed.

In contrast, Arthur S. Link and Richard L. McCormick view progressivism from the point of view of the reformers and rank it as a qualified success. They survey the criticisms of the movement made by historians since the 1950s and generally find them unconvincing. They believe that the Progressives made the first real attempts to change the destructive direction modern urban-industrial society was taking.

YES

THE FAILURE OF PROGRESSIVISM

Our first task is definitional, because clearly it would be possible to beg the whole question of "failure" by means of semantical niceties. I have no intention of being caught in that kind of critics' trap. I hope to establish that there was a distinctive major reform movement that took place during most of the first two decades of this century, that it had a mostly coherent set of characteristics and long-term objectives, and that, measured by its own criteria—not criteria I should wish, through hindsight and preference, to impose on it—it fell drastically short of its chief goals.

One can, of course, define a reform movement so broadly that merely to acknowledge that we are where we are and that we enjoy some advantages over where we were would be to prove the "success" of the movement. In many respects, Arthur Link does this sort of thing, both in his and William B. Catton's popular textbook, *American Epoch*, and in his article, "What Happened to the Progressive Movement in the 1920's?" In the latter, Link defines "progressivism" as a movement that "began convulsively in the 1890's and waxed and waned afterward to our own time, to insure the survival of democracy in the United States by the enlargement of governmental power to control and offset the power of private economic groups over the nation's institutions and life." Such a definition may be useful to classify data gathered to show the liberal sources of the enlargement of governmental power since the 1890's; but such data would not be finely classified enough to tell us much about the *non*liberal sources of governmental power (which were numerous and important), about the distinctive styles of different generations of reformers concerned with a liberal society, or even about vital distinctions among divergent reform groups in the era that contemporaries and the conventional historical wisdom have designed as progressive. . . .

Now, without going any further into the problem of historians' definitions which are too broad or too narrow—there is no space here for such an effort—I shall attempt a definition of my own, beginning with the problem that contemporaries set themselves to solve and that gave the era its cognomen, "progressive." That problem was *progress*—or more specifically,

From Richard M. Abrams, "The Failure of Progressivism," in Abrams and Levine, eds., *The Shaping of the Twentieth Century*, 2d ed. (Boston: Little, Brown, 1971). Copyright © 1971 by Richard M. Abrams. Reprinted by permission of the author.

how American society was to continue to enjoy the fruits of material progress without the accompanying assault upon human dignity and the erosion of the conventional values and moral assumptions on which the social order appeared to rest. . . .

To put it briefly and yet more specifically, a very large body of men and women entered into reform activities at the end of the nineteenth century to translate "the national credo" (as Henry May calls it) into a general program for social action. Their actions, according to Richard Hofstadter, were "founded upon the indigenous Yankee-Protestant political tradition [that] assumed and demanded the constant disinterested activity of the citizen in public affairs, argued that political life ought to be run, to a greater degree than it was, in accordance with general principles and abstract laws apart from and superior to personal needs, and expressed a common feeling that government should be in good part an effort to moralize the lives of individuals while economic life should be intimately related to the stimulation and development of individual character."

The most consistently important reform impulse, among *many* reform impulses, during the progressive era grew directly from these considerations. It is this reform thrust that we should properly call "the progressive movement." We should distinguish it carefully from reform movements in the era committed primarily to other considerations.

The progressive movement drew its strength from the old mugwump reform impulse, civil service reform, female emancipationists, prohibitionists, the social gospel, the settlement-house movement, some national expansionists, some world peace advocates, conservation advocates, technical efficiency experts, and a wide variety of intellectuals who helped cut through the stifling, obstructionist smokescreen of systematized ignorance. It gained powerful allies from many disadvantaged business interests that appealed to politics to redress unfavorable trade positions; from some ascendant business interests seeking institutional protection; from publishers who discovered the promotional value of exposés; and from politicians-on-the-make who sought issues with which to dislodge long-lived incumbents from their place. Objectively it focused on or expressed (1) a concern for responsive, honest, and efficient government, on the local and state levels especially; (2) recognition of the obligations of society—particularly of an affluent society—to its underprivileged; (3) a desire for more rational use of the nation's resources and economic energies; (4) a rejection, on at least intellectual grounds, of certain social principles that had long obstructed social remedies for what had traditionally been regarded as irremediable evils, such as poverty; and, above all, (5) a concern for the maintenance or restoration of a consensus on what conventionally had been regarded as *fixed moral* principles. "The first and central faith in the national credo," writes Professor May, "was, as it always had been, the reality, certainty, and eternity of moral values. . . . A few thought and said that ultimate values and goals were unnecessary, but in most cases this meant that they believed so deeply in a consensus on these matters that they could not imagine a serious challenge." Progressives shared this faith with most of the rest of the country, but they also conceived of themselves, with a grand sense of stewardship, as its heralds, and its agents.

The progressive movement was (and is) distinguishable from other contemporary reform movements not only by its devotion to social conditions regarded, by those within it as well as by much of the generality, as *normative*, but also by its definition of what forces threatened that order. More specifically, progressivism directed its shafts at five principal enemies, each in its own way representing reform:

1. The *socialist reform movement*—because, despite socialism's usually praiseworthy concern for human dignity, it represented the subordination of the rights of private property and of individualistic options to objectives that often explicitly threatened common religious beliefs and conventional standards of justice and excellence.

2. The corporate reorganization of American business, which I should call *the corporate reform movement* (its consequence has, after all, been called "the corporate revolution")—because it challenged the traditional relationship of ownership and control of private property, because it represented a shift from production to profits in the entrepreneurial definition of efficiency, because it threatened the proprietary small-business character of the American social structure, because it had already demonstrated a capacity for highly concentrated and socially irresponsible power, and because it sanctioned practices that strained the limits of conventionality and even legality.

3. *The labor union movement*—because despite the virtues of unionized labor as a source of countervailing force against the corporations and as a basis for a more orderly labor force, unionism (like corporate capitalism and socialism) suggested a reduction of individualistic options (at least for wage-earners and especially for small employers), and a demand for a partnership with business management in the decision-making process by a class that convention excluded from such a role.

4. *Agrarian radicalism*, and populism in particular—because it, too, represented (at least in appearance) the insurgency of a class conventionally believed to be properly excluded from a policy-making role in the society, a class graphically represented by the "Pitchfork" Bens and "Sockless" Jerrys, the "Cyclone" Davises and "Alfalfa" Bills, the wool hat brigade and the rednecks.

5. *The ethnic movement*—the demand for specific political and social recognition of ethnic or ex-national affiliations—because accession to the demand meant acknowledgment of the fragmentation of American society as well as a retreat from official standards of integrity, honesty, and efficiency in government in favor of standards based on personal loyalty, partisanship, and sectarian provincialism.

Probably no two progressives opposed all of these forces with equal animus, and most had a noteworthy sympathy for one or more of them. . . .

So much for what progressivism was not. Let me sum it up by noting that what it rejected and sought to oppose necessarily says much about what it was—perhaps even more than can be ascertained by the more direct approach.

My thesis is that progressivism failed. It failed in what it—or what those who shaped it—conceived to be its principal objective. And that was, over and above everything else, to restore or maintain the conventional consensus on a particular view of the universe, a particular set of values, and a particular constellation of behavioral modes in the country's commerce, its industry, its social relations, and its politics. Such a view, such values, such modes were challenged by the influx of diverse religious and ethnic elements into the nation's social and intellectual stream, by the overwhelming economic success and power of the corporate form of business organization, by the subordination of the work-ethic bound up within the old proprietary and craft enterprise system, and by the increasing centrality of a growing proportion of low-income, unskilled, wage-earning classes in the nation's economy and social structure. Ironically, the *coup de grâce* would be struck by the emergence of a philosophical and scientific rationale for the existence of cultural diversity within a single social system, a rationale that largely grew out of the very intellectual ferment to which progressivism so substantially contributed.

Progressivism sought to save the old view, and the old values and modes, by educating the immigrants and the poor so as to facilitate their acceptance of and absorption into the Anglo-American mode of life, or by excluding the "unassimilable" altogether; by instituting antitrust legislation or, at the least, by imposing regulations upon corporate practices in order to preserve a minimal base for small proprietary business enterprise; by making legislative accommodations to the newly important wage-earning classes—accommodations that might provide some measure of wealth and income redistribution, on-the-job safety, occupational security, and the like—so as to forestall a forcible transfer of policy-making power away from the groups that had conventionally exercised that power; and by broadening the political selection process, through direct elections, direct nominations, and direct

legislation, in order to reduce tensions caused unnecessarily by excessively narrow and provincial cliques of policymakers. When the economic and political reforms failed to restore the consensus by giving the previously unprivileged an ostensible stake in it, progressive energies turned increasingly toward using the force of the state to proscribe or restrict specifically opprobrious modes of social behavior, such as gaming habits, drinking habits, sexual habits, and Sabbatarian habits. In the ultimate resort, with the proliferation of sedition and criminal syndicalist laws, it sought to constrict political discourse itself. And (except perhaps for the disintegration of the socialist movement) *that* failed, too.

One measure of progressivism's failure lies in the xenophobic racism that reappeared on a large scale even by 1910. In many parts of the country, for example, in the far west and the south, racism and nativism had been fully blended with reform movements even at the height of progressive activities there. The alleged threats of "coolie labor" to American living standards, and of "venal" immigrant and Negro voting to republican institutions generally, underlay the alliance of racism and reform in this period. By and large, however, for the early progressive era the alliance was conspicuous only in the south and on the west coast. By 1910, signs of heightening ethnic animosities, most notably anti-Catholicism, began appearing in other areas of the country as well. As John Higham has written, "It is hard to explain the rebirth of anti-Catholic ferment [at this time] except as an outlet for expectations which progressivism raised and then failed to fulfill." The failure here was in part the inability of reform to deliver a meaningful share of the social surplus to the groups left out of the general national progress, and in part the inability of reform to achieve its objective of assimilation and consensus.

The growing ethnic animus, moreover, operated to compound the difficulty of achieving assimilation. By the second decade of the century, the objects of the antagonism were beginning to adopt a frankly assertive posture. The World War, and the ethnic cleavages it accentuated and aggravated, represented only the final blow to the assimilationist idea; "hyphenate" tendencies had already been growing during the years before 1914. It had only been in 1905 that the Louisville-born and secular-minded Louis Brandeis had branded as "disloyal" all who "keep alive" their differences of origin or religion. By 1912, by now a victim of anti-Semitism and aware of a rising hostility toward Jews in the country, Brandeis had become an active Zionist; before a Jewish audience in 1913, he remarked how "practical experience" had convinced him that "to be good Americans, we must be better Jews, and to be better Jews, we must become Zionists."

Similarly, American Negroes also began to adopt a more aggressive public stance after having been subdued for more than a decade by antiblack violence and the accommodationist tactics suggested in 1895 by Booker T. Washington. As early as 1905, many black leaders had broken with Washington in founding the Niagara Movement for a more vigorous assertion of Negro demands for equality. But most historians seem to agree that it was probably the Springfield race riot of 1908 that ended illusions that black people could gain an equitable share in the rewards of American culture by accommodationist or assimilationist methods.

The organization of the NAACP in 1909 gave substantive force for the first time to the three-year-old Niagara Movement. The year 1915 symbolically concluded the demise of accommodationism. That year, the Negro-baiting movie, "The Birth of a Nation," played to massive, enthusiastic audiences that included notably the president of the United States and the chief justice of the Supreme Court; the KKK was revived; and Booker T. Washington died. The next year, black nationalist Marcus Garvey arrived in New York from Jamaica.

Meanwhile, scientific knowledge about race and culture was undergoing a crucial revision. At least in small part stimulated by a keen self-consciousness of his own "outsider" status in American culture, the German-Jewish immigrant Franz Boas was pioneering in the new anthropological concept of "cultures," based on the idea that human behavioral traits are conditioned by historical traditions. The new view of culture was in time to undermine completely the prevailing evolutionary view that ethnic differences must mean racial inequality. The significance of Boas's work after 1910, and that of his students A. L. Kroeber and Clyde Kluckhohn in particular, rests on the fact that the racist thought of the progressive era had founded its intellectual rationale on the monistic, evolutionary view of culture; and indeed much of the progressives' anxiety over the threatened demise of "the American culture" had been founded on that view.

Other intellectual developments as well had for a long time been whittling away at the notion that American society had to stand or fall on the unimpaired coherence of its cultural consensus. Yet the new work in anthropology, law, philosophy, physics, psychology, and literature only unwittingly undermined that assumption. Rather, it was only as the ethnic hostilities grew, and especially as the power of the state came increasingly to be invoked against dissenting groups whose ethnic "peculiarities" provided an excuse for repression, that the new intelligence came to be developed. "The world has thought that it must have its culture and its political unity coincide," wrote Randolph Bourne in 1916 while chauvinism, nativism, and antiradicalism were mounting; now it was seeing that cultural diversity might yet be the salvation of the liberal society—that it might even serve to provide the necessary countervailing force to the power of the state that private property had once served (in the schema of Locke, Harrington, and Smith) before the interests of private property became so highly concentrated and so well blended with the state itself.

The telltale sign of progressivism's failure was the violent crusade against dissent that took place in the closing years of the Wilson administration. It is too easy to ascribe the literal hysteria of the postwar years to the dislocations of the War alone. Incidents of violent repression of labor and radical activities had been growing remarkably, often in step with xenophobic outbreaks, for several years before America's intervention in the War. To quote Professor Higham once more. "The seemingly unpropitious circumstances under which antiradicalism and anti-Catholicism came to life [after 1910] make their renewal a subject of moment." It seems clear that they both arose out of the sources of the reform ferment itself. When reform failed to enlarge the consensus, or to make it more relevant to the needs of the still disadvantaged and disaffected, and when in fact reform seemed to be encouraging more radical challenges to the social order, the old anxieties of the 1890's returned.

The postwar hysteria represented a reaction to a confluence of anxiety-laden developments, including the high cost of living, the physical and social dislocations of war mobilization and the recruitment of women and Negroes into war production jobs in the big northern cities, the Bolshevik Revolution, a series of labor strikes, and a flood of radical literature that exaggerated the capabilities of radical action. "One Hundred Per Cent Americanism" seemed the only effective way of meeting all these challenges at once. As Stanley Coben has written, making use of recent psychological studies and anthropological work on cultural "revitalization movements": "Citizens who joined the crusade for one hundred per cent Americanism sought, primarily, a unifying force which would halt the apparent disintegration of their culture. . . . The slight evidence of danger from radical organizations aroused such wild fear only because Americans had already encountered other threats to cultural stability."

Now, certainly during the progressive era a lot of reform legislation was passed, much that contributed genuinely to a more liberal society, though more that contributed to the more absolutistic moral objectives of progressivism. Progressivism indeed had real, lasting effects for the blunting of the sharper edges of self-interest in American life, and for the reduction of the harsher cruelties suffered by the society's underprivileged. These achievements deserve emphasis, not least because they derived directly from the progressive habit of looking to standards of conventional morality and human decency for the solution of diverse social conflicts. But the deeper nature of the problem confronting American society required more than the invocation of conventional standards; the conventions themselves were at stake, especially as they bore upon the allocation of privileges and rewards. Because most of the progressives never confronted that problem, in a way their efforts were doomed to failure.

In sum, the overall effect of the period's legislation is not so impressive. For example, all the popular government measures put together have not conspicuously raised the quality of American political life. Direct nominations and elections have tended to make political campaigns so expensive as to reduce the number of eligible candidates for public office to (1) the independently wealthy; (2) the ideologues, especially on the right, who can raise the needed campaign money from independently wealthy ideologues like themselves, or from the organizations set up to promote a particular ideology; and (3) party hacks who pay off their debt to the party treasury by whistle-stopping and chicken dinner speeches. Direct legislation through the Initiative and Referendum device has made cities and states prey to the best-financed and -organized special-interest group pressures, as have so-called nonpartisan elections. Which is not to say that things are worse than before, but only that they are not conspicuously better. The popular government measures did have the effect of shaking up the established political organizations of the day, and that may well have been their only real purpose.

But as Arthur Link has said, in his text, *The American Epoch*, the popular government measures "were merely instruments to facilitate the capture of political machinery. . . . They must be judged for what they accomplished or failed to accomplish on the higher level of substantive reform." Without disparaging the long list of reform measures that passed during the progressive era, the question remains whether all the "substantive reforms" together accomplished what the progressives wanted them to accomplish.

Certain social and economic advantages were indeed shuffled about, but this must be regarded as a short-term achievement for special groups at best. Certain commercial interests, for example, achieved greater political leverage in railroad policy-making than they had had in 1900 through measures such as the Hepburn and Mann-Elkins Acts—though it was not until the 1940's that any real change occurred in the general rate structure, as some broad regional interests had been demanding at the beginning of the century. Warehouse, farm credits, and land-bank acts gave the diminishing numbers of farm owners enhanced opportunities to mortgage their property, and some business groups had persuaded the federal government to use national revenues to educate farmers on how to increase their productivity (Smith-Lever Act, 1914); but most farmers remained as dependent as ever upon forces beyond their control—the bankers, the middlemen, the international market. The FTC, and the Tariff Commission established in 1916, extended the principle of using government agencies to adjudicate intra-industrial conflicts ostensibly in the national interest, but these agencies would develop a lamentable tendency of deferring to and even confirming rather than moderating the power of each industry's dominant interests. The Federal Reserve Act made the currency more flexible, and that certainly made more sense than the old system, as even the bankers agreed. But depositers would be as prey to defaulting banks as they had been in the days of the Pharaoh—bank deposit insurance somehow was "socialism" to even the best of men in this generation. And despite Woodrow Wilson's brave promise to end the banker's stifling hold on innovative small business, one searches in vain for some provision in the FRA designed specifically to encourage small or new businesses. In fact, the only constraints on the bankers' power that emerged from the era came primarily from the ability of the larger corporations to finance their own expansion out of capital surpluses they had accumulated from extortionate profits during the War.

A major change almost occurred during the war years when organized labor and the principle of collective bargaining received official recognition and a handful of labor leaders was taken, temporarily, into policy-making councils (e.g., in the War Labor Board). But actually, as already indicated, such a development, if it had been made permanent, would have represented a defeat, not a triumph, for progressivism. The progressives may have fought for improved labor conditions, but they jealously fought against the enlargement of union power. It was no aberration that once the need for wartime productive efficiency evaporated, leading progressives such as A. Mitchell Palmer, Miles Poindexter, and Woodrow Wilson himself helped civic and employer organizations to bludgeon the labor movement into disunity and docility. (It is possible, I suppose, to argue that such progressives were simply inconsistent, but if we understand progressivism in the terms I have outlined above I

think the consistency is more evident.) Nevertheless, a double irony is worth noting with respect to progressivism's objectives and the wartime labor developments. On the one hand, the progressives' hostility to labor unions defeated their own objectives of (1) counterbalancing the power of collectivized capital (i.e., corporations), and (2) enhancing workers' share of the nation's wealth. On the other hand, under wartime duress, the progressives did grant concessions to organized labor (e.g., the Adamson Eight-Hour Railway Labor Act, as well as the WLB) that would later serve as precedents for the very "collectivization" of the economic situation that they were dedicated to oppose.

Meanwhile, the distribution of advantages in the society did not change much at all. In some cases, from the progressive reformers' viewpoint at least, it may even have changed for the worse. According to the figures of the National Industrial Conference Board, even income was as badly distributed at the end of the era as before. In 1921, the highest 10 percent of income recipients received 38 percent of total personal income, and that figure was only 34 percent in 1910. (Since the share of the top 5 percent of income recipients probably declined in the 1910–20 period, the figures for the top 10 percent group suggest a certain improvement in income distribution at the top. But the fact that the share of the lowest 60 percent also declined in that period, from 35 percent to 30 percent, confirms the view that no meaningful improvement can be shown.) Maldistribution was to grow worse until after 1929.

American farmers on the whole and in particular seemed to suffer increasing disadvantages. Farm life was one of the institutional bulwarks of the mode of life the progressives ostensibly cherished. "The farmer who owns his land," averred Gifford Pinchot, "is still the backbone of the Nation; and one of the things we want most is more of him, . . . [for] he is the first of home-makers." If only in the sense that there were relatively fewer farmers in the total population at the end of the progressive era, one would have to say farm life in the United States had suffered. But, moreover, fewer owned their own farms. The number of farm tenants increased by 21 percent from 1900 to 1920; 38.1 percent of all farm operators in 1921 were tenants; and the figures look even worse when one notices that tenancy *declined* in the most *impoverished* areas during this period, suggesting that the family farm was surviving mostly in the more marginal agricultural areas. Finally, although agriculture had enjoyed some of its most prosperous years in history in the 1910-20 period, the 21 percent of the nation's gainfully employed who were in agriculture in 1919 (a peak year) earned only 16 percent of the national income.

While progressivism failed to restore vitality to American farming, it failed also to stop the vigorous ascendancy of corporate capitalism, the most conspicuous challenge to conventional values and modes that the society faced at the beginning of the era. The corporation had drastically undermined the very basis of the traditional rationale that had supported the nation's freewheeling system of resource allocation and had underwritten the permissiveness of the laws governing economic activities in the nineteenth century. The new capitalism by-passed the privately-owned proprietary firm, it featured a separation of ownership and control, it subordinated the profit motive to varied and variable other

objectives such as empire-building, and, in many of the techniques developed by financial brokers and investment bankers, it appeared to create a great gulf between the making of money and the producing of useful goods and services. Through a remarkable series of judicial sophistries, this nonconventional form of business enterprise had become, in law, a *person*, and had won privileges and liberties once entrusted only to men, who were presumed to be conditioned and restrained by the moral qualities that inhere in human nature. Although gaining legal dispensations from an obliging Supreme Court, the corporation could claim no theoretical legitimacy beyond the fact of its power and its apparent inextricable entanglement in the business order that had produced America's seemingly unbounded material success.

Although much has been written about the supposed continuing vitality of small proprietary business enterprise in the United States, there is no gainsaying the continued ascendancy of the big corporation nor the fact that it still lacks legitimation. The fact that in the last sixty years the number of small proprietary businesses has grown at a rate that slightly exceeds the rate of population growth says little about the character of small business enterprise today as compared with that of the era of the American industrial revolution; it does nothing to disparage the apprehensions expressed in the antitrust campaigns of the progressives. To focus on the vast numbers of automobile dealers and gasoline service station owners, for example, is to miss completely their truly humble dependence upon the very few giant automobile and oil companies, a foretold dependence that was the very point of progressives' anticorporation, antitrust sentiments. The progressive movement must indeed be credited with placing real restraints upon monopolistic tendencies in the United States, for most statistics indicate that at least until the 1950's business concentration showed no substantial increase from the turn of the century (though it may be pertinent to note that concentration ratios did increase significantly in the decade immediately following the progressive era). But the statistics of concentration remain impressive—just as they were when John Moody wrote *The Truth About the Trusts* in 1904 and Louis Brandeis followed it with *Other People's Money* in 1914. That two hundred corporations (many of them interrelated) held almost one-quarter of all business assets, and more than 40 percent of all corporate assets in the country in 1948; that the fifty largest manufacturing corporations held 35 percent of all industrial assets in 1948, and 38 percent by 1962; and that a mere twenty-eight corporations or one one-thousandth of a percentage of all nonfinancial firms in 1956 employed 10 percent of all those employed in the nonfinancial industries, should be sufficient statistical support for the apprehensions of the progressive era—*just as it is testimony to the failure of the progressive movement to achieve anything substantial to alter the situation.*

Perhaps the crowning failure of progressivism was the American role in World War I. It is true that many progressives opposed America's intervention, but it is also true that a great many more supported it. The failure in progressivism lies not in the decision to intervene but in the futility of intervention measured by progressive expectations.

NO

Arthur S. Link and Richard L. McCormick

PROGRESSIVISM IN HISTORY

Convulsive reform movements swept across the American landscape from the 1890s to 1917. Angry farmers demanded better prices for their products, regulation of the railroads, and the destruction of what they thought was the evil power of bankers, middlemen, and corrupt politicians. Urban residents crusaded for better city services and more efficient municipal government. Members of various professions, such as social workers and doctors, tried to improve the dangerous and unhealthy conditions in which many people lived and worked. Businessmen, too, lobbied incessantly for goals which they defined as reform. Never before had the people of the United States engaged in so many diverse movements for the improvement of their political system, economy, and communities. By around 1910, many of these crusading men and women were calling themselves progressives. Ever since, historians have used the term *progressivism* to describe the many reform movements of the early twentieth century.

Yet in the goals they sought and the remedies they tried, the reformers were a varied and contradictory lot. Some progressives wanted to increase the political influence and control of ordinary people, while other progressives wanted to concentrate authority in experts. Many reformers tried to curtail the growth of large corporations; others accepted bigness in industry on account of its supposed economic benefits. Some progressives were genuinely concerned about the welfare of the "new" immigrants from southern and eastern Europe; other progressives sought, sometimes frantically, to "Americanize" the newcomers or to keep them out altogether. In general, progressives sought to improve the conditions of life and labor and to create as much social stability as possible. But each group of progressives had its own definitions of improvement and stability. In the face of such diversity, one historian, Peter G. Filene, has even argued that what has been called the progressive movement never existed as a historical phenomenon ("An Obituary for 'The Progressive Movement,' " *American Quarterly*, 1970).

Certainly there was no *unified* movement, but, like most students of the period, we consider progressivism to have been a real, vital, and significant phenomenon, one which contemporaries recognized and talked and fought about. Properly conceptualized, progressivism provides a useful framework for the history of the United States in the late nineteenth and early twentieth centuries.

One source of confusion and controversy about progressives and progressivism is the words themselves. They are often used judgmentally to describe people and changes which historians have deemed to be "good," "enlightened," and "farsighted." The progressives themselves naturally intended the words to convey such positive qualities, but we should not accept their usage uncritically. It might be better to avoid the terms progressive and progressivism altogether, but they are too deeply embedded in the language of contemporaries and historians to be ignored. Besides, we think that the terms have real meaning. In this book the words will be used neutrally, without any implicit judgment about the value of reform.

In the broadest sense, progressivism was the way in which a whole generation of Americans defined themselves politically and responded to the nation's problems at the turn of the century. The progressives made the first comprehensive efforts to grapple with the ills of a modern urban-industrial society. Hence the record of their achievements and failures has considerable relevance for our own time.

WHO WERE THE PROGRESSIVES?

Ever since the early twentieth century, people have argued about who the pro-gressives were and what they stood for. This may seem to be a strange topic of debate, but it really is not. Progressivism engaged many different groups of Americans, and each group of progressives naturally considered themselves to be the key reformers and thought that their own programs were the most important ones. Not surprisingly, historians ever since have had trouble agreeing on who really shaped progressivism and its goals. Scholars who have written about the period have variously identified farmers, the old middle classes, professionals, businessmen, and urban immigrants and ethnic groups as the core group of progressives. But these historians have succeeded in identifying *their* reformers only by defining progressivism narrowly, by excluding other reformers and reforms when they do not fall within some specific definition, and by resorting to such vague, catch-all adjectives as "middle class." . . .

The advocates of the middle-class view might reply that they intended to study the leaders of reform, not its supporters, to identify and describe the men and women who imparted the dominant character to progressivism, not its mass base. The study of leadership is surely a valid subject in its own right and is particularly useful for an understanding of progressivism. But too much focus on leadership conceals more than it discloses about early twentieth-century reform. The dynamics of progressivism were crucially generated by ordinary people—by the sometimes frenzied mass supporters of progressive leaders, by rank-and-file voters willing to trust a reform candidate. The chronology of progressivism can be traced by events which aroused large numbers of people—a sensational muckraking article, an outrageous political scandal, an eye-opening legislative investigation, or a tragic social calamity. Events such as these gave reform its rhythm and its power.

Progressivism cannot be understood without seeing how the masses of Americans perceived and responded to such events. Widely circulated magazines gave people everywhere the sordid facts of corruption and carried the clamor for reform into every city, village, and county. State and national election campaigns enabled progressive candidates to trumpet their programs. Almost no literate person in the United States in, say, 1906 could have been unaware that ten-year-old children worked through the night in dangerous factories, or that many United States senators served big business. Progressivism was the only reform movement ever experienced by the whole American nation. Its national appeal and mass base vastly exceeded that of Jacksonian reform. And progressivism's dependence on the people for its objectives and timing has no comparison in the executive-dominated New Deal of Franklin D. Roosevelt or the Great Society of Lyndon B. Johnson. Wars and depressions had previously engaged the whole nation, but never reform. And so we are back to the problem of how to explain and define the outpouring of progressive reform which excited and involved so many different kinds of people.

A little more than a decade ago, Buenker and Thelen recognized the immense diversity of progressivism and suggested ways in which to reorient the study of early twentieth-century reform. Buenker observed that divergent groups often came together on one issue and then changed alliances on the next ("The Progressive Era: A Search for a Synthesis," *Mid-America*, 1969). Indeed, different reformers sometimes favored the same measure for distinctive, even opposite, reasons. Progressivism could be understood only in the light of these shifting coalitions. Thelen, in his study of Wisconsin's legislature, also emphasized the importance of cooperation between different reform groups. "The basic riddle in Progressivism," he concluded, "is not what drove groups apart but what made them seek common cause."

There is a great deal of wisdom in these articles, particularly in their recognition of the diversity of progressivism and in the concept of shifting coalitions of reformers. A two-pronged approach is necessary to carry forward this way of looking at early twentieth-century reform. First, we should study, not an imaginary unified progressive movement, but individual reforms and give particular attention to the goals of their diverse supporters, the public rationales given for them, and the results which they achieved. Second, we should try to identify the features which were more or less common to different progressive reforms.

The first task—distinguishing the goals of a reform from its rhetoric and its results—is more difficult than it might appear to be. Older interpretations of progressivism implicitly assumed that the rhetoric explained the goals and that, if a proposed reform became law, the results fulfilled the intentions behind it. Neither assumption is a sound one: purposes, rationale, and results are three different things. Samuel P. Hays' influential article, "The Politics of Reform in Municipal Government in the Progressive Era" (*Pacific Northwest Quarterly*, 1964), exposed the fallacy of automatically equating the democratic rhetoric of the reformers with their true purposes. The two may have coincided, but the historian has to demonstrate that fact, not take it for granted. The unexamined identification of either intentions or rhetoric with results is also invalid, although it is still a common feature of the scholarship on progressivism. Only within the last decade have historians begun to examine the actual achievements of the reformers. To carry out this first task, in the following . . . we will distinguish between the goals and rhetoric of individual reforms and will discuss the results of reform whenever the current literature permits. To do so is to observe the ironies, complexities, and disappointments of progressivism.

The second task—that of identifying the common characteristics of progressivism—is even more difficult than the first but is an essential base on which to build an understanding of progressivism. The rest of this chapter focuses on identifying such characteristics. The place to begin that effort is the origins of progressivism. . . .

THE CHARACTER AND SPIRIT OF PROGRESSIVISM

Progressivism was characterized, in the first place, by a distinctive set of attitudes toward industrialism. By the turn of the century, the overwhelming majority of Americans had accepted the permanence of large-scale industrial, commercial, and financial enterprises and of the wage and factory systems. The progressives shared this attitude. Most were not socialists, and they undertook reform, not to dismantle modern economic institutions, but rather to ameliorate and improve the conditions of industrial life.

Yet progressivism was infused with a deep outrage against the worst consequences of industrialism. Outpourings of anger at corporate wrongdoing and of hatred for industry's callous pursuit of profit frequently punctuated the course of reform in the early twentieth century. Indeed, antibusiness emotion was a prime mover of progressivism. That the acceptance of industrialism *and* the outrage against it were intrinsic to early twentieth-century reform does not mean that progressivism was mindless or that it has to be considered indefinable. But it does suggest that there was a powerful irony in progressivism: reforms which gained support from a people angry with the oppressive aspects of industrialism also assisted the same persons to accommodate to it, albeit to an industrialism which was to some degree socially responsible.

The progressives' ameliorative reforms also reflected their faith in progress—in mankind's ability, through purposeful action, to improve the environment and the conditions of life. The late nineteenth-century dissidents had not lacked this faith, but their espousal of panaceas bespoke a deep pessimism: "Unless this one great change is made, things will get worse." Progressive reforms were grounded on a broader assumption. In particular, reforms could protect the people hurt by industrialization, and make the environment more humane. For intellectuals of the era, the achievement of such goals meant that they had to meet Herbert Spencer head on and confute his absolute "truths." Progressive thinkers, led by Lester Frank Ward, Richard T. Ely, and, most important, John Dewey, demolished social Darwinism with what Goldman has called "reform Darwinism." They asserted that human adaptation to the environment did not interfere with the evolutionary process, but was, rather, part and parcel of the law of natural change. Progressive intellectuals and their popularizers produced a vast literature to condemn laissez faire and to promote the concept of the active state.

To improve the environment meant, above all, to intervene in economic and social affairs in order to control natural forces and impose a measure of order upon them. This belief in interventionism was a third component of progressivism. It was visible in almost every reform of the era, from the supervision of business to the prohibition of alcohol (John W. Chambers II, *The Tyranny of Change: America in the Progressive Era, 1900–1917*, 1980). Interventionism could be both private and public. Given their choice, most progressives preferred to work noncoercively through voluntary organizations for economic and social changes. However, as time passed, it became evident that most progressive reforms could be achieved only by legislation and public control. Such an extension of public authority made many progressives uneasy, and few of them went so far as Herbert Croly in glorifying the state in his *The Promise of American Life* (1909) and *Progressive Democracy* (1914). Even so, the intervention necessary for their reforms inevitably propelled progressives toward an advocacy of the use of governmental power. A familiar scenario during the period was one in which progressives called upon public authorities to assume responsibility for interventions which voluntary organizations had begun.

The foregoing describes the basic characteristics of progressivism but says little about its ideals. Progressivism was inspired by two bodies of belief and knowledge—evangelical Protestantism and the natural and social sciences. These sources of reform may appear at first glance antagonistic to one another. Actually, they were complementary, and each imparted distinctive qualities to progressivism.

Ever since the religious revivals from about 1820 to 1840, evangelical Protestantism had spurred reform in the United States. Basic to the reform mentality was an all-consuming urge to purge the world of sin, such as the sins of slavery and intemperance, against which nineteenth-century reformers had crusaded. Now the progressives carried the struggle into the modern citadels of sin—the teeming cities of the nation. No one can read their writings and speeches without being struck by the fact that many of them believed that it was their Christian duty to right the wrongs created by the processes of industrialization. Such belief was the motive force behind the Social Gospel, a movement which swept through the Protestant churches in the 1890s and 1900s. Its goal was to align churches, frankly and aggressively, on the side of the downtrodden, the poor, and working people—in other words, to make Christianity relevant to this world, not the next. It is difficult to measure the influence of the Social Gospel, but it seared the consciences of millions of Americans, particularly in urban areas. And it triumphed in the organization in 1908 of the Federal Council of Churches of Christ in America, with its platform which condemned exploitative capitalism and proclaimed the right of workers to organize and to enjoy a decent standard of living. Observers at the Progressive party's national convention of 1912 should not have been surprised to hear the delegates sing, spontaneously and emotionally, the

Christian call to arms, "Onward, Christian Solders!"

The faith which inspired the singing of "Onward, Christian Soldiers!" had significant implications for progressive reforms. Progressives used moralistic appeals to make people feel the awful weight of wrong in the world and to exhort them to accept personal responsibility for its eradication. The resultant reforms could be generous in spirit, but they could also seem intolerant to the people who were "reformed." Progressivism sometimes seemed to envision life in a small town Protestant community or an urban drawing room—a vision sharply different from that of Catholic or Jewish immigrants. Not every progressive shared the evangelical ethos, much less its intolerance, but few of the era's reforms were untouched by the spirit and techniques of Protestant revivalism.

Science also had a pervasive impact on the methods and objectives of progressivism. Many leading reformers were specialists in the new disciplines of statistics, economics, sociology, and psychology. These new social scientists set out to gather data on human behavior as it actually was and to discover the laws which governed it. Since social scientists accepted environmentalist and interventionist assumptions implicitly, they believed that knowledge of natural laws would make it possible to devise and apply solutions to improve the human condition. This faith underpinned the optimism of most progressives and predetermined the methods used by almost all reformers of the time: investigation of the facts and application of social-science knowledge to their analysis; entrusting trained experts to decide what should be done; and, finally, mandating government to execute reform.

These methods may have been rational, but they were also compatible with progressive moralism. In its formative period, American social science was heavily infused with ethical concerns. An essential purpose of statistics, economics, sociology, and psychology was to improve and uplift. Leading practitioners of these disciplines, for example, Richard T. Ely, an economist at the University of Wisconsin, were often in the vanguard of the Social Gospel. Progressives blended science and religion into a view of human behavior which was unique to their generation, which had grown up in an age of revivals and come to maturity at the birth of social science.

All of progressivism's distinctive features found expression in muckraking—the literary spearhead of early twentieth-century reform. Through the medium of such new ten-cent magazines as *McClure's*, *Everybody's* and *Cosmopolitan*, the muckrakers exposed every dark aspect and corner of American life. Nothing escaped the probe of writers such as Ida M. Tarbell, Lincoln Steffens, Ray Stannard Baker, and Burton J. Hendrick—not big business, politics, prostitution, race relations, or even the churches. Behind the exposés of the muckrakers lay the progressive attitude toward industrialism: it was here to stay, but many of its aspects seemed to be deplorable. These could be improved, however, if only people became aware of conditions and determined to ameliorate them. To bring about such awareness, the muckrakers appealed to their readers' consciences. Steffens' famous series, published in book form as *The Shame of the Cities* in 1904, was frankly intended to make people feel guilty for the corruption which riddled their cities. The muckrakers also used the social scientists' method of careful and painstaking gathering of data—and with devastating effects. The investigative function—which was later largely taken over by governmental agencies—proved absolutely vital to educating and arousing Americans.

All progressive crusades shared the spirit and used the techniques discussed here, but they did so to different degrees and in different ways. Some voiced a greater willingness to accept industrialism and even to extol its potential benefits; others expressed more strongly the outrage against its darker aspects. Some intervened through voluntary organizations; others relied on government to achieve changes. Each reform reflected a distinctive balance between the claims of Protestant moralism and of scientific rationalism. Progressives fought among themselves over these questions even while they set to the common task of applying their new methods and ideas to the problems of a modern society. . . .

In this analysis we have frequently pointed to the differences between the rhetoric, intentions, and results of progressive reform. The failure of reform always to fulfill the expectations of its advocates was not, of course, unique to the progressive era. Jacksonian reform, Reconstruction, and the New Deal all exhibited similar ironies and disappointments. In each case, the clash between reformers with divergent purposes, the inability to predict how given methods of reform would work in practice, and the ultimate waning of popular zeal for change all contributed to the disjuncture of rationale, purpose, and achievement. Yet the gap between these things seems more obvious in the progressive era because so many diverse movements for reform took place in a brief span of time

and were accompanied by resounding rhetoric and by high expectations for the improvement of the American social and political environment. The effort to change so many things all at once, and the grandiose claims made for the moral and material betterment which would result, meant that disappointments were bound to occur.

Yet even the great number of reforms and the uncommonly high expectations for them cannot fully account for the consistent gaps which we have observed between the stated purposes, real intentions, and actual results of progressivism. Several additional factors, intrinsic to the nature of early twentieth-century reform, help to explain the ironies and contradictions.

One of these was the progressives' confident reliance on modern methods of reform. Heirs of recent advances in natural science and social science, they enthusiastically devised and applied new techniques to improve American government and society. Their methods often worked; on the other hand, progressive programs often simply did not prove capable of accomplishing what had been expected of them. This was not necessarily the reformers' fault. They hopefully used untried methods even while they lacked a science of society which was capable of solving all the great problems which they attacked. At the same time, the progressives' scientific methods made it possible to know just how far short of success their programs had sometimes fallen. The evidence of their failures thus was more visible than in any previous era of reform. To the progressives' credit, they usually published that evidence—for contemporaries and historians alike to see.

A second aspect of early twentieth-century reform which helps to account for the gaps between aims and achievements was the deep ambivalence of the progressives about industrialism and its consequences. Individual reformers were divided, and so was their movement as a whole. Compared to many Americans of the late 1800s, the progressives fundamentally accepted an industrial society and sought mainly to control and ameliorate it. Even reformers who were intellectually committed to socialist ideas often acted the part of reformers, not radicals.

Yet progressivism was infused and vitalized, as we have seen, by people truly angry with their industrial society. Few of them wanted to tear down the modern institutions of business and commerce, but their anger was real, their moralism was genuine, and their passions were essential to the reforms of their time.

The reform movement never resolved this ambivalence about industrialism. Much of its rhetoric and popular passion pointed in one direction—toward some form of social democracy—while its leaders and their programs went in another. Often the result was confusion and bitterness. Reforms frequently did not measure up to popular, antibusiness expectations, indeed, never were expected to do so by those who designed and implemented them. Even conservative, ameliorative reformers like Theodore Roosevelt often used radical rhetoric. In doing so, they misled their followers and contributed to the ironies of progressivism.

Perhaps most significant, progressives failed to achieve all their goals because, despite their efforts, they never fully came to terms with the divisions and conflicts in American society. Again and again, they acknowledged the existence of social disharmony more fully and frankly than had nineteenth-century Americans. Nearly every social and economic reform of the era was predicated on the progressive recognition that diverse cultural and occupational groups had conflicting interests, and that the responsibility for mitigating and adjusting those differences lay with the whole society, usually the government. Such recognition was one of the progressives' most significant achievements. Indeed, it stands among the most important accomplishments of liberal reform in all of American history. For, by frankly acknowledging the existence of social disharmony, the progressives committed the twentieth-century United States to recognizing—and to lessening—the inevitable conflicts of a heterogeneous industrial society.

Yet the significance of the progressives' recognition of diversity was compromised by the methods and institutions which they adopted to diminish or eliminate social and economic conflict. Expert administrative government turned out to be less neutral than the progressives believed that it would be. No scientific reform could be any more impartial than the experts who gathered the data or than the bureaucrats who implemented the programs. In practice, as we have seen, administrative government often succumbed to the domination of special interests.

It would be pointless to blame the progressives for the failure of their new methods and programs to eradicate all the conflicts of an industrial society, but it is perhaps fair to ask why the progressives adopted measures which tended to disguise and obscure economic and social conflict almost as soon as they had uncovered it. For one thing, they honestly believed in the almost unlimited potentialities of science and administration. Our late twentieth-century skepticism of these wonders should not blind us to the faith with which the progressives embraced them and imbued them with what now seem magical properties. For another, the progressives were reformers, not radicals. It was one thing to recognize the existence of economic and social conflict, but quite another thing to admit that it was permanent. By and large, these men and women were personally and ideologically inclined to believe that the American society was, in the final analysis, harmonious, and that such conflicts as did exist could be resolved. Finally, the class and cultural backgrounds of the leading progressives often made them insensitive to lower-class immigrant Americans and their cultures. Attempts to reduce divisions sometimes came down to imposing middle-class Protestant ways on the urban masses. In consequence, the progressives never fulfilled their hope of eliminating social conflict. Reformers of the early twentieth century saw the problem more fully than had their predecessors, but they nonetheless tended to consider conflicts resolved when, in fact, they only had been papered over. Later twentieth-century Americans have also frequently deceived themselves in this way.

Thus progressivism inevitably fell short of its rhetoric and intentions. Lest this seem an unfairly critical evaluation, it is important to recall how terribly ambitious were the stated aims and true goals of the reformers. They missed some of their marks because they sought to do so much. And, despite all their shortcomings, they accomplished an enormous part of what they set out to achieve.

Progressivism brought major innovations to almost every facet of public and private life in the United States. The political and governmental systems particularly felt the effects of reform. Indeed, the nature of political participation and the uses to which it was put went through transitions as momentous as those of any era in American history. These developments were complex, as we have seen, and it is no easy matter to sort out who was helped and who was hurt by each of them or by the entire body of reforms. At the very least, the political changes of the progressive era significantly accommodated American public life to an urban-industrial society. On balance, the polity probably emerged neither more nor less democratic than before, but it did become better suited to address, or at least recognize, the questions and problems which arose from the cities and factories of the nation. After the progressive era, just as before, wealthier elements in American society had a disproportionate share of political power, but we can hardly conclude that this was the fault of the progressives.

The personal and social life of the American people was also deeply affected by progressivism. Like the era's political changes, the economic and social reforms of the early twentieth century were enormously complicated and are difficult to summarize without doing violence to their diversity. In the broadest sense, the progressives sought to mitigate the injustice and the disorder of a society now dominated by its industries and cities. Usually, as we have observed, the quests for social justice and social control were extricably bound together in the reformers' programs, with each group of progressives having different interpretations of these dual ends. Justice sometimes took second place to control. However, before one judges the reformers too harshly for that, it is well to remember how bad urban social conditions were in the late nineteenth century and the odds against which the reformers fought. It is also well to remember that they often succeeded in mitigating the harshness of urban-industrial life.

The problems with which the progressives struggled have, by and large, continued to challenge Americans ever since. And, although the assumptions and techniques of progressivism no longer command the confidence with early twentieth-century Americans had in them, no equally comprehensive body of reforms has ever been adopted in their place. Throughout this study, we have criticized the progressives for having too much faith in their untried methods. Yet if this was a failing, it was also a source of strength, one now missing from reform in America. For the essence of progressivism lay in the hopefulness and optimism which the reformers brought to the tasks of applying science and administration to the high moral purposes in which they believed. The historical record of their aims and achievements leaves no doubt that there were many men and women in the United States in the early 1900s who were not afraid to confront the problems of a modern industrial society with vigor, imagination, and hope. They of course failed to solve all those problems, but no other generation of Americans has done conspicuously better in addressing the political, economic, and social conditions which it faced.

POSTSCRIPT

Did the Progressives Fail?

In spite of their differences, both interpretations make concessions to their respective critics. Link and McCormick, for example, admit that the intended reforms did not necessarily produce the desired results. Furthermore the authors concede that many reformers were insensitive to the cultural values of the lower classes and attempted to impose middle-class Protestant ways on the urban masses. Nevertheless, Link and McCormick argue that in spite of the failure to curb the growth of big business, the progressive reforms did ameliorate the worst abuses of the new urban industrial society. Although the Progressives failed to solve all the major problems of their times, they did set the agenda which still challenges the reformers of the 1990s.

Abrams also makes a concession to his critics when he admits that "progressivism had real lasting effects for the blunting of the sharper edges of self-interest in American life, and for the reduction of the harsher cruelties suffered by the society's underprivileged." Yet the thrust of his argument is that the progressive reformers accomplished little of value. While Abrams probably agrees with Link and McCormick that the Progressives were the first group to confront the problems of modern America, he considers their intended reforms inadequate by their very nature. Because the reformers never really challenged the inequalities brought about by the rise of the industrial state, maintains Abrams, the same problems have persisted to the present day.

Historians have generally been sympathetic to the aims and achievements of the progressive historians. Many, like Charles Beard and Frederick Jackson Turner, came from the Midwest and lived in model progressive states like Wisconsin. Their view of history was based on a conflict between groups competing for power so it was easy for them to portray progressivism as a struggle between the people and entrenched interests.

It was not until after World War II that a more complex view of progressivism emerged. Richard Hofstadter's *Age of Reform* (Knopf, 1955) was exceptionally critical of the reformist view of history as well as of the reformers in general. Born of Jewish immigrant parents and raised in cities in New York state, the Columbia University professor argued that progressivism was a moral crusade undertaken by WASP families in an effort to restore older Protestant and individualistic values and to regain political power and status. Both Hofstadter's "status revolution" theory of progressivism as well as his profile of the typical Progressive have been heavily criticized by historians. Nevertheless, he changed the dimensions of the debate and made progressivism appear to be a much more complex issue than had previously been thought.

Most of the writing on progressivism for the past 20 years has centered around the "organizational" model. Writers of this school have stressed the role of the "expert" and the ideals of scientific management as basic to an understanding of the Progressive Era. This fascination with how the city manager plan worked in Dayton or railroad regulation in Wisconsin or the public schools laws in New York City makes sense to a 1990s generation surrounded by bureaucracies on all sides. Two books which deserve careful reading are Robert Wiebe's *The Search for Order, 1877–1920* (Hill & Wang, 1967) and the wonderful collection of essays by Samuel P. Hayes, *American Political History as Social Analysis* (Knoxville, 1980), which bring together two decades worth of articles in diverse journals that were seminal in exploring ethnocultural approaches to politics within the organizational model.

In a highly influential article written for the *American Quarterly* in the spring of 1970, Professor Peter G. Filene proclaimed "An Obituary for the 'Progressive Movement.' " After an extensive review of the literature, Filene concluded that since historians can't agree on its programs, values, geographical location, members, and supporters, there was no such thing as a Progressive movement. Few historians were as bold as Filene and wrote progressivism out of the pantheon of American reform movements. But he put the proponents of the early twentieth-century reform movement on the defensive. Students who want to see how professional historians directly confronted Filene in their refusal to attend the funeral of the Progressive movement should read the essays by John D. Buenker, John C. Burnham, and Robert M. Crunden in *Progressivism* (Schenkman, 1977).

There are three works which provide an indispensable review of the literature of progressivism in the 1980s. Link and McCormick's *Progressivism* (Harlan Davidson, 1983) deserves to be read in its entirety for its comprehensive yet concise coverage. More scholarly but still readable are the essays on the new political history in Richard L. McCormick, *The Party Period and Public Policy: American Politics from the Age of Jackson to the Progressive Era* (Oxford, 1986). The more advanced student should consult Daniel T. Rodgers, "In Search of Progressivism," *Reviews in American History* (December 1982). While admitting that Progressives shared no common creed or values, Rodgers nevertheless feels they were able "to articulate their discontents and their social visions" around three distinct clusters of ideas: "The first was the rhetoric of antimonopolism, the second was an emphasis on social bonds and the social nature of human beings, and the third was the language of social efficiency."

U.S. Department of Agriculture

PART 3

From Prosperity Through the Great Depression

In the early years of the twentieth century, America began to review its position in the world as a result of its new industrial power. New motivations were responsible for U.S. interventionist policies in Mexico, Cuba, and Central American republics and for Woodrow Wilson's reluctance to involve America in World War I.

The 1920s are often portrayed as a hedonistic interlude for everyone between the Progressive and New Deal reform eras, but there is controversy over whether the women's movement of those years lost momentum once the vote was achieved.

The onset of a more activist federal government accelerated with the Great Depression. With more than one-quarter of the work force unemployed, and with production plummeting, Roosevelt was elected on a promise to give Americans a "new deal."

Was Early Twentieth-Century American Foreign Policy in the Caribbean Basin Dominated by Economic Concerns?

Did Woodrow Wilson Fail as Commander in Chief During World War I?

Did the Women's Movement Die in the 1920s?

Was the New Deal an Effective Answer to the Great Depression?

ISSUE 9

Was Early Twentieth-Century American Foreign Policy in the Caribbean Basin Dominated by Economic Concerns?

YES: Walter LaFeber, from *Inevitable Revolutions: The United States in Central America* (W. W. Norton, 1983)

NO: David Healy, from *Drive to Hegemony: The United States in the Caribbean, 1898–1917* (University of Wisconsin Press, 1988)

ISSUE SUMMARY

YES: Professor of history Walter LaFeber argues that the United States developed a foreign policy which deliberately made the Caribbean nations its economic dependents from the early nineteenth century on.

NO: Professor of history David Healy maintains that the two basic goals of American foreign policy in the Caribbean were to provide security against the German threat and to develop the economies of the Latin American nations, whose peoples were considered to be racially inferior.

Geographically, the Caribbean area runs from the tip of the Gulf of Mexico into the Caribbean Sea and includes two major sets of countries. First, the six Central American nations of Guatemala, Honduras, El Salvador, Nicaragua, Costa Rica, and Panama stretch along a narrow 300-mile strip between Mexico and Colombia, which separates the Pacific and Atlantic oceans. Second are a number of islands—Cuba, Haiti, the Dominican Republic, and Puerto Rico—which extend below Florida eastward into the Atlantic Ocean. Ironically, parts of Cuba, which has been a major enemy of the United States for the past 30 years, lie only 90 miles from Key West, Florida.

U.S. involvement in Central America was minimal until the mid-nineteenth century, when the acquisition of California and the subsequent discovery of gold there spurred interest in the building of a canal in Panama or Nicaragua to connect the two oceans. Worried about England's desire to build a similar canal, the United States had Great Britain sign the Clayton-Bulwer Treaty in 1850, which provided that neither country would seek exclusive control over an Isthmian route.

Ironically, America's first excursions into Nicaragua were by invitation. In 1855 the Liberals in Nicaragua grew tired of trying to unseat the Conservative president who had Guatemalan aid. They hired William Walker, a Tennessee-born soldier of fortune to fight the Conservatives. In a bizarre turn of events, Walker not only assembled an army and captured the capital, he also became Nicaragua's president in 1856. During his 10 months in office, Walker tried to impose Anglo-Saxon values on the unwilling Nicaraguans. An invasion financed by Peru, Britain, Cornelius Vanderbilt, and the rest of the Central American countries succeeded in overthrowing Walker. U.S. Marines escorted him out of the country in 1857. He attempted a comeback but was caught and executed in Honduras in 1860.

During the next four decades the United States became preoccupied with its own internal affairs. But by the turn of the twentieth century, three events brought the United States back to the Caribbean area—the Spanish-American War, the Panama Canal controversy, and the Roosevelt Corollary to the Monroe Doctrine. In 1898 U.S. soldiers liberated Cuba in a "splendid little war" with Spain and acquired Puerto Rico as an American territory. Five years later President Theodore Roosevelt supported a revolution in Panama to overthrow Colombian rule and proceeded to negotiate a treaty to build a canal 15 days after the new government of Panama had been created. Finally, in 1904 Roosevelt redefined the Monroe Doctrine. Worried that European countries might intervene in the Dominican Republic because of the money owed to European banks, Roosevelt declared that America should help "backward" states pay their bills. The United States took over the customs office of the Dominican Republic and used the revenues to pay off European bill collectors. The Roosevelt Corollary stated that the United States would actively intervene on behalf of the Central American nations. The "insurrectionary habit" brought U.S. Marines to the Dominican Republic in 1916. American troops were also sent to Haiti, Honduras, and Nicaragua.

Why did the United States constantly intervene in the affairs of the Caribbean nations during the first two decades of the twentieth century? In the following essays, Walter LaFeber argues that, given the nineteenth-century racial attitudes which considered all races other than white to be inferior, the United States easily justified its expansion across the continent. Therefore, says LaFeber, the United States adopted a foreign policy which deliberately made the Caribbean nations its *economic* dependents from the early nineteenth century on. David Healy disagrees with the theory of economic neodependency, stating that U.S. interventions were motivated by two factors: to stabilize the area by having American businesses help these radically backward Caribbean nations develop their resources and to provide security against a military threat from Germany.

YES

Walter LaFeber

INEVITABLE REVOLUTIONS

AN OVERVIEW OF THE SYSTEM

Central America is the most important place in the world for the United States today.

U.S. Ambassador to the United Nations,
Jeane Kirkpatrick, 1981

What we see in Central America today would not be much different if Fidel Castro and the Soviet Union did not exist.

U.S. Ambassador to Panama,
Ambler Moss, 1980

No area in the world is more tightly integrated into the United States political-economic system, and none—as President Ronald Reagan warned a joint session of Congress in April 1983—more vital for North American security, than Central America. Washington, D.C. is closer to El Salvador than to San Francisco. Nearly two-thirds of all U.S. trade and the nation's oil imports, as well as many strategic minerals, depend on the Caribbean sea lanes bordered by the five Central American nations.

North Americans have always treated the region differently from the remainder of Latin America. The five nations cover only a little more than one-hundredth of the Western Hemisphere's land area, contain a mere one-fortieth of its population, stretch only nine hundred miles north to south and (at the widest points) less than three hundred miles from ocean to ocean. But this compact region has been the target of a highly disproportionate amount of North American investment and—especially—military intervention. Every twentieth-century intervention by U.S. troops in the hemisphere has occurred in the Central American-Caribbean region. The unusual history of the area was captured by former Chilean President Eduardo Frei, who observed that the Central American states "to a man from the deep South [of the

Americas] seem at times more remote than Europe." Frei's remark also implied that the largest South American nations (Argentina, Chile, Brazil) historically looked east to Europe, while the Central Americans have turned north to the United States.

No region in the world is in greater political and economic turmoil than Central America. And there are few areas about which North Americans are more ignorant. The following is a capsule view of the five nations which, over the past century, have become dependent on the U.S. system. Each is quite different from the other four, but all five share a dependence on the United States that is deeply rooted in history. They also share poverty and inequality that have spawned revolutions in the seventies and eighties. . . .

These five countries are changing before our eyes. Such instability, importance to U.S. security, and North American ignorance about them form a combustible mixture. One explosion has already rocked the hemisphere: the Nicaraguan revolution became the most significant political event in the Caribbean region since 1959 when Fidel Castro seized power in Cuba. Revolutionary movements have since appeared in every other Central American nation except Costa Rica, and even that democracy has not been safe from terrorism.

The United States has countered those revolutions with its military power. Washington's recent policy, this book argues, is historically consistent for two reasons: first, for more than a century (if not since 1790), North Americans have been staunchly antirevolutionary; and second, U.S. power has been the dominant outside (and often inside) force shaping the societies against which Central Americans have rebelled. The reasons for this struggle between the Goliaths and Davids of world power (or what former Guatemalan President Juan José Arévalo called "the Shark and the Sardines") lie deeply embedded in the history of U.S.-Central American relations. As U.S. Ambassador to Panama Ambler Moss phrased the problem in 1980, "What we see in Central America today would not be much different if Fidel Castro and the Soviet Union did not exist."

These two themes—the U.S. fear of revolution and the way the U.S. system ironically helped cause revolutions in Central America—form the basis of this book. Before that story is told in detail, however, a short overview introduces the two themes.

THE REVOLUTIONS OF THE 1970s AND 1770s

Washington officials have opposed radical change not because of pressure from public opinion. Throughout the twentieth century, the overwhelming number of North Americans could not have identified each of the five Central American nations on a map, let alone ticked off the region's sins that called for an application of U.S. force.

The United States consistently feared and fought such change because it was a status quo power. It wanted stability, benefited from the on-going system, and was therefore content to work with the military-oligarchy complex that ruled most of Central America from the 1820s to the 1980s. The world's leading revolutionary nation in the eighteenth century became the leading protector of the status quo in the twentieth century. Such protection was defensible when it meant defending the more equitable societies of Western Europe and Japan, but became questionable when it meant bolstering poverty and inequality in Central America.

How North Americans turned away from revolution toward defense of oligarchs is one of the central questions in U.S. diplomatic history. The process, outlined in Chapter I, no doubt began with the peculiar nature of the revolution in 1776. It was radical in that it proclaimed the ideal of personal freedom. The power of the British mercantilist state, Thomas Jefferson and some of his colleagues declared, had to be more subordinate to individual interest. North Americans, especially if they were white and male, could moreover realize such an ideal in a society that was roughly equitable at its birth, and possessed a tremendous landed frontier containing rich soil and many minerals that could provide food and a steadily growing economy for its people.

Central Americans have expressed similar ideals of freedom, but the historical sources of those ideals—not to mention the geographical circumstances in which they could be realized—have been quite different from the North American. Fidel Castro quoted the Declaration of Independence and compared burning Cuban cane fields in 1958 to the Boston Tea Party of 1773. But his political program for achieving the Declaration's principles flowed from such native Cuban revolutionaries as José Martí, not from Thomas Jefferson.

The need of Cubans and Central Americans to find different means for achieving their version of a just society arose in large part from their long experience with North American capitalism. This capitalism has had a Jekyll and Hyde personality. U.S. citizens see it as having given them the highest standard of living and most open society in the world. Many Central Americans have

increasingly associated capitalism with a brutal oligarchy-military complex that has been supported by U.S. policies— and armies. Capitalism, as they see it, has too often threatened the survival of many for the sake of freedom for a few. For example, Latin Americans bitterly observed that when the state moved its people for the sake of national policy (as in Cuba or Nicaragua), the United States condemned it as smacking of Communist tyranny. If, however, an oligarch forced hundreds of peasants off their land for the sake of his own profit, the United States accepted it as simply the way of the real world. . . .

For the United States, capitalism and military security went hand-in-hand. They have, since the nineteenth-century, formed two sides of the same policy in Central America. Early on, the enemy was Great Britain. After 1900 it became Germany. Only after World War I were those dangers replaced by a Soviet menace. Fencing out Communists (or British, or Germans) preserved the area for North American strategic interests and profits. That goal was not argued. The problem arose when Washington officials repeatedly had to choose which tactic best preserved power and profits: siding with the status quo for at least the short term, or taking a chance on radical change that might (or might not) lead to long-term stability. Given the political and economic pressures, that choice was predetermined. As former Secretary of State Dean Acheson observed, there is nothing wrong with short-term stability. "When you step on a banana peel you have to keep from falling on your tail, you don't want to be lurching all over the place all the time. Short-term stability is all right, isn't it? Under the circumstances." The "circumstances" Acheson alluded to were the revolutions that began to appear in the newly emerging countries during the 1950s.

When applied to Central America, Acheson's view missed a central tenet of the region's history: revolutions have served the functions of elections in the United States; that is, they became virtually the only method of transferring power and bringing about needed change. Acheson's short-term stability too often turned out to be Washington's method for ensuring that Central American oligarchs did not have to answer to their fellow citizens.

The revolutionaries of the 1770s thus had less and less to say to the revolutionaries of the 1970s and 1980s. The latter were more anticapitalist, pro-statist, and concerned much less with social stability than were the former. These differences appeared as the upheavals increased in number and intensity. . . . Revolutions in such areas as Central America were inevitable. The only choice was whether North Americans would work with those revolutionaries to achieve a more orderly and equitable society, or whether—as occurred in Guatemala and Nicaragua—Washington officials would try to cap the upheavals until the pressure built again to blow the societies apart with even greater force.

NEODEPENDENCY: THE U.S. SYSTEM

Central American revolutions have thus not only been different from, but opposed to, most of the U.S. revolutionary tradition. This opposition can be explained historically. For in rebelling against their own governments, Central Americans have necessarily rebelled against the U.S. officials and entrepreneurs who over many decades made Central America a part of their own nation's system. Not that day-to-day control, in Washington's view, was necessary or desirable. Actually governing such racially different and politically turbulent nations as Guatemala or Honduras was one headache that U.S. officials tried to avoid at every turn. They instead sought informal control, and they finally obtained it through a system that can be described as "neodependency."

First outlined in the 1960s, the theory of "dependency" has been elaborated until it stands as the most important and provocative method of interpreting U.S.-Latin American relations. Dependency may be generally defined as a way of looking at Latin American development, not in isolation, but as part of an international system in which the leading powers (and since 1945, the United States in particular), have used their economic strength to make Latin American development dependent on—and subordinate to—the interests of those leading powers. This dependence, the theory runs, has stunted the Latins' economic growth by forcing their economies to rely on one or two main export crops or on minerals that are shipped off to the industrial nations. These few export crops, such as bananas or coffee, make a healthy domestic economy impossible, according to the theory, because their price depends on an international marketplace which the industrial powers, not Central America can control. Such export crops also blot up land that should be used to grow foodstuffs for local diets. Thus malnutrition, even starvation, grow with the profits of the relatively few producers of the export crops.

Dependency also skews Central American politics. The key export crops are controlled by foreign investors or local elites who depend on foreigners for capital, markets, and often for personal protection. In the words of a Chilean scholar, these foreign influences become a "kind of 'fifth column' " that distorts economic and political development without taking direct political control of the country. Thus dependency theory denies outright a cherished belief of many North Americans: that if they are allowed to invest and trade freely, the result will be a more prosperous and stable Central America. To the contrary, dependency theorists argue, such investment and trade has been pivotal in misshaping those nations' history until revolution appears to be the only instrument that can break the hammerlock held by the local oligarchy and foreign capitalists. Latin American development, in other words, has not been compatible with United States economic and strategic interests.

[The next section] outlines how Central America became dependent on the United States. But as the story unfolds, it becomes clear that the economic aspects of dependency theory are not sufficient to explain how the United States gained such control over the region. Other forms of power, including political and military, accompanied the economic. In Nicaragua from 1909 to 1912, for example, or in Guatemala during the 1954 crisis, or in El Salvador during the eighties, economic leverage proved incapable of reversing trends that North American officials despised and feared. Those officials then used military force to destroy the threats. The United States thus has intervened frequently with troops or covert operations to ensure that ties of dependency remained.

In this respect, U.S. foreign policy has sharply distinguished Central America and the Caribbean nations from the countries in South America. In the latter region, U.S. political threats have been rarer. Direct, overt military intervention has been virtually nonexistent. Central American nations, however, have received special attention. Washington officials relied primarily on their nation's immense economic power to dominate Central America since 1900 . . . but they also used military force to ensure that control. Hence the term neodependency to define that special relationship.

To return to the original theme of [this discussion], no region in the world is more tightly integrated into the United States economic and security system than Central America. That region, however, is being ripped apart by revolutions that have already begun in Nicaragua, El Salvador, and Guatemala, and threaten Honduras. Even Costa Rica, with the most equitable and democratic system in Central America, is unsettled. As the dominant power in the area for a century, the United States bears considerable responsibility for the conditions that burst into revolution. The U.S. system was not designed accidentally or without well-considered policies. It developed slowly between the 1820s and 1880s, then rapidly, reaching maturity in the 1940s and 1950s. It was based on principles that had worked, indeed on principles that made the United States the globe's greatest power: a confidence in capitalism, a willingness to use military force, a fear of foreign influence, and a dread of revolutionary instability.

The application of those principles to Central America has led to a massive revolutionary outbreak. This history of U.S.-Central American relations during the past 150 years attempts to explain why this occurred. . . .

T.R. AND TAFT: JUSTIFYING INTERVENTION

In 1898 an awesome North American force needed fewer than three months to crush the remnants of Spain's New World empire and then establish bases in territory as close as the Caribbean and as distant as the Philippines. In 1901 the United States forced the British to terminate the Clayton-Bulwer treaty so Washington could fully control the building and defense of an isthmian canal. That same year William McKinley was assassinated and Theodore Roosevelt became president of the United States.

The famed Rough Rider, who fought publicly if not brilliantly in Cuba during the 1898 war, believed as much as Blaine that the United States was the "natural protector"—and should be the main beneficiary—of Central American affairs. But Roosevelt's methods were characteristically more direct than Blaine's. Nor was he reluctant to use them on Latin Americas whom he derisively called "Dagoes" because, in his view, they were incapable of either governing themselves or—most important in T. R.'s hierarchy of values—maintaining order. The U.S. emergence as a world power and Roosevelt's ascendency to the White House were accompanied by a third historic event during the years from 1898 to 1901: the largest export of North American capital to that time. The country remained an international debtor until World War I, but the force of the new U.S. industrial and agricultural complexes was felt many years before. A large-scale capital market centered in New York City allowed further expansion and concentration of those complexes.

England's investments in Central America meanwhile peaked in 1913 at about $115 million. More than two-thirds of the money, however, was in Costa Rica and Guatemala. And of the total amount, about $75 million—almost wholly in Costa Rica and Guatemala—represented British railroad holdings. Another $40 million was invested in government bonds, most of which were worthless. U.S. investments in Central America, on the other hand, climbed rapidly from $21 million in 1897 to $41 million in 1908, and then to $93 million by the eve of World War I. These differed from the British not only in the rapidity of growth, but in the overwhelming amount (over 90 percent) that went into such direct investments as banana plantations and mining, rather than into government securities, and in the power—perhaps even a monopoly power—these monies were buying in Honduran and Nicaraguan politics. Not that the two British bastions were invulnerable. In Guatemala, U.S. railroad holdings amounted to $30 million between 1897 and 1914 until they rapidly closed ground on England's investment of slightly over $40 million. U.S. fruit companies alone nearly equalled Great Britain's entire investment in Costa Rica's economic enterprises.

No one understood these movements and their implications as well as Elihu Root, T. R.'s secretary of state between 1905 and 1909, the nation's premier corporate lawyer, and perhaps his generation's shrewdest analyst of the new corporate America. Returning from a trip through Latin America in 1906, Root told a convention of businessmen that during the past few years three centuries of that nation's history had suddenly closed. The country's indebtedness had given way to a "surplus of capital" that was "increasing with extraordinary rapidity." As this surplus searched throughout the world for markets to conquer and vast projects to build, the mantle of world empire was being passed: "As in their several ways England and France and Germany have stood, so we in our own way are beginning to stand and must continue to stand toward the industrial enterprise of the world."

The northern and southern hemispheres perfectly suited each other, Root observed. People to the south needed North American manufacturers and the latter needed the former's raw materials. Even the personalities complemented each other: "Where we accumulate, they spend. While we have less of the cheerful philosophy" which finds "happiness in the existing conditions of life," as the Latins do, "they have less of the inventive faculty which strives continually to increase the productive power of men." Root closed by putting it all in historical perspective: "Mr. Blaine was in advance of his time. . . . Now, however, the time has come; both North and South America have grown up to Blaine's policy."

In important respects Root's speech of 20 November 1906 resembled Frederick Jackson Turner's famous essay of 1893 on the closing of the North American frontier. Both men understood that three centuries of U.S. development had terminated during their lifetime and that a new phase of the nation's history had begun. Both revealed social and racial views which shaped the new era's policies. Both were highly nationalistic if not chauvinistic. Most important, both used history as a tool to rationalize the present and future: the dynamic new United States necessarily prepared itself to find fresh frontiers abroad to replace the closed frontier at home.

Unfortunately for Root's plans, internal revolts and external wars tormented Central America at the time. The upheavals and the consequent danger of European intervention posed special problems after 1903. For in that year Roosevelt helped Panama break away from Colombia and he then began to build the isthmian canal. In a private letter of 1905 Root drew the lesson: "The inevitable effect of our building the Canal must be to require us to police the surrounding premises. In the nature of things, trade and control, and the obligation to keep order which go with them, must come our way." The conclusion was unarguable.

It must be noted, however, that one of Root's assumptions was faulty. The Panama Canal was only an additional, if major, reason for injecting U.S. power into Central America. That power had actually begun moving into the region a half-century before. It could claim de facto political and military predominance years before canal construction began. And as Root himself argued in his 1906 speech, United States development, especially in the economic realm, foretold a new relationship with Latin America even if the canal were never built. The Panamanian passageway accelerated the growth of U.S. power in Central America. It also magnificently symbolized that power. But it did not create the power or the new relationship.

For many reasons, therefore—to ensure investments, secure the canal, act as a "natural protector," and, happily, replace the declining presence of the British—Roosevelt announced in 1905 that henceforth the United States would act as the policeman to maintain order in the hemisphere. He focused this Roosevelt Corollary to the Monroe Doctrine on the Caribbean area, where Santo Domingo was beset by revolutions and foreign creditors, but his declaration had wider meaning: "All that this country desires is that the other republics on this continent shall be happy and prosperous; and they cannot be happy and prosperous unless they maintain order within their boundaries and behave with a just regard for their obligations toward outsiders."

Perhaps Roosevelt's major gift to U.S. statecraft was his formulation of why revolutions were dangerous to his nation's interest, and the justification he then provided to use force, if necessary, to end them. But his Corollary meant more than merely making war for peace. It exemplified North American disdain for people who apparently wanted to wage revolts instead of working solid ten-hour days on the farm. Roosevelt saw such people as "small bandit nests of a wicked and inefficient type," and to U.S. Progressives such as T.R., the only sin greater than inefficiency was instability. A top U.S. naval official called the outbreaks "so-called revolutions" that "are nothing less than struggles between different crews of bandits for the possession of the customs houses—and the loot." A fellow officer agreed that only the civilized Monroe Doctrine held "a large part of this hemisphere in check against cosmic tendencies."

Of course that view completely reversed the meaning of the original Doctrine. Monroe and Adams had originally intended it to protect Latin American revolutions from outside (that is, European) interference. Eighty years later the power balance had shifted to the United States, and the Doctrine itself shifted to mean that Latin Americans should now be controlled by outside (that is, North American) intervention if necessary. Roosevelt justified such intervention as only an exercise of "police" power, but that term actually allowed U.S. presidents to intervene according to any criteria they were imaginative enough to devise. In the end they could talk about "civilization," and "self-determination," but their military and economic power was its own justification.

Roosevelt's successor, William Howard Taft, and Secretary of State Philander C. Knox hoped that T.R.'s military "Big Stick" could be replaced by the more subtle and constructive dollar. They held to the traditional North American belief in the power of capital for political healing. To bestow such blessings Knox thought it only proper that the United States seize other nations' customs revenues so they could not become the target of "devastating and unprincipled revolutions." To stabilize Central America—and to have U.S. investors do well while doing good—Taft and Knox searched for an all-encompassing legal right for intervention. The president bluntly told a Mexican diplomat that North Americans could "not be content until we have secured some formal right to compel the peace between those Central American Governments," and "have the right to knock their heads together until they should maintain peace between them." Such a general right was never discovered because legal experts in the State Department warned Knox that such a thing did not exist. Taft and Knox fell back on straight dollar diplomacy; that instrument, given their views of Central Americans, then led them to use force in the T.R. manner. As noted below, Knox soon relied upon what he termed "the moral value" of naval power.

To argue, therefore, that the United States intervened in Central America simply to stop revolutions and bestow the blessings of stability tells too little too simply. The Roosevelt Corollary and Taft's dollar diplomacy rested on views of history, the character of foreign peoples, and politics that anticipated attitudes held by North Americans throughout much of the twentieth century. These policies were applied by presidents who acted unilaterally and set historic precedents for the global application of U.S. power in later years.

North Americans seldom doubted that they could teach people to the south to act more civilized. The potential of U.S. power seemed unlimited, and as that power grew so did the confidence with which it was wielded. Brooks Adams, the grandson and great-grandson of presidents, and a brilliant eccentric who was a friend and adviser of Roosevelt, studied history deeply, then emerged to declare that the 1898 war was "the turning point in our history. . . . I do believe that we may dominate the world, as no nation has dominated it in recent time." In a personal letter, Adams spoke for his generation when he asserted that the years from 1900 to 1914 would "be looked back upon as the grand time. We shall, likely enough, be greater later, but it is the dawn which is always golden. The first taste of power is always the sweetest."

NO

David Healy

DRIVE TO HEGEMONY

After experiencing a heady victory in the Spanish-American War, the United States acquired a small but far-flung empire and embarked upon a more energetic course in foreign affairs. For the next generation its diplomatic efforts were focused principally on two regions, northern Latin America and the Far East. In both regions Washington sought to become a leading shaper of events and fount of influence, but with very different results. In spite of its pretentious Open Door policy, the United States repeatedly met with frustration and failure in its Far Eastern efforts; by 1917 it had little to show for them but an enduring rivalry with Japan and a Philippine colony already coming to be seen as a white elephant. In the Caribbean area, by contrast, it had established an effective regional hegemony.

The reasons for the nation's differing success rate in these areas are not hard to find, for they emerge clearly in even a superficial comparison of the two. First of all, in the Far East the United States was a latecomer to a long-standing rivalry involving a number of competitors: Great Britain, Russia, Germany, France, and the rising local power, Japan. Located halfway around the globe from the United States, the region was never regarded in Washington as vital, however intense the occasional burst of diplomatic involvement might become, and certainly no one at the time ever suggested that it had any bearing upon the security of the United States.

The Caribbean region, by contrast, was close to the United States and far from the other great powers. No other major power challenged United States hegemony there. Great Britain, with a large economic presence, the world's mightiest navy, and secure bases in Jamaica, Trinidad, the Lesser Antilles, British Guiana, and British Honduras, was best positioned to mount such a challenge but consciously refrained. Although Americans [The use of *American* to mean *from the United States* is widely accepted in much of the world. In Latin America, *North American* is the term most used to denote United States origin. Since there is no generally satisfactory term available, I have used both interchangeably.] long feared that Germany would pick up the gauntlet, no significant opposition to Washington's growing power came from Berlin.

From David Healy, *Drive to Hegemony: The United States in the Caribbean* (University of Wisconsin Press, 1988). Copyright © 1988 by the University of Wisconsin Press. Reprinted by permission. Notes omitted.

The region was of secondary or marginal importance to the other nations of real weight, and of primary importance only to the United States. If necessary, the Americans were ready to fight for their aims in the Caribbean, and the other powers knew it. Locked into their own European tensions, they found nothing in the area worth a war with a rising naval and industrial power. As continental tensions rose steadily, then exploded into general war in 1914, Europe was increasingly debarred from any meaningful power commitments in the New World.

In addition to being the only major power with a free hand in the Caribbean, the United States possessed other regional advantages. Again, these emerge plainly from a regional comparison. American ambitions in the Far East initially included hopes of economic penetration, particularly into the markets of China. While these were at that time not large, Europeans and Americans alike shared a mistaken conviction that China was on the brink of rapid westernization and economic development which would make it a large consumer of western manufactures. In practice, China's trade with the developed world was not only rather static but overwhelmingly dominated by the British, while Japan emerged as a formidable regional business rival. As a result, the American economic stake in the Far East never became very large.

Once more the Caribbean was different. The British were also well entrenched in Caribbean trade, investment, and shipping in 1898, but not so strongly as in the Far East, while North American enterprise made steady inroads from the late nineteenth century on. By 1917 United States economic influence in the Caribbean had passed that of Great Britain, particularly in the countries in which Washington was most interested. The First World War clinched the American advantage by closing off the supply of European goods and money. Yankee businessmen quickly moved in to fill the void, making gains which substantially survived the end of the war.

A final contrast is even more striking: that between the vastness of China and the relative smallness of the Caribbean states. Both were vulnerable and disorganized at the turn of the century, but the teeming population of China had for centuries passively absorbed a succession of conquerors. To use force effectively in China might require considerable and expensive efforts extended over years, and the problem was compounded by the number of great-power rivals to be considered. The Russo-Japanese War of 1904–1905 was a grim warning of the price which the unwary could be obliged to pay; the winners as well as the losers suffered scores of thousands of casualties and paid dearly in gold as well as blood.

The scale of the effort required in the Caribbean was drastically smaller. Unchallenged by major rivals, Washington could overawe each small state one to one, in most cases not even needing to use its forces to make its point. When the United States did commit troops to action, seldom as many as two thousand were involved, and never more than three. There were normally enough marines stationed in the region or available nearby on the mainland to handle even small local wars without much extra expenditure, and never were they very bloody—for the North Americans, at any rate. Divided into many small, weak states, the Caribbean region posed little resistance to a determined great-power drive for hegemony.

Given these strategic and economic advantages, the United States quickly became dominant in the Caribbean. This . . . is an account of that rise to dominance, which began in 1898 and was substantially completed by 1917. The pages that follow do not, however, deal with the entire Gulf-Caribbean region. Mexico, important as it was, and however intimately entangled with the United States, constitutes another story. Like Colombia and Venezuela, it was not a part of the central system of Caribbean control erected in this period by the United States, but rather an indicator of the limits of that system. These larger countries also felt the weight of Washington's power and, in Mexico's case especially, played host to a myriad of North American enterprises, but never passed wholly within the circle of North American hegemony. Thus while Mexico's story has much in common with those of its neighbors, it is different in kind and will not be told here. Also omitted are the Caribbean colonies of Great Britain, France, and the Netherlands, with which Washington made no effort to interfere. This . . . is about United States relations, official and unofficial, with the independent states of Central America and the Greater Antilles, and the former Spanish colonies which passed under United States control in 1898. It is about the techniques developed to exercise hegemony over the small sovereign states of the Caribbean, the reasons why North Americans desired such hegemony, and some of the effects which resulted from its establishment. . . .

ASSUMPTIONS, BIASES, AND PRECONCEPTIONS

As the twentieth century got under way, the United States stood poised to extend its interests far beyond the initial Carib-

bean stepping-stones of Cuba and Puerto Rico. Even as this process began, many of the nation's people and policy makers already harbored a set of shared assumptions which would condition their future actions in the area. These assumptions touched upon the relations between the powerful industrialized states and the weaker and less developed ones, the economic potential of the Caribbean region and the capabilities of its peoples, and the probability of a European threat to the region's security.

Such preconceptions did not necessarily originate in the United States; some were borrowed from European views and experience, while many were jointly held on both sides of the Atlantic. By 1900, the European powers had a long history of interaction with other societies in every part of the world, and had established an extensive set of behavioral norms, many of which were accepted in the United States as a matter of course. The Old World was still a world of empires, and the thirty years before 1900 had witnessed a massive advance of European colonialism across Africa and Southeast Asia. Europeans of the Victorian age tended to divide the peoples of the world into the civilized and the barbarous, and their nations into the progressive and the stagnant. They saw non-European peoples lacking modern industrial societies as not merely different, but inferior, and worse yet, obstructive. These peoples, they felt, had no right to stand in the way of the world's development; "civilization" needed their raw materials, their agricultural production, and the economic opportunities which they represented. . . .

This assumed need raised problems in dealing with preindustrial nations. This was especially true of those with exotic legal and commercial codes, those prone to political violence, and those whose magnates or governments failed to honor contracts with the outside world. Once European men and money had committed themselves to enterprises in such places, their home governments must be ready to protect their lives and property against local misbehavior. The Palmerston Circular, issued by the government of Great Britain in 1849, formally claimed the right to intervene for its citizens abroad either in their individual capacity or as members of corporate organizations. Other governments claimed the same right, and the diplomatic protection of citizens' economic activities abroad became an increasingly important function of foreign offices and their legations and consulates.

It was not always clear when a citizen or corporation had been wronged, of course; frequently the disputes were murky, with much to blame on both sides. Furthermore, the issue may have been formally decided after due process by the legal system of the host country, but the imperial powers refused to accept this as decisive. . . .

The borrowers soon learned the tactics of evasion. Some Latin American governments regularly defaulted on their loans, and most did so at least once. Almost all of them contracted new loans to repay the old, usually enlarging the total in order to have fresh funds in hand for current needs. Governments regularly pledged specific sources of revenue—most often customs collections or export taxes—to the service of existing debts, then used them for other purposes in violation of their promises. It was not long before the whole process of contracting such debts became a vicious game without rules, in which each side tried to take advantage of the other. By the turn of the century some semblance of order began to emerge, as the complex and sordid controversies of the past were increasingly settled by compromise. In such settlements the debtor government paid only an agreed fraction of the sometimes fantastic totals charged against them by the bondholders. Even in 1900, however, the whole field of Caribbean government loans was still dangerous to the uninitiated, and too often tarred with scandal. . . .

If belief in special enterprisers' rights under international law commanded a consensus in the United States, so did confidence that the Caribbean countries contained a rich field for enterprise. American travelers of the period almost invariably saw vast economic promise in the region. The genuinely fertile island of Cuba set the standard, while the lush foliage of the tropics suggested a similar productivity for most of the other areas. Thus Nicaragua, for example, was widely regarded as having equal possibilities. Speaking of that country, a traveler of the 1880s concluded: "Nature has blessed it with wonderful resources, and a few years of peace and industry would make the country prosperous without comparison. . . ." Some years later the navy's Admiral James G. Walker echoed the sentiment: "The country's natural resources are immense. Millions of acres of rich land . . . need but little development to yield enormous harvests." In 1906 the United States minister drew a dismal picture of the present state of the country, then went on to contrast this with its latent potential: "This lamentable picture is one of the most fertile, beautiful countries in tropical America, which would rapidly advance in wealth and population were there security of life or property." A half dozen years later, another transient Yankee saw the future prosperity of the land in the cultivation of sugar and rubber by foreign investors, once political stability should be restored. "For these people and for this country as much can be done as we did for Cuba," he wrote, "and without firing a shot." . . .

Almost invariably, each glowing forecast of future prosperity was accompanied by harsh criticisms of the current society of the country under discussion. Thus Nicaragua had heretofore failed to flourish because "so much attention has been paid to politics that little is left for anything else," and frequently recurring civil wars disrupted labor and production. Bad government was reputed to be almost universal. The same British diplomat who saw such material promise in all of the Central American states found in their rulers a major obstacle to development. "Their dishonest methods, total lack of justice, and their shiftiness make it almost useless to endeavor to deal with these Governments as with civilized nations," he declared. "Presidents, Ministers, Judges, police and all other Government or local officials appear to have but one object, namely, to extort and steal as much as possible during their term of office." Elihu Root dismissed the public life of Santo Domingo in a sentence: "Her politics are purely personal, and have been a continual struggle of this and that and the other man to secure ascendancy and power."

To these outside observers, the failure of government was closely associated with the defects of the population. Witness after witness testified that the Caribbean peoples were ignorant, lazy, backward, perhaps vicious. The London *Times* correspondent who gave such a favorable report of Santo Domingo's land and resources described the people as "easy-going and improvident," devoid of initiative or enterprise. When he asked a rural cultivator why he did not dig a ditch and irrigate his field, the man replied that if such a thing were necessary, God would have made it. Admiral Walker saw the Nicaraguans as "dreaming the years away" without past traditions or future ambitions to inspirit them. The American author of a 1910 travel book on Central America did not attempt to conceal his contempt for the people of that region: "Barbarism, enervated by certain civilized forms, without barbarism's vigor, tells all in a word. Scenes of disgust I might repeat to the point of nausea; utter lack of sanitation, of care of body as well as mind, expose a scrofulous people to all the tropical diseases. . . ." To this writer, Central America was not properly a part of the larger Latin American whole, for the South Americans were civilized and progressive, the Central Americans not so. They would be better called "Indo-Americans," he thought, to indicate their inferiority. . . .

The truth was that the American public of the early twentieth century expected to find inferior qualities in nonwhite peoples from tropical societies. Racism in the United States was older than the nation itself; Indians and blacks had suffered from the stigma of inequality since early colonial times. The legacies of the frontier and slavery had long since hardened into fixed attitudes, only superficially changed by the passing of Indian resistance or the episodes of the Civil War and Reconstruction. By the late nineteenth century the South was resubmerging its black population under grandfather clauses, Jim Crow legislation, and lynch law, while Indians were consigned to segregated "reservations" and forgotten. Even the newer European immigrants, flocking in from Southern and Eastern Europe and bringing different cultural backgrounds into the mainstream, were received with deep suspicion and scarcely concealed intimations of inferiority. The inequality of peoples was a pervasive idea in turn-of-the-century America; the Indians, mestizos, and blacks of the Caribbean could hope for little from United States public opinion.

The period entertained not only racial, but geographical biases. A widely read book entitled *The Control of the Tropics* appeared in 1898 with a large impact in both England and America. Written by an Englishman named Benjamin Kidd, its thesis centered on the allegation that the tropical peoples were always and everywhere incapable of self-government and economic development, and their societies were typically characterized by anarchy and bankruptcy. The roots of this alleged condition were not merely racial; white men of "high efficiency," living too long amid slack standards in an enervating climate, were themselves in danger of degeneration. Such men must return regularly to their homelands to renew their mental, moral, and physical vigor, or succumb in time to the universal tropical decay. If tropical areas were to be developed, therefore, they must be governed and managed by career executives and civil servants sent out from the vigorous societies of the north, and regularly replaced by new blood. Since the last great field for the world's economic growth lay in the tropics, Kidd declared, the matter was of more than theoretical importance, and scores of reviewers and readers in the United States agreed with him. . . .

Potentially rich, but peopled by inferior stocks and retarded by inimical tropical conditions, the future of the region lay primarily with outsiders: that was the message, implicit or explicit, received by public opinion in the United States. Yet a plethora of witnesses asserted their confidence in the area's future. Given even a modest degree of order and stability, they chorused, foreign business enterprise would soon be able to tap the varied riches awaiting its fulfilling hand. With economic development under way, a generalized prosperity would soon transform the lives, the institutions, perhaps even the nature of the local populations. For the benefits of economic growth would assuredly be mutual; the native peoples of the Caribbean would gain at least as much as the entrepreneurs who came from abroad to invest their money and talents. A rising level of wealth would bring peace, education, and progress to currently benighted areas, provided of course that the developers enjoyed a relatively free hand. Furthermore, the glowing prospects so often described were typically placed, not in the remote future, but in the next decade or sooner. The driving engine of this economic miracle was to lie primarily in tropical agriculture: the sugar, coffee, bananas, or tobacco in which foreign investors were already so interested. In addition some infrastructure would be needed, particularly in the form of railroads and public utilities, while mining and lumbering represented further fields of action. . . .

In the unsparing light of hindsight, it is easy to indict these prophets of progress and prosperity for their hypocrisy. After a century of partial and selective foreign development, the Caribbean region is not rich, but poor. While the enterprisers often made money, and local elites received a more modest share, their activities produced nothing like a generalized prosperity. On the contrary, a vast inequality of incomes left many in penury and most barely above the subsistence level. And in the long run, even the investors' profits were limited; most of the twentieth century has seen agricultural products exchange at a disadvantage with industrial goods, the terms of trade being largely controlled by the industrial and financial centers. World market surpluses of sugar, coffee, and other tropical staples have further driven prices down, so that only during major wars does a true agricultural prosperity bloom in the tropical world.

In the light of these facts, it is tempting to conclude that the claims and promises by which foreign enterprisers justified themselves in the early twentieth century were insincere and self-serving. Self-serving they certainly were, but not necessarily insincere. It is, after all, easiest to believe what is welcome; belief and self-interest typically run hand in hand. More seriously, the enterpriser of 1900 or 1915 had persuasive reasons to believe in the viability of an agriculturally based economic development. At that very time, Argentina was rapidly emerging as the most prosperous and "modern" of Latin American states, making a major success of selling wheat and beef to a hungry Europe. Since the bulk of Argentina's population sprang from recent European immigrants, the lesson seemed to be that the more efficient "races" could indeed wring wealth out of the soil, and that the process was inhibited elsewhere mainly by the deficiencies of the natives. Furthermore, Argentine economic development had been managed and financed to a notable ex-

tent from England, demonstrating the efficacy of foreign enterprise. With a fast-growing productive base, a solid infrastructure, and a relatively stable political system, Argentina was widely seen as a role model for all of Latin America.

Closer to home, the enterprising Yankee had an even more compelling example of the possibilities of market agriculture. The United States itself had long flourished through the export of huge agricultural surpluses, which had played an essential role in financing nineteenth-century industrialization. Nor was this a phenomenon of the past; American food and fibers still dominated the world market, and their profitability had continued to spur the development of large sections of the nation. The Great Plains constituted the last great agricultural frontier, and in 1900 that region was just approaching full development. Within the memory of millions of living Americans, vast areas west of the Mississippi had been settled and broken to the plow. With startling speed, railroads were built, cities founded, churches, opera houses, universities created—an entire new society, comprising numerous states of the union, had appeared as if by magic in a few decades, quickly achieving American standards of wealth, productivity, and material consumption.

The undeniable fact was that united States economic development had historically been tightly linked to a varied and prosperous agriculture. Its modern industrial economy was built on a foundation of soil-based wealth; its citizens took it as a given that the one was a natural precondition for the other. What they had done at home, right up to the early twentieth century, they assumed they could do anywhere else where a reasonable resource base existed. They had little reason to doubt that a healthy economic development could spring from the export of agricultural surpluses to a world market, and every reason to have faith in the process.

In retrospect, of course, there are obvious flaws in this assumption. The relatively favorable terms of trade enjoyed by agricultural products at the beginning of the century were to disappear almost permanently after the First World War. A crop like sugar, considered as an enterprise, differed significantly from grain or meat, given sugar's special demand for cheap seasonal labor and its wildly fluctuating world price. Large-scale corporate farming by foreign businesses was hardly the same as the family farming which prevailed for so long in the United States. And nowhere in the Caribbean, except perhaps in Cuba, were there large tracts of land possessing anything like the incomparable richness of soil and climate which characterized the more prosperous farming areas of the United States. At the time, however, it appeared otherwise. The Great Plains, with their harsh climate, insect plagues, lack of trees, and inadequate rivers seemed the ultimate in nature's resistance to exploitation. Surely the nation which had brought such a region to productivity could repeat its success in the lush, warm valleys of the Caribbean, where the limitations of tropical soils were still imperfectly understood. Flush with surplus capital, confident of their new technology, and glorying in past success, it never occurred to Yankee enterprisers to doubt their ability to pluck riches from the neighboring lands to the south. Neither did they doubt that their success in this would bring the region progress and prosperity. What had happened so often at home was now to be duplicated abroad, they believed, and so did their contemporaries.

What American businessmen and policy makers feared in the Caribbean was not economic failure, but the challenge of their transatlantic rivals to United States control of the region. If they saw the principal barrier to Caribbean development in the supposed deficiencies of the native peoples, they were only slightly less concerned with the threat of European intervention in the area. France's invasion of Mexico in the 1860s, the French Panamá canal project of the 1880s, and the events leading to the Venezuelan crisis with England in the mid-1890s all mobilized long-standing fears in the United States that Europe's imperial rivalries might spill over into the Americas. As Richard Olney's "twenty-inch gun" note of 1895 had so dramatically stated, most Americans would regard such outside intervention in the hemisphere as disastrous, threatening United States security, prestige, and future economic growth. The Monroe Doctrine's dictum against the possibility had long expressed a central tenet of United States foreign policy, and commanded the most widespread popular support. . . .

In general, however, contemporary Americans were united in their opposition to European expansion in the New World, and after 1900 they came quickly to focus their strongest fears and suspicions, no longer on France or Great Britain, but on the rising power of imperial Germany. From the beginning of the twentieth century, this perceived "German threat" constituted one of the ongoing assumptions behind United States policies in the Caribbean.

Belief in a German threat to the Americas was growing rapidly even before

Theodore Roosevelt became president in 1901, and it became pervasive in the policy-making circles of the Roosevelt administration. As early as 1898, Roosevelt himself believed that "of all the nations of Europe it seems to me that Germany is by far the most hostile to us." By 1901, he was certain that only a major naval building program could deter the kaiser's ambitions. "I find that the Germans regard our failure to go forward in building up the navy this year as a sign that our spasm of preparation, as they think it, has come to an end," he wrote,

> that we shall sink back, so that in a few years they will be in a position to take some step in the West Indies or South America which will make us either put up or shut up on the Monroe Doctrine; they counting upon their ability to trounce us if we try the former horn of the dilemma.

To an English correspondent, Roosevelt confided that "as things are now the Monroe Doctrine does not touch England . . . the only power that needs to be reminded of its existence is Germany." In particular, he feared the Germans would find ways to acquire the Dutch and Danish possessions in the Americas to use as bases for the insertion of their power. By 1905, however, the president felt that his firm stance, accompanied by a continuing program of naval expansion, had become an effective deterrent: "I think I succeeded in impressing on the Kaiser, quietly and unofficially . . . that the violation of the Monroe Doctrine by territorial aggrandizement on his part around the Caribbean meant war, not ultimately, but immediately, and without any delay." It was, however, a deterrent which required continual alertness and preparation, he thought. . . .

These fears of hostile German intentions were not confined to administration insiders, but were matters of common knowledge and objects of frequent discussion in the press. They outlived the end of the Roosevelt administration, to be reinvigorated by the events of the First World War. Why were Americans so sure that Germany's power was dangerous to them, and how accurate was their assumption?

Germany, like the United States, was a fast-rising industrial power and a relative newcomer to the imperial scramble for colonies. Also like the United States, it had recently entered the international competition to become a leading naval power. Its flamboyant kaiser, fond of military show and symbolism, talked altogether too freely at times of his grandiose ambitions. The Prussian military tradition dominated the new German Empire, and if its navy aimed to become one of the strongest in due time, the position of its army was already fixed at or near the top. This was, in short, a formidable, energetic state, which appeared both ambitious and menacing to powers with established claims. . . .

There were also reasons to tie a prospective German threat to the Caribbean. Admiral Alfred von Tirpitz, the powerful German naval chief, wished to acquire bases in the western hemisphere to match those already held by Great Britain and France. He thought of finding such bases on the coast of Brazil, where three hundred thousand German immigrants had settled in the recent past, or in the Galapagos Islands on the Pacific side of South America. He also talked, however, of gaining possession for Germany of the Dutch or Danish colonies in the Caribbean area and thereby gaining a base at Curaçao, Surinam, or the Virgin Islands, a possibility that worried American naval strategists.

Between 1897 and 1905, German naval staff officers elaborated a series of war plans involving an attack upon the east coast of the United States. Their original concept of a direct descent upon New York, Norfolk, Boston, or elsewhere was eventually modified to include the prior seizure of an advanced base in Puerto Rico or Cuba. Such a staging point would make an invasion less risky, and had the added advantage that its seizure would force the American fleet to come out and fight at a time and place chosen by the Germans. By 1901 the Army General Staff had joined the Admiralty Staff in joint planning, General Alfred von Schlieffen originally estimating that fifty thousand men would be required to take and hold Cuba. A later version of the plan substituted Puerto Rico for Cuba, and reduced the troop strength for its seizure to something over twelve thousand men. Finally, in 1906, the war operations plan was reduced to a mere theoretical exercise, as rising tensions in Europe made it too dangerous to consider committing Germany's entire naval strength to operations in another part of the world. The continued increase in United States naval strength also acted to discourage German planners, and in 1909 the German navy's Caribbean–South Atlantic squadron was discontinued.

While Germany's war plans were kept secret, some idea of their nature leaked through to the United States, where American naval leaders added a real fear of invasion to their earlier anti-German bias. Repeated rumors of the German General Staff's hostile activity confirmed Theodore Roosevelt in his belief in a Teutonic threat and his determination to keep the navy strong. Interestingly, his conviction in 1905 that he had succeeded in deterring the kaiser's ambitions through a policy of firmness and strength came reasonably close to the moment when Berlin itself ceased to consider an American adventure. By 1909 President William Howard Taft would call talk of German aggression in the hemisphere "absurd," and even the navy became less convinced that a clash was imminent.

By that time, however, Americans perceived another kind of threat, as Germany's economic penetration of Latin America and success in selling its exports there identified her as a leading trade rival. The large German immigration to South America and the prominent role of resident German businessmen in many Latin American cities reinforced the picture of a drive for economic domination. Such domination was achieved in fact only in tiny, poverty-stricken Haiti, where German merchants did control the great bulk of international trade. Elsewhere, however, the growth of United States trade outpaced that of its rivals, including Germany; rapid Latin American economic growth in the early twentieth century had in fact increased the exports of all the leading suppliers to the area, but none more than the United States.

Whether there really was a "German threat" to the United States or its Caribbean interests is still a matter of debate. H. H. Herwig and David Trask have argued that the intensive German war planning at the beginning of the century indicated a serious interest in naval and military circles in an aggressive war against the United States. Admiral von Tirpitz made no secret of his ambitions in the western hemisphere, and he had considerable influence over the impressionable kaiser. True, such a war now appears adventurist and dangerous, risking German power far from home for distinctly marginal purposes, and the Germans themselves eventually thought better of it. However, they long discounted American naval, and more especially military, strength on the assumption that the United States armed forces were weakened by indiscipline and inefficiency. Thus, according to this view, it was only the growing crisis in Europe itself that finally acted to cancel out Berlin's aspirations in the New World.

Melvin Small agrees that Americans long feared a German attack, but concludes that the decision makers in Berlin never seriously considered Latin American conquest or North American aggression. Whatever intellectual gymnastics the service leaders undertook, they did not reflect actual government policy, his argument implies. Certainly after 1903, he says, the kaiser's government hoped for good relations with the United States, not confrontation. All in all, Small believes, the "German threat" had been more apparent than real. Yet Small omits a close scrutiny of the period from 1898 to 1903, where lay the strongest indications of a hostile German purpose. On the other hand, no one has made much of a case for a German threat after 1906, even if one existed earlier. One is forced to conclude that the *continuation* of the fear of German designs in the hemisphere was ill founded, even as one concedes the sincerity of most of its prophets.

Justified or not, fear of Germany played a significant part in American thinking about the area as a vital security zone. Concern for the national security blended in turn with economic objectives, status ambition, and even reforming zeal to motivate a quest for United States hegemony. As they looked southward, Americans saw a potentially rich area awaiting development. They believed its resident peoples backward and inferior, incapable by themselves of achieving progress or material development. They feared that European rivals might challenge American power and policies in the region, and in particular that Germany would do so, perhaps go even further and unleash armed aggression against the United States. And they accepted a European-made concept of international law which upheld the rights and interests of foreign enterprisers in undeveloped countries. All of these assumptions, singly and together, encouraged Americans to feel that they should play a leading role in the Caribbean, in order to benefit themselves, develop the region, and forestall foreign threats. Most Americans soon came to see United States hegemony as practical, right, legally justified, and even necessary.

POSTSCRIPT

Was Early Twentieth-Century American Foreign Policy in the Caribbean Basin Dominated by Economic Concerns?

In *Drive to Hegemony*, Healy provides us with a sophisticated summary of the most recent scholarship. Yet, in a number of ways Healy supports the views of Samuel F. Bemis, which are developed in *Latin American Policy of the United States* (Harcourt, Brace & World, 1943). Both argue that U.S. foreign policy was primarily concerned with the German threat to the security in the Caribbean. Both recognize the importance of economic factors, yet maintain that American businesses would invest or trade in the Caribbean only when encouraged by the U.S. government.

Healy gives the economic argument a new twist when he says that it was understandable why so many Yankees believed that the Caribbean was ripe for economic development. Since the United States built its industrial revolution upon its agricultural export surpluses, the assumption was that the Latin American nations could do likewise. But Healy is not willing to call the North Americans "benevolent imperialists" as Bemis does. Instead, he recognizes that American policy makers considered their neighbors to be of "racially inferior" stock and used this to partially explain the lack of economic progress in the Caribbean.

LaFeber has a different perspective than Healy in his view of U.S. relations with Central America. "From the beginning," argues LaFeber, "North American leaders believed their new republic was fated to be dominant in Spanish-held Mexico, Central America, and, indeed, the regions beyond. . . . Capitalism and military security went hand in hand . . . and since the nineteenth century, formed two sides of the same policy in Central America." LaFeber's emphasis on economic forces determining our relationship in the Caribbean is hardly new. In 1934 Charles Beard and George H. E. Smith anticipated many of Bemis's arguments and presented a detailed account of the penetration of Latin America by big business in *The Idea of National Interest* (Macmillan, 1934). LaFeber's broadened definition of imperialism is also not a new concept. Over 30 years ago, William Appleman Williams, LaFeber's graduate school mentor, in *The Tragedy of American Diplomacy*, 2d rev., enlarged ed. (Delta, 1972), argued that the United States created an informal empire in Latin America, Asia, and later Europe via the penetration of American business interests.

What distinguishes LaFeber's analysis is his application of the economic theory of "neodependency" to describe U.S. relations in the Caribbean. First outlined in the 1960s by a number of radical economists, the theory of dependency argues that the United States has used its economic strength to make the development of Latin American countries economically dependent upon the United States. Highly controversial, this theory has been criticized by David Ray in "The Dependency Model of Latin America Underdevelopment: Three Basic Fallacies," *Journal of Interamerican Studies and World Affairs* (February 1973). Ray's critique is very general, but it very easily applies to LaFeber's use of the dependency theory in his discussion of U.S. policy in the Caribbean area. He argues that "the model claims that dependency is caused by the economics of capitalism." If this is true, how can Soviet economic imperialism in Eastern Europe be explained? These countries are economically dominated by Russia, a country that lacks a capitalist economic system. The dependency model also assumes "that private foreign investment is invariably exploitative and invariably detrimental to Latin American development." But not all foreign investments are bad. Although investments in extractive industries can distort a country's economy, investments in industries that seek to expand the domestic market may be beneficial to the Central American nation. Finally, the model assumes that these countries face only two choices: dependent capitalism or nondependent "popular revolutionary governments which open the way to socialism." Consider the examples of Cuba and Nicaragua today. To what extent are they less dependent upon the Soviet bloc trade than they previously had been on trade with the West? How vulnerable are they to Soviet pressures on political and economic issues? In short, "the dependency theorists," says Ray, "conceptualize dependency/nondependency as a dichotomous variable, rather than a continuous one."

Many fine monographic studies have appeared on this subject in the last 20 years. Good overviews of this research can be found in David M. Pletcher's "United States Relations with Latin America: Neighborliness and Exploitation," *American Historical Review* (February 1977) and Richard V. Salisbury's "Good Neighbors? The United States and Latin America in the Twentieth Century," in Gerald K. Haines and J. Samuel Walker, eds., *American Foreign Relations: A Historiographical Overview* (Greenwood Press, 1981).

In a review essay of David Healy's *Drive to Hegemony* in *Diplomatic History* (Summer 1990), David M. Pletcher provides an annotated bibliographical review of all the major works on this subject for the past 75 years. An accessible and acerbic critique of the Williams-LaFeber economic analysis of United States–Caribbean relations can be found in Arthur M. Schlesinger, Jr., *The Cycles of American History* (Houghton Mifflin, 1986).

ISSUE 10

Did Woodrow Wilson Fail as Commander in Chief During World War I?

YES: George F. Kennan, from *American Diplomacy: 1900–1950* (Mentor Books, 1952)

NO: D. F. Trask, from "Woodrow Wilson and the Reconciliation of Force and Diplomacy, 1917–1918," *Naval War College Review* (January/February 1975)

ISSUE SUMMARY

YES: Former diplomat and historian George F. Kennan believes that President Wilson was an impractical idealist who led America into the right war for the wrong reasons.
NO: Historian D. F. Trask argues that Wilson developed realistic and clearly articulated war goals and coordinated his larger diplomatic aims with the use of force better than any other wartime American president.

Historians have dealt with Woodrow Wilson rather strangely. The presidential polls of Arthur Schlesinger in 1948 and 1962 as well as the 1983 Murray-Blessing poll have ranked Wilson among the top 10 presidents. William Carleton considers him the greatest twentieth-century president, only two notches below Jefferson and Lincoln. Yet, among his biographers, Wilson has been treated ungenerously. They carp at him for being naive, overly idealistic, too inflexible, rigid, uncompromising, formal, stiff, unkind, disloyal to friends, overcompromising, oratorical, preachy, messianic, and moralistic. It appears that, like many of his contemporaries, Wilson's biographers respect the man but do not like the person.

Why has Wilson been treated with a nagging pettiness which historians do not accord other presidents? Part of the reason may be Wilson's own introspective personality. He was, along with Jefferson and Theodore Roosevelt, our most intellectual president. He spent nearly 20 years as a history and political science teacher and scholar at Bryn Mawr, Wesleyan, and his alma mater, Princeton University. While his multivolume *History of the United States* appears dated, his Ph.D. dissertation on *Congressional Government*, written as a graduate student at Johns Hopkins, remains a classic statement on the weakness of leadership in the American constitutional system.

If one uses the standard categories of the late professor Clinton Rossiter, Wilson ranks very highly as a textbook president. No president, with the exception of Franklin Roosevelt and perhaps Ronald Reagan, has performed the ceremonial role of the presidency as well as Wilson. His speeches rang with oratorical brilliance and substance. No wonder he abandoned the practice of Jefferson and his successors by delivering the president's annual State of the Union Address to Congress in person rather than in writing.

During his first four years, he also fashioned a legislative program rivaled only by F.D.R.'s "New Deal." The "New Freedom" pulled together conservative and progressive, rural and urban, as well as southern and northern Democrats in passing such measures as the Underwood/Simmons Tariff, the first bill to significantly lower tariff rates since the Civil War, and the Owens/Keating Child Labor Act. It was through Wilson's adroit maneuverings that the Federal Reserve System was established. This banking measure, the most significant in our history, established the major agency which regulates the money supply in the country today. Finally, Wilson revealed his flexibility when he abandoned his initial policy of rigid and indiscriminate trust-busting for one of regulating big business through the creation of the Federal Trade Commission.

In the following essays, George F. Kennan presents the classic, realist critique of Wilsonian diplomacy. He argues that Wilson was an impractical idealist who led America into the right war for the wrong reasons. We should have entered the war not "to make the world safe for democracy" but to preserve the balance of power in the world. D. F. Trask counters with a very favorable assessment of Wilson as commander in chief and chief diplomat during World War I. In a tightly constructed essay, Trask argues that Wilson developed realistic and clearly articulated war goals and coordinated his larger diplomatic aims with the use of force better than any other wartime U.S. president.

YES
George F. Kennan

WORLD WAR I

I would first like to say a word about the total result of these two world wars in Europe. These wars were fought at the price of some tens of millions of lives, of untold physical destruction, of the destruction of the balance of forces on the Continent—at the price of rendering western Europe danger-ously, perhaps fatefully, vulnerable to Soviet power. Both wars were fought, really, with a view to changing Germany: to correcting her behavior, to making the Germans something different from what they were. Yet, today, if one were offered the chance of having back again the Germany of 1913—a Germany run by conservative but relatively moderate people, no Nazis and no Communists, a vigorous Germany, united and unoccupied, full of energy and confidence, able to play a part again in the balancing-off of Russian power in Europe—well, there would be objections to it from many quarters, and it wouldn't make everybody happy; but in many ways it wouldn't sound so bad, in comparison with our problems of today. Now, think what this means. When you tally up the total score of the two wars, in terms of their ostensible objective, you find that if there has been any gain at all, it is pretty hard to discern. . . .

Eclipsed for many of us by the fresher and more vivid recollections of World War II, this first World War has become in many respects the forgotten factor. Yet all the lines of inquiry, it seems to me, lead back to it. World War II seemed really so extensively predetermined; it developed and rolled its course with the relentless logic of the last act of a classical tragedy. And the main elements of that tragic situation—the sickness and impatience of Germany, the weakness of eastern Europe, the phenomenon of bolshevism in Russia, and the weariness and debility in France and England—all these things took their origin so clearly in the period of 1914–20 that it seems to be here, if anywhere, that the real answers should be sought. . . .

So we come back to the fact that much of the cause for the decline in our security in the West lay with the course and outcome of the first World War. And for this reason our own part in it deserves the most careful scrutiny.

What was the problem for our statesmen? Let us review it again in our minds.

You all remember how war broke out in 1914. The origins of this war were complex in the extreme. I will not try to describe them in detail here. Some were of a long-term nature: the still-unsolved problems of the breakup of the old Turkish Empire, the restlessness of subject peoples in the Danubian basin, the loss of what the French call the *elan vital* in Austria-Hungary, the relative growth of German power, the rivalry between Germany and England. Others were of a short-term nature: the stupidities and timidities of statesmen, the pressures of public opinion, the vagaries of coincidence. If you tried to compute the various degrees of guilt, you got a rather fuzzy pattern: the Austrians and the Russians no doubt in first place, the Germans with less but certainly with a goodly share, and no one with none at all. Above all, you could not say that anyone had deliberately started the war or schemed it. It was a tragic, helpless sort of war from the beginning. Poor old Europe had got herself into a box. The structure of her international life had a weak spot. The shot at Sarajevo struck into that weak spot—and suddenly no one knew how *not* to go to war. . . .

Now it would be pleasant, and would ease our task, if we could say that, as a war so sickening ran its course, peoples and governments on both sides sobered and became thoughtful, became aware of the increasing emptiness of victory, aware that no political objectives could be worth this price, amenable to any reasonable suggestion for a compromise peace that would put an end to the slaughter. Unfortunately, we cannot say this. There are certain sad appreciations we have come to about human nature on the basis of the experiences of these recent wars. One of them is that suffering does not always make men better. Another is that people are not always more reasonable than governments; that public opinion, or what passes for public opinion, is not invariably a moderating force in the jungle of politics. . . .

In 1916 people in Europe had not yet learned this, any more than many people in the United States have learned it today; and, by consequence, the progress of World War I did not bring reasonableness, or humility, or the spirit of compromise to the warring peoples. As hostilities ran their course, hatreds congealed, one's own propaganda came to be believed, moderate people were shouted down and brought into disrepute, and war aims hardened and became more extreme all around.

The Allies came to be interested only in a total victory over Germany: a victory of national humiliation, of annexations, of crushing reparations. They resented suggestions for an end of hostilities on any other basis.

The Germans wanted to retain military facilities in Belgium. They wanted to hold Belgium for the future in the status of a subordinate state. They wanted a slight increase in their own territory, for economic reasons, at the expense of France. They wanted an indemnity for evacuating France and Belgium. These aims were of course utterly unacceptable to the Allies.

Now, plainly, all this posed no easy problem for American statesmanship, and I would not want it thought that anything I am about to say indicates any lack of sympathy for Woodrow Wilson or of appreciation for the depth and bitterness of his problems. But none of this absolves us from the duty of looking coldly and critically at the nature of our national reaction to such a challenge.

In the first place, with respect to the origins of the war: let us note that there was for long no understanding in this country that either the origins or the issues of the war were of any concern to us. Speaking in 1916, President Wilson said that with the objects and causes of the war "we are not concerned. The obscure foundations from which its stupendous flood has burst forth we are not interested to search for or explore." "America," he said on a later occasion, "did not at first see the full meaning of the war. It looked like a natural raking out of the pent-up jealousies and rivalries of the complicated politics of Europe." Here, we may note, there was not recognition that what might be at issue in the European war was anything that concerned us. There was the same denial we saw in the case of the Far East—of the legitimacy of the real interests and aspirations of other peoples, the same dismissal of these things as unsubstantial and unworthy of our attention, as "jealousies and rivalries" too silly, too "complicated" to deserve our respect.

Proceeding on this basis, it was logical that the only American interest in the war we were inclined to recognize for a long time was the defense of our neutral rights, according to the established laws of maritime warfare, as they had been known in the past. We did not understand that new modalities of warfare and new weapons—above all, the total blockade and the submarine—had rendered obsolete some of the more important of these rules. Not only had their observance become physically impracticable, but each side had come to feel that its chances of victory and survival depended on the violation of one or another of them. Either side would have preferred to accept war with us rather than refrain from violating certain ones of them. This meant that a strict insistence by us on their observance could eventually lead us, theoretically, into war with both belligerents—a paradoxical ending for a policy designed to keep us out of war.

Looking backward today on these endless disputes between our government and the belligerents over neutral rights, it seems hard to understand how we could have attached so much importance to them. They irritated both belligerents and burdened our relations with them, and I find it hard to believe that they involved our national honor. It might be our privilege to defend the rights of our citizens to travel on belligerent vessels, but it was hardly a duty, unless we chose to define it as a duty to ourselves.

As time went on, there grew up, of course, alongside this outlook, something quite different: a realization of the danger of defeat that confronted the Entente powers and an awareness of the damage that would be done to our world position by the elimination of England as a strong force in the world. In addition to this, the superiority of British propaganda, and other factors, began to work to the benefit of the Allied cause. The result was a gradual growth of pro-Allied sentiment, and particularly in the minds of the responsible American leaders. This sentiment was enough to cause Wilson and House to water down our neutrality policy to the benefit of the British and to make cautious efforts to stop the war, in 1915 and 1916, as the best means of averting the danger of a British defeat. But this pro-Ally feeling was never sufficient to constitute, for the national consciousness as a whole, adequate justification for entering the war; and you will remember that our entry, when it came, was over an issue of neutrality.

Once in the war, we had no difficulty in discovering—and lost no time in doing so—that the issues involved in it were of the greatest significance to us.

It is surely a curious characteristic of democracy: this amazing ability to shift gears overnight in one's ideological attitudes, depending on whether one considers one's self at war or at peace. Day before yesterday, let us say, the issues at stake between ourselves and another power were not worth the life of a single American boy. Today, nothing else counts at all; our cause is holy; the cost is no consideration; violence must know no limitations short of unconditional surrender.

Now I know the answer to this one. A democracy is peace-loving. It does not like to go to war. It is slow to rise to provocation. When it has once been provoked to the point where it must grasp the sword it does not easily forgive its adversary for having produced this situation. The fact of the provocation then becomes itself the issue. Democracy fights in anger—it fights for the very reason that it was forced to go to war. It fights to punish the power that was rash enough and hostile enough to provoke it—to teach that power a lesson it will not forget, to prevent the thing from happening again. Such a war must be carried to the bitter end.

This is true enough, and if nations could afford to operate in the moral climate of individual ethics, it would be understandable and acceptable. . . . You wonder whether it would not have been wiser for him to have taken a little more interest in what was going on at an earlier date and to have seen whether he could not have prevented some of these situations from arising instead of proceeding from an undiscriminating indifference to a holy wrath equally undiscriminating.

In any case, once we were at war, it did not appear to us that our greatest danger might still lie precisely in too long a continuation of the war, in the destruction of Europe's equilibrium, and in the sapping of the vital energies of the European peoples. It did not appear to us then that the greatest interest we had in the war was still that it should be brought to an end as soon as possible on a basis involving a minimum maladjustment and as much stability as possible for the future. Prior to our entry into the war, many people had thought that way. As late as January, 1917, Wilson was still arguing against total victory. A "peace forced upon the loser, a victor's terms imposed upon the vanquished," he said, "would be accepted in humiliation, under duress, at an intolerable sacrifice, and would leave a sting, a resentment, a bitter memory upon which terms of peace would rest . . . as upon quicksand." But, once we were in the war, these ideas were swept away by the powerful currents of war psychology. We were then as strong as anybody else in our determination that the war should be fought to the finish of a total victory.

Considerations of the power balance argued against total victory. Perhaps it was for this very reason that people in this country rejected them so emphatically and sought more sweeping and grandiose objectives, for the accomplishment of which total victory could plausibly be represented as absolutely essential. In any case, a line of thought grew up, under Wilson's leadership, which provided both rationale and objective for our part in fighting the war to a bitter end. Germany was militaristic and antidemocratic. The Allies were fighting to make the world safe for democracy. Prussian militarism had to be destroyed to make way for the sort of peace we wanted. This peace would not be based on the old balance of power. Who, as Wilson said, could guarantee equilibrium under such a system? It would be based this time on a "community of power," on "an organized common peace," on a League of Nations which would mobilize the conscience and power of mankind against aggression. Autocratic government would be done away with. Peoples would themselves choose the sovereignty under which they wished to reside. Poland would achieve her independence, as would likewise the restless peoples of the Austro-Hungarian Empire. There would be open diplomacy this time; peoples, not governments, would run things. Armaments would be reduced by mutual agreement. The peace would be just and secure.

In the name of such principles you could fight a war to the end. A future so brilliant would surely wash away the follies and brutalities of the war, redress its injuries, heal the wounds it had left. This theory gave us justification both for continuing the war to its bitter and terrible end . . . and at the same time for refusing to preoccupy ourselves with the practical problems and maladjustments to which the course of hostilities was leading. Under the protecting shadow of this theory, the guns continued their terrible work for a final year and a half after our entry. Under the shadow of this theory Wilson went to Versailles unprepared to face the sordid but all-important details of the day of reckoning. Under this theory he suffered his tragic and historic failure. Under this theory things advanced with a deadly logic and precision to a peace which was indeed "forced upon the loser, a victor's terms imposed upon the vanquished, accepted in humiliation, under duress"—a peace that did indeed leave a sting, a resentment, a bitter memory, and upon which its own terms came later to rest "as upon quicksand."

And the tragedy of this outcome was not substantially mitigated by the fact that we were not signatories to the Treaty of Versailles and kept ourselves aloof from its punitive provisions. The damage had been done. The equilibrium of Europe had been shattered. Austria-Hungary was gone. There was nothing effective to take its place. Germany, smarting from the sting of defeat and plunged into profound social unrest by the breakup of her traditional institutions, was left nevertheless as the only great united state in Central Europe. Russia was no longer there, as a possible reliable ally, to help France contain German power. From the Russian plain there leered a single hostile eye, skeptical of Europe's values, rejoicing at all Europe's misfortunes, ready to collaborate solely for the final destruction of her spirit and her pride. Between Russia and Germany were only the pathetic new states of eastern and Central Europe, lacking in domestic stability and the traditions of statesmanship—their peoples bewildered, uncertain, vacillating between brashness and timidity in the exercise of the unaccustomed responsibilities of independence. And to the other side of Germany were France and England, reeling, themselves, from the vicissitudes of the war, wounded far more deeply than they themselves realized, the plume of their manhood gone, their world positions shaken.

Truly, this was a peace which had the tragedies of the future written into it as by the devil's own hand. It was a peace, as the French historian Bainville said, which was too mild for the hardships it contained. And this was the sort of peace you got when you allowed war hysteria and impractical idealism to lie down together in your mind, like the lion and the lamb; when you indulged yourself in the colossal conceit of thinking that you could suddenly make international life over into what you believed to be your own image; when you dismissed the past with contempt, rejected the relevance of the past to the future, and refused to occupy yourself with the real problems that a study of the past would suggest.

But suppose you hadn't taken this line. Would things have been different? Was there another line you could take?

It does seem to me there was.

You might have begun, I should think, with a recognition of the importance to us of what was brewing in Europe in those years before the outbreak of war. You will remember that Wilson dismissed all this as something we were not even interested to examine.

Yet, was it all so silly, so unworthy of attention? I said in the beginning that some of the causes of the war were deep ones. The absence of a major war on the Continent during the century before 1914 had rested on a balance of power which presupposed the existence of France, Germany, Austria-Hungary, and Russia as dominant elements—and all of this flanked by an England instinctively conscious of her stake in the preservation of the balance among them and prepared to hover vigilantly about the fringes of the Continent, tending its equilibrium as one might tend a garden, yet always with due regard for the preservation of her own maritime supremacy and the protection of her overseas empire. In this complicated structure lay concealed not only the peace of Europe but also the security of the United States. Whatever affected it was bound to affect us. And all through the latter part of the nineteenth century things were happening which *were* bound to affect it: primarily the gradual shift of power from Austria-Hungary to Germany. This was particularly important because Austria-Hungary had not had much chance of becoming a naval and commercial rival to England, whereas Germany definitely did have such a chance and was foolish enough to exploit it aggressively, with a chip on her shoulder, in a way that gave the British a deep sense of concern and insecurity.

It is not only in retrospect that these things are visible.

In the winter of 1913 there appeared, anonymously, and in an English magazine (because no American magazine would take it), an article written by an American diplomatist of the time, Mr. Lewis Einstein. In this article, Mr. Einstein drew attention to the storm clouds gathering over Europe, to the depth of the Anglo-German antagonism, to the danger that war might arise from some relatively insignificant incident, and to the effect that such a war might have on the equilibrium and stability of Europe. He then went on to trace out the significance of such a European war for the security of the United States. He never doubted that we would have to intervene to save England, if the alternative were clearly her destruction. But he warned against the assumption that we would not be affected by any drastic alteration either way in the balance of forces in Europe:

Unperceived by many Americans, the European balance of power is a political necessity which can alone sanction on the Western Hemisphere the continuance of an economic development unhandicapped by the burden of extensive armaments.

. . . The disappearance or diminution of any one state in Europe would be a calamity, varying with its degree. . . .

It is no affair of the United States even though England were defeated, so long as the general balance is preserved. But if ever decisive results are about to be registered of a nature calculated to upset what has for centuries been the recognized political fabric of Europe, America can remain indifferent thereto only at its own eventual cost. If it then neglects to observe that the interests of the nations crushed are likewise its own, America will be guilty of political blindness which it will later rue.

Now you could, it seems to me, have taken this view—so well substantiated by the subsequent course of events—as your point of departure, let us say, from 1913. You might then, departing from the recognition that serious troubles *were* brewing in Europe and that our own interests *were* endangered, have seen to it that this country provided itself right then and there with something in the way of an armed establishment, so that our word would carry some weight and be listened to in the councils of the powers. When war broke out, you could have ignored the nonsensical timidities of technical neutrality and used our influence to achieve the earliest possible termination of a war that nobody could really win. Admittedly, if there were any possibility of this, it was in the first months of the war, and we would have had to be armed. If this had not succeeded, then you would have had to carry on through the war, exercising what moderating influence you could, avoiding friction with the belligerents on minor matters, hold-

ing your power in reserve for the things that counted. And if you finally had to intervene to save the British from final defeat (which I am quite prepared to accept as a valid ground for intervention), then you could have gone in frankly for the avowed purpose both of doing this and of ending the war as rapidly as possible; you could have refrained from moralistic slogans, refrained from picturing your effort as a crusade, kept open your lines of negotiation to the enemy, declined to break up his empires and overthrow his political system, avoided commitments to the extremist war aims of your allies, retained your freedom of action, exploited your bargaining power flexibly with a view to bringing its full weight to bear at the crucial moments in order to achieve the termination of hostilities with a minimum prejudice to the future stability of the Continent.

All these things, as I say, you might conceivably have done. If you ask me, "Can you guarantee that this would have produced a better outcome and a happier future?" my answer is, "Of course not." I can say only that I fail to see how it could have produced a much worse one. And I can say that it would have been a conceptual framework more closely related to the realities of the world we live in and that in the long run—in the law of averages—conduct realistically motivated is likely to be more effective than conduct unrealistically motivated.

But I think I hear one great, and even indignant, objection to what I have suggested; and I must speak to it before I close. People will say to me: You know that what you have suggested was totally impossible from the standpoint of public opinion; that people in general had no idea that our interests were affected by what was going on in Europe in 1913; that they would never have dreamed of spending real money for armaments in time of peace; that they would never have gone into a war deliberately, as a result of cold calculation about the balance of power elsewhere; that they would have made war only upon direct provocation; that they could never have been brought to forgive such provocation and to refrain from pressing such a war to its final conclusion. And you know that they would not have been happy unless they had been able to clothe their military effort in the language of idealism and to persuade themselves that anything so important as Americans fighting on foreign soil had to end with a basic alteration of the terms of life among nations and a settlement of this business for once and for all. You—these people will say to me—hold yourself out as a realist, and yet none of these things you are talking about were even ever within the realm of practical possibility from the standpoint of domestic realities in our country.

I have no quarrel with this argument. I am even going to concede it. I do think that political leaders might have made greater efforts than they did, from time to time, to inform themselves and to tell people the true facts, and I think people might even have understood them and been grateful to them if they had. But let us let that go and say that basically the argument is sound. I still have one thing to say about it.

I am not talking here about the behavior of Woodrow Wilson or Colonel House or Robert Lansing. I am talking about the behavior of the United States of America. History does not forgive us for national mistakes because they are explicable in terms of our domestic politics. If you say that mistakes of the past were unavoidable because of our domestic predilections and habits of thought, you are saying that what stopped us from being more effective than we were was democracy, as practiced in this country. And, if that is true, let us recognize it and measure the full seriousness of it—and find something to do about it. A nation which excuses its own failures by the sacred untouchableness of its own habits can excuse itself into complete disaster. I said in the first of these lectures that the margin in which it is given to us to commit blunders has been drastically narrowed in the last fifty years. If it was the workings of our democracy that were inadequate in the past, let us say so. Whoever thinks the future is going to be easier than the past is certainly mad. And the system under which we are going to have to continue to conduct foreign policy is, I hope and pray, the system of democracy.

NO

D. F. Trask

WOODROW WILSON AND THE RECONCILIATION OF FORCE AND DIPLOMACY, 1917-1918

The questions most frequently addressed by historians in their study of American foreign policy during World War I normally concern either why the United States entered the war or why she ultimately rejected the postwar settlement. These questions lead scholars primarily to the study of neutrality from August 1914 to April 1917 and to an examination of peacemaking from November 1918 to March 1920. Unfortunately, the period of actual combat has, until recently, been all but neglected.

One significant aspect of belligerency that has never been thoroughly examined is the process by which President Wilson sought to apply the military and naval power of the United States in the service of larger political purposes during 1917-1918. Indeed, most historians seem to have assumed that Wilson, specifically, and the U.S. Government, in general, paid scant attention to this question. It is certainly true that Wilson gave less time to day-to-day operations than perhaps any other wartime President; but if ever an American President put into practice the famous Clausewitzian dictum that warfare should be conducted to achieve fundamental political purposes, it was Woodrow Wilson. This notion of Wilson being a grand strategist par excellence is a direct contradiction to the generally held image of Wilson as a lofty and impractical idealist who knew little and cared less about the real world. Nevertheless, although the evidence supports the proposition that he was a profound idealist with high hopes for his country and for mankind, it also establishes Wilson as an example of the fact that realism and idealism often coexist in the statecraft of national leaders. Another unsound dialectical proposition is that Wilson was either a nationalist or an internationalist. He was both, and those who ignore this circumstance do so at the risk of seriously distorting the historical facts.

Woodrow Wilson, during 1917-1918, calculated most carefully the disposition of American military and naval power in order to achieve his larger

From D. F. Trask, "Woodrow Wilson and the Reconciliation of Force and Diplomacy, 1917-1918," *Naval War College Review*, vol. 27 (January/February 1975), pp. 23-31. Copyright © 1975 by *Naval War College Review*, Newport, RI 02841. Reprinted by permission.

political objects, and he also succeeded not only in preserving the vital democratic principle of civilian control over the military but also in avoiding a serious civil-military rift with the U.S. Government.

In the development of this theme, it is first necessary to outline the general political objectives which Wilson hoped to attain through warfare by examining in broad terms the course of his diplomacy during American neutrality. The onset of war in Europe initially involved Wilson in the defense of neutral rights on the high seas. As the operations of the United States during this period are well known, it is sufficient here to note that as of May 1916, Wilson had been forced to threaten war against Germany if that country attempted a campaign of unrestricted submarine warfare against neutral and noncombatant shipping. Since Germany did indeed launch such a campaign as of 1 February 1917, most historians have concluded that this decision accounts for the American intervention in April 1917.

This interpretation, however, fails to take sufficiently into account another less dramatic but even more significant diplomatic enterprise to which Wilson committed himself during the period of neutrality. When the war began, Wilson adopted a conventional version of strict neutrality, assuming that the struggle in Europe concerned only the interests of the Old World and that it would be a relatively short contest. Soon, however, it became apparent that the war was no ordinary affair—that it represented a truly imposing event in world history and that it would not be decided quickly. It had turned into an unprecedented bloodbath that threatened to alter not only the long-established European power relationships, but the balance between Eastern and Western Hemispheres might ultimately create dangers for the Republic. In these circumstances Wilson's thoughts turned to the question of how to bring the war to a close. This policy cohered with both the national interest and the dictates of humanity. The President quickly decided that the proper course would be to offer mediation—to use American influence without American power to arrange a negotiated peace. To further this purpose he sent Edward M. House to Europe on two occasions—early in 1915 and early in 1916—to sound the belligerents about their war aims and to discover a basis upon which the war might be ended through the exercise of America's good offices. House's private inquiries came to naught, but, undaunted, Wilson persisted as the war lengthened and as its potential consequences became more and more apparent. After his reelection, he launched in December 1916 another campaign to bring about a negotiated peace. Asking the belligerents to declare their war aims publicly, he gambled that in their responses he could discern a basis for negotiation. This initiative culminated in one of the President's most famous speeches—the so-called "peace without victory" address of 22 January 1917.

The gallant project failed abjectly. There was never any likelihood that mediation could succeed or even that serious negotiation would be undertaken so long as each coalition believed that it could force a decisive victory.

However, in the context of seeking mediation, Wilson was able to develop the broad outlines of a proper postwar settlement. His plan rested on two fundamental elements. One was a scheme to bring about a restabilization of the European and world balance, but on a much more equitable foundation rooted in the democratic process of self-determination, government by consent. Wilson also recognized that mere adjustment in the balance of power could not guarantee both a just and lasting peace. He therefore came to the conclusion that the world needed international mechanisms capable of policing the balance—adjusting power relationships among nation-states to preclude the development of causes for war. In addition, such mechanisms could sponsor a gradual but general improvement in the lives and fortunes of all mankind, particularly among the less advanced peoples of the world.

Wilson announced this program in his speech of 22 January 1917. The term "peace without victory" served as Wilsonian shorthand for an equitable territorial settlement designed to reconstitute international stability, and the term "League for Peace" summarized his conception of an international organization dedicated to preserving the created stability. In this pronouncement Wilson made clear his profound antipathy to what he considered the principal diseases eating away at international peace and progress: Europe's inveterate proclivities for imperialism and for militarism.

Wilson's program reflected faithfully, if dramatically, both the self-interest of his own Nation and its historic tradition as an exemplar of peace and justice throughout the world. The President himself had become profoundly committed to his project and came to believe that anything short of it would fail to resolve the disequilibrium which had brought on the war and insure the future of peace.

Fatefully, Wilson learned only a week or so after his speech that no prospect remained for a negotiated peace along the lines he had urged, and on 1 February 1917, Germany began its unrestricted submarine campaign against world shipping. Hindenburg and Ludendorff assumed supreme command in Germany during 1916 and had soon concluded that, while Russia could be conquered, Germany could not hope to achieve a decision on land against France and Britain. Accordingly, they eventually fell in with a naval plan to achieve a decision at sea. The naval staff argued that an unrestricted submarine campaign would so disorganize the Allied economies that they would be forced to capitulate within 6 months. Civilian leaders, long opposed to a thoroughgoing *guerre de course* in the belief that it would lead to American intervention, were put off by the argument that the war would be decided at sea before the Americans could bring sufficient power to bear. The Kaiser, as usual, bowed to his warriors.

Wilson, after much hesitation, finally opted for war not because of the submarine decision, *per se*, but because he saw in intervention the only means by which he could insure that the world would find a just and lasting peace. From this perspective the submarine crisis becomes more an occasion for war than a cause. The President, philosophically committed to peaceful rather than violent resolution of political conflict, could not have overcome his abhorrence of war for any less imposing purpose than the one he embraced.

There is no room for real doubt as to what Woodrow Wilson hoped to accomplish when he intervened in April 1917. His war aims had been announced in general terms prior to the American entry, and during the intervention itself Wilson expanded on these guidelines to spell out the details of his plan. He had not only to maneuver during the war so that he could force acceptance of his program upon the Central Powers, but he also had to consider probable opposition from his partners in the Allied coalition. He knew well that the war aims of France, Britain, Italy, Russia, and Japan diverged markedly from those he had in mind, to wage war so as to become *arbiter mundi*. Here, indeed, was a grand design—one of the most extraordinary ever undertaken in world history.

The United States, aside from a limited campaign of "preparedness" had adopted no real program of rearmament and indulged in no detailed planning prior to the intervention. Wilson had hoped desperately to avoid war; he made his decision only when it became clear that he could accomplish his grand design only through belligerency. Also, he did not want to take martial steps that might prejudice the mediation project. However, after making his decision to fight, he lost little time in working out a comprehensive political-military approach to intervention.

The first component of his political-military approach to belligerency was to avoid any further declaration of war aims until he could safely do so without prejudicing the unity of the Western coalition. He fully appreciated the crisis of 1917 and the exhaustion that had overtaken the Allies and consciously avoided political activity that might interfere with the immediate goal of Germany's defeat.

The second component was a decision to cooperate as fully as possible with the European Allies while at the same time avoiding political or military forms of cooperation that might lessen his freedom of action at war's end; that is, he would utilize his political and military influence in ways to further his own purposes and to protect the Republic

against activities that served competitive interests—including those desires of the Allies he deemed incompatible with his own. To convey the limits of cooperation he referred to the United States not as an "allied power" but as an "associated power."

In order to implement this program, the United States first did what it could to confute the German assumption that the war would end before the Americans could contribute to its outcome. Wilson authorized immediate economic assistance and financial support to the Allies in generous measure. He also employed a significant portion of the only force then available to him, the U.S. Navy, as part of the Allied antisubmarine campaign. Toward this goal, Adm. William S. Sims was sent to London to direct the American naval effort in Europe.

In pursuit of the long-term objectives of his policy, Wilson decided to mobilize a great military effort by the formation of an expeditionary force and the expansion of the Navy. At home this released a remarkable surge of energy as the American people actively supported the growth of instruments of government to develop the speed and efficiency dictated by the requirements of war. Wilson went to these lengths because he recognized that nothing less would develop a preponderance sufficient to overwhelm the enemy. In addition to this military motive, the President also calculated the political consequences. If the American contribution meant the difference between victory and defeat, it would greatly enhance American prestige and thereby strengthen the President's bargaining position after the war. Moreover, a great army and navy in being at the end of the war and during the postwar negotiations would constitute an important influence on anyone who might challenge the President's wishes at a peace conference, especially if one assumes that at war's end both the enemy and Allied forces would be exhausted. American military and naval strength would reach its zenith just as European strength approached its nadir.

There remained to President Wilson and his advisers the important decisions concerning how the American Army and Navy were to be employed. A most crucial element was an American reinforcement of the Allies in certain critical theaters of war. Well before the war, France and Britain had arrived at certain fundamental strategic commitments. Although they launched what were called "sideshows" in the Mediterranean and the Middle East, partially for imperial reasons, their primary objective had always been to achieve victory on land by holding the German forces on the western front in France and then achieving a decisive breakthrough. Their naval strategy centered on confining the German High Sea Fleet to its home bases, a task assigned to the British Grand Fleet, and on deploying a huge antisubmarine force to contain the U-boat offensive. The United States quickly accepted these central principles and never deviated from support of them. Furthermore the United States considered Germany the prime enemy. It showed an interest in the other Central Powers only incidentally—rarely unless in some way such attention became part of the way of destroying Germany's will to resist. If Germany collapsed, the Americans correctly assumed that the other Central Powers would also fall.

Even after the United States accepted the hold-and breakthrough strategy in France and a containment strategy at sea, there were still difficult decisions to be made on the deployment of forces.

Since the submarine campaign had not forced victory during 1917, Hindenburg and Ludendorff staked everything on a last desperate gamble in France—a series of end-the-war offensives timed to begin in March 1918. Facing an enormous German concentration of men and material along the western front, the Allies desperately tried to convince the United States to send its manpower across the Atlantic in small units to be integrated into the French and British Armies. This proposal became known as "amalgamation."

Despite the most intense pressure, especially as the crisis of 1918 materialized in France, Wilson never wavered from support of the Army's desire to mobilize, train, transport, and maneuver an independent American Army under its own commanders within its own sector of the western front. Wilson resisted the Allies on this most significant issue partially in response to public opinion at home, but more importantly, in deference to his military advisers who contended that the deployment of an independent force would in the long run make a more effective contribution. There also existed an important political consideration—an independent army which contributed importantly to victory would constitute a much more potent political support for American diplomacy during and after the war than a replacement army under European control. Despite profound irritation in London and Paris, and predictions of impending doom, the American decision to fight an independent force did not lead to disaster, and its existence at war's end did, in fact, greatly strengthen Wilson's hand as *arbiter mundi*.

I turn now to the question of the American Navy. Given the extreme emergency stemming from the unrestricted submarine campaign of 1917, the Allies pressed the United States not to maneuver an independent battle fleet but to concentrate most of its naval energies on providing support for the antisubmarine campaign. This recommendation entailed use of destroyers, torpedo boats, and other small craft as part of antisubmarine operations against the U-boats. It also required use of cruisers, auxiliaries, and other vessels as escorts for convoys of merchant ships. Admiral Sims, reporting from Europe, strongly supported this concept and it was accepted in Washington.

President Wilson's acceptance of a subordinate and supportive rather than an independent role for the Navy was based primarily on the absolute necessity of responding quickly and forcefully to counteract the submarine campaign. Moreover, Wilson foresaw no particularly dangerous political consequences—especially any that might unduly prejudice his postwar aspirations. Ships, unlike individual soldiers, were still easily recognizable elements of the U.S. Government distinct from the foreign fleets with which they operated. The desperate situation at sea required immediate and effective response, and Wilson did not hesitate to act. Had he not done so, the Allies might not have been able to sustain their civilian populations and armies in the field, and the United States might not have been able to transport a huge army to Europe in 1918.

Almost all the fundamental components of America's political-military approach to belligerency were established during the earliest months of the intervention. Their application helped achieve the desired decision over the Central Powers, and it produced no serious disputation between the civilian and military sectors of the American Government. Rarely in the national experience of war

has the exercise of force and the objects of diplomacy been so consistently coordinated and so broadly accepted within the armed services.

Wilson's approach to the war had far-reaching and largely successful results. Despite continuing anxiety, the Allies contained, although they did not defeat, the submarine campaign by the use of the convoy system. In London, Sims quickly decided to support the convoy solution, and in this initiative he gradually gained wholehearted support from the President and the Navy Department. Once Germany opted for unrestricted submarine warfare, its High Sea Fleet abandoned the idea of important fleet actions in the North Sea and served thereafter as support for the submarine campaign, holding the British Fleet in the North Sea so that it could not be used for operations elsewhere against the U-boats. If at Jutland in May 1916 the German Fleet had achieved some tactical success against the British Fleet, the outcome of that confused combat also demonstrated rather conclusively that the British would probably defeat the Germans in a full-scale engagement at sea. This realization, indeed, was part of the rationale for recourse to unrestricted submarine warfare. The American decision to concentrate its naval effort on antisubmarine activity made important contributions to the victory at sea, and the outcome confirmed the overall expediency of President Wilson's naval policy.

On land the Allies during 1917 suffered through bitter frustration and even defeat. Offensive operations along the western front failed to achieve a breakthrough. Then the Italians suffered a catastrophic defeat at Caporetto in October 1917. Most important, the eastern front disintegrated, and after the Bolshevik takeover in Russia during November 1917, Lenin and Trotsky removed the Russians from the war. The only victories came in a peripheral theater—the Middle East.

As intelligence had revealed the outlines of the German end-the-war offensive of 1918, the Allies made their response. It is instructive to analyze the American reactions to various Allied projects since they illumine the wartime workings of Wilson's overall plan.

Prime Minister David Lloyd George and other European leaders accurately attributed a great part of their frustration in France to the lack of sufficient inter-Allied cooperation. During the crisis that developed late in 1917, Lloyd George finally moved to establish numerous organs of inter-Allied cooperation—all of which were to be directed by an Inter-Allied Supreme War Council charged with planning and coordinating both political and military initiatives. Wilson, for his part, reacted favorably to the military planning concept but bitterly opposed any large political role for the Supreme War Council. It might take steps during the war incompatible with his grand design. His reasoning was perfectly consistent with his larger conception of postwar objectives. The President was prepared to abet practical projects to encompass the defeat of Germany, but he was unalterably opposed to any institutional arrangements which might lessen his freedom of action at war's end.

This pattern appeared again when, just after the beginning of the German offensive in France in March 1918, the Allies finally decided to establish unity of command on the western front. Wilson strongly supported the elevation of General Foch to the supreme command. He saw in this a necessary and proper command arrangement which promised to assist in defeating the Germans but which entailed no great political risk.

Other plans also received the required scrutiny. Given the difficulties they faced in France, various Allied leaders—and none more actively than Lloyd George—entertained thoughts of concentrating an offensive not against the Germans but against their tottering junior partners—the Austrians and the Turks. Wilson disagreed. In his mind the prime enemy was Germany, and the quickest and best way to victory was to concentrate in France against the German Army. He showed no inclination to support campaigns in the Mediterranean or Middle Eastern theaters which would delay the ultimate decision and which, he suspected, were related more to European imperial interests than to the immediate object of defeating the Central Powers. During World War II President Roosevelt sought less successfully to pursue a similar course.

No American policy, however, was more revealing of Wilson's motivations than his response to sustained pressure from London and Paris to participate in armed intervention against Bolshevik Russia. Ostensibly, the purpose of such incursions was to reconstitute some part of the eastern front in order to minimize German reinforcement of depleted formations in France. There was also, of course, a covert political motive—the embarrassment and even the overthrow of the Bolshevik regime which had taken Russia out of the war. Yet Wilson stubbornly refused to authorize any extensive intervention in Russia. In July 1918 Wilson agreed only to very small expeditions designed principally to protect military stores at Murmansk, Archangel, and Vladivostok and to expedite the withdrawal of Czech prisoners of war. Indeed he became a party to this venture more to exercise some restraint on the British, French, and Japanese than to further either of the objectives entertained by the Allies. The later expansion of these expeditions came about not because of, but in spite of, American views, and the United States wavered from this course only temporarily during 1919 when it briefly condoned support for the abortive Siberian campaign of Admiral Kolchak.

President Wilson did not resist an incursion into Russia because he in any sense approved of bolshevism. Like practically all bourgeois political leaders, he recognized in the Russian revolution a truly dangerous movement. His solution to it, however, was predicated on a belief that the extremism of the Bolshevik movement related directly to the exhausting effect of the war on civilian populations. If the great conflict could be quickly ended by a success in the west, Wilson hoped that the healing effects of a recovered peace would facilitate the eventual collapse of the Bolshevik revolution.

Wilson had a number of other reasons for opposing massive Allied intervention in Russia. First, it would require a great military and naval effort to achieve success. As such it would divert resources from the theater where the United States wished to concentrate—namely the western front—resources that simply could not be spared. But perhaps more important, Wilson did not fail to consider a critical political question. Armed intervention in Russia aimed at the Bolshevik regime would violate the prime political concept underlying the postwar territorial arrangements that the President wished to sponsor, namely, the principle of self-determination. To condone an obvious violation of this principle might seriously undermine the President's moral authority when he entered into postwar peace negotiations. Why compromise so important a principle for, at best, dubious prospects of military success, particularly when another solution to the Bolshevik menace seemed much more viable as well as morally defensible? Therefore, bearing in mind both political and military considerations of great moment, Wilson took his stand in the face of the most desperate appeals of the European Allies. It is unfortunate that some historians persist in attributing to the United States a desire to destroy bolshevism by force, despite overwhelming evidence to the contrary.

During 1918 the Allies held the line sufficiently in France to preclude a German breakthrough. From March to July, Hindenburg and Ludendorff threw their men futilely against the British, French, Belgian, and American forces ranged against them. Once the German reserve had been eaten up, Foch correctly turned to the offensive. During the emergency the United States had temporarily modified its demand for an independent army under its own commanders in its own sector to the extent of taking over quiet sectors of the front and allowing the French and British to move veteran diversions to active sectors. Nevertheless, General Pershing never faltered in his determination to fight an independent campaign. This policy found limited expression at least in two distinctive operations—the reduction of the St. Mihiel salient in September 1918 and the difficult advance in the Meuse-Argonne sector.

The combination of German exhaustion and growing Allied strength—through American reinforcement—finally forced a decision in western Europe. As the German army began to disintegrate and domestic unrest approached crisis proportions, Ludendorff informed the Kaiser that Germany must seek an armistice. By doing so, he stimulated an irreversible process leading to peace. He may have intended simply to gain some time in order to recoup, as he later claimed, but, whatever his purposes, the decision to inaugurate negotiations for a cessation of hostilities led inexorably to final defeat.

Early in October, Germany approached President Wilson with a proposal to end the war. Wilson then engaged in a brilliant bilateral exchange with Germany—one of the most competent examples of this species of diplomacy in our national experience—which culminated in a German agreement to negotiate along the lines of Wilson's grand design. This outcome infuriated the European Allies, who were systematically excluded from the discussions. Germany agreed to the American conditions because, although they contained much that was unpalatable, they offered a program relatively far more lenient than any put forward by the Allies. Once Wilson had obtained German agreement, which implied the consent of all the other Central Powers, he sent Colonel House to Paris for further negotiations with the Allies themselves.

After the United States entered the war, Wilson had refrained both from negotiations and comments concerning war aims, which might have threatened inter-Allied unity. However, by early 1918 it was clear to both Wilson and the Allies that the events of 1917 had placed Allied destinies in American hands. The result was Wilson's pronouncement of the Fourteen Points in January 1918. Making explicit his commitment to certain general principles—open covenants openly arrived at, absolute freedom of the seas, equal conditions of international trade,

disarmament, and equitable adjustment of colonial claims—Wilson then outlined his conception of the territorial settlement based on the principle of self-determination and concluded with his recommendation that the powers establish a league of nations. Wilson simply announced this program unilaterally and did not discuss it with the Allies. Later, in February, July, and September, Wilson made public an additional 13 points which amended and clarified the original 14. While these points were general in nature and susceptible of diverse interpretation, they constituted by far the most specific and detailed program of war aims announced by any belligerent.

By late October and early November, House had persuaded his European associates to accept a postwar negotiation based on Wilson's peace plans. He made only two important concessions. Britain successfully reserved acceptance of the American version of freedom of the seas, and France guaranteed the right of the victors to exact postwar reparations. In all other respects, however, Wilson's program received the grudging but unavoidable seal of Allied approval before the Armistice of 11 November. Britain, France, and Italy had therefore accepted a peace program which precluded them from achieving many of the war aims for which they had fought so long and so desperately. They had no choice. In order to compel their acquiescence, House had only to suggest delicately that their failure to do so would result in an American withdrawal from the war. Any such step by the United States would have given Germany an opportunity to continue fighting. Moreover, it would have deprived the Allies of American aid and comfort after the conflict, something that all Europe knew had to be forthcoming, at least for some period of time. American support was essential to the Allies not only to facilitate their own recovery but to frustrate any postwar revolutions, following the Russian precedent, that might occur.

Thus, by November 1918 Wilson had sustained the supreme object for which he had gone to war in 1917. He had indeed made himself *arbiter mundi*, and he had done so because he made a remarkably accurate calculation of what was necessary to accomplish this purpose, because he developed a cogent political program, because he controlled the American war effort so that it supported his diplomacy, and because he possessed the iron will essential to the execution of a grand design.

Historians who believe that Wilson, at heart a pacifist or near-pacifist, lacked an appreciation of how to reconcile force and diplomacy or who think that Wilson was either ignorant of or uninterested in problems of grand strategy must examine more carefully the strategic program outlined and followed by the President during the war. The search for the historical Wilson as against the mythic Wilson of past imagining will no doubt lead scholars of the future to abandon certain basic assumptions they have long propagated about the man and award to him the accolade of a great captain.

POSTSCRIPT

Did Woodrow Wilson Fail as Commander in Chief During World War I?

Kennan's *American Diplomacy: 1900–1950* (Mentor, 1951) remains the classic, "realist" critique of American foreign policy. Having spent many years as a diplomat in Germany and Russia, he observed firsthand the breakdown of the balance of power in Europe after both world wars. His essay on World War I is part of Kennan's overall criticism of America's twentieth-century diplomacy. Written at the height of the cold war in 1950, Kennan argues that America exaggerated the role of legal and moral principles in diplomacy and neglected the pursuit of realistic goals in defense of the national interest. Woodrow Wilson was not wrong in bringing the United States into the war, argues Kennan; however, he should have entered the war with more limited realistic goals and not waged a total crusade to make the world safe for democracy.

Kennan, whom Truman's secretary of state Dean Acheson once called "the most intelligent man in America," has spent the better part of three decades at Princeton University's Institute for Advanced Study. Among the best-known works are his two volumes on Soviet-American relations from 1917–1920 entitled *Russia Leaves the War* and *The Decision to Intervene* (W. W. Norton, 1984).

A vocal critic of America's participation in the Vietnam War, again on the grounds of its unrealistic goals, Kennan also has become obsessed with the fear that another breakdown of the balance of power could lead to a nuclear holocaust. His latest book *The Fateful Alliance: France, Russia and the Coming of the First World War* (Pantheon, 1984) has been correctly described as a "masterpiece of diplomatic narrative." Yet it is full of overtones which suggest that a breakdown in present-day Soviet-American relations could bring about the destruction of the human race.

Trask takes a more sympathetic view of Wilson's diplomatic efforts during World War I. Trask has published a number of important scholarly works on this period, including *The United States in the Supreme War Council* (Wesleyan University Press, 1961) and *Captains and Cabinets: Anglo-American Naval Relations, 1917–1918* (University of Missouri Press, 1972). His research on this period, with the exception of Russian history, is more firmly grounded in primary sources than is Kennan's in his essay.

Trask's essay clearly explains Wilson's efforts to apply the military and naval power of the United States for the larger political purposes of defeating Germany and its Austro-Hungarian allies, thereby preserving the balance of power in the Western world. Trask demonstrates that Wilson abandoned his stance of neutrality not only because Germany violated its pledge not to engage in unrestricted submarine warfare, but also because the entrance of the United States into the war was the only way to guarantee that the balance of power in Europe would be maintained.

Most present-day historians accept the viewpoint advanced by Trask that Wilson was a realistic statesman. Not all historians, however, agree with Trask that Wilson coordinated his larger diplomatic goals with the use of force better than any other war president in American history. In *The Ultimate Decision* (George Braziller, 1960), Professor Ernest May argues that Wilson was not interested in the daily military operations, a point which Trask concedes. Moreover, says May, Wilson was hesitant to provide strategic direction for the military because if he became too involved it might compromise his ability to negotiate a peace settlement.

Wilson's negotiations for the Treaty of Versailles as well as his failure to secure its ratification by the United States have often been criticized by historians. Trask, who sees Wilson as a master reconciliator of force and diplomacy during World War I, is forced to admit, in *Victory Without Peace: American Foreign Relations During the Twentieth Century* (Wiley, 1968), that Wilson committed a number of political errors which prevented ratification of the treaty. Some of those mistakes included a failure to communicate "the content and purpose of his peace plans to the American people" and a tendency to use "moralistic oratory," which obscured the harsh realities behind the treaty. Finally, says Trask, "Wilson was a tormented man, caught in the grip of certain neurotic compliances which had helped him politically in the past but tended to injure him during the fight for the League of Nations."

During the past decade, a number of important works have been published about our 28th president. Arthur S. Link is the editor of the Wilson papers and author of the definitive multivolume biography of Wilson. His latest assessment of Wilson's foreign policy can be found in his short, concise study, *Woodrow Wilson: Revolution, War, and Peace* (Harlan Davidson, 1979), an updating of the Albert Shaw Lectures on Diplomatic History at the Johns Hopkins University originally delivered in 1957. Link has also edited a useful collection of articles entitled *Woodrow Wilson and a Revolutionary World, 1913–1921* (University of North Carolina, 1982). More critical than Link is Robert H. Ferrell, *Woodrow Wilson and World War I: 1917–1921* (Harper & Row, 1985). Finally, students who are interested in political power should read John Milton Cooper, Jr., *The Warrior and the Priest: Woodrow Wilson and Theodore Roosevelt* (Harvard University Press, 1983), an intriguing study of perhaps the two most powerful American figures in the early twentieth century.

ISSUE 11

Did the Women's Movement Die in the 1920s?

YES: Lois W. Banner, from *Women in Modern America: A Brief History* (Harcourt Brace Jovanovich, 1974)

NO: Anne Firor Scott, from *The Southern Lady: From Pedestal to Politics, 1830–1930* (University of Chicago Press, 1970)

ISSUE SUMMARY

YES: Professor of history Lois W. Banner concludes that, following the ratification of the Nineteenth Amendment, antifeminist trends and a lack of unity among women's organizations combined to hinder further progress on women's issues in the 1920s.

NO: Professor of history Anne Firor Scott insists that the suffrage victory produced a heightened interest in further social and political reform, which inspired Southern women to pursue these goals throughout the 1920s.

On March 31, 1776, Abigail Adams wrote to her husband, John: "I long to hear that you have declared an independency—and by the way in the new Code of Laws which I suppose it will be necessary for you to make I desire you would Remember the Ladies, and be more generous and favourable to them than your ancestors." Apparently, John Adams did not heed his wife's supplication. Consequently, following the American Revolution, women benefited very little from the democratic forces that swept through the United States. Their failure to enjoy the same progress as men in terms of political democracy produced a status characterized by historian Gerda Lerner as "relative deprivation." It was this sense of deprivation that helped fuel the women's movement during the "age of reform," which culminated in the Women's Rights Convention of 1848 in Seneca Falls, New York.

The tone of the meeting was set by Elizabeth Cady Stanton's presentation of the Declaration of Sentiments and Resolutions, which called for the elimination of the separate status of the two sexes by proclaiming that "all men and women are created equal." All of the resolutions passed unanimously except one demanding women's suffrage. This proposal finally was adopted, but not without a floor fight. The right to vote, it appeared, was too radical. After 1890, the National American Woman's Suffrage Association

(NAWSA) began to view women's suffrage as a primary goal for the reform of American society. Benefiting from the organizational skills of Carrie Chapman Catt, who formulated her "Winning Plan" to gain the suffrage, American women won their campaign with the passage and ratification of the Nineteenth Amendment.

For many participants, the suffrage victory signaled the last step to full equality. For others, it marked only another beginning. Certainly there was no evidence that voting rights brought full equality for American women after 1920. On the other hand, there is some doubt about whether women in the 1920s developed the collective self-consciousness that had been displayed in the suffrage campaign and that would be required to achieve further gains in their status. What *did* happen to the women's movement in the 1920s?

In the following selections, Lois W. Banner argues that, following the enactment of the Nineteenth Amendment, the women's movement splintered into numerous groups that focused upon separate concerns, preventing feminists from uniting around a single issue in the 1920s as they had during the suffrage battle. She adds that the decline of membership in women's organizations and the various antifeminist trends that promoted a new female image worked to dissolve the momentum of the women's movement. Anne Firor Scott concentrates on Southern women and concludes that the 1920s witnessed significant efforts by women to secure reforms in areas of interest to members of their sex and society as a whole. She claims that women contributed significantly to the success of progressivism in the South in the 1920s and that many women of the post-suffrage era desired to increase their opportunities beyond the purely domestic sphere.

YES   Lois W. Banner

THE 1920s: FREEDOM
OR DISILLUSIONMENT?

What characterized the woman's movement of the 1920s more than anything else was its splintering into a number of groups, each involved with a separate concern. True, most established women's organizations continued to function, and several major new ones were organized as the war ended and suffrage was achieved. The formation in 1919 of the National Federation of Business and Professional Women's Clubs (BPW) and of the Women's Bureau in the federal Department of Labor as well as the Women's Joint Congressional Committee (WJCC) and the League of Women Voters in 1920 seemed to promise further striking progress for women. But such was not to be. Soon after the passage of the suffrage amendment, Anna Howard Shaw remarked to Emily Newell Blair, then a young suffragist and later vice president of the National Committee of the Democratic party, "I am sorry for you young women who have to carry on the work for the next ten years, for suffrage was a symbol, and now you have lost your symbol." Shaw could not foresee that political conservatism and an emphasis on personal gratification would come to characterize the decade of the 1920s. But she realized the potential for a breakup into factions within the united woman's movement. Essentially there were four groups: social feminists, pacifists, professional women, and feminists.

The largest faction of women was clustered around social feminism. With suffrage won, the NAWSA disbanded. Instead of Alice Paul's Woman's Party being designated as its successor, however, a new organization, the League of Women Voters, was formed. During the 1920s, the League came to concentrate on three goals: general social reform; the elimination of state laws that discriminated against women; and the education of women to their responsibilities as citizens.

As an agency of reform, the League was not without effect. Its efforts at local, state, and national levels on behalf of municipal reform, conservation, tighter consumer laws, a Child Labor Amendment, and public support of indigent mothers have earned for it the accolade of historian Stanley

Lemons. In his study of social feminism in the 1920s, he argues that women's organizations, and particularly the League, were primarily responsible for whatever Progressive impulse still existed in an essentially conservative decade. State chapters of the League were successful, too, in whittling down the number of discriminatory marriage and property laws still on the books. They also successfully fought for the repeal of laws that prohibited women from serving on juries or holding office—laws that a number of state legislatures passed after ratification of the suffrage amendment. The League often served as a training ground for women interested in politics. The career of Lavinia Engle was not exceptional. After serving seven years as a field secretary for the NAWSA, she became director of the Maryland League in 1920. Later she was elected to the Maryland legislature, and in 1936 she became an official in the federal Social Security Administration.

In function and approach, however, the League has always been a conservative organization. Not only was this apparent in its commitment to social reform but also in its emphasis on education. True, its early history, in many ways traumatic, determined its destiny. As former suffragists who had expected the vote to produce a national reformation, League leaders were shaken when the elections of the early 1920s revealed that the turnout of eligible women voters was light and that their voting patterns did not differ from those of men. Moreover, the League retained no more than a small percentage of the NAWSA's sizable membership. In reaction to this turn of events, League leaders decided that the education of women for responsible citizenship, rather than their mobilization to reform the political system, must be one of their primary functions.

As this concept of education was worked out, it took on conservative and nonpartisan overtones that influenced the entire League approach. Instead of using education as a means of proselytizing for feminist or social-reform goals, as the suffragists and the Progressives had done, the League came to view education in its classic sense, as study to arrive at truth. In the typical local League, women met to study the problems of government in an objective manner. The state and national organizations were no less cautious. . . .

Behind this notion of nonpartisan study lay the idealistic hope that the entire political system might follow the League's example. But the problem was that lengthy inquiry delayed taking a firm stand on any issue. It also re-enforced the belief that women were insecure in the political world and ignorant about politics. In the male world of politics it was dangerous to project a female image and expect to be taken seriously. But, committed to social welfare and education, the League accepted the fiction that the political parties were open to women, even though representation on party governing committees was token, and few women actually ran for political office. Indeed, members of the League who became candidates for political office were required to resign from the League so as not to jeopardize its nonpartisan stance. Moreover, although the League used the political techniques of lobbying and letter writing in its social feminist campaigns, its approach was genteel. The League method was "wooing our legislators in a dignified and league-like [ladylike] manner."

That another approach might have been more effective in challenging the political system is apparent in the striking campaigns of Florence Allen for the Ohio State Supreme Court in 1922 and 1928. In both elections, Allen won the judgeship without party support. Instead she formed an organization made up of women activists. The plan was simple. Her managers contacted women in every county who had been suffragists, and these women handled publicity, arranged meetings, and distributed campaign literature. But it was difficult to form an effective coalition of women around any issue in the 1920s. Many former activists were exhausted from their exertions as suffragists before the war. One former Connecticut suffragist explained: "After we got the vote, the crusade was over. It was peacetime and we went back to a hundred different causes and tasks that we'd been putting off all those years. We just demobilized." Indeed, membership in women's organizations in general dropped off, and the national leadership of the League complained of a dearth of able women willing to take leadership positions in local chapters.

A number of organizations active in the Progressive coalition before the war turned away from activism. Most important, local women's clubs, which before the war had led the social-welfare coalition, often developed in the 1920s into social organizations in which women played bridge or discussed fashions, gardening, and cooking. One ex-president of a formerly flourishing suburban club in the Midwest bemoaned the fact that her clubhouse had once echoed with brilliant speeches, while "now it rings with such terms as 'no trump' and 'grand slam'." Only with difficulty did the national leadership of these clubs arouse the members' interest in reform legislation. This change in the character of wom-

en's clubs was partly due to the general conservatism of the decade; but also, other organizations with a social feminist emphasis, such as the League of Women Voters, were drawing away their reform-minded members, while professional women were more and more deserting them to join professional organizations.

Social workers and settlement-house workers, too, were dropping away from the social activist coalition. To postwar college graduates, themselves influenced by the conservative and individualist tenor of the decade, settlement work, by now in its fourth decade of existence, no longer held out the same appeal as it had to the first generation of settlement workers. Public and private sources of funding similarly fell off, while the movement of blacks into the formerly Jewish, Italian, and Slavic neighborhoods that the settlements served made the challenge of living in the midst of their clientele ever more difficult. Moreover, settlement workers themselves were influenced by general trends within the profession of social work. After several decades of more or less uncontrolled growth, the calling had entered a time of rationalization, of concern with issues of professional standards, training, and pay. At the same time, the influence of Freudian psychology made the individual client and not the social environment seem important to the caseworker.

Organizations like the Women's Trade Union League and the Consumers' League, still headed by Florence Kelley, remained in existence. The prewar activists in these groups were joined by vigorous lieutenants like Frances Perkins, a former Hull House resident who worked for the Consumers' League in the 1920s before becoming head of the New York State Department of Labor under Governor Franklin Roosevelt, and in the 1930s Secretary of Labor in the federal government (the first woman to hold a cabinet position) under President Franklin Roosevelt. Like the League of Women Voters, settlement and social-welfare groups lobbied for a Child Labor Amendment, for special legislation for working women, for federal relief for indigent mothers, among other social-welfare goals. But in the 1920s their support and successes were limited. The old issues of Progressivism no longer prevailed.

At the same time, many former influential suffragists took up pacifism rather than domestic welfare as their primary concern. Carrie Chapman Catt established the National Conference on the Cause and Cure of War, while Jane Addams became involved in the Women's International League for Peace and Freedom (WILPF). For some long-time suffragists, like Rheta Childe Dorr, internationalism promised a new and exciting crusade: their change of heart was in the nature of a "conversion." With the onset of the First World War, Dorr found herself no longer interested in the woman's movement, but rather in "humanity." She resigned from Heterodoxy, of which she had been a devoted member, because "alternate Saturday lunches had no more attractions for me." World events took precedence.

For others, pacifism was a logical extension of their feminism. Organized women were outraged by the outbreak of the First World War, which they saw as the most menacing example possible of male aggressiveness. At the very time that the suffragists and the social feminists were working for a national reformation, men were threatening to destroy the social order. Women as mothers, pacifist rhetoric stressed, had a "peculiar

moral passion against both the cruelty and the want of war." To Jane Addams, pacifism meant "the replacement of the war virtues by virtues which sublimate the heroic but anachronistic energies of the soldier into aspirations towards harmony and justice in society." Pacifist leaders, too, criticized preexisting antiwar societies, dominated by men, for their failure to respond quickly to the war's outbreak. By 1916 most women's organizations advocated peace.

In the 1920s the efforts of women pacifists were not without success. The WILPF, for example, was an important pressure group behind the various disarmament and peace conferences that national governments and pacifist groups held throughout the decade. They played no small part in pressuring the United States and foreign governments into signing the Kellogg-Briand Pact of 1927, which outlawed war as national policy. It is perhaps only in retrospect that their actions appear somewhat futile. Yet one inevitable byproduct of their praiseworthy campaign for peace was a further scattering of the feminist effort at home.

Professional women, too, were becoming an increasingly difficult group to activate behind goals other than equal pay and equal employment opportunities. During the war the absence of men had offered greater advancement possibilities to them, while the government, as part of its general program of bolstering citizen morale, had encouraged them to organize. These experiences had heightened their consciousness of their role as professionals and of discrimination within their professions. With the ending of the war, new professional women's associations appeared in many fields, including dentistry, architecture, and journalism. In 1919, under the sponsorship of the

YWCA, to which many women professionals had previously belonged, representatives of these groups founded the National Federation of Business and Professional Women's Clubs. Its focus was on the attainment of equal rights for women within the professions, although on occasion it supported social feminist causes.

In the 1920s the inheritors of the prewar feminist mantle split off from their sometime associates in the suffragist coalition. The Woman's Party, founded by Alice Paul in 1916, refused to endorse the League of Women Voters' program of social feminism and education for women. Instead, the Woman's Party centered its efforts on attaining an Equal Rights Amendment (ERA) which would, they believed, be the surest way of ending the many state and national laws that discriminated against women. In 1916 and after, Paul's technique of pressuring Congress for the suffrage amendment had seemed fruitful; now she and her associates decided to follow the same course. The amendment—which read simply that "men and women shall have equal rights throughout the United States and every place subject to its jurisdiction"—was first introduced in Congress in 1923. The League, as well as most women's organizations, opposed the ERA. They did want to eliminate the legal strictures against women in areas like marriage and property holding, but they judged that factory women still required special legislation.

The membership of the Woman's Party was small, but it contained numerous women of wealth and professional eminence. It was not a radical group. Crystal Eastman—socialist, pacifist, and an associate of Henrietta Rodman in the prewar Feminist Alliance and of Alice Paul in the prewar Woman's Party—charged that when she presented Paul with a list of militant demands, including the legalization of birth control, Paul refused to consider them. The concern of the Woman's Party was to be the ERA. The strategy was not without effect. Even though Congress consistently refused to vote on the ERA, all commentators were impressed by the lobbying skill of Woman's Party members—a skill that may have stemmed from experience and from the fact that they were working for just one measure.

For many women who were concerned specifically about women's rights, an equal rights amendment was too broad a concept. Some young New York professional women, led by journalists Jane Grant and Ruth Hale, wife of newsman Heywood Broun, formed the Lucy Stone League after Hale was unable to obtain a passport under her maiden name. The purpose of the organization was to persuade married professional women, following Lucy Stone's nineteenth-century example, to use their maiden names and to pressure the government to make this usage legal. In support of this limited reform, the women wrote editorials, held rallies, and lobbied. For a number of years even the BPW did not support the ERA. It was a signal triumph when, in 1928, through the efforts of members influential in professional groups, the Woman's Party secured the support of the BPW, which was convinced by the argument that the ERA was essential to advancing the position of women within the professions.

If any strong sense of common purpose existed among women in the 1920s, that common purpose was social feminism. In 1919 a number of women's organizations formed the Women's Joint

Congressional Committee to work as a common lobby. At one time or another, the League of Women Voters, the BPW, and the General Federation of Women's Clubs were members of the committee, as were the National Congress of Parents and Teachers, the WCTU, the American Association of University Women (AAUW), and the National Council of Jewish Women. In many states similar legislative councils emerged. The national committee worked for improved education, maternal and infant health care, the Child Labor Amendment, the World Court, and increased funding for the Children's Bureau and the Women's Bureau. Its successes, however, were limited. Even its major triumph, the 1921 Sheppard-Towner Act, which provided matching federal grants to set up maternity and pediatric clinics, was to all intents and purposes overturned in 1929. Part of the difficulty lay in the ambivalence of the members of many of these organizations about social welfare; part lay in the evident fact that a woman's voting bloc—which might have forced Congress to pay more heed to social-welfare and feminist campaigns—had not emerged.

In addition to the WJCC, the Women's Bureau in the Department of Labor, established as the result of women's work during wartime and the vigorous lobbying of women's organizations, might have served as an agency to unify women's organizations. But more than anything else in its early years, the Women's Bureau played the role of a fact-finding and publication service. It concerned itself almost exclusively with women's employment. Its first and long-term president, Mary Anderson, had come from the ranks of the Women's Trade Union League. For the first few decades of its existence, the bureau was a firm supporter of special legislation for women.

Although one can discern a certain unified spirit among women in the 1920s around social feminism, the prewar suffrage coalition had largely disintegrated. Organizations like the League of Women Voters tried to keep faith with the Progressive spirit, and some historians think that, especially on the state level, their efforts were not insubstantial. But the very lack of unity among women's organizations made further progress on the feminist front difficult.

ANTIFEMINIST UNDERCURRENTS

Unity or no unity, the general mood of the country was not receptive to feminist reform. Americans in the 1920s were tired of reform causes and dazzled by seeming prosperity and mass-produced consumer goods: automobiles, radios, and, for women in particular, washing machines, vacuum cleaners, and electric kitchens. What need was there for social service when industry was apparently fulfilling its promise of providing material prosperity to all Americans? What concerned Americans—at least of the middle class—were their cars, the availability of illicit liquor, the opportunities for stock-market and land speculation, the radio serials and the latest movie, the exploits of sports stars and cultural heroes, and the pursuit of beauty and youth. The women's clubs, which turned from social service to bridge, were indicative of the general mood of the middle class. Vida Scudder, a Wellesley College professor active in Boston settlements and in the Women's Trade Union League, concluded that "those ten exhausted years [the 1920s] were the worst I have ever known."

By the mid-1920s it had become a matter of belief, proclaimed by press and radio, businessmen and politicians, that women had in fact achieved liberation. Suffrage had been won. The number of women's organizations had not diminished. Women had been employed in large numbers during the First World War in positions of responsibility; they had become men's comrades in the office and factory, or so it seemed. Legions of Vassar and Smith graduates descended on New York City every year to become secretaries, copy editors, and management trainees in department stores. Women were smoking in public, wearing short skirts, and demanding and gaining entry into saloons, speakeasies, men's clubs, and golf courses. Female sports stars, like Helen Wills in tennis and Gertrude Ederle in swimming, were challenging any remaining notions that women could not excel in athletics. And sports promoters were promoting them as vigorously as any male athlete. Even Suzanne LaFollette, author of one of the few militant feminist treatises of the decade, wrote in 1926 that the woman's struggle "is very largely won."

The premise that women had achieved liberation gave rise to a new antifeminism, although it was never stated as such. In essence, it involved the creation of a new female image, certainly more modern than before but no less a stereotype and still based on traditional female functions. It was subtle in argument and compelling to a generation tired of reform causes and anxious to enjoy itself. By the late 1920s numerous articles appeared in popular journals contending that in gaining their "rights," women had given up their "privileges." What these privileges amounted to in this literature were self-indulgence, leisure, and freedom from working. The new antifeminists did not openly question women's right to work. They simply made it clear that they did not think women were capable of combining marriage and a career. Women's world in the home was pictured as exotic and self-gratifying. One representative writer contended that working women simply did not have the strange and delightful experience of taking "an hour to dress," of "spending the day in strictly feminine pursuits," of "actually making the kind of cake that [now] comes from the bakery."

The proponents of this new antifeminism not only borrowed the rhetoric of the prewar feminists but claimed that they were the real feminists of the 1920s. "It [the return to the home] is going to be almost as long and hard a struggle . . . as the struggle for women's rights." Prewar feminists were attacked as unfeminine and asexual. In 1927 writer Dorothy Dunbar Bromley defined a "feminist—new style." She bore no relationship to "the old school of fighting feminists who wore flat heels and had very little feminine charm, or the current species who antagonize men with their constant clamor about maiden names, equal rights, women's place in the world." The "new-style feminist" was well-dressed, admitted that she liked men, did not care for women in groups, and was convinced that "a full life calls for marriage and children as well as a career," with the stress on the former.

Other molders of public opinion spread the message far and wide. Advertising, which doubled in volume in the 1920s, found its major market in women, who spent the bulk of the family income. To sell dishwashers, refrigerators, and cleaning products, advertisers pictured the woman as the model consumer whose existence was devoted to the improvement of family life through the purchase of new products. As the clothing and cosmetic industries began their phenomenal growth in the 1920s (a growth that was largely a product of advertising), women were shown as beings for whom fashion, beauty, and sex appeal were the most important concerns in life.

New writings on the nature of women's sexuality drove the message home. Before the First World War, a few bold feminists and doctors had suggested that women could enjoy sex; now marriage manuals advocating sexual pleasure for women and spelling out erotic techniques were readily available. Their message was underlined by the scientific theories of Sigmund Freud, who had argued as early as the 1890s that unconscious drives, and especially sex, were central forces in human behavior. A small number of doctors and Greenwich Village intellectuals had known of Freud's work before the war, but it was not until the 1920s—an age preoccupied with the notion of pleasure—that Freudian theories became popular. Yet Freud's ideas were as confining for women as they were liberating. While Freud gave the final scientific refutation to the old belief that sex was an unpleasant duty for women, he also argued that women were prey to a particular disability besides the basic human irrationality. The crucial factor in female personality formation, according to him, was the female child's envy for the male sex organ—an envy that produced a lifelong dissatisfaction with being a woman. The only way to overcome this discontent, according to Freud, was through motherhood.

However, the influence of Freudian theories in the 1920s must not be overemphasized. In the later years of the decade, the behaviorist ideas of John B. Watson were in vogue. Watson played down the importance of suppressed drives as factors controlling human actions and stressed that, through will power, the individual could control his or her behavior. His message to women was nonetheless ambiguous. In his *Psychological Care of Infant and Child* (1928), the standard reference on child-rearing for a decade or more, Watson argued that most women were failures as mothers and that they should decide either not to have children or to realize that child-rearing was a skill so complex that it required extensive training and complete dedication. Unlike Freud, Watson did not view motherhood as the natural role for all women, but his prescriptions for child-rearing, which centered around the conscious withholding of paternal affection and the establishment of fixed schedules of activity for the child in order to nurture self-reliance, placed heavy demands on the mother who wanted to seek employment outside the home. . . .

. . . The arguments of those feminists who had wanted a "single standard" of sexuality and who had attacked male sex drives seemed antiquated: Charlotte Perkins Gilman, for example, found it almost impossible in the 1920s to secure speaking engagements or to get her books published. The arguments of those feminists who had preached a doctrine of the erotic or who had upheld motherhood did not really seem to disagree with the new ideas. Nor were the two schools of thought necessarily antagonistic. The new sexuality did represent new freedom for women. Feminists themselves were taking an interest in the new theories. Gilman reported that by the mid-1920s Heterodoxy was devoting discussions to sex psychology, a topic that, she admitted, did not particularly interest her. The Greenwich Village feminists who before the war had formed the Feminist Alliance were dispirited as a result of the war experience, and they left New York City. The next generation of women in Greenwich Village in the 1920s were primarily interested in the pursuit of pleasure, according to historian June Sochen. It was the experience of bohemia, not the hope of a reorganized society, that captivated them.

Finally, antifeminism was aided by extraordinary accusations of communism lodged against many feminist leaders by organizations like the American Legion and the Daughters of the American Revolution (which had evolved from a sometime advocate of social feminism into a right-wing supporter of military preparedness). Jane Addams was charged with being a communist because of her involvement in pacifist causes; Florence Kelley was similarly accused because of her socialist past and her support for the Child Labor Amendment, which the extreme right saw as a socialist measure. Such charges did not create a major stir in the 1920s, but they contributed to the popular belief that feminism was foreign and dangerous.

"FLAMING YOUTH": NEW LIBERTIES, OLD ATTITUDES

Feminism also failed to take roots in the 1920s because by and large it did not appeal to the young women of that generation. No movement can long prosper without attracting younger members to its ranks. In 1910 the suffrage campaign had been reactivated by a group of younger women, including Alice Paul and Rheta Childe Dorr. Such was not the case with the feminist cause in the 1920s, nor, indeed, until the 1960s. . . .

Young people had other preoccupations. Foremost was their rebellion against Victorian culture, its mores and especially its sex taboos. They set the tone of the 1920s. They were the leaders in fashion, in dance, in the introduction of a freer morality. Young women were "flappers," and they lived for fun and freedom, which they saw in terms of short skirts, cigarettes, automobiles, dancing, sports, and speakeasies. The cult of the young had been a muted theme before the First World War. Some among the well-to-do had owned automobiles and had affairs; some young working-class women had been free and easy in their behavior; daring young women had smoked cigarettes and danced new dances like the bunny hug and the turkey trot; and hems had risen as early as 1920. But in about 1920 these qualitative changes took a quantitative jump, and the age of "flaming youth" was on.

In 1921 the conservative *Ladies' Home Journal* first recognized the existence of a "rebellion of the young," moved to do so by letters from frantic mothers throughout the country. "It would be a fine thing for this generation," said the *Journal*, "if the word 'flapper' could be abolished." Before the war (and the *Journal* held the war responsible for the changed attitudes of the young) the word *flapper* meant " 'a sprightly and knowing miss in her early teens.' " Since the war, its "morbid" side had emerged, under which rubric was included cigarette smoking, short skirts, obscene dancing, one-piece bathing suits, jazz, psychoanalysis, birth control, and Bolshevism. . . .

THE NEW HEROINES

Every age has its heroines, and those chosen by the 1920s generation tell us much about the prevailing attitudes toward women. In the 1910s, Jane Addams had been the national heroine, the secular saint whose deep compassion and forceful personality endeared her to a generation of humanitarian Americans. The heroines of the 1920s were of a different stamp. Among them, the pilot Amelia Earhart, the movie actress Mary Pickford, and the "vamp," a standard film character, stand out as representative. Each was strikingly different; and although their careers seemed to give weight to the notion of women's emancipation, together they signaled the demise of feminism as the prewar generation had known it. . . .

The emblem of the change was the beauty queen. In 1920 the hotel owners of Atlantic City, New Jersey, thought up a promotional scheme to lengthen the summer season at the beach. Their idea was to host a beauty contest late in September when most vacationers had gone home—a contest to select America's reigning beauty, its Miss America. They raised the beauty contest to a level of national attention and enshrined it as a typically American institution. And more than anything else, they provided the ultimate symbol of what the American woman in the 1920s was supposed to be.

NO

Anne Firor Scott

WOMEN WITH THE VOTE

Women had been saying for years that the world, and they themselves, would be changed if they were granted the right to vote. When Tennessee ratified the Nineteenth Amendment, the old dream became reality. Would the predicted consequences follow?

For more than two decades increasing numbers of southern women had become deeply engaged in efforts to build a system of public schools, to clean up prisons and abolish the convict lease system, to restrict the use of child labor, to improve the working conditions and reduce the hours of work of women and of factory workers generally, and to diminish racial discrimination in the South. Progress in all these areas had been slow, and the World War diverted the energies of many reformers. Now the war was over, women had the ballot, and the time had come when it was possible to believe, as one young North Carolina woman put it, that "the advent of women into political life would mean the loosening of a great moral force which will modify and soften the relentlessly selfish economic forces of trade and industry . . . the ideals of democracy and of social and human welfare will undoubtedly receive a great impetus."

Whatever the future was destined to reveal about the long-run consequences of adding women to the electorate, at the outset there was a burst of energy, a new drive for accomplishment. Among those who had long supported the idea of suffrage there was no lack of confidence that women would live up to their new opportunity. In Baton Rouge the daughter of a former governor edited a weekly paper entitled *Woman's Enterprise* with the goal of proving to the world that women "are as fully alive to the demands of the times as are the sterner sex." The newspaper encouraged women to register and vote, urged them to run for office, and issued constant reminders to officeholders that women now intended to be heard on all important issues. Women, the *Enterprise* thought, far from voting as their menfolk directed, were on the way to becoming the politically influential members of their families. "Place one energetic woman on a commission and a general house cleaning will result such as Baton Rouge has never enjoyed," the editors confidently asserted; "inefficiency in every department will disappear."

In addition to politics the *Enterprise* carried a steady stream of articles on working women's problems, education for women, and the "new concept of marriage." It also directed a good deal of attention to the accomplishments of young women enrolled at the Louisiana State University.

For those who had taken it seriously the suffrage movement had been an excellent school in political methods. In the first flush of post-suffrage enthusiasm, the old hands undertook to try to teach the ways and means of political action to as many of the newly enfranchised as they could persuade to be interested. Even before the Nineteenth Amendment was ratified, state suffrage organizations transformed themselves into leagues of women voters, to educate women and work for "needed legislation." Charles Merriam, a well-known political scientist, was persuaded to offer an intensive training course for women leaders at the University of Chicago. "Citizenship schools" blossomed over the landscape, offering everything from the most serious reading in political theory to the simplest instruction in ballot marking. Meanwhile women established legislative councils in a concerted effort to attain the laws they felt were needed. The Alabama council, for example, was made up of sixteen organizations ranging from the Woman's Trade Union League to the Methodist Home Missionary Council. In Texas the Joint Legislative Council published a carefully compiled record of the work of congressmen, state legislators, and judges.

The central political concern had to do with the problems of children. In nearly every state women were active in the effort to secure better child labor laws. The case of Virginia is instructive. In 1921 women's groups urged the legislature to establish a Children's Code Commission, and when the legislature took their suggestion, they persuaded the governor to appoint five of their number to the commission. When the commission, in turn, brought in twenty-four recommendations for new laws, ranging from a statewide juvenile court system to compulsory education, the women went to work to secure legislative approval of the recommendations. Eighteen of the twenty-four were adopted.

Also in 1921 a combination of women's groups in Georgia secured the passage of a children's code, a child-placement bill, and a training school bill. In 1923 Georgia women tried, but failed, to persuade the state legislature to ratify the federal child labor amendment. In Arkansas, by contrast, a woman member of the legislature, working in conjunction with the members of the women's clubs, was given credit for that state's ratifying the amendment. The wife of the man who led the floor fight against ratification was reported to be unable to conceal her delight that he had failed. In other states when women failed to secure ratification of the child labor amendment they turned their attention to strengthening state labor laws, an effort in which they were more successful.

In 1921 southern women, along with women from over the nation, brought pressure upon the Congress to pass the Sheppard-Towner Act for maternal and infant health. Nineteen of 26 southern senators voted for the bill. In the House, 91 of the 279 votes in support of the bill came from the South and only 9 of 39 votes against it. This law, which pioneered federal-state cooperation in welfare, was the first concrete national achievement of newly enfranchised women. Since the law provided for federal-state cooperative financing, it was necessary for the women to follow up their congressional efforts with work to secure the matching appropriations from state legislatures. This campaign elicited a great deal of enthusiasm among women in every southern state. It was in those states particularly, where the machinery of public health was not well developed, that the favorable effects of the Act were most visible.

Next to children the subjects of most general interest to politically minded women had to do with the working conditions and wages of women workers. In Arkansas, for example, as early as 1919 the suffrage organization began to work for minimum wages and maximum hours in cotton mills. In Georgia women joined the Federation of Labor in an effort to secure a limit on hours of work for women. The hearing on this last measure brought out "every cotton mill man in Georgia," and while a woman's eloquent testimony persuaded the committee to report the bill, the millowners had enough influence to prevent its being brought to a vote. As a result of what they had learned about the conditions in which many factory women worked, clubwomen and the League of Women Voters developed a deepening concern for the problems of industrial labor generally. This concern often brought them into conflict with husbands and friends. The businessman's cherished "cheap labor" might be seen by his wife as an exploited human being, especially when the worker was a woman or a child. For years southern ladies had been praised for their superior sensitivity to human and personal problems, and now that their "sphere" was enlarging, such sensitivity took them in directions not always welcome to their husbands.

This particular drama of wives against husbands was played out, among other places, in North Carolina. Textile manufacturing was a major economic interest in that state, and working conditions in many mills were far from ideal. Wages were low, and it was common to find numbers of young children at work. Soon after the passage of the Nineteenth Amendment, North Carolina women began to develop an aggressive interest in these matters. In occurred to them to ask the state government to invite the Woman's Bureau of the United States Department of Labor to investigate working conditions in North Carolina mills. This suggestion aroused a strong opposition among millmen and their business colleagues. The governor was polite to the women but adamant: North Carolina had no need for the federal government to tell it how to run its affairs. Textile journals and newspapers accused the offending women of being unwomanly, of mixing in things about which they knew nothing, and of being the dupes of northern manufacturers bent on spoiling the competitive advantage which child labor and cheap female labor gave the South. The YWCA, one of the groups supporting the idea of a survey, was warned that it would soon find itself without funds. The state president of the League of Women Voters was summoned before a self-constituted panel of millmen and lectured severely. She was told that her husband's sales of mill machinery would diminish as long as she and the league continued their unseemly interest in working conditions in the mills.

The progressive movement came fully into being in the South in the 1920s, especially in relation to state government. Southern women contributed significantly to the political effort which led to the adoption of a wide range of social legislation in those years. In public, women continued to defer to men, but in their private correspondence they described their own efforts as more practical than those of men.

As time went by a small number of very respectable southern women became deeply involved in what could only be called, in the southern context, the radical aspect of the labor movement. Lucy Randolph Mason, whose name testified to her Virginia lineage, began by working with the YWCA in Richmond and became, as she said, more and more concerned about the lack of social control in the development of southern industry. In her YWCA work she became acutely aware of industrial problems, for the young women in the Y, during the twenties, were preoccupied with the study of the facts of industrial life. They worked out a legislative program which included the abatement of poverty, abolition of child labor, a living wage in every industry, the eight-hour day, and protection of workers from the hardships of continued unemployment. At Randolph-Macon members of the Y studied the problems of coal miners, and at Westhampton those of unemployment. College girls across the South formed a committee for student industrial cooperation, seeking, as they put it, to Christianize the social order.

In January 1923 the National Consumers League sponsored a conference on industrial legislation for the Mississippi Valley states. The session on hours of work for women was chaired by a New Orleans woman, and the one on minimum wages by a Kentucky woman. In the same year the chairman of the Women in Industry Committee of the Mississippi League of Women Voters urged members of local leagues to inform themselves about the working conditions of the 15,000 working women in Mississippi "in restaurants and shops, in bakeries and laundries and fisheries," about their inadequate wages, and their need for safety and sanitary protection. All this was to be in preparation for the next session of the Mississippi legislature.

Middle-class southern women set up two schools for factory girls. One, sponsored by the YWCA at Lake Junaluska in North Carolina, offered what its founders called a brief social-religious education. Although the organizers of this school realized that political action to improve their wages and working conditions could not be accomplished by the working women alone, they felt that these summer conferences might stimulate girls to begin to study and think about their own problems. The other experiment was the Southern Summer School for Women Workers in Industry, founded at Burnsville, North Carolina, in 1927. An outgrowth of the famous Bryn Mawr workers summer school, it offered training to factory girls many of whom, when the upsurge of unionization occurred in the 1930s, would become labor organizers.

By 1931 the Southern Council on Women and Children in Industry, made up of women, had been formed to work for shorter hours and to try to bring an end to night work in the textile industry. Lucy Mason worked for this group too, before she went on to her major effort in the 1930s as an organizer for the CIO.

It is curious in view of the deep conservatism of the majority of southern women, many of whom never registered to vote, that those who did choose to live an active life were often found on the progressive side of the political spectrum. Part of the explanation is that the person who was bold enough to assume a role unusual for women was also likely to be radical on social questions generally. As the president of the Tennessee League of Women Voters remarked:

> Some good souls are pleased to call our ideas socialistic. They are indeed uncomfortable often for some folk. Some timid souls of both sexes are only half converted to the new order . . . [yet] every clear thinking, right feeling and high minded man and woman should consecrate his best talents to the gradual reorganization of society, national and international.

One evidence of the advanced thinking of many of the southern women who were most active in public life was the important part they played in what came to be called the interracial movement. Beginning in 1919, at a time when many Negroes were leaving the South and many others were coming home from the war with a new view of life, the interracial movement of the twenties was built on the foundation laid in the previous decades. . . .

In 1920 at a meeting of southern churchwomen in Memphis four Negro women came on invitation to speak of the needs of southern Negroes. One of them, Charlotte Hawkins Brown, head of a school for Negroes in North Carolina, told the gathering that she had been forcibly removed from a Pullman car on her way to the meeting. In the emotional stir of the moment the ninety-odd white churchwomen constituted themselves the Woman's Department of Will Alexander's Commission on [Interracial Cooperation].

The first head of this group was Mrs. Luke Johnson of Griffin, Georgia, under whose leadership interracial committees were organized in every southern state. Mrs. Johnson thought race was "one of the livest issues of the day and . . . a real test of Christianity and of citizenship."

In Texas the women's interracial organization was put together by an energetic widow, businesswoman, and former suffrage worker, Jessie Daniel Ames. By 1924 women there were working to improve Negro housing, schools, libraries, to secure Negro farm agents to work with Negro farmers, for better health care, a school for delinquent girls, adequate railroad accommodations, and for textbooks dealing with the economic and racial development of the Negro people. They proposed an anti-lynching law which would have made every member of a mob liable to murder charges. The group also attempted to investigate particular problems of intimidation, and organized a speakers' bureau to take the discussion of race issues to the state. In North Carolina Mrs. Bertha Newell, superintendent of the Bureau of Christian Social Relations of the Women's Missionary Council of the Methodist Church, and Clara Cox, a Friend from High Point, carried on the same kind of effort. In 1926 Mrs. Newell began working to secure better job opportunities for educated Negro girls.

Women tried to deal with racial conflict and black problems in many ways. When the National League of Women Voters decided in 1924 to establish a committee on Negro problems with membership from every state that had more than 15 percent Negro population, women in eight southern states accepted appointment. Many of these same women served on local interracial committees, of which there were finally about eight hundred in the South. In Tennessee white women organized a special citizenship school for Negro women. Some individuals offered personal support to their Negro fellow citizens. Mary Cooke Branch Munford of Richmond made a room of her house permanently available to Negroes for public meetings, and a busy doctor's wife in Alabama waged a one-woman campaign for better Negro education. When the Richmond city council considered a segregation statute in 1929, it was Lucy Randolph Mason who, almost single-handedly, persuaded the council to defeat it. In April 1924 the Mississippi Federation of Women's Clubs set up a committee on the condition of the colored people, and the president of the Colored Women's Federation was invited to tell the white convention about the problems of Negro domestic workers.

The most dramatic aspect of women's interracial work was the crusade against lynching, which began in the early twenties. A group of Georgia women sent a message to the *New York World:*

> We are convinced that if there is any one crime more dangerous than others, it is that crime which strikes at the roots of and undermines constituted authority, breaks all laws and restraints of civilization, substitutes mob violence and masked irresponsibility for established justice and deprives society of a sense of protection against barbarism.

By 1930 under the leadership of Jessie Daniel Ames, who by that time had left Texas for Atlanta, the Association of Southern Women for the Prevention of Lynching took shape. At its peak this organization enrolled 40,000 small-town and rural churchwomen in an effort to bring to an end this most spectacularly disgraceful form of race conflict.

In the meantime southern white women inaugurated an increasing number of interracial meetings, in which there was fairly open discussion of the problems Negroes faced. Though Negro women leaders, for the most part, took care to eschew any demand for social equality, they did hammer away on such things as discrimination in the administration of justice, housing, Jim Crow cars, inferior education, and the need for the ballot. It seems likely that these efforts, ineffectual as they seemed in the face of the magnitude of the problem, nevertheless represented the opening wedge which would ultimately bring an end to the monolithic position of southerners on the issue of white supremacy. From slavery through Reconstruction and into the twentieth century, relationships between white and black women were quite unlike those common between white and black men, sharing as they did many concerns about children and home life across the color line. The fact that women were very active in the interracial movement is not surprising.

In the twenties white women were speaking of their sympathy for Negro women who were, like themselves, mothers and homemakers. One point they made over and over was the need to protect the chastity of Negro women from the aggression of white men. Just as one antebellum woman had candidly remarked that she did not know whether her grandmother's sympathy for abolition stemmed from sympathy for slaves or for white women, so it might be wondered whether part of the concern for the chastity of Negro women was a reflection of the white women's distaste for the half-hidden miscegenation which existed in every southern community.

The interest of women in humanitarian causes had deep roots in traditional feminine philanthropy. However, the twenties also witnessed the beginning of some newer interests. As they studied the mechanics of government in order to vote, women began to develop a concern for efficient organization. One of the tools for educating new voters to their responsibilities was the study of state and local government. As women went about looking at the way such governments actually operated they began to wonder whether they could be made more efficient. As early as 1922 women's groups in Virginia were working for improved election laws, and in the following year they undertook to learn about the executive budget. In 1924 the Virginia League of Women Voters concentrated upon tax administration, a subject which the controlling Democratic machine was not anxious to discuss. The same group successfully supported a bill to create a uniform fiscal year but failed in an effort to secure civil service, a conservation department, and reform of the county government and the state educational machinery.

Such interests were not confined to Virginia. Women in Georgia and Tennessee became convinced that outmoded constitutions were the source of much inefficiency; and in both states campaigns for constitutional revisions were launched and eventually succeeded. Kentucky women in 1927 began to work for home rule for cities, improvements in local charters, and the adoption of city manager government.

Women were interested not only in the structure of government; they wanted to make it more democratic. Their own long

exclusion had made them sensitive to citizen participation. It was newly enfranchised women who invented the now commonplace idea of getting out the vote. In some places their efforts led to spectacular increases. In Alabama, for example, 54.4 percent of the qualified voters voted in 1924 following a get-out-the-vote effort, compared to less than 30 percent in 1920. One county, where women had been particularly active, turned out 84.1 percent of its qualified voters. Florida in the same year reported a 65.9 percent increase over 1920 in the number of voters going to the polls.

The poll tax was a subject of twofold concern. Women's groups opposed the tax on principle, but as long as it remained in force, they set out to collect it in order to increase the number of qualified voters. In 1925 Louisiana women collected $30,000 to this end. The work of North Carolina women for the Australian ballot, which finally succeeded in 1929, was another example of an effort to improve democratic procedures.

Close to home, yet a long way from women's traditional concerns, were two other political issues that developed strength in southern women's groups in the twenties: government ownership of Muscle Shoals and the regulation of utility rates. Interest in both these questions resulted from studies of the cost of living. The movement that would lead to the Tennessee Valley Authority gained the enthusiastic support of women in Alabama and Tennessee. On these as on other questions politically active women took a pragmatic view without reference to traditional free enterprise arguments. . . .

Many southern women showed an interest in running for elective office; and, though numerous obstacles lay between almost any woman and nomination, by 1930 only Louisiana had yet to have women in the state legislature. During the twenties women served as secretaries of state in Kentucky, Texas, and Louisiana, as clerks or deputy clerks of the Supreme Court in Georgia and Oklahoma, as commissioners of public welfare in North Carolina and Oklahoma, as commissioner of state lands in Arkansas, railroad commissioner in Florida, and superintendent of public instruction in Texas.

One woman who made her way to the center of power was Mrs. Nellie Nugent Somerville of Greenville, Mississippi, who had been an active politician long before the Nineteenth Amendment. At the first election after it was legal to do so, in 1923, she ran for the state legislature, in a campaign that was a model of thorough organization, and was elected. She had been observing party organization long enough to understand it rather well, and she hoped the newly enfranchised women would be similarly observant. She advised them to be certain they had a hand in choosing county committees and reminded them: "It now becomes the duty of women voters to take lively interests in the details of political machinery. When any meeting or election is ordered by your political party be sure you take part in it." . . .

Another politically minded woman who reached a position of genuine power in the party was Sue Shelton White of Tennessee, an independent court reporter, secretary to members of the Tennessee Supreme Court, and from 1920 to 1926 secretary to Senator Kenneth McKellar. In 1915 she drafted the first mother's pension law to be presented to the Tennessee legislature, which finally passed in 1920. She went from her job in Senator McKellar's office to practice law in Jackson, Tennessee, and was sufficiently effective in Democratic politics to be invited to work for the Democratic National Committee. With Nellie Davis (Tayloe) Ross she helped lay the groundwork for the extensive women's program of the party during the early Franklin D. Roosevelt years. . . .

An increasing number of southern women undertook simple party work of the doorbell-ringing and envelope-stuffing variety—a trend that still continues. And whether they helped make policy or not, women voters believed they were affecting the outcome of elections. Women claimed to have defeated James E. Ferguson and elected William P. Hobby governor of Texas in 1920. In Mississippi Henry L. Whitfield, former president of Mississippi State College for Women, was elected governor in 1923, largely through the efforts of alumnae of the college. South Carolina women thought they had a large hand in the defeat of Cole Blease. One South Carolina woman who worked through the whole campaign remarked innocently, "We made no partisan stand, we merely got out the vote." Tennessee Democrats, perhaps looking for a scapegoat, blamed women for the Republican victory in Tennessee in the 1920 election. The women themselves claimed credit for the return of Cordell Hull to Congress three years later.

In North Carolina in 1921 the federated women persuaded a reluctant governor to appoint their former president, Kate Burr Johnson, commissioner of charities and welfare. The legislature showed an equal reluctance to confirm the appointment, but, as Mrs. Johnson recalled it, "They were scared to death of what women with the vote might do, and one legislator was heard to remark, 'Well, we might as well put her in; she's pretty and won't give us any trouble.' " The forecast was inaccurate, since Mrs. Johnson, with the organized women behind her, became a prime mover in the struggle to secure a survey of working conditions in North Carolina mills, and by so doing soon stood high on the legislature's list of troublemakers. . . .

Many of the women . . . who had been trained during the two or three decades before suffrage, and who had been acutely aware of the disadvantage of being barred from the polls, were eager to move into a more active and effective political role in 1920. Their general goals had been worked out in the preceding decades. Their underlying motivation was complex, but at least two main drives were clear: first, the drive to assert themselves as individual human beings with minds and capacities that could be used; and, second, the drive to improve the world in which they lived. The balance of these motives varied from person to person. Some, like Lucy Mason, were primarily interested in social reform:

> When I was fourteen, a missionary's sermon made me want to be a missionary myself. Later I recognized that religion can be put to work right in one's own community. It was this belief that took me into the Equal Suffrage League, and later the League of Women Voters, both of which were interested in labor and social legislation.

Others thoroughly enjoyed the game of politics and the feeling of power that occasionally accompanied it. Nearly all felt that significant reforms would be more easily achieved with women's help.

The Nineteenth Amendment changed a good many things, but it only partially modified southern culture. A number of difficulties remained in the way of women's full participation in public life. One major obstacle, in addition to the demands of home and family, was widespread male opposition, typified, perhaps, by the Texan who burned his wife's poll tax receipt to prevent her from voting. Equally important was the unwillingness of many women to assume and carry through large responsibilities. Often they had a vague desire to "do something" but needed leadership to find out what to do and how to do it, and there were never enough leaders to tap all the potential resources. A good example, no doubt an extreme one, was a Virginia town of which it was reported that when a certain Miss Terry was at home the town was alive with women's political activities but when she went to Europe all was quiet.

Around the handful of leaders there gathered a slowly growing number of supporters and workers, and when this support was effectively channeled, specific goals were achieved. In almost every instance—as in child labor reform, for example—groups of men were working to the same ends, and frequently there was cooperation. Women's efforts were crucial in the areas of race relations and factory regulation. Through it all, the outward aspect of the southern lady continued to be maintained as the necessary precondition for securing a hearing. For some women, this was a perfectly compatible outward role, so long as their freedom of action was not seriously limited. Others impatiently called for an end to pedestals, but even they found it effective to operate within the ladylike tradition. The other side of the coin was that women were accused of not being proper southern ladies by those who objected to the substantive goals for which they were working, and who hoped thus to discredit the goals themselves. . . .

When all this is said, however, the fact remains that the post-suffrage burst of political and social effort created a milieu in which the emerging new woman could try her powers. Along with expanding opportunities for work, education, and associated activity, the franchise added another dimension to women's lives, and another option for women who wanted more than purely domestic experience.

POSTSCRIPT

Did the Women's Movement Die in the 1920s?

Most students today associate the Equal Rights Amendment (ERA) with the women's liberation movement of the 1960s and 1970s, but, as Banner points out, the history of this amendment dates back to the 1920s. Proposed for the first time in 1923, the amendment stated that: "Men and women shall have equal rights throughout the United States and every place subject to its jurisdiction." This notion of full equality met significant opposition, as it has in recent years, including numerous challenges from women's organizations. Groups such as the League of Women Voters complained that the Equal Rights Amendment, if ratified, would roll back protective legislation with respect to minimum wage and maximum hour laws and would jeopardize penalties for rape and sexual offenses against women. Hence, many of the fruits of the Progressive Era would be lost. For Alice Paul, leader of the National Women's Party, which supported the amendment, the protective legislation enacted in the past represented a conspiracy to deny women full equality by singling them out for special treatment. These laws, Paul argued, set women apart as a separate and unequal class. The ideological struggle suggested by these divergent positions continued into the 1930s and reflected the serious divisions that surfaced in the women's movement following the suffrage victory.

The status of women in the decade after suffrage receives general treatment in William H. Chafe, *The American Woman: Her Changing Social, Economic, and Political Roles, 1920–1970* (Oxford University Press, 1972); June Sochen, *Herstory: A Woman's View of American History* (Alfred Publishing Company, 1974); Mary P. Ryan, *Womanhood in America: From Colonial Times to the Present* (New Viewpoints, 1975); Sheila M. Rothman, *Woman's Proper Place: A History of Changing Ideals and Practices, 1870 to the Present* (Basic Books, 1978); and Nancy Woloch, *Women and the American Experience* (Knopf, 1984). Discussions of feminism in the 1920s are presented in William L. O'Neill, *Everyone Was Brave: The Rise and Fall of Feminism in America* (University of Illinois Press, 1973); Susan D. Baker, *The Origins of the Equal Rights Amendment: Feminism Between the Wars* (Greenwood Press, 1981); and Nancy F. Cott, *The Grounding of Feminism* (Yale University Press, 1987). Cott's study argues that the diversity within the women's movement created important paradoxes. For example, although feminists in the 1920s desired equality with men, unity among themselves, and gender consciousness, they also focused upon their differences from men, the diversity of women, and the elimination of gender roles. David M. Kennedy, *Birth Control in America: The Career of Margaret Sanger* (Yale University Press, 1970), examines an important issue that attracted the interest of many women's groups in the 1920s, while Jacqueline Dowd Hall, *Revolt Against Chivalry: Jessie Daniel Ames and the Women's Campaign Against Lynching* (Columbia University Press, 1979), explores the role of women in the area of race relations. A valuable historiographical essay is presented in Estelle B. Freedman, "The New Woman: Changing Views of Women in the 1920s," *Journal of American History* (September 1974).

ISSUE 12

Was the New Deal an Effective Answer to the Great Depression?

YES: William E. Leuchtenburg, from "The Achievement of the New Deal," in Harvard Sitkoff, ed., *Fifty Years Later: The New Deal Evaluated* (Temple University Press, 1985)

NO: N. V. Sivachev, from "The New Deal of F. Roosevelt," in Otis L. Graham, Jr., ed., *Soviet-American Dialogue on the New Deal* (University of Missouri Press, 1989)

ISSUE SUMMARY

YES: Professor of history William E. Leuchtenburg contends that the New Deal extended the power of the national government in order to humanize the worst features of American capitalism.

NO: N. V. Sivachev, former director of the Department of Modern and Contemporary History at Moscow State University, criticizes the Roosevelt administration for adopting bourgeois socioeconomic policies that benefited industrial and agricultural capitalists ("state monopolism") while stifling legitimate social protest.

The catastrophe triggered by the 1929 Wall Street debacle crippled the American economy, deflated the optimistic future most Americans assumed to be their birthright, and ripped apart the values by which the country's businesses, farms, and governments were run. In the 1920s, the whirlwind of a boom economy had sucked people into its vortex. During the next decade, the inertia of the Great Depression stifled their attempts to make ends meet.

The world depression of the 1930s began in the United States, which is where some of the most serious effects were felt. The United States had suffered periodic economic setbacks—in 1873, 1893, 1907, and 1920—but those slumps had been limited and temporary. The omnipotence of American productivity, the ebullient American spirit, and the self-deluding thought "it can't happen here" blocked out any consideration of an economic collapse which might devastate the capitalist economy and threaten U.S. democratic government.

All aspects of American society trembled from successive jolts; there were four million unemployed people in 1930 and nine million more by 1932.

Those who had not lost their jobs took pay cuts or worked for scrip. Charitable organizations attempted to provide for millions of homeless and hungry people, but their resources were not adequate. There was no security for those whose savings were lost forever when banks failed or stocks declined. Manufacturing halted, industry shut down, and farmers destroyed wheat, corn, and milk rather than sell them at a loss. Worse, there were millions of homeless Americans; refugees from the cities roaming the nation on freight trains, victims of the drought of the Dust Bowl seeking a new life farther west, and hobo children estranged from their parents. Physicians reported increased cases of malnutrition. Some people plundered grocery stores rather than starve.

Business and government leaders alike seemed immobilized by the economic giant that had fallen to its knees. "In other periods of depression there has always been hope, but as I look about, I now see nothing to give ground for hope—nothing of man," said former president Calvin Coolidge on New Year's Day 1933. Herbert Hoover, the incumbent president at the start of the Great Depression, attempted some relief programs. They were, however, ineffective considering the magnitude of the unemployment, hunger, and distress. Nor did Hoover's initiatives recognize the need for serious changes in the relationship between the federal government and society or for any modification of its relationship with individual Americans.

As governor of New York, Franklin D. Roosevelt (who was elected president in 1932) had introduced some relief measures, such as industrial welfare and a comprehensive system of unemployment remedies, to alleviate the social and economic problems facing the citizens of the state. Yet his campaign did little to reassure his critics that he was more than a "Little Lord Fauntleroy" rich boy who wanted to be president. In light of later developments, Roosevelt may have been the only presidential candidate to deliver more programs than he actually promised.

In the following selections, William E. Leuchtenburg claims that Roosevelt's New Deal revolutionized American politics, reorganized the government to increase the powers of the presidency, and assumed responsibility for managing the economy. As a Marxist historian, N. V. Sivachev analyzed history from a class-oriented perspective. His essay argues that the New Deal brought about the transition of the economy from a system of monopolistic capitalism to one run by state-based monopolistic agencies, such as the NRA and the AAA. Furthermore, as he sees it, it was the masses that pressured the government to issue social reforms, such as minimum wage laws and social security.

YES

William E. Leuchtenburg

THE ACHIEVEMENT OF THE NEW DEAL

The fiftieth anniversary of the New Deal, launched on March 4, 1933, comes at a time when it has been going altogether out of fashion. Writers on the left, convinced that the Roosevelt experiment was either worthless or pernicious, have assigned it to the dustbin of history. Commentators on the right, though far less conspicuous, see in the New Deal the origins of the centralized state they seek to dismantle. Indeed, the half-century of the age of Roosevelt is being commemorated in the presidency of Ronald Reagan, who, while never tiring of quoting FDR, insists that the New Deal derived from Italian fascism. . . .

During the 1960s historians not only dressed up these objections as though they were new revelations but carried their disappointment with contemporary liberalism to the point of arguing either that the New Deal was not just inadequate but actually malign or that the New Deal was so negligible as to constitute a meaningless episode. This estimate derived in large part from disaffection with the welfare state, which Herbert Marcuse in *One-Dimensional Man* characterized as "a state of unfreedom," and which, as one critic noted, some considered "the ultimate form of repressive super-ego." The New Deal was now perceived to be elitist, since it had neglected to consult the poor about what legislation they wanted, or to encourage the participation of ghetto-dwellers in decision-making. Roosevelt's policies, historians maintained, redounded to the benefit of those who already had advantages—wealthier staple farmers, organized workers, business corporations, the "deserving poor"—while displacing sharecroppers and neglecting the powerless. An "antirevolutionary response to a situation that had revolutionary potentialities," the New Deal, it was said, missed opportunities to nationalize the banks and restructure the social order. Even "providing assistance to the needy and . . . rescuing them from starvation" served conservative ends, historians complained, for these efforts "sapped organized radicalism of its waning strength and of its potential constituency among the unorganized and discontented." The Roosevelt Administration, it has been asserted, failed to achieve more than it did not as a result of the

From William E. Leuchtenburg, "The Achievement of the New Deal," in Harvard Sitkoff, ed., *Fifty Years Later: The New Deal Evaluated* (Alfred A. Knopf, 1985). Copyright © 1985 by Alfred A. Knopf, Inc. Reprinted by permission of the publisher.

strength of conservative opposition but because of the intellectual deficiencies of the New Dealers and because Roosevelt deliberately sought to save "large-scale corporate capitalism." In *Towards a New Past*, the New Left historian Barton Bernstein summed up this point of view: "The New Deal failed to solve the problem of depression, it failed to raise the impoverished, it failed to redistribute income, it failed to extend equality and generally countenanced racial discrimination and segregation."

Although the characterization of Bernstein as "New Left" suggests that he represents a deviant persuasion, the New Left perspective has, in fact, all but become the new orthodoxy, even though there is not yet any New Left survey of the domestic history of the United States in the 1930s. This emphasis has so permeated writing on the New Deal in the past generation that an instructor who wishes to assign the latest thought on the age of Roosevelt has a wide choice of articles and anthologies that document the errors of the New Deal but no assessment of recent vintage that explores its accomplishments.

The fiftieth anniversary of the New Deal provides the occasion for a modest proposal—that we reintroduce some tension into the argument over the interpretation of the Roosevelt years. If historians are to develop a credible synthesis, it is important to regain a sense of the achievement of the New Deal. As it now stands, we have a dialectic that is all antithesis with no thesis. The so-called "debate" about the New Deal is not truly a debate, for even some of the historians who dispute the New Left assertions agree that one can only take a melancholy view of the period. The single question asked is whether the failure of

the New Deal was the fault of the Roosevelt Administration or the result of the strength of conservative forces beyond the government's control; the fact of failure is taken as the basic postulate. As a first step toward a more considered evaluation, one has to remind one's self not only of what the New Deal did not do, but of what it achieved.

NEW DEAL CHANGES

Above all, one needs to recognize how markedly the New Deal altered the character of the State in America. Indeed, though for decades past European theorists had been talking about *der Staat*, there can hardly be said to have been a State in America in the full meaning of the term before the New Deal. If you had walked into an American town in 1932, you would have had a hard time detecting any sign of a federal presence, save perhaps for the post office and even many of today's post offices date from the 1930s. Washington rarely affected people's lives directly. There was no national old-age pension system, no federal unemployment compensation, no aid to dependent children, no federal housing, no regulation of the stock market, no withholding tax, no federal school lunch, no farm subsidy, no national minimum wage law, no welfare state. As late as Herbert Hoover's presidency, it was regarded as axiomatic that government activity should be minimal. In the pre-Roosevelt era, even organized labor and the National Conference of Social Workers opposed federal action on behalf of the unemployed. The New Deal sharply challenged these shibboleths. From 1933 to 1938, the government intervened in a myriad of ways from energizing the economy to fostering unionization. . . .

This vast expansion of government led inevitably to the concentration of much greater power in the presidency, whose authority was greatly augmented under FDR. Rexford Tugwell has written of Roosevelt: "No monarch, . . . unless it may have been Elizabeth or her magnificent Tudor father, or maybe Alexander or Augustus Caesar, can have given quite that sense of serene presiding, of gathering up into himself, of really representing, a whole people." The President became, in Sidney Hyman's words, "the chief economic engineer," to whom Congress naturally turned for the setting of economic policy. Roosevelt stimulated interest in public affairs by his fireside chats and freewheeling press conferences, shifted the balance between the White House and Capitol Hill by assuming the role of Chief Legislator, and eluded the routinized traditional departments by creating emergency agencies. In 1939 he established the Executive Office of the President, giving the Chief Executive a central staff office for the first time. "The verdict of history," wrote Clinton Rossiter, "will surely be that he left the Presidency a more splendid instrument of democracy than he found it."

To staff the national agencies, Roosevelt turned to a new class of people: the university-trained experts. Before FDR, professors had not had an important role in the national government, save briefly in World War I, but when Roosevelt ran for president in 1932, he recruited advisers, most of them from Columbia University, who supplied him with ideas and helped write his speeches. During the First Hundred Days, large numbers of professors, encouraged by FDR's reliance on the Brain Trust, flocked to Washington to draft New Deal legislation and to ad-minister New Deal agencies. The radical literary critic Edmund Wilson wrote, "Everywhere in the streets and offices you run into old acquaintances: the editors and writers of the liberal press, the 'progressive' young instructors from the colleges, the intelligent foundation workers, the practical idealists of settlement houses." He added: "The bright boys of the Eastern universities, instead of being obliged to choose, as they were twenty years ago, between business, the bond-selling game and the field of foreign missions, can come on and get jobs in Washington." . . .

This corps of administrators made it possible for Roosevelt to carry out a major change in the role of the federal government. Although the New Deal always operated within a capitalist matrix and the government sought to enhance profitmaking, Roosevelt and his lieutenants rejected the traditional view that government was the handmaiden of business or that government and business were co-equal sovereigns. As a consequence, they adopted measures to discipline corporations, to require a sharing of authority with government and unions, and to hold businessmen accountable. . . .

Through a series of edicts and statutes, the administration invaded the realm of the banker by establishing control over the nation's money supply. The government clamped an embargo on gold, took the United States off the gold standard, and nullified the requirement for the payment of gold in private contracts. In 1935 a resentful Supreme Court sustained this authority, although a dissenting justice said that this was Nero at his worst. The Glass-Steagall Banking Act (1933) stripped commercial banks of the privilege of engaging in investment banking, and established federal insurance of bank deposits, an innovation which the leading monetary historians have called "the structural change most conducive to monetary stability since bank notes were taxed out of existence immediately after the Civil War." The Banking Act of 1935 gave the United States what other industrial nations had long had, but America lacked—central banking. This series of changes transformed the relationship between the government and the financial community from what it had been when Grover Cleveland had gone, hat in hand, to beseech J. P. Morgan for help. As Charles Beard observed: "Having lost their gold coins and bullion to the Federal Government and having filled their vaults with federal bonds and other paper, bankers have become in a large measure mere agents of the Government in Washington. No longer do these powerful interests stand, so to speak, 'outside the Government' and in a position to control or dictate to it."

A number of other enactments helped transfer authority from Wall Street to Washington. The Securities Act of 1933 established government supervision of the issue of securities, and made company directors civilly and criminally liable for misinformation on the statements they were required to file with each new issue. The Securities and Exchange Act of 1934 initiated federal supervision of the stock exchanges, which to this day operate under the lens of the Securities and Exchange Commission (SEC). The Holding Company Act of 1935 levelled some of the utility pyramids, dissolving all utility holding companies that were more than twice removed from their operating companies, and increased the regulatory powers of the SEC over public utilities. Robert Sobel has concluded that

the 1934 law marked "a shift of economic power from the lower part of Manhattan, where it had been for over a century, to Washington." To be sure, financiers continued to make important policy choices, but they never again operated in the uninhibited universe of the Great Bull Market. By the spring of 1934, one writer was already reporting:

> Financial news no longer originates in Wall Street. . . . News of a financial nature in Wall Street now is merely an echo of events which take place in Washington. . . . The pace of the ticker is determined now in Washington not in company boardrooms or in brokerage offices. . . . In Wall Street it is no longer asked what some big trader is doing, what some important banker thinks, what opinion some eminent lawyer holds about some pressing question of the day. The query in Wall Street has become: "What's the news from Washington?"

The age of Roosevelt focused attention on Washington, too, by initiatives in fields that had been regarded as exclusively within the private orbit, notably in housing. The Home Owners' Loan Corporation, created in 1933, saved tens of thousands of homes from foreclosure by refinancing mortgages. In 1934 the Federal Housing Administration (FHA) began its program of insuring loans for the construction and renovation of private homes, and over the next generation more than 10 million FHA-financed units were built. Before the New Deal, the national government had never engaged in public housing, except for the World War I emergency, but agencies like the Public Works Administration now broke precedent. The Tennessee Valley Authority laid out the model town of Norris, the Federal Emergency Relief Administration

(FERA) experimented with subsistence homesteads, and the Resettlement Administration created greenbelt communities, entirely new towns girdled by green countryside. When in 1937 the Wagner-Steagall Act created the U.S. Housing Authority, it assured public housing a permanent place in American life.

A NEW DEAL
FOR THE COMMON MAN

The New Deal profoundly altered industrial relations by throwing the weight of the government behind efforts to unionize workers. At the outset of the Great Depression, the American labor movement was "an anachronism in the world," for only a tiny minority of factory workers were unionized. Employers hired and fired and imposed punishments at will, used thugs as strikebreakers and private police, stockpiled industrial munitions, and ran company towns as feudal fiefs. In an astonishingly short period in the Roosevelt years a very different pattern emerged. Under the umbrella of Section 7(a) of the National Industrial Recovery Act of 1933 and of the far-reaching Wagner Act of 1935, union organizers gained millions of recruits in such open-shop strongholds as steel, automobiles, and textiles. Employees won wage rises, reductions in hours, greater job security, freedom from the tyranny of company guards, and protection against arbitrary punishment. Thanks to the National Recovery Administration and the Guffey acts, coal miners achieved the outlawing of compulsory company houses and stores. Steel workers, who in 1920 labored twelve-hour shifts seven days a week at the blast furnaces, were to become so powerful that in the postwar

era they would win not merely paid vacations but sabbatical leaves. A British analyst has concluded: "From one of the most restrictive among industrially advanced nations, the labour code of the United States (insofar as it could be said to exist before 1933) was rapidly transformed into one of the most liberal," and these reforms, he adds, "were not the harvest of long-sustained agitation by trade unions, but were forced upon a partly skeptical labor movement by a government which led or carried it into maturity."

Years later, when David E. Lilienthal, the director of the Tennessee Valley Authority, was being driven to the airport to fly to Roosevelt's funeral, the TVA driver said to him:

I won't forget what he did for me. . . . I spent the best years of my life working at the Appalachian Mills . . . and they didn't even treat us like humans. If you didn't do like they said, they always told you there was someone else to take your job. I had my mother and my sister to take care of. Sixteen cents an hour was what we got; a fellow can't live on that, and you had to get production even to get that, this Bedaux system; some fellows only got twelve cents. If you asked to get off on a Sunday, the foreman would say, "All right you stay away Sunday, but when you come back Monday someone else will have your job." No, sir, I won't forget what he done for us.

Helen Lynd has observed that the history of the United States is that of England fifty years later, and a half century after the welfare state had come to Western Europe, the New Deal brought it to America. The NRA wiped out sweatshops, and removed some 150,000 child laborers from factories. The Walsh-Healey Act of 1936 and the Fair Labor Standards

Act of 1938 established the principle of a federally imposed minimal level of working conditions, and added further sanctions against child labor. If the New Deal did not do enough for the "one-third of a nation" to whom Roosevelt called attention, it at least made a beginning, through agencies like the Farm Security Administration, toward helping sharecroppers, tenant farmers, and migrants like John Steinbeck's Joads. Most important, it originated a new system of social rights to replace the dependence on private charity. The Social Security Act of 1935 created America's first national system of old-age pensions and initiated a federal-state program of unemployment insurance. It also authorized grants for the blind, for the incapacitated, and for dependent children, a feature that would have unimaginable long-range consequences. . . .

Roosevelt himself affirmed the newly assumed attitudes in Washington in his annual message to Congress in 1938 when he declared: "Government has a final responsibility for the well-being of its citizenship. If private co-operative endeavor fails to provide work for willing hands and relief for the unfortunate, those suffering hardship from no fault of their own have a right to call upon the Government for aid; and a government worthy of its name must make fitting response."

A NEW DEAL
FOR THE UNEMPLOYED

Nothing revealed this approach so well as the New Deal's attention to the plight of the millions of unemployed. During the ten years between 1929 and 1939, one scholar has written, "more progress was made in public welfare and relief than in the three hundred years after this country was first settled." A series of alphabet agencies—the FERA, the CWA, the WPA —provided government work for the jobless, while the National Youth Administration (NYA) employed college students in museums, libraries, and laboratories, enabled high school students to remain in school, and set up a program of apprentice training. In Texas, the twenty-seven-year-old NYA director Lyndon Johnson put penniless young men like John Connally to work building roadside parks, and in North Carolina, the NYA employed, at 35 cents an hour, a Duke University law student, Richard Nixon.

In an address in Los Angeles in 1936, the head of FDR's relief operations, Harry Hopkins, conveyed the attitude of the New Deal toward those who were down and out:

I am getting sick and tired of these people on the W.P.A. and local relief rolls being called chiselers and cheats. . . . These people . . . are just like the rest of us. They don't drink any more than us, they don't lie any more, they're no lazier than the rest of us—they're pretty much a cross section of the American people. . . . I have never believed that with our capitalistic system people have to be poor. I think it is an outrage that we should permit hundreds and hundreds of thousands of people to be ill clad, to live in miserable homes, not to have enough to eat; not to be able to send their children to school for the only reason that they are poor. I don't believe ever again in America we are going to permit the things to happen that have happened in the past to people. We are never going back . . . to the days of putting the old people in the alms houses, when a decent dignified pension at home will keep them there. We are coming to the day when we are going to have decent houses for the poor, when there is genuine and real security for everybody. I have gone all over the moral hurdles that people are poor because they are bad. I don't believe it. A system of government on that basis is fallacious.

Under the leadership of men like Hopkins, "Santa Claus incomparable and privy-builder without peer," projects of relief agencies and of the Public Works Administration (PWA) changed the face of the land. The PWA built thoroughfares like the Skyline Drive in Virginia and the Overseas Highway from Miami to Key West, constructed the Medical Center in Jersey City, burrowed Chicago's new subway, and gave Natchez, Mississippi, a new bridge, and Denver a modern water-supply system. Few New Yorkers today realize the long reach of the New Deal. If they cross the Triborough Bridge, they are driving on a bridge the PWA built. If they fly into La Guardia Airport, they are landing at an airfield laid out by the WPA. If they get caught in a traffic jam on the FDR Drive, they are using yet another artery built by the WPA. Even the animal cages in Central Park Zoo were reconstructed by WPA workers. In New York City, the WPA built or renovated hundreds of school buildings; gave Orchard Beach a bathhouse, a mall, and a lagoon; landscaped Bryant Park and the campus of Hunter College in the Bronx; conducted examinations for venereal disease, filled teeth, operated pollen count stations, and performed puppet shows for disturbed children; it built dioramas for the Brooklyn Museum; ran street dances in Harlem and an open-air night club in Central Park; and, by combining neglected archives, turned up forgotten documents like the court proceedings in the Aaron Burr libel case and the marriage license issued to Captain Kidd. In New York City alone the WPA employed more people than the entire War Department. . . .

The New Deal showed unusual sensitivity toward jobless white-collar workers, notably those in aesthetic fields. The Public Works of Art Project gave an opportunity to muralists eager for a chance to work in the style of Rivera, Orozco, and Siqueiros. The Federal Art Project fostered the careers of painters like Stuart Davis, Raphael Soyer, Yasuo Kuniyoshi, and Jackson Pollock. Out of the same project came a network of community art centers and the notable *Index of American Design*. . . .

The Federal Writers' Project provided support for scores of talented novelists and poets, editors and literary critics, men like Ralph Ellison and Nelson Algren, John Cheever and Saul Bellow. These writers turned out an exceptional set of state guides, with such features as Conrad Aiken's carefully delineated portrayal of Deerfield, Massachusetts, and special volumes like *These Are Our Lives*, a graphic portfolio of life histories in North Carolina, and *Panorama*, in which Vincent McHugh depicts "the infinite pueblo of the Bronx." Project workers transcribed chain-gang blues songs, recovered folklore that would otherwise have been lost, and collected the narratives of elderly former slaves, an invaluable archive later published in *Lay My Burden Down*. . . .

Some thought it an ill omen that the Federal Theatre Project's first production was Shakespeare's *Comedy of Errors*, but that agency not only gave employment to actors and stage technicians but offered many communities their first glimpse of live drama. . . .

Roosevelt, it has been said, had a "proprietary interest in the nation's estate," and this helps account for the fact that the 1930s accomplished for soil conservation and river valley development what the era of Theodore Roosevelt had done for the forests. The Tennessee Valley Authority, which drew admirers from all over the world, put the national government in the business of generating electric power, controlled floods, terraced hillsides, and gave new hope to the people of the valley. In the Pacific Northwest the PWA constructed mammoth dams, Grand Coulee and Bonneville. Roosevelt's "tree army," the Civilian Conservation Corps, planted millions of trees, cleared forest trails, laid out picnic sites and campgrounds, and aided the Forest Service in the vast undertaking of establishing a shelterbelt—a windbreak of trees and shrubs: green ash and Chinese elm, apricot and blackberry, buffalo berry and Osage orange from the Canadian border to the Texas panhandle. Government agencies came to the aid of drought-stricken farmers in the Dust Bowl, and the Soil Conservation Service, another New Deal creation, instructed growers in methods of cultivation to save the land. As Alistair Cooke later said, the favorite of the New Dealers was the farmer with the will to "take up contour plowing late in life."

These services to farmers represented only a small part of the government's program, for in the New Deal years, the business of agriculture was revolutionized. Roosevelt came to power at a time of mounting desperation for the American farmers. Each month in 1932 another 20,000 farmers had lost their land because of inability to meet their debts in a period of collapsing prices. On a single day in May 1932, one-fourth of the state of Mississippi went under the sheriff's hammer. The Farm Credit Administration of 1933 came to the aid of the beleaguered farmer, and within eighteen months, it had refinanced one-fifth of all farm mortgages in the United States. In the Roosevelt years, too, the Rural Electrification Administration literally brought rural America out of darkness. At the beginning of the Roosevelt era, only one farm in nine had electricity; at the end, only one in nine did not have it. But more important than any of these developments was the progression of enactments starting with the first AAA (the Agricultural Adjustment Act) of 1933, which began the process of granting large-scale subsidies to growers. As William Faulkner later said, "Our economy is not agricultural any longer. Our economy is the federal government. We no longer farm in Mississippi cotton fields. We farm now in Washington corridors and Congressional committee rooms."

GOVERNMENT OF AND FOR MORE OF THE PEOPLE

At the same time that its realm was being expanded under the New Deal, the national government changed the composition of its personnel and of its beneficiaries. Before 1933, the government had paid heed primarily to a single group—white Anglo-Saxon Protestant males. The Roosevelt Administration, however, recruited from a more ethnically diverse group, and the prominence of Catholics and Jews among the President's advisers is suggested by the scintillating team of the Second Hundred Days, Corcoran and Cohen. The Federal Writers' Project turned out books on Italians and Albanians, and the Federal Theatre staged productions in Yiddish and wrote a history of the Chinese stage in Los Angeles. In the 1930s women played a more prominent role in government than they ever had before, as the result of such appointments as that of Frances Perkins as the first female cabinet member, while the influence of Eleanor Roosevelt was pervasive. . . .

Although in some respects the New Deal's performance with regard to blacks added to the sorry record of racial discrimination in America, important gains were also registered in the 1930s. Blacks, who had often been excluded from relief in the past, now received a share of WPA jobs considerably greater than their proportion of the population. Blacks moved into federal housing projects; federal funds went to schools and hospitals in black neighborhoods; and New Deal agencies like the Farm Security Administration (FSA) enabled 50,000 Negro tenant farmers and sharecroppers to become proprietors. "Indeed," one historian has written, "there is a high correlation between the location of extensive FSA operations in the 1930s and the rapidity of political modernization in black communities in the South in the 1960s." Roosevelt appointed a number of blacks, including William Hastie, Mary McLeod Bethune, and Robert Weaver, to high posts in the government. Negroes in the South who were disfranchised in white primaries voted in AAA crop referenda and in National Labor Relations Board plant elections, and a step was taken toward restoring their constitutional rights when Attorney General Frank Murphy set up a Civil Liberties Unit in the Department of Justice. The reign of Jim Crow in Washington offices, which had begun under Roosevelt's Democratic predecessor, Woodrow Wilson, was terminated by Secretary of the Interior Harold Ickes who desegre-gated cafeterias in his department. Ickes also had a role in the most dramatic episode of the times, for when the Daughters of the American Revolution (DAR) denied the use of their concert hall to the black contralto Marian Anderson, he made it possible for her to sing before thousands from the steps of Lincoln Memorial; and Mrs. Roosevelt joined in the rebuke to the DAR. Anderson's concert on Easter Sunday 1939 was heard by thousands at the Memorial, and three networks carried her voice to millions more. Blacks delivered their own verdict on the New Deal at the polling places. Committed to the party of Lincoln as late as 1932, when they voted overwhelmingly for Hoover, they shifted in large numbers to the party of FDR during Roosevelt's first term. This was a change of allegiance that many whites were also making in those years.

THE DURABLE LEGACY OF THE NEW DEAL

The Great Depression and the New Deal brought about a significant political realignment of the sort that occurs only rarely in America. The Depression wrenched many lifelong Republican voters from their moorings. In 1928, one couple christened their newborn son "Herbert Hoover Jones." Four years later they petitioned the court, "desiring to relieve the young man from the chagrin and mortification which he is suffering and will suffer," and asked that his name be changed to Franklin D. Roosevelt Jones. In 1932 FDR became the first Democrat to enter the White House with as much as 50 percent of the popular vote in eighty years—since Franklin K. Pierce in 1852. Roosevelt took advantage of this opportunity to mold "the FDR coalition," an alliance centered in the low-income districts of the great cities and, as recently as the 1980 election, the contours of the New Deal coalition could still be discerned. Indeed, over the past half-century, the once overpowering Republicans have won control of Congress only twice, for a total of four years. No less important was the shift in the character of the Democratic party from the conservative organization of John W. Davis and John J. Raskob to the country's main political instrumentality for reform. "One political result of the Roosevelt years," Robert Burke has observed, "was a basic change in the nature of the typical Congressional liberal." He was no longer a maverick, who made a fetish of orneriness, no longer one of the men Senator Moses called "the sons of the wild jackass," but "a party Democrat, labor-oriented, urban, and internationalist-minded."

Furthermore, the New Deal drastically altered the agenda of American politics. When Arthur Krock of the *New York Times* listed the main programmatic questions before the 1932 Democratic convention, he wrote: "What would be said about the repeal of prohibition that had split the Republicans? What would be said about tariffs?" By 1936, these concerns seemed altogether old fashioned, as campaigners discussed the Tennessee Valley Authority and industrial relations, slum clearance and aid to the jobless. That year, a Little Rock newspaper commented: "Such matters as tax and tariff laws have given way to universally human things, the living problems and opportunities of the average man and the average family."

The Roosevelt years changed the conception of the role of government not just in Washington but in the states, where a series of "Little New Deals"—

under governors like Herbert Lehman in New York—added a thick sheaf of social legislation, and in the cities. In Boston, Charles Trout has observed, city council members in 1929 "devoted endless hours to street paving." After the coming of the New Deal, they were absorbed with NRA campaigns, public housing, and WPA allotments. "A year after the crash the council thought 5,000 dollars an excessive appropriation for the municipal employment bureau," but during the 1930s "the unemployed drained Boston's treasury of not less than 100,000,000 dollars in direct benefits, and the federal government spent even more."

In a cluster of pathbreaking decisions in 1937, the Supreme Court legitimized this vast exercise of authority by government at all levels. As late as 1936, the Supreme Court still denied the power of the United States government to regulate agriculture, even though crops were sold in a world market, or coal mining, a vital component of a national economy, and struck down a minimum wage law as beyond the authority of the state of New York. Roosevelt responded with a plan to "pack" the Court with as many as six additional Justices, and in short order the Court, in what has been called "the Constitutional Revolution of 1937," sounded retreat. Before 1937 the Supreme Court stood as a formidable barrier to social reform. Since 1937 not one piece of significant social legislation has been invalidated, and the Court has shifted its docket instead to civil rights and civil liberties. . . .

The New Deal accomplished all of this at a critical time, when many were insisting that fascism was the wave of the future and denying that democracy could be effective. . . .

In these "dark and leaden thirties," Professor Berlin [wrote], "the only light in the darkness that was left was the administration of Mr. Roosevelt and the New Deal in the United States. At a time of weakness and mounting despair in the democratic world Mr. Roosevelt radiated confidence and strength. . . . Even to-day, upon him alone, of all the statesmen of the thirties, no cloud rested neither on him nor on the New Deal, which to European eyes still looks a bright chapter in the history of mankind."

For the past generation, America has lived off the legacy of the New Deal. Successive administrations extended the provisions of statutes like the Social Security Act, adopted New Deal attitudes toward intervention in the economy to cope with recessions, and put New Deal ideas to modern purposes, as when the Civilian Conservation Corps served as the basis for both the Peace Corps and the VISTA program of the War on Poverty. Harry Truman performed under the shadow of FDR, Lyndon Johnson consciously patterned his administration on Roosevelt's, Jimmy Carter launched his first presidential campaign at Warm Springs, and Ronald Reagan has manifested an almost obsessive need to summon FDR to his side. Carl Degler has observed:

Conventionally the end of the New Deal is dated with the enactment of the Wages and Hours Act of 1938. But in a fundamental sense the New Deal did not end then at all. Americans still live in the era of the New Deal, for its achievements are now the base mark below which no conservative government may go and from which all new reform now starts. . . . The reform efforts of the Democratic Truman, Kennedy, and Johnson administrations have been little more than fulfillments of the New Deal. . . .

By restoring to the debate over the significance of the New Deal acknowledgment of its achievements, we may hope to produce a more judicious estimate of where it succeeded and where it failed. For it unquestionably did fail in a number of respects. There were experiments of the 1930s which miscarried, opportunities that were fumbled, groups who were neglected, and power that was arrogantly used. Over the whole performance lies the dark cloud of the persistence of hard times. The shortcomings of the New Deal are formidable, and they must be recognized. But I am not persuaded that the New Deal experience was negligible. Indeed, it is hard to think of another period in the whole history of the republic that was so fruitful or of a crisis that was met with as much imagination.

NO

N. V. Sivachev

THE NEW DEAL OF F. ROOSEVELT

The socioeconomic reforms and ideopolitical changes in the middle and late 1930s known as the New Deal (from the beginning of Roosevelt's administration on 4 March 1933 until the problems connected with World War II at the end of the decade) constitute one of the most important periods in American history. During the past decade the historiography of the New Deal has been shaped by differing views on the relationship of reform to sharp class and political conflict. The meaning of what occurred from 1933 to 1939 has become an integral part of American political and intellectual life. History and contemporaneity merged. . . .

The works of bourgeois historians ignored the process of governmentalization that underlay Roosevelt's reforms, overestimated the roles of Hoover and Roosevelt, and underestimated the role of the working class in bringing about progressive social reform. The critical potential of radical historians, who came close to an understanding of the class character of the New Deal, was weakened by the absence of a dialectical approach to the historical process. Their vision of the history of the 1930s was inadequate to the extent that they did not understand the complexity of American capitalism's state-monopolistic development.

In Soviet historiography the New Deal is studied as a "categoric shift in the social development of the country." It is the result of the process by which American monopolistic capitalism developed into state-monopolism. [Editorial note: For more information about terms used by Soviet historians in describing American history, see N. V. Sivachev and E. F. Yazkov, *History of the USA Since World War I* (Moscow, 1976), and E. F. Yazkov, ed., *The U.S. Two-Party System: Past and Present* (Moscow, 1988).] The Leninist theory and analysis of state-monopolistic capitalism explains the nature of governmentalization that ran its full course in the United States in the beginning of the twentieth century, the catalytic role of the crisis of 1929–1933, the significance of political activity among certain bourgeois groups adept at social maneuvering to prompt and accelerate action, and the bourgeois character of governmentalization. Leninist analysis shows both the speculation of raising

From N. V. Sivachev, "The New Deal of F. Roosevelt," in Otis L. Graham, Jr., ed., *Soviet-American Dialogue on the New Deal* (University of Missouri Press, 1989). Copyright © 1989 by the Curators of the University of Missouri. Reprinted by permission of the University of Missouri Press. Notes omitted.

questions about a "Roosevelt revolution" and the dogmatism of radical historians who found nothing new in the New Deal because its supporters defended and strengthened capitalism.

New Deal economic policy took two directions. One involved deep institutional reforms that brought an increased government role in production; the other involved deficit financing. Both these directions intertwined; both prompted the private monopolies that formed the economic base to show sympathy for the idea of state-monopoly. . . .

Once they had been handed the reigns of government, Democrats were convinced it was impossible to fulfill their election promises of cutting government spending and balancing the budget. Practical needs of the day forced New Dealers to turn to deficit financing. Increased government spending was dictated by two important conditions: first, the already difficult economic situation was made worse by the failure of private business to undertake industrial capital investment; and second, and more evident and urgent, an unemployed army of many millions expected material aid from government. Investments in industrial and social life were linked inseparably. Both demanded repudiation of traditional wisdom about the budget— which mostly rested on reducing the limit on what could be spent during a fiscal year.

The argument over when, whether, and to what degree Roosevelt became a Keynesian economist persists in American literature to this day. The state-monopolistic theory of J[ohn Maynard] Keynes featured an active role for government in the economy and sanctioned expansion of government spending without regard to possible budget deficit.

Both were features of the New Deal, not as a result of reading Keynes (although his works were studied attentively by many American economists, including some of Roosevelt's advisors and aides), but due to the pressure of circumstances. In 1933 the government revealed plans for a grandiose hydroelectric station in the basin of the Tennessee River and created a special Tennessee Valley Authority (TVA). By means of government investment, numerous aspects of life in the region would be reconstructed. But the political right wing bitterly attacked the TVA as the embodiment of "socialism"—even though it was the very image of state-monopoly. While New Dealers caused government to intervene in the economy quite apart from any influence of Keynes, in the area of budgeting they departed from orthodoxy because of real needs and the inculcation of Keynesian thought in the United States.

The specific character of New Deal economic policy was determined by tension between deficit financing (the policy of "priming the pump") and the belief of most New Dealers in balancing the budget. Very few supporters of deficit financing came forward in 1933–1934 during the early stage of the New Deal, but those crisis years proved to be a great teacher. During the second stage of the New Deal, which became evident in 1935, advocates of deficit spending had much greater influence in Roosevelt's circle. Then, the economic crisis of 1937–1938 further opened the science of economics and economic policy to Keynesian thinking. From 1936 to 1937 the budget deficit had decreased sharply—from $3.5 billion to $0.2 billion. But in an address to Congress on 14 April 1938, Roosevelt recommended a major increase in government spending. In his subsequent "fireside chat" he admitted that a precipitate drop in state spending during 1936–1937 had been one of the basic causes of the recession of 1937–1938. The budget deficit rose significantly; it amounted to $2 billion in 1938 and $2.2 billion in 1939. The war greatly heightened this trend.

Although New Dealers did not acknowledge Keynesian ideas about deficits as consistent and positive weapons in economic policy, they nevertheless implemented this primary aspect of Keynesian theory more than did the English. In 1929 general private investment amounted to $35 billion (in 1954 prices), and the value of goods and services purchased by government agencies came to $18.5 billion (of which $2.9 billion was spent by the federal government). In 1938 the relation between the two categories had changed. Private investment had fallen to $15.5 billion, and government purchases had increased to $28.8 billion (of which $11.4 billion was attributable to the federal government). This change encouraged the growth of the government debt. In 1929 government debt amounted to $29.7 billion, with $16.5 billion of that amount incurred by the federal government. By 1939, government debt was $58.9 billion, with $42.6 billion owed by the federal government. The increase of the federal portion was particularly important. In 1929 it was 58.9 percent of all government debt, and in 1939 it was 72.3 percent. Government circles gradually had to change their thinking about Keynesianism in order to rationalize the deficit and the debt. At the end of the decade the president himself was among those who, though not yet Keynesian, had ceased to feel their former trepidation about deficits.

New Deal financial and economic measures, which were seen by their initiators as devices for rescuing the economy from depression and as barriers against a new recession, fell far short of the intent. The beginning of a new, unexpected economic crisis in 1937 was the best proof. Compared to 1936, the index of industrial production had fallen by 16.4 percent by 1938. The dubious means of applying anticrisis therapy, through the "built-in stabilizers" created by New Dealers' economic policies, undoubtedly strengthened the development of state-monopoly. The index of industrial production in 1938 was 53.3 percent higher than in 1932, and 120 percent higher by 1940. The pattern of federal spending also had changed: from 1932 to 1938 expenditures rose by almost 100 percent, from $4.266 billion to $8.449 billion, and from 1932 to 1940 by 136 percent—to $10.061 billion. Admittedly, using 1932 (the lowest point in the Depression) as the date for comparison weakens proof of the thesis that federal expenditures outstripped other economic growth; but the figures are nevertheless convincing. The great change in the movement of these indicators would be particularly striking if the latter years of the 1920s were used as the point of comparison: production from 1927 to 1940 increased by 32 percent, and federal expenditures by 185 percent. Government expenditures are one of the most important components in state-monopolistic capitalism. The sharp and steady growth of government expenditures over a relatively short time is a persuasive quantitative measurement of proof of the transformation of monopolistic capitalism in America into state-monopolism.

While the New Deal economy was evolving into state-monopolism, the approach to resolving social problems was becoming that of state socialism. In the United States state socialism was particularly liberal; it was reflective of the broad and deep maneuvering of the masses in behalf of a number of urgent demands. For the first time in American history social policy was consistent with needs. Such factors as the deepening socioeconomic crisis and the rise of democratic movements among the masses had a decisive influence on its formation. According to official data, 13 million people did not have work in 1933. In 1937 the number of the unemployed had decreased to 7.7 million, but in 1938 it jumped again to 10.4 million. And in 1939, the figure was 9.5 million, that is, 17.2 percent of the work force. Indeed, the number of unemployed for all these years was actually significantly higher. Secretary of Labor F[rances] Perkins stated that in 1933 it reached 18 million. According to trade union statistics, nearly 12 million were unemployed in January 1940, and 8.2 million in April 1941 (at a time official data showed only 5.6 million unemployed). The most important trait of international political development was the rise of the workers' and democratic movement. During the Depression and particularly during the New Deal, the United States entered this movement and the country seethed.

The workers' and democratic movement of the period under review was a militant offensive in support of broad sociopolitical goals. Foremost were demands for effective aid to the unemployed. These included legislation to create social insurance, legislation to set a minimum wage and a maximum work day, recognition of trade unions and collective bargaining, help for debt-ridden farmers and other workers, and guarantees of civil rights for even the most discriminated-against minority. The masses demanded a stop to the spread of fascism and a stop to events that threatened the unleashing of a new world war. The country experienced the most dramatic shift to the left since the second American revolution [i.e., the Civil War and Reconstruction]. A powerful new alliance of industrial unions arose—the Congress of Industrial Organizations (CIO)—in which the Communists exercised great influence. In 1932, there were 2,857,000 members of trade unions in the United States. By 1939 the two federations of unions (AFL and CIO) had enrolled 8,980,000 workers. During the middle and second half of the 1930s, the Communist Party of the United States occupied a stable position in unions and other organizations of the masses for the first time. In 1938 the ranks of the Communist party contained 75,000 members. Socialist thinking was having considerable influence among American intellectuals. American Socialist leader N[orman] Thomas had every reason to call the 1930s the "red decade." In the midst of the Depression and the powerful expression of popular will, there was still perceptible the authority of the monopolies, entities that during the years of "prosperity" considered themselves to be "in the saddle." After 1929, in the words of one American business leader, business was "in the doghouse." This decisively weakened the opposition of monopoly capital to progressive social innovations.

Resolving social problems through state socialist methods was accelerated by international conditions and events—signs of the general breakdown of capitalism. The revolutionary practice of socialistic construction in the USSR had a visible influence. The principles of socialist planning, successfully realized in the USSR by fulfilling the first five-year plan, strengthened the position of believers in government regulation of the economy in the United States. Many Americans, not particularly concerned about accurate terminology, drew an analogy between government regulation of the economy and the Soviet experiment in "planning." The social aspects of transformations in the Soviet Union had an even stronger influence on American society. Elimination of unemployment in the USSR together with success in the fields of education and social and health insurance proved convincingly that government responsibility for the fate of each citizen led not to the destruction of individuality, but to improved well-being and to conditions in which individual abilities could be most fully developed. Americans were also influenced from the opposite end of the political spectrum. Spokesmen for world fascism speculated on the inability of traditional parliamentary regimes to resolve social problems, and the false slogans of the fascists about the "final solution" for all problems alienated the masses from bourgeois democracy.

More than anything, the Roosevelt administration had to concern itself with the problem of unemployment. The administration tried to resolve the problem through three basic steps: distribution of monetary subsidies to the unemployed, execution of all possible public works projects, and passage of social insurance legislation. . . .

The reforms of the New Deal and the conflicts that accompanied them called for certain changes in the functioning of government institutions, in ideology, and in the two-party system. In each area there were marks left by the terrible crisis of 1929-1933 and the aftermath that lasted until World War II. Change re-

sulted from sharp class and political conflict, which in turn deepened social antagonisms. This dynamic caused the New Deal period to be one of the stormiest in United States history.

At the beginning of the New Deal, during the "hundred days" (the period of the special session of the Seventy-third Congress, 9 March to 16 June 1933), laws were passed usually without discussion and, by American standards, at a fantastic speed. Although petty skirmishes arose over individual bills, on the whole congressmen from both the majority and minority parties obediently endorsed the initiatives that seemed to pour from some legislative cornucopia in the White House. There seemed to be an atmosphere of "national unity" for a time, although in fact it was only a temporary muting of traditional interparty conflict. When the spirit of national unity disintegrated, there were several consequences. Foremost among them was the fact that New Dealers did not pull the economy out of crisis or end the outbreaks of social protest. When the initial response proved so ineffective, Roosevelt's circle was pushed into new experimentation, but that promoted simultaneous opposition from the traditionalists. Having been forced to adjust to the feverish activity of the "hundred days," they now saw the New Deal's shortcomings. And when government became active in matters that were traditionally the province of private enterprise, some considered it threateningly close to "socialism." The rise of the workers' and democratic movements—the main reasons for the New Deal's shift to the left—intensified ideopolitical conflict inside the ruling class. Some in these groups came to believe that New Dealers indulged the masses in order to grab power and to achieve "dictatorial" goals. Such feelings deepened the opposition of business to economic regulatory measures.

At the same time, Roosevelt's reforms were criticized by leftists, including the Communists. But all the heaviest attacks came from the right, from the reactionary-conservative camp. . . .

After the 1934 election, opponents of reform put their hope in the United States Supreme Court, the last stronghold of tradition in the system. It must be said that when the New Deal shifted to the left, the majority of the ruling class did not embrace the Liberty League or fascist demagogues. They supported traditional conservatives, who were particularly strong in the judiciary and reasonably influential in Congress, and reasonably strong in both political parties, especially the Republican. The Supreme Court in 1935 and 1936 raised hopes in the rightist camp by annulling twelve New Deal laws, among them two of the most important passed during the "hundred days"—the NIRA and the act to regulate agricultural production. The NIRA was unanimously declared unconstitutional for two reasons: there was an improper transfer of legislative power to the executive branch, and the federal government undertook regulation of commerce over which it lacked jurisdiction. The acts of suppression, of active government interference in socioeconomic relations, of banning concessions to the workers, were based on those rationales. That is to say, the court decisions were in conflict with the liberal state of socialism of the New Dealers.

Thus the courts were severely tested during the Depression; their very existence, in fact, was threatened by efforts of Roosevelt's government to strengthen the bourgeoisie. The ruling class itself seemed deeply split over questions of political strategy. . . .

If, after the shattering defeat of the Republicans and the whole reactionary bunch in the 1936 election, the Supreme Court had invalidated the highly important social legislation passed during 1935 (as well it might have in light of its recent performance), there could have been extremely dangerous social outbursts with unpredictable results. The president fully realized that he was mandated to fight for those laws. However, a decision to confront the Supreme Court openly was not easy, for in the United States the image of the Court had long been one of a judicial Olympus of unquestionable authority. Instead, the situation called for plotting a blow to forestall the Supreme Court—something to deter the Court from rashly liquidating the laws passed in 1935 that had found such favor among the masses. The noisy campaign in 1937 to reform the courts should be viewed in this light. Inasmuch as his plan for judicial reform was never enacted, Roosevelt was defeated. But the very debates over the plan played a role in reorienting the Supreme Court—and that was Roosevelt's main objective. Even as the heated political arguments continued, the Supreme Court favorably reviewed three exceptionally important cases—the Wagner Act, the law on social insurance, and state laws to regulate industrial working conditions. These decisions weakened the attacks against the Supreme Court and in many ways warded off a congressional decision to impose unwanted changes.

Contemporaries and, later, bourgeois historiography showed not a few misunderstandings about events and the debates over judicial reform. Roosevelt's opponents clearly exaggerated the extent of his defeat. They lost sight of something more essential—the fact that this campaign helped "reeducate" the judicial body and facilitated the approval of New Deal enactments. Roosevelt's supporters, and some of his opponents, exaggerated another way. They vastly overcredited the 1937 reform campaign with forcing a change in the Court's positions. In so doing, they ignored or underestimated the power of the mass movement for progressive social reform. In its decisions during 1937, the Supreme Court broadly applied socioeconomic arguments and repudiated the legalism of the reactionary Right that permeated its earlier opinions. It was a victory for the ideas of the rightist sociological school, a position to which O[liver] W[endell] Holmes, member of the Supreme Court from 1902 to 1932, had made a great contribution. To the sociological school, formal-legal logic was not of paramount importance; the facts of real socioeconomic life were. Only at the end of the 1930s did Holmes's classical formula receive recognition: "The life of the law has not been logic; it has been experience." He had first put the idea forward in 1881 in a book, *The Common Law*. The United States judicial system henceforth stood solidly on the course of state-monopoly, the course set by the socioeconomic measures of the New Deal, the course to which the executive and legislative branches of government already had adapted themselves.

Understanding that saving capitalism as a system demanded repudiation of "rugged individualism" created state-socialist, state-monopolistic ideology. This doctrine was developed from roots that grew in American soil in the last quarter of the nineteenth century. The traditional liberalism of the New Deal years completed the evolution begun at the end of the nineteenth century from a negative view of strong government in socioeconomic processes to a positive view. Thus Manchester liberalism was turned into a new, state-monopolistic ideology—neo-liberalism. Asked to provide an alternative to socialism from one side and to extreme reaction from the other, "neo-liberalism looked for a means of combing individualistic traditions with the concepts of a regulated economy and reformist social theory."

Neo-liberalism was a left-central variant of state-monopolistic ideology that found institutional and political refuge in government agencies run by New Dealers and in the Roosevelt wing of the Democratic party. Mass movements encouraged the formation of neo-liberalism as left-central bourgeois state socialism. Although no "Roosevelt revolution" occurred, the New Deal, as a declaration of the American Communist party put it in December 1962, was "one of the most progressive chapters" in the history of the United States. The pace of reform was so swift that many American ideologues could not keep up. They remained preoccupied with the dogma of "rugged individualism" and with the myth of the downfall of the "old order." In fact, they were experiencing the transformation, the broad and all-encompassing transformation, of the "old order" to the spirit of state-monopolistic capitalism and to neo-liberal forms.

During the New Deal a change occurred in the power relationship between America's two main bourgeois parties. A fundamental realignment occurred, and a new stage was opened in the history of the two-party system. In the configuration of parties that resulted from the Civil War and Reconstruction, the Republican party led a two-party system with Republicans dominant over Democrats. This conservative and dynamic political combination was unable to resolve the problems that accompanied the general crisis of capitalism. Also unable to overcome the dogma of individualism, the combination suffered its deepest crisis at the beginning of the 1930s. The ideopolitical catastrophe particularly affected the Republican party. The Democratic party assumed first place in the two-party system from the middle of the 1930s, and thereafter the system functioned as a configuration of Democrats dominant over Republicans. Changes in its social base, primarily the urbanization of its electorate, rendered the Democratic party most capable of understanding the ideas of bourgeois collectivism and social maneuvering. The overwhelming majority of workers (particularly those in unions), farmers, the middle class, and intellectuals crossed to the Democratic camp. The black community broke away from the Republicans, and ethnic and religious minorities rallied to Roosevelt's party. The result was an amorphous political union known as the "Roosevelt coalition." Roosevelt himself played an enormous role in this evolution; he was the strongest U.S. government official and political party functionary in the twentieth century. . . .

The party alignment of the 1930s took place within the bounds of the traditional parties: the power balance between them was changed, and there were basic changes in the ideopolitical foundations of each. The Democrats had crossed the line to neo-liberalism by the end of the 1930s, and the Republicans had begun to master the principles of neo-conservatism. Neo-conservatism was a right-central variation of state-monopolistic ideology and policy. It differed from the left-central neo-liberal system primarily in that, although it acknowledged the positive aspects of state socialism, it was less active than neo-liberalism in instilling the principles of governmentalization. The major exception to this generalization was that the neo-conservatives used the increased role of government against the laboring masses to a significantly larger degree than did the neo-liberals. As the Republicans developed neo-conservatism, the major contribution was made by a group of new leaders who came to prominence in the party at the end of the decade—W[endell] Wilkie, T[homas] Dewey, R[obert] Taft, H[arold] Stassen, and J[ohn D.] Hamilton. The tenets of right-central state socialism reverberated through the party's election campaign in 1940. By visibly stretching the definition, one can speak of the "neo-conservative character of the Republican platform."

If the New Deal is examined as two integral processes—the development of state-monopolistic regulation and the implementation of major social reforms demanded by the masses—it can be considered ended in 1939. After the election of 1938, according to assessments by the bourgeois press, the Roosevelt camp seemed "confused over the next phase of the New Deal." The president was "inclined to move cautiously" and to show "moderation" in his dealings with Congress. Newspapers unanimously considered that the White House had proposed nothing essential to the lawmakers who convened a new legislative session in January 1939. In contemplating the work before the Seventy-sixth Congress, the Speaker of the House of Representatives, conservative Alabama Democrat W[illiam] Bankhead, declared that the main goals of the New Deal "have been practically completed" and that the necessity of further reform was less urgent. In his annual State of the Union message on 4 January 1939, Roosevelt proposed no reforms. New Dealers made significant concessions to the rightists by accepting lower appropriations for social programs and the end of some experimental projects. Then the president officially proclaimed an end to the "period of internal conflict in the launching of our program of social reform." The purveyors of bourgeois propaganda applauded this signal of retreat.

But this turn of events did not mean the dismantling of the New Deal. New Deal socioeconomic legislation lasted and, more importantly, state socialism, state-monopolistic structures and principles, became an organic part of American society. The transition to state-monopoly achieved during the New Deal appears irreversible, although as a result of World War II it has taken other, more conservative forms. Government regulation of the economy and the social infrastructure was the most important legacy of the New Deal. To a lesser degree it contributed to the capacity of American capitalism to adapt to modern conditions. However, the "brokers" already had managed to show their inability to offset the blows dealt them by capitalism's ever-deepening crisis. The economic shocks of the following decade confirmed their helplessness.

POSTSCRIPT

Was the New Deal an Effective Answer to the Great Depression?

Leuchtenburg's 50th-anniversary assessment of the legacy of the "New Deal" should be compared with the summary chapter from his classic treatment, *Franklin D. Roosevelt and the New Deal, 1932–1940* (Harper & Row, 1963). Both essays make a number of the same points and are generally very sympathetic to the accomplishments of the New Deal.

In the second selection, Sivachev takes issue not only with New Left scholars but also with the interpretations of bourgeois liberal and conservative writers. He argues that the New Deal brought about two major transformations. First, a transition in the economy from a monopolistic system of capitalism to one of state capitalism, and second, a resolution of social problems through the emergence of state socialism.

Sivachev's summary has not satisfied bourgeois critics. In a commentary on this piece, Leuchtenburg chides the Russian scholar for the vague meanings of the terms "monopolistic capitalism," "state capitalism," and "state socialism." He also criticizes Sivachev for underestimating the clashing interest groups that supported or opposed changes in America's economic and social systems. Leuchtenburg accuses Sivachev of "exaggerating the role of the masses, the unions, and the American Communists in bringing about 'state socialism.' " He also exaggerates, says Leuchtenburg, the achievements of the nation's social welfare policies, which even bourgeois historians would admit have never adequately dealt with the problems of American poverty. Finally, Sivachev falsely concludes that the "economic shocks of the 1940s" reflected the inability of America's politicians "to offset the blows dealt them by capitalism's deepening crisis." In fact, the decade of the 1940s was extremely prosperous. The major problem was not unemployment but an inflation caused by the inability of the business sector to produce goods quickly enough to meet the needs of a consumer-oriented middle class.

There is voluminous literature on the Depression and the New Deal. Comprehensive and up-to-date syntheses and bibliographies can be found in Robert S. McElvaine, *The Great Depression: America, 1929–1941* (Times Books, 1984), and Anthony J. Badger, *The New Deal: The Depression Years, 1933–1940* (Farrar, Straus, & Giroux, 1989). For a convenient reproduction of approximately 150 of "the most important" articles on all aspects of this topic, see *The Great Depression and the New Deal* (Garland Publishing, Inc., 1990), edited by Melvyn Dubofsky and Stephen Burwood.

A knowledge of economic history is essential to understanding the Depression. John Kenneth Galbraith in *The Great Crash, 1929* (Houghton

Mifflin, 1955), discusses the events which caused the Depression, aiming daggers at Presidents Coolidge and Hoover and the members of the economic establishment. Conservative economists Milton Friedman and Ann Jacobson Schwartz disagree with Galbraith and emphasize the failure of the changing monetary policies of the Federal Reserve Board in *The Great Contraction, 1929–1933* (Princeton University Press, 1965). Studs Terkel presents interviews with hundreds of people who suffered through the economic dislocation in *Hard Times* (Pantheon, 1970). Robert S. McElvaine edited a sample of the 15 million letters in the Franklin D. Roosevelt library that were sent to federal agencies in *Down and Out in the Great Depression: Letters from the Forgotten Man* (University of North Carolina Press, 1983).

Radical criticisms of the New Deal and its legacy became common in the 1960s. Howard Zinn's extended essay is a good starting point in his edited collection, *New Deal Thought* (Bobbs-Merrill, 1966). Two of the most sophisticated New Left criticisms are Barton J. Bernstein, *The New Deal: The Conservative Achievements of Liberal Reform* (Pantheon, 1967), and Paul K. Conklin, *The New Deal*, 2d ed. (Harlan Davidson, 1975). Steve Fraser and Gary Gerstle edited a series of social and economic essays, which they present in *The Rise and Fall of the New Deal Order, 1930–1980* (Princeton, 1989).

Contemporary left-wing critics have been dissected in Arthur M. Schlesinger, Jr.'s *The Politics of Upheaval*, 3d vol. (Houghton Mifflin, 1960), but the standard work is now Alan Brinkley's overview *Voices of Protest: Huey Long, Father Coughlin and the Great Depression* (Knopf, 1982).

The standard conservative critique of the New Deal is Edgar E. Robinson's scathing *The Roosevelt Leadership, 1933–1945* (Lippincott, 1955). The most recent collection of neoconservative essays critical of FDR's imperial presidency and how it changed the constitutional structure of government and emasculated individual liberties can be found in *The New Deal and its Legacy: Critique and Reappraisal* (Greenwood Press, 1989), edited by Robert Eden.

The celebration of the 100th birthday of FDR in 1982 and the 50th anniversary of the New Deal in 1983 inspired a number of conferences and the subsequent publication of the papers. Among the most important are Harvard Sitkoff, ed., *Fifty Years Later: The New Deal Evaluated* (Temple University Press, 1985), which includes the Leuchtenburg essay reprinted here; Wilbur J. Cohen, ed., *The Roosevelt New Deal: A Program Assessment Fifty Years After* (Lyndon B. Johnson School of Public Affairs, 1986); and Herbert D. Rosenbaum and Elizabeth Barteline, eds., *Franklin D. Roosevelt: The Man, the Myth, the Era, 1882–1945* (Greenwood Press, 1987). Many of the essays in these collections deal with the new interest in African Americans, women, and other aspects of social history, as well as more traditional subjects, such as the New Deal agencies, approached from a more sophisticated institutional and policy-oriented angle.

AP/Wide World Photos

PART 4

The Cold War and Beyond

The nation emerged from World War II in a position of global responsibility and power, but the struggle between the United States and the Soviet Union that began at the war's end has dominated U.S. foreign policy for more than 40 years. The battle against world communism was part of the rationale for U.S. involvement in the war in Vietnam. The indecisive outcome of that war continues to shape the views of historians and present-day policy makers.

The 1960s were tumultuous. Old standards were challenged. Protest movements seemed to appear everywhere. The civil rights movement dominated the era and resulted in many positive political and economic changes for middle-class blacks. There is some speculation, however, that America's position in the world declined in the 1970s and 1980s and continues to drop in the 1990s.

Was It Necessary to Drop the Atomic Bomb to End World War II?

Was Dwight Eisenhower a Great President?

Could the United States Have Prevented the Fall of South Vietnam?

Was Martin Luther King, Jr.'s Leadership Essential to the Success of the Civil Rights Movement?

Is the United States in a Period of Decline?

ISSUE 13

Was It Necessary to Drop the Atomic Bomb to End World War II?

YES: McGeorge Bundy, from *Danger and Survival* (Random House, 1988)

NO: Martin J. Sherwin, from *A World Destroyed: Hiroshima and the Origins of the Arms Race* (Random House, Vintage Books, 1987)

ISSUE SUMMARY

YES: Professor of history McGeorge Bundy maintains that President Truman wisely dropped the atomic bomb in order to end the war as quickly as possible.
NO: Professor of history Martin J. Sherwin argues that American policy-makers ruled out all other options and dropped the atomic bomb, an understandable but unnecessary act.

America's development of the atomic bomb began in 1939 when a small group of scientists led by well-known physicist Albert Einstein called President Franklin D. Roosevelt's attention to the enormous potential uses of atomic energy for military purposes. In his letter, Einstein warned Roosevelt that Nazi Germany was already experimenting in this area. The program to develop the bomb, which began very modestly in October 1939, soon expanded into the two-billion-dollar Manhattan Project, which combined the talents and energies of scientists (many of whom were Jewish refugees from Hitler's Nazi Germany) from universities and research laboratories across the country. The Manhattan Project was the beginning of the famed military-industrial-university complex that we take for granted today.

Part of the difficulty in reconstructing the decision to drop the atomic bomb lies in the rapidity with which events moved in the spring of 1945. On May 8, 1945, Germany surrendered. Almost a month earlier the world was stunned by the death of FDR, who was succeeded by Harry Truman, a former U.S. senator who was chosen as a compromise vice-presidential candidate in 1944. The man from Missouri had never been a confidant of Roosevelt. Truman did not even learn of the existence of the Manhattan Project until 12 days after he became president, at which time Secretary of War Henry L. Stimson advised him of a "highly secret matter" that would have a "decisive" effect upon America's postwar foreign policy.

Because Truman was unsure of his options for using the bomb, he approved Stimson's suggestion that a special committee of high-level political, military, and scientific policymakers be appointed to consider the major issues. The committee recommended unanimously that "the bomb should be used against Japan as soon as possible . . . against a military target surrounded by other buildings . . . without prior warning of the nature of the weapon."

A number of scientists disagreed with this report. They recommended that the weapon be tested on a desert island before representatives of the United Nations and that an ultimatum be sent to Japan warning of the destructive power of the bomb. Should the Japanese reject the warning, these young scientists suggested that the bomb be used only "if sanction of the United Nations (and of public opinion at home) were obtained."

A second scientific committee created by Stimson rejected both the test demonstration and warning alternatives. This panel felt that if the bomb failed to work during the demonstration, there would be political repercussions both at home and abroad.

Thus, by the middle of June 1945, the civilian leaders were unanimous that the atomic bomb should be used. During the Potsdam Conference in July, Truman learned that the bomb had been successfully tested in New Mexico. The big three—Truman, Atlee, and Stalin—issued a warning to Japan to surrender or suffer prompt and utter destruction. When the Japanese equivocated in their response, the Americans replied by dropping an atomic bomb on Hiroshima on August 6, which killed 100,000 people, and a second bomb on August 9, which leveled the city of Nagasaki. During this time the emperor pleaded with the Japanese military to end the war. On August 14 the Japanese accepted the terms of surrender with the condition that the emperor not be treated as a war criminal.

Was it necessary to drop the atomic bomb on Japan in order to end the war? In the following selections, McGeorge Bundy, a former high-level governmental official who helped Stimson write his memoirs in the late 1940s, advances a modified traditional view of the events. American policymakers, he argues, were guided by short-run considerations and dropped the bomb for military reasons. The successful explosion at Hiroshima also shortened the war because it led to the Russian declaration of war on Japan a week ahead of schedule and forced the Japanese militarists to adhere to the emperor's wishes and surrender less than a week later. Martin J. Sherwin takes issue with Bundy's analysis and advances a modified revisionist thesis. The atomic bomb was dropped, he says, because policymakers preferred it over options such as a modification of unconditional surrender, the continuation of a naval blockade and conventional air bombardment, or the awaiting of a Russian declaration of war against Japan and its invasion of Manchuria.

YES

McGeorge Bundy

DANGER AND SURVIVAL

In the decades since Hiroshima a number of writers have asserted a quite different connection between the American thinking on the bomb and the Soviet Union—namely that a desire to impress the Russians with the power of the bomb was a major factor in the decision to use it. This assertion is false, and the evidence to support it rests on inferences so stretched as to be a discredit both to the judgment of those who have argued in this fashion and the credulity of those who have accepted such arguments. There is literally no evidence whatever that the timetable for the attack was ever affected by anything except technical and military considerations; there is no evidence that anyone in the direct chain of command from [President Harry S.] Truman to [Secretary of War Henry L.] Stimson to [Secretary of State George C.] Marshall to [Brigadier General Leslie R.] Groves ever heard of or made any suggestion that either the decision itself or the timing of its execution should be governed by any consideration of its effect on the Soviet Union.

What is true—and important—is that these same decision makers were full of hope that the bomb would put new strength into the American power position. As we shall see, they were in some confusion as to how this "master card" (Stimson's term) should be played, but they would have been most unusual men if they had thought it irrelevant. It is also true that Byrnes [James F. Byrnes, who headed the office of War Mobilization] in particular was eager to get the war in Japan over before the Russians came in, thinking quite wrongly that their moves on the mainland might thus be forestalled. In May he also argued with Leo Szilard [a physicist who predicted the problem of uncontrolled nuclear weapons proliferation] on the question whether the use of the bomb in Japan would make the Soviet Union harder or easier to deal with—but this was merely an argument with a scientist who was presenting a contrary view, not a statement of basic reasons for the decision. That decision belonged, by all the accepted practices of wartime Washington, in the hands of the commander in chief and the Pentagon; Byrnes supported it, but he did not originate it or modify it in any way. At the most the opinions of Byrnes deprived Truman of the different advice that he might have heard from a different secretary of state. But the name of a man who would have been ready and able to sway Truman from the course so powerfully supported by Stimson and Marshall, and so deeply consonant with the wartime attitudes of the American people and with his own, does not leap to mind. Ending the war in complete victory just as fast as possible was a totally dominant motive in its own right. This preemptive purpose, along with the compulsive secrecy of the whole business, certainly made men slow to attend to other considerations, one of which could well have been a more thoughtful look at the real effect the use of the bomb would have on Moscow. But this is a totally different point well made by later and more careful critics.

Each of the realities that produced the Japanese surrender was purposely concealed from Japan, and each of these concealments was governed on the American side by the conviction that for use against Japan the bomb was indeed *a military weapon like any other,* if more so. Keep the value of surprise and do not give warning; use it to bring your enemy to the very brink of surrender *before* you make a concession on the emperor that might otherwise seem weak or embarrass you at home, and use it right on schedule if its use can help to minimize the role of an increasingly troubling ally.

What you do not think of separately, you seldom think of all at once, so it is not surprising that no one fully examined the possibilities of a triple demarche: warning of the bomb, warning of Soviet entry, and assurances on the emperor. Obviously Potsdam was no place for such thoughts [the Potsdam Conference was held between Truman,

Soviet premier Joseph Stalin, and British prime minister Winston Churchill to discuss possible action against Japan]; by then the basic decisions had been made, and no senior American at Potsdam was in a mood for reversing them. A more interesting question is what might have happened in May and June, in Washington, if there had been a group charged with the duty of considering the bomb, the emperor, and the Soviet pledge, all together, in the context of achieving early surrender, and if that group had been charged to consider also the possible advantages of *not* having to use the bomb. Or better yet, what might have happened if the same questions had been examined even earlier, by Roosevelt and a few advisers?

There are several tantalizing hints that Franklin Roosevelt was troubled about the basic question of using the weapon against Japan in a way that his successor never was. In a most secret private memorandum that no other senior American saw until after he was dead, Roosevelt agreed with Churchill, at Hyde Park on September 18 or 19, 1944, that "when a 'bomb' is finally available, it might perhaps, after mature consideration, be used against the Japanese . . ." Four days later he asked [Office of Scientific Research and Development director Vannevar] Bush, in a long and general exchange, whether the bomb should actually be used against the Japanese or tested and held as a threat. The two men agreed that the question should be carefully discussed, but Roosevelt also accepted Bush's argument that it could be "postponed for quite a time" in view of the fact that "certainly it would be inadvisable to make a threat unless we were distinctly in a position to follow it up if necessary." So twice in less than a week

Roosevelt thought about *whether* and *how* to use the bomb.

Six weeks later, in a fireside chat on the eve of the election, he made his one public reference to the bomb. It was cryptic and not much noticed at the time, but its meaning is plain enough now. Speaking of the need to put a lasting end to "the agony of war," he warned of terrible new weapons:

Another war would be bound to bring even more devilish and powerful instruments of destruction to wipe out civilian populations. No coastal defenses, however strong, could prevent these silent missiles of death, fired perhaps from planes or ships at sea, from crashing deep within the United States itself.

The records at Hyde Park show that this extraordinary forecast was the product of the president's own changes in the speechwriter's draft, and it takes no great leap of imagination to suppose that a man facing a decision on the use of just such a "devilish" device would have thought about it pretty hard. Yet in the same speech Roosevelt called it an all-important goal to win the war "at the earliest moment." In 1944 he said to his secretary Grace Tully, without telling her what the Manhattan Project was about [Manhattan Project refers to the coordinated efforts to develop the atomic bomb], that "if it works, and pray God it does, it will save many American lives." He also told his son James in January 1945 that there was a new weapon coming along that would make an invasion of Japan unnecessary. It would therefore be wrong to conclude that Roosevelt would not have used the bomb *in some fashion*. Nevertheless the joint memorandum with Churchill and the conversation with

Bush do give the impression that the question of actually dropping an atomic bomb on a Japanese target was for Roosevelt a real question as it was not for Truman, or indeed for Stimson and Byrnes. The men at the top when the time came had the rapid ending of the war as their wholly dominant purpose.

Sometime in December Roosevelt heard a recommendation for an international demonstration from Alexander Sachs, the friend who had brought him Einstein's letter back at the beginning. But he did not follow up on this conversation with anyone else; indeed he never again pressed his September question to Bush. Here, as on still larger questions of long-run atomic policy, he kept his counsel. In his last few months a posture that had been established by the combined force of his passionate concern for secrecy and his desire not to be crowded by advice was reinforced by the dreadful weight of his own growing fatigue. If something did not have to be done now, he would not do it. In the winter of 1944-45 both the first nuclear test and the final climax of the war on Japan still seemed far away. Given the orders for secrecy that he had given so explicitly in October 1941 and reinforced so strongly ever since, his own delay meant delay by everyone.

But what was too far away in the winter was also too near in the spring. Consider the case of [Undersecretary of the Navy] Ralph Bard: In early May he joins a committee whose first business is to plan the actions required by an expected use of the bomb. He is exposed to the problems and possibilities of warning and demonstration only on May 31; both the soldiers and the physicists, well ahead of him in both exposure and expertise, argue that sudden surprise use is more likely to work. Nowhere in this meeting or in a second discussion on June 18 is he asked to relate this problem to that of the emperor, or to that of Russian entry. Is it surprising that it takes him until June 27 to work out those connections for himself, probably helped by talks with [Assistant Secretary of War John J.] McCloy? But by then it is really too late; his committee has long since been recorded the other way, and in any case Bard has no standing on two of the three questions he has correctly pulled together; even his second thoughts on explicit warning about the bomb have an air of indecisiveness.

Or consider the effort of McCloy. He gets his one big chance on June 18 almost by accident. He is present and prepared because Stimson, feeling unwell, has not initially intended to come. But when he does speak, at the president's direction, one part of his proposal, for an explicit warning on the bomb, is not supported by his own secretary or indeed by the president. They have already decided the matter the other way two weeks earlier. His proposal on the emperor is referred to the unenthusiastic Byrnes. McCloy impressed the president; on August 14 Truman called him up and ordered him over to the White House to attend the announcement of the Japanese surrender. After the ceremony, the president told the assistant secretary that he had given more help than anyone else. But what Truman clearly meant was help in ending the war before an invasion, not in ending it before using the bomb. Helping Harry Truman to be ready to "let 'em keep the emperor" was not trivial, but it was not the same as a full study of the fateful choices on the use of the bomb, and no one knew that better than McCloy himself. Like Bard, but with the advantage of a direct order to speak his mind, he did what he could. Through no fault of his, it was too little and too late.

It is hard to avoid the conclusion that the real opportunities had been missed earlier. Let us suppose Roosevelt himself had established a council not unlike the Interim Committee, but with an earlier start and a wider charge. Might not all these possible ways to peace have been examined, at least, and possibly tried? The use of Alamogordo [an air base in New Mexico where the first atomic bomb was successfully detonated] for demonstration and warning could have been imagined more easily before its imminence made men tense. The role of the emperor, which divided the government so sharply when stated in terms of its effect on the Japanese political future, might not have been so divisive if considered in the context of trying to start the atomic age the right way. I find it relevant that two of those most wary of the emperor, [Assistant Secretaries of State Dean] Acheson and [Archibald] MacLeish, later showed themselves intensely aware of the magnitude of the issues presented by nuclear weapons. In July 1945 they were not authorized parties to the secret.

In earlier months, with Soviet participation still clearly desired, it might not have been impossible to think through a pattern of combined action that was at least worth consideration—and quite possibly action. The inclusion of the Soviets is difficult; it inevitably engages wider questions about the bomb in relation to the Soviet Union that we have yet to consider. Yet American decisions to give assurances on the emperor and to demonstrate the bomb, if announced in time to Moscow, might in themselves have produced prompt Soviet action of a sort that would help bring surrender from Tokyo. Moreover the later fear of an unwanted Russian role in the main islands of Japan was not a fear of what the Soviets could insist on, but rather of what the Americans themselves might unwisely concede. The forces occupying these islands would always be those allowed ashore by the United States Navy, and in any case a Russian claim to an occupation zone in the main islands would have failed by the precedents already established in Europe. Certainly the Russians wanted such a zone, but there was no good reason, still less any need, to let them have it.

All these possible means of ending the war without using the bomb are open to question; they remain possibilities, not certainties. It remains remarkable that nothing remotely like them was ever even considered, by any senior body, or by any single individual except Ralph Bard. After the war Colonel Stimson, with the fervor of a great advocate and with me as his scribe, wrote an article intended to demonstrate that the bomb was not used without a searching consideration of alternatives. That some effort was made, and that Stimson was its linchpin, is clear. That it was as long or wide or deep as the subject deserved now seems to me most doubtful. Franklin Roosevelt, the great man who himself had the earliest recorded doubts of use without warning, was probably also the principal obstacle to such consideration.

Yet if Stimson claimed too much for the process of consideration, his basic defense remains strong, within his own assumption that in the context of the war against Japan the bomb was a weapon like any other. Its use did surely help to end the war. The attack on Hiroshima, by the persuasive evidence of the Japa-

nese best placed to know, provided a shock of just the sort the peace party and the emperor needed to force the issue. It also served to accelerate the Soviet entry (a point that Stimson and I, among other defenders of the decision, later failed to emphasize). Stalin at Potsdam had said he would be ready by August 15, but after Hiroshima, on August 6, he decided on an earlier date and thus provided a second and nearly simultaneous shock. When the Soviet Union broadcast its declaration of war, before dawn on August 9, three Soviet armies were already invading Manchuria. The Japanese decision for surrender came less than twenty-four hours later. Efforts to measure the two shocks against each other are futile; both were powerful, and different Japanese advisers weighed them differently. The two together brought a Japanese response that led in turn to the American assurance on the emperor. So in the event the use of the bomb did catalyze the rapid convergence of the three actions that both forced and permitted surrender.

Even today we cannot know *by how much* this extraordinary set of events shortened the war—whether by days, weeks, or months. None of the retrospective estimates, long or short, is entitled to high credibility; in particular one should be skeptical of the estimates of officers who thought their own preferred weapons had almost finished the job. No such guesswork, in advance, could be a basis for action or inaction at the time. I have argued my own present belief that there were things that might have been done to increase the chance of early surrender, but I have also had to recognize how hard it was to decide to do those things as matters actually stood in May, June, and July.

And if perhaps, or even probably, there were better courses, we must also recognize that we are measuring a real decision against might-have-beens. The bomb did not win the war, but it surely was responsible for its ending when it did. To those who cheered at the time—and they were the vast majority—that was what mattered most. The bomb did shorten the war; to those in charge of its development that had been its increasingly manifest destiny for years.

MORAL QUESTIONS

There remain two questions of morality, one specific and one general: Even if Hiroshima was necessary, or at least defensible, what of Nagasaki? Long before Alamogordo and Potsdam it was agreed to seek authority for more than one attack in a single decision, and Truman accepted that arrangement. This decision was defended later on the ground that it was not one bomb or even two, but the prospect of many, that was decisive.

But Hiroshima alone was enough to bring the Russians in; these two events together brought the crucial imperial decision for surrender, just *before* the second bomb was dropped. The news of Nagasaki arrived during a meeting that had been called by Prime Minister Suzuki Kantarō after the emperor had told him expressly that he wanted prompt surrender on whatever terms were necessary. There can be little doubt that the news of a second terrible attack strengthened the peace party and further shook the diehards, but the degree of this effect cannot be gauged. It is hard to see that much could have been lost if there had been more time between the two bombs. If the matter had not been settled long since, in a time when victory seemed much less close than it did on August 7, or if the authority to order the second attack had simply been retained in Washington, one guesses that the attack on Nagasaki would have been delayed for some days; the bomb in actual use was a shock in Washington too. Such a delay would have been relatively easy, and I think right.

More broadly, what if the notion of dropping the bomb on a city was simply wrong—not just hasty because there should have been warning, or gratuitous because assurance on the emperor could have done the job, or excessive because a smaller target could have been used just as well, or even dangerous because of its impact on the Russians (an argument we have yet to consider)—but just plain wrong? This fundamental question has been addressed most powerfully by Michael Walzer [editor of *Dissent*], and his argument deserves respectful attention, although—or perhaps because—*no one* put it forward before Hiroshima.

All of the alternatives to surprise attack on a city that were proposed or considered by anyone who knew about the bomb, in 1944–45, were put forward in terms that allowed for such possible use if other alternatives failed. Roosevelt asked Bush about a demonstration and a threat, but he recognized in the same conversation that you do not make a threat you are not able to carry out if necessary. The Franck committee [consisting of Szilard, physicist James Franck, and others who understood the destructive potential of nuclear weapons] proposed a demonstration, and George Marshall at one point considered a uniquely military installation (as distinct from a city full of such installations), but both recognized that it might be necessary to go on to urban targets. Bard, with all his desire for a complex diplomatic demarche, never argued against using the bomb if the demarche failed, nor did McCloy. No one ever went beyond the argument that we should use up other forms of action—warnings, demonstrations, or diplomacy—before an urban attack. Szilard came closest; in a petition Truman almost surely never saw—he was already at Potsdam when it was signed on July 17—Szilard and sixty-seven colleagues asked Truman not to decide on use "without seriously considering the moral responsibilities which are involved." Yet even this petition conceded that "the war has to be brought to a successful conclusion and attacks by atomic bombs may very well be an effective method of warfare." No one ever said simply, do not use it on a city *at all*.

That is what Walzer says, and he says it powerfully. To underline the strength of his conviction he accepts in its strongest form the contention that the bomb was less terrible than the kinds of warfare it helped to end. His reply is that the attack on Hiroshima was still wrong, because it violated a fundamental rule of war—that the rights of noncombatants must be respected. The citizens of Hiroshima had done nothing that justified the terrible fate that overtook them on August 6; to kill them by tens of thousands merely in order to shock their government into surrender was a violation of the great tradition of civilized warfare under which "the destruction of the innocent, whatever its purposes, is a kind of blasphemy against our deepest moral commitments." Walzer grants an exception for "supreme emergency"—for the British, perhaps, when they were embattled alone against Hitler. But where, he asks, was the supreme emergency for the United States in August 1945? Even if Hiroshima was less murderous than con-

tinued firebombings and blockade, it was wrong, and all that the comparison can demonstrate is the equal wickedness of the existing "conventional" unlimited war. You might justify any one of these kinds of war against civilians if it was all that stood between you and a Hitler: If we don't do X to him, *he* will do Y (much worse) to us. But it is quite another matter to say, "If we don't do X, *we* will do Y."

Walzer's is a powerful argument, but it runs as forcefully against incendiaries as against nuclear bombs. His moral argument against the use of the bomb requires an equal moral opposition to the whole long, brutal tendency of modern war makers to accept, and sometimes even to seek, the suffering of civilians in the search for victory. He may well be deeply right, but we have seen already the enormous distance between this view of war making and what Americans actually thought in 1945. To reject the climactic acts as immoral Walzer must reject so very much else that his judgment becomes historically irrelevant. The change in strategy and tactics required by his argument is one that no political leader could then have imposed. By requiring too much he proves too little.

The war against Japan that had such momentum by the summer of 1945 may well have involved much immorality and in more ways than Walzer had space to catalogue. But that was the war that needed ending, and so much the weapon did. To those who were caught up in that war on both sides, it was no small service. I should declare a personal interest: If the war had gone on to a campaign in the main Japanese islands, the infantry regiment of which I was then a member would have been an early participant, and I do not to this day see how that campaign could have been readily avoided if there had been no urban bombing and no threat of an atomic bomb. If as a company commander I had ventured to take Walzer's view, with officers or men, I think I would have been alone, and even to reach the question of taking such a lonely view I would have had to have more understanding than I did.

There remains a final question: Was not the nuclear weapon, in and of itself, morally or politically different from firebombs and blockades, and in ways that should have required that it not be used? Cannot Walzer's argument be amended and strengthened, by remarking that even these "primitive" nuclear weapons were so terrible, not only in their explosive and incendiary effect but also in their radiation, that it was morally wrong to be the first to use them? And especially because the American effort had uncovered, as early as 1942, the still more terrible prospect of thermonuclear weapons, was there not also a political imperative to set an example of restraint? Although none of them ever presented such an argument in categorical terms, thoughts like these were strong among men like Franck, Szilard, and Bard. But since they all agreed that the bomb might be used on an inhabited target if all else failed to bring surrender, they accepted the terms of debate that in fact were followed. When their proposals were judged unlikely to end the war as quickly as direct military use, they could not fall back on a claim that here was a moral or political imperative against killing civilians in this new and terrible way. Even the doubters were in some measure prisoners of the overriding objective of early victory.

Yet it is right for us all to ponder these more absolute questions. I do not myself find Hiroshima more *immoral* than Tokyo or Dresden, but I find the *political* question more difficult. The nuclear world as we now know it is grimly dangerous; might it be less dangerous if Hiroshima and Nagasaki had never happened? If so, a stretchout of the anguish of war might have been a small price to pay. No one can make such an assessment with certainty: as we move on to later events we shall encounter evidence that weighs on both sides. All that we can say here is that the Americans who took part in the decisions of 1945 were overwhelmingly governed by the immediate and not the distant prospect. This dominance of clear present purpose over uncertain future consequences is a phenomenon we shall meet again.

Historically almost predestined, by the manner of its birth and its development, made doubly dramatic by the fateful coincidence that it was ready just when it might be decisive, and not headed off by any carefully designed alternative—of threat, assurance, demonstration, or all of them together—the bomb dropped on Hiroshima surely helped to end a fearful war. It was also the fierce announcement of the age of nuclear weapons. To the men who made and used it, or at least to many of them much of the time, this double meaning of what they were doing was evident. . . . In the summer of 1945 their overriding present purpose was to shorten the war, and in that they succeeded.

Given this overriding purpose it was natural for most of them to accept the argument for using the new weapons by surprise just as soon and just as impressively as possible. The president with doubts never acted on them or set others free to work them through. The president without such doubts never looked behind the assumptions of April, the recommendations of June, or the final approvals of July, nor did anyone close to him ever press him to do so. Whether broader and more extended deliberation would have yielded a less destructive result we shall never know. Yet one must regret that no such effort was made.

NO

Martin J. Sherwin

A WORLD DESTROYED

On July, 16, 1945, dawn broke twice over the Alamagordo desert in New Mexico. At 5:30 A.M., thirty minutes before the sun rose, science preempted nature with "a lighting effect . . . equal to several suns at midday." Just five and a half years after the discovery of nuclear fission, Manhattan Project scientists had constructed and successfully tested an atomic bomb. By raising the consequences of war to the level of Armageddon, the atomic bomb elevated the stakes of peace beyond historical experience. In physicist I. I. Rabi's cryptic phrase: "Suddenly the day of judgment was the next day and has been ever since." . . .

HIROSHIMA AS MORAL HISTORY

More than four decades after the destruction of Hiroshima and Nagasaki, the relevance of the fate of those cities has not diminished, nor have the debates they ignited. No one who looks closely at those debates will fail to recognize that there are issues at stake that go beyond military history. There are questions of morality, national character, and this nation's responsibility for the shape of the postwar world. Hiroshima not only introduced the nuclear age, it also served as the symbolic coronation of U.S. global power. The atomic bomb, as more than one contemporary cartoonist depicted it, was our scepter, and its use contributed to the image of our international authority.

But military power was not the only foundation for authority. "The position of the United States as a great humanitarian nation" was also important, Under Secretary of the Navy Ralph Bard wrote to the Secretary of War on June 27, 1945. Urging that the Japanese be warned several days prior to the attack, Bard sought to modify the decision taken on May 31 that "we could not give the Japanese any warning; that we could not concentrate on a civilian area; but that we should seek to make a profound psychological impression on as many of the inhabitants as possible." "At the suggestion of Dr. [James B.] Conant the Secretary [of War Henry L. Stimson] agreed," the minutes of the Interim Committee continued: "*the most desirable target would*

Martin J. Sherwin, *A World Destroyed: Hiroshima and the Origins of the Arms Race* (Vintage Press, 1987). Copyright © 1987 by Martin J. Sherwin. Reprinted by permission of Vintage Press, a division of Random House, Inc. Notes omitted.

be a vital war plant employing a larger number of workers and closely surrounded by workers' houses" (emphasis added).

Bard's advice went unheeded, however, and an early irony of Hiroshima was that the very act symbolizing our wartime victory was quickly turned against our peacetime purposes. At the 1946–1948 Tokyo War Crimes Trials, which, like the Nuremberg trials, were a symbolic expression of our moral authority, Justice Radhabinod Pal of India cited Hiroshima and Nagasaki as evidence against our claim to rule by right of superior virtue. The atomic bombings, he wrote in a dissenting opinion, were "the only near approach [in the Pacific War] to the directive . . . of the Nazi leaders during the Second World War."

President Truman's earliest public explanations for the bombings of Hiroshima and Nagasaki addressed the issues of just cause and morality that Pal later raised. "We have used [the atomic bomb]," he stated, "in order to shorten the agony of war, in order to save the lives of thousands and thousands of young Americans." But several days later he added less lofty reasons. Responding to a telegram criticizing the atomic bombings, the President wrote:

Nobody is more disturbed over the use of Atomic bombs than I am but I was greatly disturbed over the unwarranted attack by the Japanese on Pearl Harbor and their murder of our prisoners of war. The only language they seem to understand is the one we have been using to bombard them.

When you have to deal with a beast you have to treat him as a beast. It is most regrettable but nevertheless true.

But in the aftermath of Hiroshima, many thoughtful commentators began to view the bomb itself as the "beast." "For all we know," H. V. Kaltenborn, the dean of radio news commentators, observed on August 7, "we have created a Frankenstein! We must assume that with the passage of only a little time, an improved form of the new weapon we use today can be turned against us."

At some level, this thought has been the enduring nightmare of the nuclear age, a vision of an inevitable holocaust imbedded deep within our culture. "How does the universe end?" Billy Pilgrim, the protagonist in Kurt Vonnegut's *Slaughterhouse Five*, asks his omniscient Trafalmadorian captors. The novel continues:

"We blow it up, experimenting with new fuels for our flying saucers. A Trafalmadorian test pilot presses a starter button, and the whole Universe disappears."

"If you know this," said Billy, "isn't there some way you can prevent it? Can't you keep the pilot from pressing the button?"

"He has always pressed it, and he always will. We always let him and we always will let him. The moment is structured that way."

The structure of the nuclear age—deterrence and the inexorable accumulation of the weapons designed to promote its purposes—has encouraged a deadening sense that there are forces at work beyond political control. The American public's feeling of powerlessness before those forces may be the single most important reason behind the belief that a massive arsenal of nuclear weapons is needed to guarantee our national security. Even here, the moral dimension of the debate over the atomic bombings of Hiroshima and Nagasaki is relevant, for it is of paramount importance to those who wish to rely upon nuclear weapons that they are not tarnished with a sense of guilt that could inhibit their use as an instrument of diplomacy.

This concern about the practical effects of "Hiroshima guilt" was discussed soon after the war by the Manhattan Project's chief science administrator, James Conant, who had returned full time to his post as president of Harvard University. Raising the issue in a letter to former Secretary of War Henry L. Stimson, he wrote of his concern about the "spreading accusation that it was entirely unnecessary to use the atomic bomb at all," particularly among those he described as "verbal minded citizens not so generally influential as they were influential among the coming generations of whom they might be teachers or educators." To combat that view, he urged Stimson to write an article on "the decision to use the bomb," which subsequently appeared in the February 1947 issue of *Harper's* magazine.

If "the propaganda against the use of the atomic bomb had been allowed to grow unchecked," Conant wrote to Stimson after reading a prepublication version of the article, "the strength of our military position by virtue of having the bomb would have been correspondingly weakened," and the chances for international control undermined. "Humanitarian considerations" that led citizens to oppose the strengthening of the U.S. atomic arsenal, in Conant's opinion, were likely to subvert the common effort to achieve an international atomic energy agreement. "I am firmly convinced," he told Stimson, "that the Russians will eventually agree to the American proposals for the establishment of an atomic energy authority of world-wide scope,

provided they are convinced that we would have the bomb in quantity and would use it without hesitation in another war."

Stimson's article responded to Conant's practical concerns. Explaining the steps in the decision strictly in the context of the Pacific War and the objective of "avoiding the enormous losses of human life which otherwise confronted us," he left no room for the suggestion that considerations beyond the war could have been factors, or that in future similar circumstances the government would not be compelled to take similar actions. The war had not ended when the bomb became available; the decision flowed inexorably out of those circumstances: "In light of the alternatives which, on a fair estimate, were open to us I believe that no man, in our position and subject to our responsibilities," Stimson wrote, "holding in his hands a weapon of such possibilities, could have failed to use it and afterwards looked his countrymen in the face."

The primary argument for the "necessity" of using the atomic bomb was saving American lives. President Truman wrote in his memoirs that half a million U.S. soldiers would have been killed had the planned invasions been launched. Winston Churchill claimed that the figure was closer to a million. Could any responsible Commander-in-Chief send so many young men to die on foreign shores when an alternative like the atomic bomb was readily at hand?

As stated, the question answers itself. As stated, it also distorts the nature of the historical problem. Before the decision to use atomic bombs can be properly understood, many other questions need to be considered. They range from the expected impact of the use of the bomb on the Japanese during the war to the influence such a demonstration might have on the Soviet behavior afterward. They include questions related to bureaucratic momentum and political expediency; to the instinct for revenge as well as the pressure for results; to scientific pride and economic investments; to Roosevelt's legacy and Truman's insecurity.

In the original edition of *A World Destroyed* I sought to analyze these questions within their historical context, limiting the discussion to what was said and done before the bombs were dropped. My narrative tacitly accepted the published casualty estimates as a compelling influence limiting decision makers' choices. But recently discovered estimates of invasion casualties dramatically contradict the figures released by Truman, Churchill, and Stimson. These require some comments on the information that has shaped the postwar debate.

Historians have known for decades that several alternatives to atomic bombing or an invasion of Japan were considered during May and June 1945. The first was to modify unconditional surrender. Having broken the Japanese diplomatic code, the Department of State's Far Eastern specialists were sanguine that the peace advocates in the Imperial Cabinet could win capitulation if the United States assured Japan that it would maintain the Emperor and the Imperial Dynasty. The second alternative was to delay the atomic bombings until after August 8, the final day on which Stalin could live up to his agreement to enter the war against Japan within three months of Germany's surrender. [On August 8 the Soviet Union declared war on Japan.] The third alternative, Admiral William D. Leahy wrote to the Joint Chiefs of Staff on June 14, 1945, was "to

defeat Japan by isolation, blockade, and bombardment by sea and air forces."

All of these suggestions were viable alternatives, but none of them was without its particular disadvantages.

The first option, modifying unconditional surrender, was politically risky. Introduced by Roosevelt and accepted by the Allies, the unconditional surrender had become the basis upon which the public expected the war to be concluded. From the point of view of Truman and his advisers, tampering with this doctrine appeared fraught with unattractive political dangers. [Nevertheless, *after* the Soviets declared war on Japan and *after* both available bombs had been dropped, unconditional surrender was modified according to the terms stated above.]

Second, a Japanese surrender (precipitous or otherwise) following the entry of the Soviet Union into the Pacific War would have facilitated the expansion of Soviet power in the Far East. By summer of 1945 such an option was anathema to Truman and his advisers.

Finally, continuing the blockade and bombardment promised no immediate results and might, as the Joint War Plans Committee wrote to the President, "have an adverse effect upon the U.S. position vis-à-vis other nations who will, in the meantime, be rebuilding their peacetime economy."

In the summer of 1945 it was therefore not the lack of an alternative that might induce Japan's surrender that led to the use of atomic bombs. It was the undesirability of relying on the available alternatives *given the nuclear option*. The nuclear option was preferred because it promised dividends—not just the possibility that it would end the war but the hope that it would eliminate the need to rely on one of the other alternatives.

The question of how policymakers came to understand their choices is probed throughout *A World Destroyed*. It is a question we should keep before us as the recent discovery of the actual invasion casualty estimates should make clear. The casualty estimates announced by Truman in the aftermath of Hiroshima were grossly exaggerated. . . . For example, on June 15, 1945, the Joint War Plans Committee (JWPC) estimated that about 40,000 Americans would be killed and 150,000 wounded if *both* southern Kyushu and the Tokyo plain had to be invaded (on November 1, 1945, and March 1, 1946, respectively). General George C. Marshall, Army Chief of Staff, who Truman cited in his memoirs as the source of the estimate that an invasion would cost "half a million American lives," endorsed an estimate on June 7 that was similar to the one produced a week later by the Joint War Plans Committee. On June 18, General Douglas MacArthur, the commander of U.S. Pacific forces, concurred with the range of JWPC's estimates. On July 9 a memorandum to the Joint Staff Planners entitled "Note by the Secretaries" included a revised casualty estimate of 31,000 killed, wounded, and missing for the first 30 days of the planned operation against Kyushu. [During the first 30 days of the Normandy invasion, the killed/wounded/missing count for U.S. troops was 42,000.]

In the end the most destructive conventional war of the century was concluded with the first nuclear warfare in history. Many who advocated that alternative hoped it would contribute to a postwar settlement that would banish those weapons—others hoped it would establish their value. But whatever they believed, those who felt called upon to defend the bombing of Hiroshima and Nagasaki came to recognize more clearly in retrospect what a few had warned in prospect: that nuclear war was beyond the reach of conventional moral categories.

Though no American President could be expected to have chosen an invasion of Japan if a plausible alternative was available, the fact that several available alternatives had been rejected increased the moral burden of justifying the extraordinary consequences of Hiroshima and Nagasaki. Americans had self-consciously fought World War II to preserve the values of their civilization. Is it surprising that in its aftermath those who had directed the war conspired to explain its terrible conclusion as unavoidable and consistent with those values?

Reflecting on the choices the administration had faced in the summer of 1945, former Secretary of War Stimson felt compelled to admit the possibility that refusing to modify unconditional surrender might have been a mistake—a mistake that could have *delayed* the end of the war. Composing his memoirs several years after the war, he wrote "that history might find that the United States, by its delay in stating its position [on the conditions of surrender], had prolonged the war."

Despite Stimson's singular remark, and the general availability of information about the other options, the invasion has remained *the* alternative to the atomic bombings in public discussions. Perhaps this is because the invasion remains the least ambiguous of the options. Or perhaps it is because it lends to the bombings an implicit moral legitimacy. According to the figures released, the magnitude of the projected slaughter of invading Americans was even greater than the actual slaughter of Japanese civilians. As reports, images, and tales of death, dying, and suffering from nuclear warfare filtered into the American press, the alternatives to the invasion were filtered out.

The manipulation of the estimated casualty figures, and thereby the history of the decision-making process that led to the atomic bombings of Hiroshima and Nagasaki, has masked an important lesson. The choice in the summer of 1945 was not between a conventional invasion or a nuclear war. It was a choice between various forms of diplomacy and warfare. While the decision that Truman made is understandable, it was not inevitable. It was even avoidable. In the end, that is the most important legacy of Hiroshima for the nuclear age.

LOS ALAMOS AND HIROSHIMA

The confluence of the invention of weapons that could destroy the world and a foreign policy of global proportions removed the physical and psychological barriers that had protected the United States from the full force of international affairs before World War II. In the context of the cold war, politics no longer stopped at the water's edge. On the contrary, politics often began there. No group of Americans was more alert to this change than the scientists of the Manhattan Project, who had brought it about. To Robert Oppenheimer, the new alignment of science and power threatened "the life of science [and] the life of the world." The change in scale and stakes involved scientists more, he said, "than any other group in the world." The existence of the atomic bomb linked science to national security and made scientists into military assets. The twin "evils of secrecy and control strike at the very roots of what science is and what it is for," Oppenheimer warned his former colleagues at Los Alamos in November 1945.

The question of the meaning and uses of science raised by Oppenheimer took on a new sense of immediacy for all scientists after the war. With the advent of the atomic age, the answer to the question of science and the state inevitably became tied to the political and national defense issues generated by the cold war. As a result, the boundary between science and politics blurred, and the public's attitude toward science was increasingly defined by political criteria. In such an environment Bernard Baruch could suggest that "science should be free but only when the world has been freed from the menaces which hang over us."

The scientists disagreed. Fearing that science would become the first political victim of their success, Percy W. Bridgman, the president of the American Physical Society, responded to the threat of external control of science with the declaration that "society is the servant of science. . . . Any control which society exerts over science and invention must be subject to this condition."

With Bridgman, the scientist's, view at one pole and the converse approach expressed by Baruch at the other, it is not too much to suggest that there arose a split between "two cultures." But it was not, as C. P. Snow argued, a division having to do with a nonscientist's knowledge of the second law of thermodynamics or a scientist's ability to quote Shakespeare. It touched upon a deeper issue—the nature of freedom and power in a democratic society.

Oppenheimer spoke of this issue from a scientific perspective in answering the question he raised. "If you are a scientist," he said, "you believe that it is good to find out how the world works . . . that it is good to turn over to mankind at large the greatest possible power to control the world and to deal with it according to its lights and its values." It was not for the scientist to judge, he implied, whether those lights and values were adequate to control new understandings. Nor was it for society to judge, he added explicitly, what the scientist should and should not seek to discover. Any such external control "is based on a philosophy incompatible with that by which we live, and have learned to live in the past." If society was not the servant of science, it certainly was a collaborator. To politicize science was to destroy it. A free state could only be well served by science if scientists were free to publish and discuss their research. A state was not free, he implied, if the life of science was not open and free of political control.

To keep politics out of science, scientists responded politically. Some counseled the Administration privately against policies that would lead to military control, while others led a successful campaign against military domination of the Atomic Energy Commission. However, in the ensuing cold war, civilian control of atomic energy proved to be illusory. Military requirements held sway, loyalty and security programs were vigorously enforced, and government support led to far more control than anticipated. Though scientists gained greater opportunities to participate in policy formulation, their advice was expected to support basic policies decided by others. This was the clear message communicated by the removal of Oppenheimer's security clearance in 1954.

After the war, the scientific community itself appeared to divide "culturally."

Scientists such as Oppenheimer, Vannevar Bush, James Conant, Ernest Lawrence, and Karl and Arthur Compton worked closely with the government. In contrast, Leo Szilard, Eugene Rabinowitch, and other leaders of the Federation of American (Atomic) Scientists became vocal critics of the Truman Administration's policies. The division among scientists was fundamentally political, yet both groups shared an abiding faith in science. The scientific community was united by an unstated assumption that what was good for science was good for world peace. But how was peace best attained?

All scientists agreed that avoiding an atomic arms race with the Soviet Union was the most important issue of the day. The revolution in weapons technology, they maintained, could lead either to a peaceful diplomatic revolution or a nuclear-armed world. If an arms-control plan was not adopted, an arms race would harness science to military requirements. To avoid this catastrophe the veterans of the Manhattan Project lobbied vigorously to scuttle the military's attempt to capture the atom.

The outlines of that debate emerged during the war and became established soon afterward. Though only 13 atomic bombs existed in 1947, by 1948 the number had escalated to 50. In 1949, when the Soviet Union exploded its first atomic bomb, President Truman faced conflicting recommendations. One group of scientists and politicians urged him to opt for a program to develop a hydrogen bomb, a proposal that represented a "quantum leap" into the realm of megaton weapons. On the other side of the argument were the scientists of the Atomic Energy Commission's General Advisory Committee (GAC), who recommended against such an escalation, proposing instead that the President adhere to the principle of sufficiency. "To the argument that the Russians may succeed in developing [the hydrogen bomb]," the members of GAC wrote in October 1949 to the President, "we would reply that our undertaking it will not prove a deterrent to them. Should they use the weapon against us, reprisals by our large stock of atomic bombs would be comparably effective to the use of a super [H]bomb." The moral consequences of technology were also at issue. "We base our recommendation," the committee members also wrote, "on our belief that the extreme dangers to mankind inherent to the proposal [for a super] wholly outweigh any military advantage that could come from this development."

But in January 1950 Truman opted for the hydrogen bomb. The principle of the nuclear containment of the Soviet Union —an idea that was first developed during the war in the context of the decision to use the atomic bomb against Japan—was now firmly set in place.

On October 16, 1945, his last day as director of the Los Alamos Scientific Laboratory, Robert Oppenheimer, who would write the GAC's report opposing the "super," accepted a certificate of appreciation from the Secretary of War on behalf of the laboratory with these words:

It is our hope that in years to come we may look at this scroll, and all that it signifies with pride.

Today that pride must be tempered with a profound concern. If atomic bombs are to be added as new weapons to the arsenals of a warring world, or to the arsenals of nations preparing for war, then the time will come when mankind will curse the names of Los Alamos and Hiroshima.

In the context of a nuclear-armed world, "how well they meant" and "how well we mean" cannot be the central points.

POSTSCRIPT

Was It Necessary to Drop the Atomic Bomb to End World War II?

Though appalled by the use of the atomic bomb, Bundy argues that the alternatives of a test demonstration and specific warning were rejected because Truman, along with everybody else, wanted the war to end as quickly as possible. The achievement of this goal is substantiated by an important work by Robert J. C. Butow, *Japan's Decision to Surrender* (Stanford University Press, 1954), whose thorough examination of Japanese sources demonstrates the importance of the bomb on the emperor's decision to pressure the Japanese military to surrender.

Since Sherwin's book was first published in 1975, new documents have come to light which seriously question the 300,000 to 500,000 American casualties that were estimated to result from the alternative plan of invading Japan. According to a document issued by the Joint War Plans Committee (JWPC) on June 15, 1945, approximately 40,000 U.S. soldiers would be killed and 15,000 wounded if both southern Krushu and the Tokyo plain were invaded in late 1945 and early 1946. Other analyses by Generals Marshall and MacArthur agree with the JWPC estimates. Sherwin's 1987 edition of *A World Destroyed* contains these documents, and a full discussion of whether or not a landed invasion should have been considered is in Barton Bernstein's "A Postwar Myth: 500,000 U.S. Lives Saved," *Bulletin of Atomic Scientists* (June/July 1986).

Two other issues deserve consideration: FDR's untimely death and the use of a second bomb at Nagasaki. Bundy shows that in 1944 FDR questioned whether the bomb should be "used against Japan or tested and held as a threat." He became ill in 1945 and died before the bomb was dropped, which allows us to speculate whether Roosevelt would have chosen a different alternative than his successor, Truman.

Both writers agree that military considerations were paramount. Sherwin, though, argues that U.S. officials viewed the bomb as a political/diplomatic weapon. This was why Roosevelt refused to share information about the Manhattan Project with Stalin as he did with Churchill. It also explains why Truman was not willing to wait for a Russian invasion of Manchuria, which may have given Russia the claim to an occupation zone in postwar Japan.

J. Samuel Walker has written the most recent and important article on the use of the bomb, entitled "The Decision to Use the Bomb: A Historiographical Update," *Diplomatic History* (Winter 1990).

ISSUE 14

Was Dwight Eisenhower a Great President?

YES: Stephen E. Ambrose, from *Eisenhower: The President, vol. 2* (Simon & Schuster, 1984)

NO: Arthur M. Schlesinger, Jr., from *The Cycles of American History* (Houghton Mifflin, 1986)

ISSUE SUMMARY

YES: Professor of history Stephen E. Ambrose maintains that Eisenhower was a greater president than his predecessors and successors because he balanced the budget, stopped inflation, and kept the peace.
NO: Professor of the humanities Arthur M. Schlesinger, Jr., argues that Eisenhower failed as a president because he refused to tackle the moral and environmental issues at home and because he established a foreign policy which relied on covert CIA activities and threats of nuclear arms.

David Dwight Eisenhower (he reversed his name in high school) was the third of seven sons raised in the 1890s in Abilene, Kansas, in a very modest household. After graduating from high school, he worked for a year and then passed a competitive examination for an appointment to the U.S. Naval Academy. He was not accepted because he was considered too old.

Instead he entered West Point in 1911, against the wishes of his pacifist parents. According to his major biographer, Stephen E. Ambrose, "sports were his all-consuming passion." During his sophomore year a twisted knee ruined the potential All-American's football career. In 1915, a disconsolate Eisenhower graduated 61st in a class of 164.

At first his military career looked very unpromising. During World War I he took command of a tank training center and learned a good deal about armored warfare but gained no combat experience. In the early 1920s he spent most of his time coaching football teams on army posts and seemed disinterested in his profession.

Fortunately he met General Fox Conner, a man who stimulated Eisenhower's thinking about military strategy. With Conner's assistance he went to the Command and General Staff School in Leavenworth, Kansas, and graduated first in his class. Conner convinced the young officer of two things which would greatly impact his future career: (1) The next war would be global, and (2) a certain General George C. Marshall would lead the American troops in this future worldwide conflict.

Why contemporary observers of Eisenhower's presidency underestimated his intellectual abilities to think and write clearly remains puzzling when one examines his early career. The young officer had developed a reputation as an excellent staff officer who was uncommonly good at preparing reports. In 1927 he wrote an excellent guidebook detailing the major battles of World War I. In the summer of 1941 Eisenhower's organizational skills gained public notoriety when he distinguished himself as the chief planner of the 3rd Army in the Louisiana maneuvers. Therefore, it was no accident that Army Chief of Staff George C. Marshall called Eisenhower to Washington a week after the Pearl Harbor attack and put him in the War Plans Division.

During World War II Eisenhower, as the head of the Combined Chiefs of Staff, was forced to make numerous military decisions. He performed brilliantly. In November 1942 he directed the combined American and British invasion of North Africa. His organizational skills were stretched to the limit when he directed the largest landed invasion in history. More than 156,000 men hit the beaches of Normandy, France, on D-Day, June 6, 1944, to establish the long-awaited second front. Germany surrendered less than a year later.

Like his predecessors Washington, Jackson, and Grant, the emergence of General Eisenhower as a war hero made him presidential timber. Democratic leaders asked him to be Truman's replacement in 1948. He turned them down because of his hostility to the New Deal. He served a short stint as the first NATO commander before he accepted the bid of the "establishment" Republican leaders to become their candidate in 1952. After a successful run in the primaries and a bruising floor fight at the Republican convention against the leading conservative candidate, Ohio senator Robert Taft, the general was nominated.

The main issues of the campaign were an unpopular war and corruption and communism in government. Candidate Eisenhower made a trip to Korea and promised to end the war. The public believed him and he easily defeated his Democratic opponent, Illinois governor Adlai Stevenson.

In the following selections, Stephen E. Ambrose argues that Eisenhower ranks as one of America's greatest presidents because he balanced the budget, stopped inflation, and gave the nation eight years of peace and prosperity. Arthur M. Schlesinger, Jr., disagrees with this assessment. He emphasizes the negative side of Eisenhower's administration: his refusal to tackle the moral and environmental issues at home and his establishment of a foreign policy which relied upon covert CIA activities and too often went to the brink with threats of nuclear war.

YES

Stephen E. Ambrose

THE EISENHOWER PRESIDENCY:
AN ASSESSMENT

Any attempt to assess Eisenhower's eight years as President inevitably reveals more about the person doing the assessing then it does about Eisenhower. Assessment requires passing a judgment on the decisions Eisenhower made on the issues of his time, and every issue was political and controversial. Further, all the major and most of the minor issues of the 1950s continued to divide the nation's political parties and people in the decades that followed. To declare, therefore, that Eisenhower was right or wrong on this or that issue tends to be little more than a declaration of the current politics and prejudices of the author. The temptation to judge, however, is well-nigh irresistible, and most of the authors who write about the 1950s give in to it.

Thus William Ewald, in *Eisenhower the President*, concludes "that many terrible things that could have happened, didn't. Dwight Eisenhower's presidency gave America eight good years—I believe the best in memory." There were no wars, no riots, no inflation—just peace and prosperity. Most white middle-class and middle-aged Republicans would heartily agree with Ewald. But a black American could point out that among the things that did not happen were progress in civil rights or school desegregation. People concerned about the Cold War and the nuclear arms race could point out that no progress was made in reducing tensions or achieving disarmament. People concerned about the Communist menace could point out that no Communist regimes were eliminated, and that in fact Communism expanded into Vietnam and Cuba. On these and every issue, in short, there are at least two legitimate points of view. What did not happen brought joy to one man, gloom to another.

One of the first serious attempts at assessment was by Murray Kempton in a famous article in *Esquire* magazine in September 1967. Kempton called the piece "The Underestimation of Dwight D. Eisenhower," and in it he admitted that Eisenhower was much shrewder and more in control of events than he, or other reporters, had ever imagined during the fifties. Eisenhower was

From Stephen E. Ambrose, *Eisenhower: The President, vol. 2* (Simon Schuster, 1984). Copyright © 1984 by Stephen E. Ambrose. Reprinted by permission of Simon & Schuster, Inc.

"the great tortoise upon whose back the world sat for eight years," never recognizing "the cunning beneath the shell." Garry Wills took up the same theme in his 1970 book *Nixon Agonistes*. Such judgments were little more than confessions on the part of the reporters, and they shed little light on the Eisenhower Presidency.

Members of the academic community also confessed. Thus Arthur Schlesinger, Jr., who wrote speeches for Stevenson during the presidential campaigns of 1952 and 1956, was—at the time—critical of Eisenhower for failing to exercise vigorous executive leadership, as Schlesinger's heroes, Andrew Jackson, Franklin Roosevelt, and Harry Truman, had done. Later, after Watergate, Schlesinger wrote *The Imperial Presidency*. In that book, Schlesinger's major criticism of Eisenhower was that Eisenhower went too far in his use of executive powers, especially in his proclamation of the principle of executive privilege when he refused to turn over documents or personnel to McCarthy's investigating committee, and in his insistence on exclusive executive responsibility during foreign-policy crises.

To repeat, then: To say that Eisenhower was right about this or wrong about that is to do little more than announce one's own political position. A more fruitful approach is to examine his years in the White House in his own terms, to make an assessment on the basis of how well he did in achieving the tasks and goals he set for himself at the time he took office.

By that standard, there were many disappointments, domestic and foreign. Eisenhower had wanted to achieve unity within the Republican Party, on the basis of bringing the Old Guard into the modern world and the mainstream of American politics. In addition, he wanted to develop within the Republican Party some young, dynamic, trustworthy, and popular leaders. He never achieved either goal, as evidenced by the 1964 Republican Convention, where the Old Guard took control of the party, nominating a candidate and writing a platform that would have delighted Warren Harding, or even William McKinley. Franklin Roosevelt did a much better job of curbing the left wing of the Democratic Party than Eisenhower did of curbing the right wing of the Republican Party.

Eisenhower wanted to see Senator McCarthy eliminated from national public life, and he wanted it done without making America's record and image on civil-liberties issues worse than it already was. But because Eisenhower would not denounce McCarthy by name, or otherwise stand up to the senator from Wisconsin, McCarthy was able to do much damage to civil liberties, the Republican party, numerous individuals, the U.S. Army, and the Executive Branch before he finally destroyed himself. Eisenhower's only significant contribution to McCarthy's downfall was the purely negative act of denying him access to executive records and personnel. Eisenhower's cautious, hesitant approach—or nonapproach—to the McCarthy issue did the President's reputation no good, and much harm.

Eisenhower had wanted, in January of 1953, to provide a moral leadership that would both draw on and illuminate America's spiritual superiority to the Soviet Union, indeed to all the world. But on one of the great moral issues of the day, the struggle to eliminate racial segregation from American life, he provided almost no leadership at all. His failure to speak out, to indicate personal approval of *Brown v. Topeka*, did incalculable harm to the civil-rights crusade and to America's image.

Eisenhower had hoped to find a long-term solution for American agriculture that would get the government out of the farming business while strengthening the family farm. In this area, he and Secretary Benson suffered abject failure. The rich grew richer thanks to huge government payments for the Soil Bank, the government in 1961 was more closely and decisively involved in agriculture than it had been in 1953, and the number of family farms had dropped precipitously.

In 1953 Eisenhower had entertained wildly optimistic hopes for the peaceful uses of nuclear power. Electricity too cheap to meter, he believed, was just around the corner, as soon as nuclear power plants went into operation. New trans-ocean canals would be blasted open, artificial harbors created, enormous strides in medicine taken, the world's fertilizer problems solved, the energy for the industrialization of the Third World created. But as he left office in 1961, there had not been any such significant application of nuclear power to civilian purposes.

In foreign affairs, Eisenhower's greatest failure, in his own judgment, which he expressed on innumerable occasions, was the failure to achieve peace. When he left office, the tensions and dangers and costs of the Cold War were higher than they had ever been. In large part, this was no fault of his. He had tried to reach out to the Russians, with Atoms for Peace, Open Skies, and other proposals, only to be rebuffed by Khrushchev. But his own deeply rooted anti-Communism was certainly a contributing factor to the failure. Eisenhower refused to trust the Russians to even the slightest degree. He continued and expanded the economic, political, diplomatic, and covert-operations pressure on the Kremlin for his entire two terms. This was good policy for winning votes, and may even have been good for achieving limited victories in the Cold War, but it was damaging to the cause of world peace.

Allied with the failure to achieve peace was the failure to set a limit on the arms race (never mind actual disarmament, another of his goals). Better than any other world leader, Eisenhower spoke of the cost of the arms race, and its dangers, and its madness. But he could not even slow it down, much less stop it. The great tragedy here is opportunity lost. Eisenhower not only recognized better than anyone else the futility of an arms race; he was in a better position than anyone else to end it. His prestige, especially as a military man, was so overwhelming that he could have made a test ban with the Russians merely on his own assurance that the agreement was good for the United States. But until his last months in office, he accepted the risk of an expanding arms race over the risk of trusting the Russians.

When finally he was ready to make an attempt to control the arms race by accepting an unsupervised comprehensive test ban, the U-2 incident intervened. Fittingly, the flight that Powers made was one Eisenhower instinctively wanted to call off, but one that his technologists insisted was necessary. In this case, as in the case of building more nuclear weapons, holding more tests, or building more rockets, he allowed the advice of his technical people to override his own common sense. That this could happen to Eisenhower illustrates vividly the tyranny of technology in the nuclear/missile age.

Another area of failure came in the Third World, which Eisenhower had hoped to line up with the Western democracies in the struggle against Russia. In large part, this failure was caused by Eisenhower's anti-Communism coupled with his penchant for seeing Communists wherever a social reform movement or a struggle for national liberation was under way. His overthrow of popularly elected governments in Iran and Guatemala, his hostility toward Nasser, his refusal to seek any form of accommodation with Castro, his extreme overreaction to events in the Congo, were one result. Another was a profound mistrust of the United States by millions of residents of the Third World. A third result of his oversimplifications was an overcommitment in Indochina, based on an obsession with falling dominoes.

In Central and Eastern Europe, Eisenhower had hoped to take the offensive against Communism. But his unrealistic and ineffective belligerency, combined with his party's irresponsible advocacy of uprisings and liberation within a police state, produced the tragedy of Hungary in 1956, which will stand forever as a blot on Eisenhower's record. In his Administration, "roll back" never got started, as "stand pat" became the watchword. But the free world was not even able to stand pat, as Eisenhower accepted an armistice in Korea that left the Communists in control in the north, another in Vietnam that did the same, and the presence of Castro in Cuba.

These failures, taken together, make at first glance a damning indictment. According to Eisenhower's critics, they came about because of the greatest shortcoming of all, the failure to exert leadership. In contrast to FDR and Truman, Eisenhower seemed to be no leader at all, but only a chairman of the board, or even a figurehead, a Whig President in a time that demanded dramatic exercise of executive power. Eisenhower was sensitive about this charge, which he had heard so many times. When Henry Luce made it, in an August 1960 *Life* editorial, Eisenhower took time to provide Luce with a private explanation of his methods—"not to defend," Eisenhower insisted, "merely to explain."

He realized, he told Luce, that many people thought "I have been too easy a boss." What such people did not realize, he pointed out, was that except for his "skimpy majority" in his first two years, "I have had to deal with a Congress controlled by the opposition and whose partisan antagonism to the Executive Branch has often been blatantly displayed." To make any progress at all, he had to use methods "calculated to attract cooperation," and could not afford "to lash out at partisan charges and publicity-seeking demagogues." In addition, the government of the United States had become "too big, too complex, and too pervasive in its influence for one individual to pretend to direct the details of its important and critical programming." Nothing could be accomplished without competent assistants; to command their loyalty, the President had to be willing to show patience, understanding, a readiness to delegate authority, and an acceptance of responsibility for honest errors.

Finally, Eisenhower concluded, "In war and in peace I've had no respect for the desk-pounder, and have despised the loud and slick talker. If my own ideas and practices in this matter have sprung from weakness, I do not know. But they were and are deliberate or, rather, natural to me. They are not accidental."

Shortly after Eisenhower left office, his successor suffered an embarrassing defeat at the Bay of Pigs. In passing his own judgment on the event, Eisenhower concentrated his criticism on Kennedy's failure to consult with the NSC before deciding to act. He chided Kennedy for not gathering together in one room representatives of every point of view, so that he could hear both the pros and the cons. Since Eisenhower made such a major point of this failure to consult, it is only fair to apply the same standard to Eisenhower's own Administration. How well did he listen to every point of view before acting?

In some cases, fully. In other cases, hardly at all. In the various Far East crises that began with Korea in 1952 and continued through Dien Bien Phu, the Geneva Conference of 1954, and Formosa, he consulted with every appropriate department and agency, listened carefully to every point of view, and acted only after he was satisfied he had taken everything into consideration and was prepared for all possible consequences. But in other areas, he was surprisingly remiss. He did not give the anti-McCarthy people a full hearing, for example, and only once met with Negro leaders on civil-rights issues. Until 1958, he allowed himself to be isolated from the nuclear scientists opposed to testing. On national defense, he gave the proponents of more spending every opportunity to express their views, but except for one meeting with Senator Taft in 1953 he never listened to those who urged dramatic cuts. Advocates of more spending for domestic social programs or for tax cuts seldom got near Eisenhower. He kept the U-2 such a closely guarded secret that only insiders who were proponents of the program ever gave him advice on how to utilize the spy plane.

But on major questions involving the European allies, he consulted with the heads of government in Paris, Bonn, and London before acting (except at Suez, and the failure to consult there was no fault of his). His record, in short, was mixed, and hardly pure enough to justify his extreme indignation at Kennedy for Kennedy's failure to consult the NSC before acting at the Bay of Pigs.

How effective, if not dramatic, Eisenhower's leadership techniques were can be seen in a brief assessment of his accomplishments as President, an assessment once again based on his own goals and aspirations. First and foremost, he presided over eight years of prosperity, marred only by two minor recessions. By later standards, it was a decade of nearly full employment and no inflation.

Indeed by almost every standard—GNP, personal income and savings, home buying, auto purchases, capital investment, highway construction, and so forth—it was the best decade of the century. Surely Eisenhower's fiscal policies, his refusal to cut taxes or increase defense spending, his insistence on a balanced budget, played some role in creating this happy situation.

Under Eisenhower, the nation enjoyed domestic peace and tranquillity—at least as measured against the sixties. One of Eisenhower's major goals in 1953 was to lower the excesses of political rhetoric and partisanship. He managed to achieve that goal, in a negative way, by not dismantling the New Deal, as the Old Guard wanted to do. Under Eisenhower, the number of people covered by Social Security doubled as benefits went up. The New Deal's regulatory commissions stayed in place. Expenditures for public works were actually greater under Eisenhower than they had been under FDR or Truman. Nor were Eisenhower's public works of the boondoggle variety—the St. Lawrence Seaway and the Interstate

Highway System made an enormous contribution to the economy. Eisenhower, in effect, put a Republican stamp of approval on twenty years of Democratic legislation, by itself a major step toward bringing the two parties closer together.

Eisenhower's positive contribution to domestic peace and tranquillity was to avoid partisanship himself. His close alliance with the southern Democrats, his refusal to ever denounce the Democratic Party as a whole (he attacked only the "spender" wing), his insistence on a bipartisan foreign policy, his careful cultivation of the Democratic leaders in Congress, all helped tone down the level of partisan excess. When Eisenhower came into the White House, his party was accusing the other party of "twenty years of treason." The Democrats in turn were charging that the Republicans were the party of Depression. When Eisenhower left office, such ridiculous charges were seldom heard.

In 1953, Eisenhower had also set as a major goal the restoration of dignity to the office of the President. He felt, strongly, that Truman had demeaned the office. Whether Truman was guilty of so doing depended on one's perception, of course, but few would argue against the claim that in his bearing, his actions, his private and social life, and his official duties as head of state, Eisenhower maintained his dignity. He looked, acted, and sounded like a President.

He was a good steward. He did not sell off the public lands, or open the National Wilderness Areas or National Parks to commercial or mineral exploitation. He retained and expanded TVA. He stopped nuclear testing in the atmosphere, the first world statesman to do so, because of the dangers of radiation to the people who had chosen him as their leader.

In the field of civil rights, he felt he had done as well as could be done. His greatest contribution (albeit one that he had grown increasingly unhappy about) was the appointment of Earl Warren as Chief Justice. In addition, he had completed the desegregation of the armed forces, and of the city of Washington, D.C., as well as all federal property. He had sponsored and signed the first civil-rights legislation since Reconstruction. When he had to, he acted decisively, in Little Rock in 1957. These were all positive, if limited, gains. Eisenhower's boast was that they were made without riots, and without driving the white South to acts of total desperation. Progress in desegregation, especially in the schools, was painfully slow during the Eisenhower years, but he was convinced that anything faster would have produced a much greater and more violent white southern resistance.

In 1952, when he accepted the Republican nomination for the Presidency, Eisenhower called the party to join him in a "crusade." Its purpose was to clean the crooks and the Commies (really, the Democrats) out of Washington. Once those tasks had been accomplished, Eisenhower's critics found it difficult to discover what his crusade was aiming at. There was no stirring call to arms, no great moral cause, no idealistic pursuit of some overriding national goal. Eisenhower, seemingly, was quite content to preside over a fat, happy, satisfied nation that devoted itself to enjoying life, and especially the material benefits available in the greatest industrial power in the world. There was truth in the charge. Eisenhower's rebuttal also contained an elementary truth. The Declaration of Independence stated that one of man's inalienable rights was the pursuit of happiness. Eisenhower tried, with much success, to create a climate in the 1950s in which American citizens could fully exercise that right.

His greatest successes came in foreign policy, and the related area of national defense spending. By making peace in Korea, and avoiding war thereafter for the next seven and one-half years, and by holding down, almost single-handedly, the pace of the arms race, he achieved his major accomplishments. No one knows how much money he saved the United States, as he rebuffed Symington and the Pentagon and the JCS and the AEC and the military-industrial complex. And no one knows how many lives he saved by ending the war in Korea and refusing to enter any others, despite a half-dozen and more virtually unanimous recommendations that he go to war. He made peace, and he kept the peace. Whether any other man could have led the country through that decade without going to war cannot be known. What we do know is that Eisenhower did it. Eisenhower boasted that "the United States never lost a soldier or a foot of ground in my administration. We kept the peace. People asked how it happened—by God, it didn't just happen, I'll tell you that."

Beyond keeping the peace, Eisenhower could claim that at the end of his eight years, the NATO alliance, that bedrock of American foreign policy, was stronger than ever. Relations with the Arab states, considering the American moral commitment to Israel, were as good as could be expected. Except for Cuba, the Latin-American republics remained friendly to the United States. In the Far East, relations with America's partners, South Korea, Japan, and Formosa, were excellent (they were still nonexistent with the Chinese). South Vietnam seemed well on

the road to becoming a viable nation. Laos was admittedly in trouble, but it appeared to be the only immediate danger spot.

What Eisenhower had done best was managing crises. The crisis with Syngman Rhee in early 1953, and the simultaneous crisis with the Chinese Communists over the POW issue and the armistice; the crisis over Dien Bien Phu in 1954, and over Quemoy and Matsu in 1955; the Hungarian and Suez crises of 1956; the Sputnik and Little Rock crises of 1957; the Formosa Resolution crisis of 1958; the Berlin crisis of 1959; the U-2 crisis of 1960—Eisenhower managed each one without overreacting, without going to war, without increasing defense spending, without frightening people half out of their wits. He downplayed each one, insisted that a solution could be found, and then found one. It was a magnificent performance.

His place in history is, of course, a relative matter. He has to be judged against other Presidents, which means that no judgment can be fair, because he did not have the opportunities, nor face the dangers, that other Presidents did. We cannot know how great a leader he might have been, because he ruled in a time that required him, at least in his own view, to adopt a moderate course, to stay in the middle of the road, to avoid calling on his fellow citizens for some great national effort. He did not face the challenges that Washington did, or Lincoln, or Franklin Roosevelt. How he would have responded to setting precedents, rather than following them, or to a Civil War, or to a Depression, or to a world war, we cannot know. What we do know is that he guided his country safely and securely through a dangerous decade.

Shortly after Eisenhower left office, a national poll of American historians placed him nearly at the bottom of the list of Presidents. By the early 1980s, a new poll placed him ninth. His reputation is likely to continue to rise, perhaps even to the point that he wil be ranked just below Washington, Jefferson, Jackson, Lincoln, Wilson, and Franklin Roosevelt.

In attempting to assess th Eisenhower Presidency, certain comparisons must be made. Since Andrew Jackson's time, only four men have served eight consecutive years or more in the White House—Grant, Wilson, Franklin D. Roosevelt, and Eisenhower. Of these four, only two—Grant and Eisenhower—were world figures before they became President. Of the four, only two—Eisenhower and Roosevelt—were more popular when they left office than when they entered. In contrast to his Democratic predecessors and successors, Eisenhower kept the peace; in contrast to his Republican successors, Eisenhower both balanced the budget and stopped inflation.

Eisenhower gave the nation eight years of peace and prosperity. No other President in the twentieth century could make that claim. No wonder that millions of Americans felt that the country was damned lucky to have him.

NO

Arthur M. Schlesinger, Jr.

THE CYCLES OF AMERICAN HISTORY

EISENHOWER

Eisenhower never sank so low as Hoover in the esteem of historians, but his comeback has been still more impressive. The fashion in the 1980s is to regard Hoover rather as Hoover himself regarded Prohibition—"a great social and economic experiment, noble in motive and far-reaching in purpose." He is seen as a deep social thinker but as a failed statesman. Eisenhower, on the other hand, has come with time to be seen as above all a successful statesman. The year after he left office, historians and political scientists in my fathers's poll of 1962 rated him twenty-second among American Presidents. In a poll taken by Steve Neal of the *Chicago Tribune* twenty years later, Eisenhower rose to ninth place. In Professor Robert K. Murray's poll the next year he finished eleventh. (Hoover meanwhile, despite revisionist ardor, dropped from nineteenth in 1962 to twenty-first in 1982 and 1983 polls.)

There are obvious reasons for Eisenhower's upward mobility. At the time the 1950s seemed an era of slumber and stagnation, the bland leading the bland. After intervening years of schism and hysteria, the Eisenhower age appears in nostalgic retrospect a blessed decade of peace and harmony. Moreover, the successive faults of Eisenhower's successors—Kennedy's activism, Johnson's obsessions, Nixon's crookedness, Ford's mediocrity, Carter's blah, Reagan's ideology—have given his virtues new value. Historians should not overlook the capacity of Presidents to do more for the reputations of their predecessors than for their own. The final impetus was provided by the swing of the political cycle back to the private-interest mood of Eisenhower's own Presidency.

THE OPENING OF THE PAPERS IN THE EISENHOWER LIBRARY IN ABILENE, KANSAS, has speeded the revaluation by placing his character in striking new light. When he was President, most Americans cherished him as the national hero reigning benignly in the White House, a wise, warm, avuncular man who grinned a lot and kept the country calm and safe. His critics, whom he routed in two presidential elections, saw him as an old duffer who neglected his job, tripped up in his syntax, read Westerns, played golf and bridge with millionaires and let strong associates run the country in his name, a "captive hero." Both views assumed his kindness of heart and benevolence of spirit.

The Eisenhower papers powerfully suggest that the pose of guileless affability was a deliberate put-on and that behind the masquerade an astute leader moved purposefully to achieve his objectives. Far from being an openhearted lover of mankind, Eisenhower now appears a wily fellow, calculating, crafty and unerringly self-protective. Far from being a political innocent, he was a politician of the first water, brilliantly exploiting the popular illusion that he was above politics. Far from being an amiable bumbler, he feigned his incoherence to conceal his purposes. Far from being passive and uninterested, he had large and vigorous concerns about public policy.

The man who emerges, for example, from *The Eisenhower Diaries* is shrewd, confident and masterful. He is hard and cold in his judgement of his associates. Some entries reveal the famous Eisenhower temper. ("One thing that might help win this war is to get someone to shoot King," he wrote in 1942 about the imperious Chief of Naval Operations.) Others betray, while denying, his ambition. Occasional passages of ponderous philosophizing read as if they had been carefully indited for posterity.

We thought at the time that he lacked political experience. How wrong we were! Politics has few tougher training schools than the United States Army. Eisenhower, who began as a protégé of

General MacArthur and then rose to eminence as a protégé of MacArthur's detested rival, General Marshall, was obviously endowed with consummate political talent. His later skill as President in distancing himself from his unpopular party infuriated Republican professionals but testified to his dazzling instinct for survival.

We must assume now that, however muddled he often appeared, Eisenhower knew perfectly what he was up to most of the time—not least when he encouraged his fellow citizens to think of him as (Good Old) Ike. Once, when the State Department pleaded with him to say nothing in a press conference about the then explosive question of Quemoy and Matsu, the besieged islands off the coast of China, he told James Hagerty, his press secretary, "Don't worry, Jim, if that question comes up, I'll just confuse them." He confused us all. As Richard Nixon put it, Eisenhower was "a far more complex and devious man than most people realized, and in the best sense of those words."

Martin Van Buren, John Randolph of Roanoke once said, "rowed to his object with muffled oars." Phrased less elegantly, this is Fred I. Greenstein's thesis in his influential study of Eisenhower's administrative techniques. Greenstein ascribes six "political strategies" to Eisenhower— "hidden-hand" leadership; "instrumental"—i.e., manipulative—use of language; refusal to engage in personalities; taking action nevertheless on the basis of private personality analysis; selective delegation; and building public support. While the author concedes that these strategies were hardly exclusive to Eisenhower, the loving care with which they are described gives the impression of attributing uniquely to Eisenhower practices that are the stock in trade of political leaders. Thus: "Eisenhower ran organizations by deliberately making simultaneous use of both formal and informal organizations." What President does not?

I do not think that Greenstein fully considers the implications of a "hidden-hand Presidency." For in a democracy, politics must be in the end an educational process, resting above all on persuasion and consent. The Presidency, in Franklin D. Roosevelt's words, is "preeminently a place of moral leadership." The hidden-hand Presidency represents an abdication of the preeminent presidential role. The concept is even a little unjust to Eisenhower, who was not entirely averse to using the Presidency as a pulpit.

On the whole, however, as his political confidant Arthur Larson later wrote, "He simply did not believe that the President should exploit his influence as a dominant national figure to promote good causes that were not within his constitutional function as Chief Executive." In consequence, Larson regretfully continued, Eisenhower denied the country the "desperately needed . . . educational guidance and moral inspiration that a President with a deep personal commitment to the promotion of human rights could supply." Larson was talking about civil rights. His point applies equally to civil liberties.

Racial justice and McCarthyism were the great moral issues of the Eisenhower years. Eisenhower evaded them both. This may be in part because of his severely constricted theory of the Presidency. But it was partly too because Eisenhower did not see them as compelling issues. He did not like to use law to enforce racial integration, and, while he disliked McCarthy's manners and methods, he basically agreed with his objectives. His failure, as his biographer Stephen E. Ambrose has said, "to speak out directly on McCarthy encouraged the witch-hunters, just as his failure to speak out directly on the *Brown v. Topeka* [school integration] decision encouraged the segregationists." It can be added that Eisenhower's failure to speak out directly on the Pentagon, at least before his Farewell Address, encouraged the advocates of the arms race.

Yet, whatever his defects as a public leader, we may stipulate that behind the scene Eisenhower showed more energy, interest, purpose, cunning and command than many of us understood in the 1950s; that he was the dominant figure in his administration whenever he wanted to be (and he wanted to be more often than it seemed at the time); and that the very talent for self-protection that led him to hide behind his reputation for muddle and to shove associates into the line of fire obscured his considerable capacity for decision and control. . . .

IT IS ON HIS HANDLING OF THE PROBLEMS of peace and war that Eisenhower's enhanced reputation rests. Robert A. Divine conveniently sums up the case for "a badly underrated President" in his *Eisenhower and the Cold War* (1981):

For eight years he kept the United States at peace, adroitly avoiding military involvement in the crises of the 1950s. Six months after taking office, he brought the fighting in Korea to an end; in Indochina, he resisted intense pressure to avoid direct American military intervention; in Suez, he courageously aligned the United States against European imperialism while maintaining a staunch posture toward the Soviet Union. He earnestly sought a reduction in Cold War tensions.

Professor Divine draws a particular contrast with his predecessor, claiming that the demands of foreign policy outran Truman's ability and that the result was "overreaction and tragedy for the nation and the world."

In fact, Eisenhower thought that Truman underreacted to the Soviet menace. "In the fiscal years, 1947, 1948, 1949, and 1950," Eisenhower wrote in his diary the day after his inauguration, "the defense fabric continued to shrink at an alarming extent — and this in spite of frequent . . . warnings that people like Jim Forrestal had been expressing time and time again." Forrestal had been Eisenhower's mentor regarding the "threat by the monolithic mass of communistic imperialism." When Forrestal killed himself in 1949, Eisenhower recalled their talks in 1945 about the Russians: "He insisted they hated us, which I had good reason to believe myself. I still do." In May 1953 Eisenhower complained to the legislative leaders that Truman "had let our armed forces dwindle after World War II and had thus invited the attack on Korea. . . .

Eisenhower fully accepted the premises of the Cold War. He appointed the high priest of the Cold War as his Secretary of State. He allowed Dulles to appease Joe McCarthy, to purge the Foreign Service, to construct a network of military pacts around the globe and to preach interminably about godless communism and going to the brink and massive retaliation. Lord Salisbury, the quintessential British Tory and a leading figure in the Churchill cabinet, found Eisenhower in 1953 "violently Russophobe, greatly more so than Dulles," and believed him "personally responsible for the policy of useless pinpricks and harassing tactics the U.S. is following against Russia in Europe and the Far East."

Eisenhower's superiority to the other Cold War Presidents, revisionists argue, lay not in the premises of policy but in the "prudence" with which he conducted the struggle. It is true that, as a former general, Eisenhower was uniquely equipped among recent Presidents to override the national security establishment. Convinced that excessive government spending and deficits would wreck the economy, he kept the defense budget under control. He knew too much about war to send regular troops into combat lightly, especially on unpromising Third World terrain. Perhaps for this as well as for budgetary reasons—nuclear weapons cost less than large conventional forces—he contrived a military posture that made it almost impossible for the United States to fight anything short of nuclear war.

The doctrine of massive retaliation left the United States the choice, when confronted by local aggression in a distant land, of dropping the bomb or doing nothing. Eisenhower's critics feared he would drop the bomb. Most of the time his preference was for doing nothing—not always a bad attitude in foreign affairs. When the Democrats took over in 1961, they briskly increased conventional forces. Their theory was that enlarging the capability to fight limited wars would reduce the risk of nuclear war. The result was the creation of forces that enabled and emboldened us to Americanize the war in Vietnam. Had the Eisenhower all-or-nothing strategy survived, we might have escaped that unmitigated disaster. Or we might have had something far worse.

Eisenhower's budgetary concerns—"a bigger bang for a buck"—and his skepticism about the regular Army and Navy also had their disadvantages. They led him to rely exceptionally, and dangerously, on unconventional forms of coercive power: upon the covert operations of the Central Intelligence Agency, and upon nuclear weapons.

PROFESSOR DIVINE IN HIS APOLOGIA DECLINES to write about CIA covert action "because the evidence on Eisenhower's role is not yet available." This is surprising from such a competent historian. *Eisenhower and the Cold War* was published five years after the many revealing volumes of the Church Committee inquiry had become available. Indeed, in the same year of *Eisenhower and the Cold War* two other books—*Ike's Spies* by Stephen E. Ambrose with R. H. Immerman and *The Declassified Eisenhower* by Blanche Wiesen Cook—submit an impressive amount of evidence about Eisenhower and the CIA. Moreover, the CIA is central to any work purporting to discuss Eisenhower and the Cold War.

Instead of sending regular forces into combat abroad, Eisenhower silently turned the CIA into the secret army of the executive branch. The CIA, as originally conceived in 1947, was supposed to concentrate on the collection and analysis of intelligence. Covert action began in 1948 under the Truman administration, and there was more of it than Truman later remembered (or knew about?). But it was mostly devoted to supporting friends—socialist and Christian trade unions, Italian Christian Democrats, anti-Stalinist intellectuals—rather than to subverting foes. As Kermit Roosevelt, the CIA operative in Iran, has written about his project of overthrowing the Mossadegh government, "We had, I felt sure, no chance to win approval from the outgoing administration of Truman and Acheson. The new Republicans, however, might be quite different."

Indeed they were. Where Truman had seen Mossadegh as an honest if trying nationalist, Eisenhower saw him as a tool of Moscow. Eisenhower, as Anthony Eden, the British Foreign Minister, reported to Churchill, "seemed obsessed by the fear of a Communist Iran." The new President promptly gave Kim Roosevelt the green light. In August 1953 the CIA overthrew Mossadegh and restored the Shah. (One result of this disruption of indigenous political evolution in Iran was to stir resentments that after festering a quarter century overthrew the Shah in 1979. By that time Washington would have been delighted if it could have had a Mossadegh rather than a Khomeini.)

His thorough and generally approved biographer Stephen E. Ambrose has noted Eisenhower's "penchant for seeing Communists wherever a social reform movement or a struggle for national liberation as under way." He saw Communists next in the reformist Arbenz government in Guatemala. The domino theory was already forming itself in Eisenhower's mind. "My God," he told his cabinet, "just think what it would mean to us if Mexico went Communist!" Exhilarated by success in Iran, the CIA overthrew the Arbenz regime in 1954.

Exhilarated once more, the CIA helped install supposedly pro-western governments in Egypt (1954) and Laos (1959), tried to overthrow the Indonesian government (1958) and organized the expedition of Cuban exiles against Castro (1960). In December 1955 Eisenhower specifically ordered the CIA to "develop underground resistance and facilitate covert and guerrilla preparations . . . to the extent practicable" in the Soviet Union, China, and their satellites; and to "counter any threat of a party or individuals directly or indirectly responsive to Communist control to achieve dominant power in a free-world country."

The CIA evidently construed the verb "counter" in drastic fashion. There are indications that CIA operatives in 1955 blew up the plane on which Chou En-lai was scheduled to fly to the Afro-Asian conference in Bandung, Indonesia. There is no question about later CIA assassination attempts in the Eisenhower years against Castro and against the Congolese leader Patrice Lumumba. There is no evidence, however, that these operations were undertaken with Eisenhower's knowledge or approval. Given the strong evidence that the CIA so often acted on its own, one may well conclude that assassination was another of its private initiatives.

By 1956 the CIA was spending $800 million a year for covert action as against $82 million in 1952. That same year Eisenhower created a President's Board of Consultants on Foreign Intelligence Activities. Its members were private citizens of unimpeachable respectability. (One was Joseph P. Kennedy, who remarked about the CIA after the Bay of Pigs, "I know that outfit, and I wouldn't pay them a hundred bucks a week.") The Board promptly commissioned Robert A. Lovett and David Bruce to take a look at the CIA's covert action boom.

Lovett had been Secretary of Defense and Undersecretary of State. Bruce had run the Office of Strategic Services in the European Theater of Operations and was a distinguished diplomat. Their report was stern and devastating. Those who made the 1948 decision to start a program of covert action, Lovett and Bruce said, "could not possibly have foreseen the ramifications of the operations which have resulted from it." CIA agents were making mischief around the planet, and "no one, other than those in the CIA immediately concerned with their day to day operation, has any detailed knowledge what is going on." Should not someone in authority, Lovett and Bruce asked, be continuously calculating "the long-range wisdom of activities which have entailed our virtual abandonment of the international 'golden rule,' and which, if successful to the degree claimed for them, are responsible in a great measure for stirring up the turmoil and raising the doubts about us that exist in many countries of the world today?" If we continue on this course, they concluded, "Where will we be tomorrow?"

Where indeed? The Board endorsed the report and warned Eisenhower in February 1957 that CIA covert action was "autonomous and free-wheeling" and that few projects received the formal approval of the 5412 Special Group, the National Security Council's review mechanism. In 1958 the Board asked Eisenhower to reconsider "programs which find us involved covertly in the internal affairs of practically every country to which we have access." Eisenhower paid no attention. In 1959 his own Special Assistant for National Security, Gordon Gray, told him that the 5412 Committee had little control over covert operations. The Committee began to meet more regularly, but the CIA continued to keep it in the dark—on assassination plots, for example. In its last written report to Eisenhower (January 1961) the Board declared that CIA covert action was not worth the risk, money and manpower it involved and had detracted "substantially" from the execution of the CIA's "primary intelligence-gathering mission." The Board begged still one more time for "a total reassessment of our covert action policies."

Though this material was published in 1978, it was ignored both by Divine and by Ambrose. Eisenhower revisionism generally obscures Eisenhower's decisive personal role in converting the CIA from an intelligence agency into an instrument for American intervention around the world. This was a sea change from Truman's CIA. As Lovett told the Bay of Pigs board of inquiry in 1961, "I have never felt that the Congress of the United States ever intended to give the United States Intelligence Agency authority to conduct operations all over the earth."

Eisenhower did not bring this change about through inattention or inadvertence. The Second World War had persuaded him of the value of covert action, and CIA excesses during his Presidency did not shake his faith. He strongly opposed Senator Mike Mansfield's resolution calling for a joint congressional committee to oversee the CIA, telling one Republican congressman that "this kind of bill would be passed over my dead body." In his conference with President-elect Kennedy the day before the inauguration, Eisenhower observed of the CIA's anti-Castro expedition, "It was the policy of this government to help such forces to the utmost" and urgently recommended to Kennedy that "this effort be continued and accelerated."

Eisenhower's faith in covert action produced mindless international meddling that exacerbated the Cold War, angered American allies and in later years rebounded fiercely against American interests. Moreoover, by nourishing and cherishing the CIA more than any President before Reagan had done, Eisenhower released a dangerous virus in American society and life.

WE ARE SENSITIVE THESE DAYS ABOUT THE limitless horror of nuclear war. Revisionist historians condemn Truman for his allegedly unrepentant decision to drop the bomb in 1945. In fact, Truman behaved like a man much shaken by the decision. He had directed that the bomb be used "so that military objectives . . . are the target and not women and children," and he was considerably disturbed when he learned that most of those killed at Hiroshima were civilians. . . .

Revisionist historians are similarly severe in condemning Kennedy for running the risk of nuclear war to get the Soviet missiles out of Cuba in 1962. They seem strangely unconcerned, however, that Eisenhower used the threat of nuclear war far more often than any other American President has done, before or since. Nuclear blackmail was indeed the almost inevitable consequence of the military posture dictated by "massive retaliation." It is said in his defense that Eisenhower used the threat in a context of American nuclear superiority that minimized the risk. But the same condition of nuclear superiority prevailed for, and must equally absolve, Truman and Kennedy.

Eisenhower began by invoking the nuclear threat to end the fighting in Korea. He let the Chinese know, he later told Lyndon Johnson, that "he would not feel constrained about crossing the Yalu, or using nuclear weapons." Probably the effectiveness of this threat has been exaggerated. The Chinese had compelling reasons of their own to get out of the war. The decisive shift in their position away from the forced repatriation of prisoners of war took place, as McGeorge Bundy has pointed out, after the death of Stalin in March 1953—and before Eisenhower sent his signals to Peking. In May 1953 General J. Lawton Collins, the Army Chief of Staff, declared himself "very skeptical about the value of using atomic weapons tactically in Korea." Eisenhower replied that "it might be cheaper, dollar-wise, to use atomic weapons in Korea than to continue to use conventional weapons." If the Chinese persisted, "it would be necessary to expand the war outside of Korea and . . . to use the atomic bomb." In December, Eisenhower said that, if the Chinese attacked again, "we should certainly respond by hitting them hard and wherever it would hurt most, including Peiping itself. This . . . would mean all-out war." A joint memorandum from the State Department and the Joint Chiefs of Staff called for the use of atomic weapons against military targets in Korea, Manchuria and China.

The next crisis came in 1954 in Vietnam. In March, according to Divine, Eisenhower was "briefly tempted" by the idea of American intervention, refusing, as he put it, to "exclude the possibility of a single [air] strike, if it were almost certain this would produce decisive results. . . . Of course, if we did, we'd have to deny it forever." As envisaged by General Twining of the Air Force and Admiral Radford, the strike would involve three atomic bombs. Opposition by Congress and by the British killed the idea. Whether this was Eisenhower's hope when he permitted Dulles to carry the air strike proposal to London remains obscure. It was at this time that he propounded what he called "the 'falling domino' principle . . . a beginning of a

disintegration that would have the most profound influences," a disintegration that, he said, could lead to the loss of Indochina, then Burma, then Thailand, Malaya, Indonesia, then Japan, Formosa and the Philippines. This theory of the future entrapped Eisenhower's successors in the quicksands of Vietnam. The dominos did indeed fall in Indochina, as we all know now. But, with communist China invading communist Vietnam because communist Vietnam had invaded communist Cambodia, the dominos fell against each other, not against the United States.

Whatever Eisenhower's intentions regarding Vietnam, he definitely endorsed in May 1954 the recommendation by the Joint Chiefs to use atomic bombs in case of Chinese intervention if Congress and allies agreed. "The concept" in the event of a large-scale Vietminh attack, Dulles said in October, "envisions a fight with nuclear weapons rather than commitment of ground forces."

Eisenhower tried nuclear blackmail again during the Quemoy-Matsu crisis of 1955. In March of that year Dulles publicly threatened the use of atomic weapons. Eisenhower added the next day in his press conference, "I see no reason why they shouldn't be used just exactly as you would use a bullet or anything else." In the 1958 replay of the Quemoy-Matsu drama, Dulles said that American intervention would probably not be effective if limited to conventional weapons; "the risk of a more extensive use of nuclear weapons, and even of general war, would have to be accepted." "There [is] no use of having stuff," Dulles remarked over the phone to General Twining "and never being able to use it."

"The beauty of Eisenhower's policy," Divine writes with regard to Quemoy and Matsu, "is that to this day no one can be sure whether or not . . . he would have used nuclear weapons." Nuclear blackmail may strike some as the beauty part, though we did not used to think so when Khrushchev tried it. In Eisenhower's case it was associated with an extraordinary effort to establish the legitimacy of nuclear war. One restraint on the use of the bomb was the opposition of American allies and of world opinion. This resistance Eisenhower was determined to overcome. As Dulles told the National Security Council on 31 March 1953, while "in the present state of world opinion we could not use an A-bomb, we should make every effort now to dissipate this feeling." The minutes of the meeting add: "The President and Secretary Dulles were in complete agreement that somehow or other the tabu which surrounds the use of atomic weapons would have to be destroyed." . . .

In December 1954 Eisenhower ordered the Atomic Energy Commission to relinquish control of nuclear weapons to the Department of Defense. At the same time, he ordered Defense to deploy overseas a large share of the nuclear arsenal—36 percent of the hydrogen bombs, 42 percent of the atomic bombs—many on the periphery of the Soviet Union. The movement of American policy continued to disturb our British allies. . . .

Eisenhower's persevering effort was to abolish the "firebreak" between conventional and nuclear weapons. Fortunately for the world, this effort failed. By 1964 nearly everyone agreed with Lyndon Johnson when he said, "Make no mistake. There is not such thing as a conventional nuclear weapon."

IN THE FIRST YEARS IN THE WHITE HOUSE, Eisenhower regarded nuclear attack as a usable military option. He had no compunction about threatening such attack. He hoped to destroy the taboo preventing the use of nuclear weapons. But in fact he never used them. As Ambrose points out, "Five times in one year [1954] the experts advised the President to launch an atomic strike against China. Five times he said no." His campaign to legitimate the bomb was happily only a passing phase.

As the Soviet Union increased its nuclear arsenal, Eisenhower came to believe more and more strongly in the horror of nuclear war. The outlook was ever closer, he said in 1956, "to destruction of the enemy and suicide for ourselves." When both sides recognized that "destruction will be reciprocal and complete, possibly we will have sense enough to meet at the conference table with the understanding that the era of armaments has ended and the human race must conform its actions to this truth or die."

For all his early talk about the "same old whore," Eisenhower now sought better relations with the Soviet Union. As Sherman Adams, Eisenhower's chief of staff on domestic matters, later observed, "The hard and uncompromising line that the United States government took toward Soviet Russia and Red China between 1953 and the early months of 1959 was more a Dulles line than an Eisenhower line." But Dulles retained his uses for Eisenhower, both in frightening the Russians and in enabling the President to reserve for himself the role of man of peace.

In his later mood, Eisenhower strove, less anxiously than Churchill and later Macmillan but a good deal more anxiously than Dulles, to meet the Russians at the conference table. In 1953 at the United Nations he set forth his Atoms for

Peace plan, by which the nuclear powers would contribute fissionable materials to an International Atomic Energy Agency to promote peaceful uses of atomic energy. This well-intentioned but feckless proposal assumed that atoms for peace could be segregated from atoms for war—an assumption abundantly refuted in later years and the cause of dangerous nuclear proliferation in our own time. In 1955 at the Geneva summit he came up with a better idea, the creative Open Skies plan. A system of continuous reciprocal monitoring, Eisenhower argued, would reduce fears of surprise attack. The Russians turned Open Skies down as an American espionage scheme. Open Skies was a good idea; it deserves revival. In his second term, against the opposition of many in his own administration, Eisenhower fitfully pursued the project of a nuclear test ban.

He resented the mounting pressure from the Democrats and from the Pentagon to accelerate the American nuclear build-up. The Pentagon did not impress him. He knew all the tricks, having employed them himself. He used to say that he "knew too much about the military to be fooled." He refused to be panicked by perennial Pentagon alarms about how we were falling behind the Russians and dismissed the 'missile gap' of the late 1950s with richly justified skepticism.

Yet he weakly allowed the build-up to proceed. In 1959 he complained that the Pentagon, after agreeing a few years earlier that hitting seventy key targets would knock out the Soviet system, now insisted on hitting thousands of targets. The military, he said, were getting "themselves into an incredible position— of having enough to destroy every conceivable target all over the world, plus a threefold reserve." The radioactivity

from atomic blasts at this level, he said, would destroy the United States too. The United States already had a stockpile of "five thousand or seven thousand weapons or whatnot." Why did the Atomic Energy Commission and the Department of Defense want more? "But then," writes Ambrose, "he reluctantly gave way to the AEC and DOD demands."

In 1960, when informed at a National Security Council meeting that the United States could produce almost 400 Minuteman missiles a year, Eisenhower with "obvious disgust" (according to his science adviser George Kistiakowsky) burst out, "Why don't we go completely crazy and plan on a force of 10,000?" The nuclear arsenal had now grown to a level that the Eisenhower of 1954 had considered "fantastic," "crazy" and "unconscionable." There were approximately 1000 nuclear warheads when Eisenhower entered the White House, 18,000 when he left.

For all his concern about nuclear war, for all his skepticism about the Pentagon, for all the unique advantage he enjoyed as General of the Armies in commanding confidence on defense issues, he never seized control of the military-industrial complex. "Being only one person," he lamely explained, he had not felt he could oppose the "combined opinion of all his associates." In the measured judgment of the Regius Professor of History at Oxford, the military historian Michael Howard, "The combination of his constant professions of devotion to disarmament and peace with his reluctance to take any of the harsh decisions required to achieve those professed objectives leaves an impression, if not of hypocrisy, then certainly of an ultimate lack of will which, again, denies him a place in the first rank of world statesmen."

Though Eisenhower carefully avoided war himself, he was surprisingly bellicose in his advice to his successors. He told Kennedy before the inauguration not only to go full speed ahead on the exile invasion of Cuba but, if necessary, "to intervene unilaterally" in Laos. So bent was Eisenhower on American intervention in Laos that Kennedy persuaded Macmillan to explain to him in detail the folly of such an adventure. When Vietnam became the issue in the mid-1960s, Eisenhower advised Lyndon Johnson to avoid gradualism, "go all out," declare war, seek victory, not negotiations, warn China and the Soviet Union, as Eisenhower himself had done over Korea, that the United States might feel compelled to use nuclear weapons to break the deadlock, and, if the Chinese actually came in, "to use at least tactical atomic weapons." The antiwar protest, Eisenhower declare, "verges on treason." When Johnson announced in 1968 that he was stopping most of the bombing of North Vietnam, Eisenhower, Ambrose writes, "was livid with anger, his remarks [to Ambrose] about Johnson's cutting and running unprintable." Eisenhower was more a hawk than a prince of peace.

"It would perhaps have been better for him, as in the last century for Wellington and Grant," Sir John Colville concludes, "if he had rested on his military laurels." Walter Lippmann remarked in 1964 that Eisenhower's was "one of the most falsely inflated reputations of my experience"—and he was speaking before the inflation was under way. In later years the Eisenhower boom has gathered momentum in cyclical response to a need and a time.

In due course the pendulum will doubtless swing back toward the view of Eisenhower presented in the illuminating early memoirs by men close to him—Sherman Adams's *Firsthand Report* (1961), Emmet Hughes's *The Ordeal of Power* (1963), Arthur Larson's *Eisenhower: The President Nobody Knew* (1968). In these works of direct observation, Eisenhower emerges as a man of intelligence, force and restraint who did not always understand and control what was going on, was buffeted by events and was capable of misjudgment and error. I lunched with Emmet Hughes in 1981. "Eisenhower was much more of a President than you liberals thought at the time," he said. "But Eisenhower revisionism has gone too far. Take Fred Greenstein of Princeton, for example. He is a nice fellow. But his thesis these days—Eisenhower the activist President—is a lot of bullshit."

Yet we were wrong to have underestimated Eisenhower's genius for self-presentation and self-preservation—the best evidence of which lies in his capacity to take in a generation of scholars.

POSTSCRIPT

Was Dwight Eisenhower a Great President?

How will historians rank Eisenhower in the year 2000? Ambrose believes his reputation will continue to rise to just a notch below Washington, Jefferson, Jackson, Lincoln, Wilson, and Roosevelt. Schlesinger thinks the pendulum will push him back to the middle of the pack. Historians may quibble with Schlesinger's view that Eisenhower has fooled the current generation of scholars, but nobody will ever again view him as a kindly, grinning grandfather who read westerns and played golf with millionaires while his aides ran the country.

Most early assessments of Eisenhower were generally lukewarm or critical of his presidency. A good collection of these early appraisals appears in *Eisenhower as President* (Hill & Wang, 1963), edited and introduced by Dean Albertson. Revisionist assessments were started in the late 1960s by journalists Murray Kempton and Garry Wills. The fullest portrait is Stephen E. Ambrose's two-volume *Eisenhower* (Simon & Schuster, 1983, 1984), a portion of which was reprinted as the first article in this issue. The most recent assessment, Anthony James Joe's "Eisenhower Revisionism and American Politics," in Joann P. Krieg, ed., *Dwight Eisenhower: Soldier, President, Statesman* (Greenwood Press, 1987), is a part of a symposium held at Hofstra University in March 1984.

The most carefully constructed revisionist analysis of Eisenhower is by Princeton University political scientist Fred I. Greenstein, *The Hidden-Hand Presidency: Eisenhower as Leader* (Basic Books, 1982). His arguments are summarized in "Eisenhower as an Activist President: A Look at New Evidence," *Political Science Quarterly* (Winter 1979-80) and most recently in "Dwight D. Eisenhower: Leadership Theorist in the White House," in Greenstein, ed., *Leadership in the Modern Presidency* (Howard University Press, 1988). The latter book is extremely useful because it contains detailed sketches of every U.S. president from Truman through Reagan.

Greenstein's thesis is fairly simple. Based upon a close examination of Eisenhower's diaries and most intimate personal papers, the author concludes that Eisenhower deliberately employed a convoluted speaking style at his press conferences and used his subordinates to carry out his policies. Greenstein's critics have argued that Ike's hidden-hand methods are not that unique. It remains to be seen whether Greenstein's analysis of Eisenhower's presidency will be substantiated by future historians. The postrevisionist critics, as Schlesinger predicted, have already begun to emerge. British historian Piers Brendon recalls how, as a boy of seven, he admired the leader of D-Day and savior of the Western world. Years later he became disillusioned with his hero and has accused Eisenhower of chronic vacillation and moral obtuseness in *Ike: His Life and Times* (Harper & Row, 1986).

ISSUE 15

Could the United States Have Prevented the Fall of South Vietnam?

YES: Guenter Lewy, from *America in Vietnam* (Oxford, 1978)

NO: George C. Herring, from "The 'Vietnam Syndrome' and American Foreign Policy," *Virginia Quarterly Review* (Spring 1981)

ISSUE SUMMARY

YES: Professor emeritus of political science Guenter Lewy believes that the South Vietnamese government might not have lost the war if the United States had followed "a strategy of surprise and massed strength at decisive points" against North Vietnam.

NO: Professor of history George C. Herring argues that the policy makers exaggerated the strategic importance of Vietnam and deluded themselves about America's power.

At the end of World War II, imperialism was coming to a close in Asia. Japan's defeat spelled the end of her control over China, Korea, and the countries of southeast Asia. Attempts by the European nations to reestablish their empires were doomed. Anti-imperialist movements emerged all over Asia and Africa, often producing chaos.

The United States faced a dilemma. America was a nation conceived in revolution and was sympathetic to the struggles of Third World nations. But the United States was afraid that many of the revolutionary leaders were Communists who would place their countries under the control of the expanding empire of the Soviet Union. By the late 1940s, the Truman administration decided that it was necessary to stop the spread of communism. The policy that resulted was known as containment.

Vietnam provided a test of the containment doctrine in Asia. Vietnam had been a French protectorate from 1885 until Japan took control during World War II. Shortly before the war ended, the Japanese gave Vietnam its independence, but the French were determined to reestablish their influence in the area. Conflicts emerged between the French-led nationalist forces of South Vietnam and the Communist-dominated provisional government of the Democratic Republic of Vietnam (DRV) that was established in Hanoi in August 1945. Ho Chi Minh was the president of the DRV. An avowed Communist since the 1920s, Ho had also become the major nationalist figure in Vietnam. As the leader of the anti-imperialist movement against French and Japanese colonialism for over 30 years, Ho managed to tie together the Communist and Nationalist movements in Vietnam.

A full-scale war broke out in 1946 between the Communist government of North Vietnam and the French-dominated country of South Vietnam. The war lasted eight years. After the Communists defeated the French at the battle of Dien Bien Phu in May 1954, the latter decided to pull out. At the Geneva Conference the following summer, Vietnam was divided at the 17th parallel pending elections.

The United States became directly involved in Vietnam after the French withdrew. In 1955 the Republican president Dwight Eisenhower refused to recognize the Geneva Accords but supported the establishment of the South Vietnamese government. Its leader was Ngo Dinh Diem, an authoritarian Catholic who was more popular with U.S. politicians than he was with the Buddhist peasants of South Vietnam who resented his oppressive rule. In 1956 Diem, with U.S. approval, refused to hold elections, which would have provided a unified government for Vietnam in accordance with the Geneva agreement. The Communists in the south responded by again taking up the armed struggle. The war continued for another 19 years.

Both President Eisenhower and his Democratic successor, John F. Kennedy, were anxious to prevent South Vietnam from being taken over by the Communists, so economic assistance and military aid were provided.

A major problem for President Kennedy lay in the unpopularity of the South Vietnamese government. He supported the overthrow of the Diem regime in October 1963 and hoped that the successor government would establish an alternative to communism. It didn't work. Kennedy himself was assassinated three weeks later. His successor, Lyndon Johnson, changed the character of American policy in Vietnam by escalating the air war and increasing the number of ground forces from 21,000 in 1965 to a full fighting force of 550,000 at its peak in 1968.

The next president, Richard Nixon, adopted a new policy of "Vietnamization" of the war. Military aid to South Vietnam was increased to ensure the defeat of the Communists. At the same time, American troops were gradually withdrawn from Vietnam. South Vietnamese president Thieu recognized the weaknesses of his own position without the support of U.S. troops. He reluctantly signed the Paris Accords of January 1973 only after being told by Secretary of State Henry Kissinger that the United States would sign them alone.

Once U.S. soldiers were withdrawn, Thieu's regime was doomed. In the spring of 1975 a full-scale war broke out and the South Vietnamese government collapsed. Could the United States have prevented a North Vietnamese victory? In the following selections, Guenter Lewy argues that South Vietnam might not have lost the war if the United States had adopted a more consistent military policy in the years from 1954 to 1975. George Herring believes that a succession of American presidents misapplied the containment policy to an inherently unstable situation in Vietnam with disastrous results.

YES
Guenter Lewy

COULD THE UNITED STATES HAVE WON IN VIETNAM?

One can begin to answer this difficult question by pointing to certain mistakes made by American leaders in holding together the home front, though this task, for reasons to be discussed below, would probably have presented almost insuperable difficulties even to the most adroit leadership. There was the failure, especially on the part of the Johnson administration, to provide a convincing explanation and justification of the American involvement. Simplistic rhetoric like "fighting for democracy in Vietnam" or halting "communist aggression," though not without some element of truth, was inappropriate to the complex situation faced in Southeast Asia; it also was highly vulnerable to the retort of the critics who pointed to the undemocratic character of the Saigon government and to the extensive involvement of Southerners in the conflict.

The government in its pronouncements spoke of success and light at the end of the tunnel, but continued to dispatch additional troops while casualties mounted steadily. As the director of the *Pentagon Papers* task force, Leslie H. Gelb, has observed, optimism without results could only work so long; after that, it had to produce a credibility gap. To be sure, the Johnson administration had never expected to become engaged in a protracted ground war on such a scale, and even when the involvement deepened it attempted to keep the war limited, a war without full mobilization of the home front and without a hated enemy. President Johnson is said to have rejected the view of some of his advisers that in order to hold the support of the country he would have to engage in some outright chauvinistic rabble-rousing and provide the American people with a vivid foe. Such a mobilization of patriotic sentiments, he apparently concluded, could force him into unduly risky actions such as unrestricted bombing and even an invasion of North Vietnam—which, in turn, could lead to a confrontation with Communist China or Russia. At the very least, a widening of the war would prevent the achievement of his domestic "Great Society" programs.

From Guenter Lewy, *America in Vietnam* (Oxford University Press, 1978). Copyright © 1978 by Guenter Lewy. Reprinted by permission of Oxford University Press, Inc. Notes omitted.

For the same reasons, Johnson refrained from asking Congress for a declaration of war, which until 1967 he probably could have gotten without much difficulty. It is well to remember that at the time even critics of the president's Vietnam policy did not want to press for a formal declaration of war by Congress on the grounds that it would have undesirable consequences—it might trigger secret treaties between North Vietnam and Russia and China, thus risking a dangerous expansion of the conflict, and it could lead to the enactment of wartime curbs on free speech and press. Only years later did charges of an abuse of the Gulf of Tonkin resolution arise. Even though this resolution, considered by most legal authorities a functional equivalent of a declaration of war, was repealed by Congress in January 1971, the Nixon administration did not rely on it for its policy of withdrawal, and Congress did not end military appropriations for Vietnam until the last U.S. serviceman had left Vietnam and the prisoners of war had returned in 1973. Citing these appropriations, the courts consistently rejected charges of an unconstitutionally conducted war. And yet in retrospect it is apparent that Presidents Johnson and Nixon would have been spared much opposition and grief if Johnson had asked Congress for a declaration of war.

As a result of many different considerations, then, the nation fought a limited war, with the full employment of its military power restricted through elaborate rules of engagement and limitations on operations beyond the borders of South Vietnam, while for its determined opponent the war was total. The U.S. fought a limited war whose rationale was never convincingly explained and which, in any event, even an able leader would have had a most difficult time justifying. How does one tell a young conscript that he should be prepared to die in order to create a balance of power in Asia or in order to improve the American bargaining position at the upcoming negotiations that would lead to a compromise settlement?

If the Vietnam war had occurred in a different age some of these difficulties might have been surmountable. There was a time when the mass of the people were deferential to any official definition of the national interest and of the objectives of the nation's foreign policy. For good or for bad, this situation no longer holds in a modern democracy. Moreover, the war was fought at a time when major social evils had come to light in America and when a social transformation at home, the achievement of the "Great Society," was widely and urgently expected. Attacks on the mounting cost of the war in Asia were given special pertinence by the rioting in the urban black ghettos in 1967 and 1968 and by the deterioration of American cities which these racial explosions held up for all to see.

But the most important reason for the steadily spreading acceptance of the view that the American involvement in Vietnam had been a mistake was probably neither the implausibility of the rationale given for the war nor the preoccupation of both the educated classes and the poor with social reform. The decisive reason for the growing disaffection of the American people was the conviction that the war was not being won and apparently showed little prospect of coming to a successful conclusion. There was a clear correlation between declining support and a mounting casualty toll; the increasing cost in lives, occurring in a war without decisive battles or conquered territory, was the most visible symbol of failure. Hanoi's expectation that the American democracy would not be able to sustain a long and bloody conflict in a faraway land turned out to be more correct than Westmoreland's strategy of attrition, which was supposed to inflict such heavy casualties on the Communists as to force them to cease their aggression.

Had the intervention succeeded, say, by 1967, the public's disaffection probably would not have arisen and President Johnson would have emerged as a highly popular figure. As John F. Kennedy is supposed to have said of the reaction to the Bay of Pigs invasion: Success has a thousand fathers, but failure is an orphan. The capacity of people in a modern democracy to support a limited war is precarious at best. The mixture of propaganda and compulsion which a totalitarian regime can muster in order to extract such support is not available to the leaders of a democratic state. Hence when such a war for limited objectives drags on for a long time it is bound to lose the backing essential for its successful pursuit. It may well be, as an American political scientist has concluded, that "unless it is severely provoked or unless the war succeeds fast, a democracy cannot choose war as an instrument of policy."

That American public opinion, as Leslie Gelb has put it, was "the essential domino" was, of course, recognized by both American policy-makers and the Vietnamese Communists. Each geared his "strategy—both the rhetoric and the conduct of the war—to this fact." And yet, given the limited leverage which the leaders of a democracy have on public opinion, and in view of the various liabilities to which the American war effort was subject, the ability of American decision-makers to control this "essential domino" was always precarious. For the Vietnamese Communists, on the other hand, ideological mobilization at home and carrying the propaganda effort to the enemy was relatively easy, and they worked at both objectives relentlessly and with great success. Enormous amounts of effort, manpower and money were devoted to creating the image of the Viet Cong as a highly motivated, honest and noble human being, who was engaged in a just war against an imperialist aggressor and his corrupt puppets. This concerted activity, Douglas Pike stresses, was not just pretense and sham. "The communists worked hard to create their image. They altered policy in its name. They shot looters, purged cadres, refused alliances, ordered military offensives, all for the sake of perception abroad." The outcome of this uneven contest was predictable. The Western observer, essentially unable to check out the claims of the communist camp, was left with the image of a tough and highly effective enemy while at the same time he was daily exposed to the human and bureaucratic errors and shortcomings of his own side. Image was bound to triumph over reality.

The coverage of the war by television was a crucial factor in this one-sided publicity. The VC were notoriously uncooperative in allowing Western cameramen to shoot pictures of the disemboweling of village chiefs or other acts of terror, while scenes of South Vietnamese brutality, such as the mistreatment of prisoners, were often seen on American TV screens. Television stresses the dramatic and contentious, and the Vietnam war offered plenty of both. The result was a one-dimensional coverage of the conflict—apparently meaningless destruction of lives and property in operations which rarely led to visible success. War has always been beastly, but the Vietnam war was the first war exposed to television cameras and seen in practically every home, often in living color. Not surprisingly this close-up view of devastation and suffering, repeated daily, strengthened the growing desire for peace. The events of Tet and the siege of Khe Sanh in 1968, in particular, shook the American public. The nightly portrayal of violence and gore and of American soldiers seemingly on the brink of disaster contributed significantly to disillusionment with the war. Gallup poll data suggest that between early February and the middle of March 1968 nearly one person in five switched from the "hawk" to the "dove" position.

Despite the small percentage of individuals actively involved in organized opposition to the war, the antiwar movement had a significant impact on both the Johnson and Nixon administrations. Not only does a small percentage of a country of 200 million constitute a sizable number of people, but the active and articulate few, often strategically placed, can have an importance well beyond their proportion of the population. The tactics of the antiwar movement were often unpopular, and the association of the drive for peace with other causes and groups regarded as radical by most Americans further contributed to its political isolation. Some of the leaders were old-time or New leftists; others were admirers of the Viet Cong, whose struggle and tactics they romanticized. To politically seasoned Americans it was obvious that many of these men and the organizations and committees they spawned were not so much for peace and against the war as they were partisans of Hanoi, whose victory they sought to hasten through

achieving an American withdrawal from Vietnam. But the great majority of those who joined peace demonstrations were ordinary Americans—Democrats, Republicans and independents—simply fed up with the seemingly endless bloodletting.

The impact of the antiwar movement was enhanced by the widely publicized charges of American atrocities and lawlessness. The inability of Washington officials to demonstrate that the Vietnam war was not in fact an indiscriminate bloodbath and did not actually kill more civilians than combatants was a significant factor in the erosion of support for the war, especially among the media and the intellectual community generally. The view held by many of these critics that the war did not involve any important national stakes further contributed to their unwillingness to accept a level of violence that was probably less extreme than in many previous wars fought by this country. To attempt such an effort at explanation without appearing to have a callous disregard for human life would, of course, have been extremely difficult. Moreover, there can be little doubt that while the casualties inflicted on the civilian population of Vietnam were not out of line in comparison with World War II and Korea, they did have a highly detrimental effect in a counterinsurgency setting like Vietnam. The realization on the part of many civilian policy-makers that this was so, combined with the unwillingness of the military to forego the highly destructive tools of heavy weaponry, may be one of the reasons why no meaningful effort at explanation was ever undertaken.

In the absence of a frank and convincing official justification of the high level of violence in Vietnam, speculation and unsupported allegations of wrongdoing held sway. Given respectability by the support of well-known public figures, this agitation eventually had an effect upon the larger educated public. Self-flagellation for the alleged gross immorality of America's conduct in the war and its moral decline as a nation became rampant, and calls for the trial of "Amerika's" leaders for crimes against peace and humanity fell on sympathetic ears. Unable to end the war on their terms, many intellectuals vented their frustration in verbal overkill which probably will not be remembered as their finest hour. Shrill rhetoric created a world of unreality in which the North Vietnamese Communists were the defenders of national self-determination, while U.S. actions designed to prevent the forceful takeover of South Vietnam stood branded as imperialism and aggression. Many of those who complained of the repressive character of the Thieu regime were uncritical of or found nothing but praise for the totalitarian regime in Hanoi. Politically innocent citizens paid hundreds of thousands of dollars for newspaper advertisements which recorded their support of charges concerning American actions and motives which they could not possibly have confirmed by any kind of evidence. Academics lent these ads an aura of authority by signing them with their titles and university affiliations. Everyone—from clergyman and biologist to movie actor and pediatrician—could become an instant expert on international law, Southeast Asia, and foreign policy generally. Professors who would never have dared treat their own disciplines in such a cavalier fashion proclaimed with assurance solutions to the Vietnam problem at "teach-ins," complete with folk singers, mime troupes and other forms of entertainment.

The disaffection of large segments of the country's intellectual leadership—in the media, the professions, on the college campuses, and increasingly in Congress—reinforced the growing war-weariness and disillusionment in the country, often quite unrelated to wider political or humanitarian concerns. The Vietnam war ended up as the longest and most unpopular war in the nation's history.

As was to be expected, North Vietnam sought to make the most of the antiwar movement in America. North Vietnamese officials, at meetings with radical antiwar activists held in Cuba, Hungary, Czechoslovakia and North Vietnam, provided tactical advice and helped coordinate worldwide antiwar demonstrations. Communist propaganda regularly reported peace demonstrations as proof that the American people were weakening in their resolve. The North Vietnamese were convinced that just as the Viet Minh had defeated France not only, or primarily, on the battlefield but rather by outlasting the patience of the French people for the war in Indochina, so North Vietnam and the Viet Cong would eventually triumph over the United States on account of their own determination and the failure of the American people to last the course. As Assistant Secretary of Defense John T. McNaughton put it with considerable understatement in a memorandum in May 1967: "The state of mind in the US generates impatience in the political structure of the United States. It unfortunately also generates patience in Hanoi." Well-meaning as most participants in the peace movement were, James Reston wrote in October 1965, "the truth is that . . . they are not promoting peace but postponing it. They are not persuading the President and the Congress to end the war, but deceiving Ho Chi Minh and General Giap into prolonging it."

The opponents of the war had a constitutional right to express their views, but it was folly to ignore the consequences of this protest. American public opinion indeed turned out to be a crucial "domino"; it influenced military morale in the field, the long-drawn-out negotiations in Paris, the settlement of 1973, and the cuts in aid to South Vietnam in 1974, a prelude to the final abandonment in 1975. A more supportive public opinion in America would probably have led to a slower pace of disengagement, but whether this additional time would have materially changed the fighting ability of the South Vietnamese armed forces and thus could have prevented an ultimate collapse remains, of course, an open question.

Opposition to the war in Vietnam benefited from America's moralistic approach to world affairs which, as the political scientist Lucian Pye has suggested, makes Americans uneasy about being identified with governments striving to suppress rebellions. "We tend to suspect that any government confronted with a violent challenge to its authority is probably basically at fault and that a significant number of rebels can be mobilized only if a people has been grossly mistreated. Often we are inclined to see insurgency and juvenile delinquency in the same light, and we suspect that, as 'there is no such thing as bad boys, only bad parents,' so there are no bad people, only evil and corrupt governments." In point of fact, while the communist insurgency in Vietnam undoubtedly for a long time drew strength from the failure of the government of South Vietnam to address and remedy the social and economic problems of its rural population, the GVN eventually carried out a far-reaching land reform and undertook other successful measures to better relations with its people. Just as the internal strength and cohesion of the Republic of Korea did not save it from attack in 1950 and would not have staved off a communist victory without American military intervention, so the strengthening of the GVN did not prevent the North Vietnamese invasions in 1972 and 1975 which finally led to the collapse of South Vietnam. Indeed, at least in part, it was this very improvement of the GVN and the greatly weakened posture of the VC which led to the decision of Hanoi to abandon the tactic of revolutionary war and to resort to conventional warfare with tanks and heavy artillery.

And yet it is also true that the way in which both the Americans and South Vietnamese carried out the effort to suppress the communist insurgency often alienated the population of the countryside. The record . . . does not bear out charges of genocide or indiscriminate killings of civilians and wholesale violations of the law of war. However, the strategy and tactics of the allied counterinsurgency, especially the lavish use of firepower, did undermine the efforts of the GVN to win the allegiance of its people. There is reason to believe that the suffering inflicted upon large segments of South Vietnam's rural population during long years of high-technology warfare contributed to the spread of a feeling of resignation, war-weariness and an unwillingness to go on fighting against the resolute opponent from the North. It is also well to remember that revulsion at the fate of thousands of hapless civilians killed and maimed by the deadly arsenal of a modern army may undercut the willingness of a democratic nation to fight communist insurgents and that reliance upon high-technology weapons in an insurgency setting therefore may be counterproductive on still another level.

Despite much talk about "winning hearts and minds," the U.S. failed to understand the real stakes in a revolutionary war and for all too long ignored the conflicts in Vietnamese society which the VC exploited and used to motivate their forces. The U.S. also never really learned to fight a counterinsurgency war and used force in largely traditional ways, and the South Vietnamese copied our mistakes. The military, like all bureaucracies encountering a new situation for which they are not prepared and in which they do not know what to do, did what they knew to do. That happened to be the inappropriate thing. "The Vietnamese Communist generals," Edward G. Lansdale has written, "saw their armed forces as instruments primarily to gain political goals. The American generals saw their forces primarily as instruments to defeat enemy military forces. One fought battles to influence opinions in Vietnam and in the world, the other fought battles to finish the enemy keeping tabs by body count." As it turned out, the enemy's endurance and supply of manpower proved stronger than American persistence in keeping up the struggle. More importantly, the strategy of attrition downgraded the crucial importance of pacification and ignored the fact that the enemy whom it was essential to defeat was in the hamlets and not in the jungles. American forces, applying classic Army doctrines of aggressively seeking out the enemy and destroying his main-force units, won most of the battles but lost the war.

Many of American's military leaders argue to this day that their ability to conduct a winning strategy was hamstrung not only by overly restrictive rules of engagement, designed to protect civilian life and property, but also by geo-graphical constraints imposed on them for fear of a collision with Communist China and the Soviet Union. This argument is less than persuasive, for the war, in the final analysis, had to be won in South Vietnam. Military action in Laos and Cambodia at an early stage of the war, seeking permanently to block the Ho Chi Minh Trail, would have made the North Vietnamese supply effort far more difficult, but basically an expansion of the conflict would not have achieved the American task. Certainly, an invasion of North Vietnam would only have magnified the difficulties faced.

The war not only had to be won in South Vietnam, but it had to be won by the South Vietnamese. Unfortunately, to the end South Vietnamese performance remained the Achilles' heel of the allied effort. A totalitarian state like Communist North Vietnam, possessing a monopoly of indoctrination and social control, was bound to display greater military morale and unity than a fragmented and barely authoritarian country like South Vietnam. Also, the Republic of Vietnam, under American prodding, gradually did improve its stability and cohesion. But progress in building a viable political community was painfully slow, and it was not far-reaching enough to create the sense of purpose necessary for a successful defense against the communist enemy. The ignominious collapse of ARVN in 1975, as I have tried to show, was due not only to ARVN's inferiority in heavy weapons and the shortage of ammunition but in considerable measure was also the result of lack of will and morale.

All this does not mean that the U.S. could not have succeeded in achieving its objectives in Vietnam. It may well be, as Barbara Tuchman has argued, that the American goal of saving Nationalist China after World War II from communist domination was unachievable. "China was a problem for which there was no American solution." But South Vietnam in the early 1970s was not China in the 1940s, and the U.S. position, too, was incomparably stronger.

The U.S. in the years from 1954 to 1975 could have pursued policies different from those actually followed. What if, instead of making a piece-meal commitment of military resources and adopting a policy of gradualism in their use, America had pursued a strategy of surprise and massed strength at decisive points? What if the mining of North Vietnamese harbors had taken place in 1965 instead of 1972? What if the U.S. from the beginning had implemented a strategy of population security instead of fighting Westmoreland's war of attrition, perhaps utilizing the Marines' CAP concept or the village defense program developed by the Special Forces-trained Civilian Irregular Defense Group? What if Vietnamization had begun in 1965 rather than 1968? While one cannot be sure that these different strategies, singly or in combination, would necessarily have brought about a different outcome, neither can one take their failure for granted.

Relations with the South Vietnamese and Vietnamization, too, could have followed a different course. As a result of anticolonialist inhibitions and for other reasons, the U.S. refrained from pressing for a decisive reorganization of the South Vietnamese armed forces and for a combined command, as America had done in Korea under the mantle of a UN mandate. Similarly, in regard to pacification and matters of social policy generally, America sought to shore up a sovereign South Vietnamese government and therefore, for the most part, limited itself to an advisory and supporting role, always mindful of the saying of Lawrence of Arabia: "Better they do it imperfectly than you do it perfectly, for it is their country, their war, and your time is limited." Western aggressiveness and impatience for results, it was said, ran counter to oriental ways of thinking and doing things and merely created increased resistance to change and reform. But if internal weaknesses in South Vietnamese society and the high level of corruption were as important a factor in the final collapse as the evidence . . . seems to suggest, might a radically different approach perhaps have been indicated?

Should the U.S. initially have accepted full responsibility for both military and political affairs, as suggested by experienced Vietnam hands like John Paul Vann, and only gradually have yielded control over the conduct of the war to a newly created corps of capable military leaders and administrators? Should America have played the role of the "good colonialist" who in this way slowly prepares a new country for viable independence? At the very least, should the U.S. have exerted more systematic leverage on its Vietnamese ally? The long record of American failure to move the GVN in directions which in retrospect would clearly have been desirable—for both the people of South Vietnam and America—writes Robert Komer, suggests "that we would have had little to lose and much to gain by using more vigorously the power over the GVN that our contributions gave us. We became their prisoners rather than they ours—the classic trap into which great powers have so often fallen in their relationships with weak allies."

We will never know, of course, whether any of these different approaches would have yielded better results. However, these alternative policy options must be mentioned in order to challenge facile and unhistorical assumptions of an inevitable collapse of South Vietnam. Just as the success of a policy does not prove that it was the only possible successful course of action, a policy can be correct even if for a variety of reasons it fails. The commitment to aid South Vietnam was made by intelligent and reasonable men who tackled an intractable problem in the face of great uncertainties, including the future performance of an ally and the actions and reactions of an enemy. The fact that some of their judgments in retrospect can be shown to have been flawed and that the outcome has been a fiasco does not make them villains or fools. If Hitler in 1940 had succeeded in conquering Britain, this would not have proven wrong Churchill's belief in the possibility and moral worth of resistance to the Nazis. Policy-makers always have to act on uncertain assumptions and inadequate information, and some of the noblest decisions in history have involved great risks. As long as there exists a reasonable expectation of success, the statesman who fails can perhaps be pitied, but he should not be condemned.

Both critics and defenders of American policy in Vietnam can agree that, as Kissinger put it in June 1975, "outside effort can only supplement, but not create, local efforts and local will to resist. . . . And there is no question that popular will and social justice are, in the last analysis, the essential underpinning of resistance to subversion and external challenge." To bolster local ability, effort and will to resist was, of course, the basic purpose of the American policy of Vietnamization. The fact that South Vietnam, abandoned by its ally, finally succumbed to a powerful and ruthless antagonist does not prove that this policy could not have had a less tragic ending. Neither does it vitiate the moral impulse which played a significant part in the original decision to help protect the independence of South Vietnam. Indeed, the sad fate of the people of Indochina since 1975 lends strength to the view that the American attempt to prevent a communist domination of the area was not without moral justification.

NO

George C. Herring

THE "VIETNAM SYNDROME" AND AMERICAN FOREIGN POLICY

During the past few months, a new phrase has entered the American political vocabulary. It is called the "Vietnam syndrome." It was apparently coined by Richard Nixon. As employed by the Reagan administration, it presumably means that America's failure in Vietnam and the backlash from it have been primarily responsible for the malaise that has allegedly reduced the United States to a state of impotence in a menacing world. Doctor Reagan and his associates seem determined to cure the disease. Some of the administration's defenders have even justified intervention in El Salvador as essential to that end; and although the White House and State Department may not go that far, their public statements leave no doubt of their determination to exorcise the Vietnam syndrome.

The notion of a Vietnam syndrome presupposes a view of the war which, although rarely articulated in full, nevertheless clearly influences the administration's foreign policy. Reagan himself has stated—contrary to a long-prevailing view—that Vietnam was "in truth a noble war," an altruistic attempt on the part of the United States to help a "small country newly free from colonial rule" defend itself against a "totalitarian neighbor bent on conquest." He and Secretary of State Alexander M. Haig, Jr. have also insisted that it was a necessary war, necessary to check the expansionist designs of the Soviet Union and its client states and to uphold the global position of the United States. They have left no doubt that they regard it as a war that we should have won. America failed, Reagan recently stated, not because it was defeated but because the military was "denied permission to win." Haig had argued that the war could have been won at any of several junctures if American leaders had been willing to "apply the full range of American power to bring about a successful outcome." The defeat was thus self-inflicted, and the consequences have been enormous. "America is no longer the America it was," Haig has stated, and "that is largely attributable to the mistakes of Vietnam."

From George C. Herring, "The 'Vietnam Syndrome' and American Foreign Policy," *Virginia Quarterly Review* (Autumn 1981). Copyright © 1981 by *Virginia Quarterly Review*. Reprinted by permission.

These views are not, of course, new, nor is it surprising that they have gained credence in recent years. The aggressiveness of the Soviets and the Hanoi regime have made it easier for us to justify our own actions morally in terms of national security. An explanation of failure which places blame on ourselves rather than elsewhere is probably easier for us to live with. Scholars had begun to revise conventional dovish views of the war well before Reagan took office, and films such as the *Deerhunter,* whatever their artistic merit, promoted a form of redemption. What *is* significant is that this now seems to be the official view and is also a partial basis for major policy decisions. Equally important, it is getting little challenge from Congress and the media, the centers of respectable dissent in the late 1960's and early 1970's. From all appearances, to apply an Oriental usage, 1981 is the year of the hawk.

It seems particularly urgent, therefore, that we examine this view critically in terms of the following very difficult questions: was Vietnam a just and necessary war as is now being proclaimed? Was it a winnable war, our failure primarily the result of our own mistakes? Has the so-called Vietnam syndrome been responsible for our recent inability to control world events and meet foreign challenges?

Let me begin with a caveat. The questions I have just raised cannot now be answered definitively. We are still very close to Vietnam, and it is difficult to appraise the war with the sort of detachment and perspective we would like. The evidence is far from complete. We have no more than roughly 15 percent of the documentation on the American side, and Hanoi has given no indication that it plans to initiate a freedom of information act. More important, some of the major questions concerning the war can never be answered with finality. We cannot know, for example, what would have happened if we had not intervened in Vietnam or if we had fought the war differently. We can do no more than speculate, an inexact science at best.

With these qualifications in mind, we can turn to the essential questions that have been raised about the war and its consequences. For many of those who experienced the Vietnam era, Reagan's "noble war" statement seemed so far off the wall that it could not be taken seriously. But it touched a responsive chord, and this is not surprising. The charges of American atrocities and war guilt that echoed across the land just a few years ago ran across the grain of our traditional sense of our own righteousness. Every war has its elements of nobility, moreover, and it is perhaps proper and even necessary for us to recognize the acts of heroism, sacrifice, and compassion that were as much a part of Vietnam as the atrocities. Certainly it was wrong for us to lay on the veterans the guilt which all of us share in one way or another, and Reagan's statement may have been addressing this point, at least obliquely.

His argument was based on the specific premise that we intervened in defense of a "free government" against "outside aggression," however, and this interpretation badly distorts the origins and nature of the war. In fact, we tried to contain an indigenous revolution that, although Communist led, expressed the deepest and most powerful currents of Vietnamese nationalism. The Vietnam conflict cannot be understood by looking at the situation in 1965, when the major U.S. commitments were made. It is necessary to go back to 1945 or even earlier.

The revolution that erupted in Vietnam at the end of World War II sought to eliminate French colonialism and to unify a country that had been divided for several centuries. During the ensuing war against France, the revolution generated widespread popular support, and its leader, Ho Chi Minh, came to symbolize for many Vietnamese the spirit of national independence just as George Washington did for the revolutionary generation of Americans. Ho's Vietminh defeated the French in 1954, despite the massive aid given France by the United States. It would probably have unified Vietnam after 1954, had the United States not stepped in and helped to make permanent a division at the 17th parallel the Geneva Conference had intended to be temporary. The Vietcong revolution, which erupted spontaneously in the south in the late 1950's, and subsequent North Vietnamese support of it, were extensions of the revolution of 1945, a fact which explains their unusual staying power in the face of tremendous adversity. This is not to endow the revolution with a higher morality, as the rhetoric of the antiwar movement frequently did. Its leaders were ruthless in pursuit of their goals and were capable of great brutality toward their own people and others. The point rather is that throughout much of the 30-year war, Ho's revolution represented the most powerful political force in Vietnam, and we can talk of outside aggression only in the most narrow, ahistorical sense. . . .

Finally, I would argue that the major American decisions in Vietnam were made primarily on the basis of self-interest, not altruism. This is a sticky wicket, to be sure. It is difficult to separate the two, and American policy makers certainly felt they were acting on the basis of principle as well as self-interest. To put it another way, however, had it been merely a matter of saving a free people from outside aggression, they would not have acted as they did. At every step along the way, they were convinced that the national interests of the United States required them to escalate the commitment.

What were these interests and why were they felt to be so compelling? From 1950 at least into the late 1960's, we viewed Vietnam primarily in terms of the Cold War and the doctrine of containment, the overarching principle of our Cold War foreign policies. The basic assumption of that policy was that we faced a monolithic, tightly unified world Communist movement, orchestrated by Moscow, and committed to world revolution. We viewed the world as split into two hostile blocs, irreconcilably divided by ideology and existing in a precarious equilibrium. Particularly after the fall of China to communism in 1949, we saw the Cold War as a zero sum game in which any gain for communism was automatically a loss for what we called the "free world." To contain the global Communist menace, we constructed a worldwide network of alliances, intervened freely in the affairs of other nations, and went to war in Korea.

From the beginning to near the end, we viewed the conflict in Vietnam primarily from this perspective. Because the revolution was led by Moscow-trained Communists, we assumed it was but an instrument of the Kremlin's drive for world domination. In the early stages, we felt it necessary to block Communist conquest of Vietnam lest it set off a domino effect which could cause the loss of all of Southeast Asia, with presumably incalculable strategic, political, and economic consequences for the United States. Later, we escalated the commitment because of a felt need to uphold our credibility. We had to prove that we would stand by our commitments to dissuade the Communists from further aggressions that could drastically undermine our global position or perhaps plunge us into a global war.

II

This leads directly to question number two: were these assumptions valid? Was the war necessary, as many now allege, to stop the advance of communism and uphold our world position? It is impossible to answer these questions with absolute certainty because we can never know precisely what would have happened if we had not intervened. It seems probable that there would have been war of some kind and that Vietnam would have been unified by force. What then? Would the dominoes have fallen in Southeast Asia? Would there have been a new wave of aggression elsewhere? Obviously, we can never know. I would argue, however, that we badly misperceived the nature of the struggle in Vietnam and that we may have exaggerated the possible consequences of a Communist victory.

The containment policy was misguided both generally and in its specific application to Vietnam. The simplistic, black and white assumptions from which it derived never bore much resemblance to reality. Soviet goals were (and remain) as much the product of traditional Russian nationalism as ideology, and they fell considerably short of world domination. The so-called Communist bloc was never a monolith—it was torn by divisions from the start, and the fragmentation has become more pronounced. In the Third World, nationalism and resistance to any form of outside influence have been the driving force. And there has never been a zero sum game. What appeared to be a major victory for the Soviet Union in China in 1949, for example, has turned out to be a catastrophic loss. In most parts of the world, neither the Soviet Union nor the United States has prevailed, and pluralism and fragmentation have been the norm.

In applying the containment policy to Vietnam, we drastically misjudged the internal dynamics of the conflict. We attributed the war to an expansionist communism bent on world domination. In fact, as I have suggested, it began as a revolution against French colonialism. Ho Chi Minh and his cohorts were Communists, to be sure, rigid and doctrinaire in their views and committed to structure their society along Marxist-Leninist lines. But they were never mere instruments of Moscow. The Soviet Union did not instigate the revolution and in fact exerted very little influence on it until after the United States initiated the bombing in 1965. The Chinese Communists exerted some influence in the early stages, but traditional Vietnamese suspicions of China, the product of a long history of Chinese imperialism, restricted the closeness of these ties. "I would rather sniff French dung for a few years than eat Chinese for a lifetime," Ho Chi Minh once said, expressing Vietnam's deep-seated fear of its larger northern neighbor. Throughout the 30-year war, the Soviet Union and China supported Vietnam when it was expedient to do so, but they also abandoned it at several critical junctures. North Vietnam played the two off against each other for essentially Vietnamese ends—to rid the country of foreign influence and unify it under one government.

Our rigid application of the containment doctrine in Vietnam had fateful consequences. By placing ourselves against the strongest force in an otherwise politically fragmented country, first in the war against France, later on our own, we may have ensured our ultimate failure. By ascribing the war to international rather than local forces, we underestimated the enemy's commitment, a vital point to which I will return later. Our intervention probably gave the war an international significance it did not have at the outset. Indeed, we may have driven the Vietnamese closer into the arms of their Communist allies than they would have preferred to go.

I also believe that we exaggerated the possible consequences of nonintervention. We will never know whether the domino theory would have operated if Vietnam had fallen earlier, but there is reason to doubt that it would have. Nationalism has proven the most potent and enduring force in recent history, and the nations of Southeast Asia, with their long tradition of opposition to China and Vietnam, would have resisted mightily. By making the war a test case of our credibility, we may have made its consequences greater than they would otherwise have been. By rigidly adhering to a narrow, one-dimensional world view, without adequately taking into account the nature and importance of local forces, we may have placed ourselves in an untenable position.

III

Question number three: was Vietnam a winnable war, our failure there primarily the result of our mistakes, our lack of

will, the disunity within our society? Because it has such profound implications for future policy decisions, this is the most important of our questions and deserves the most extended commentary. Those who argue that our defeat was self-inflicted focus on the misuse of our admittedly vast military power. Instead of using air power to strike a knockout blow against the enemy, they contend, Lyndon Johnson foolishly hedged it about with restrictions, applied it gradually, and held back from the sort of massive, decisive bombing attacks that could have assured victory. Similarly, they argue, had Johnson permitted U.S. ground forces to invade North Vietnamese sanctuaries in Laos, Cambodia, and across the 17th parallel, General Westmoreland's strategy of attrition could have worked and the war could have been won.

These criticisms are not without merit. Johnson's gradual expansion of the bombing did give North Vietnam time to disperse its resources and develop a highly effective air defense system, and the bombing may have encouraged the will to resist rather than crippled it as Johnson had intended. A strategy of attrition could not work as long as the enemy enjoyed sanctuary. If losses reached unacceptable proportions, the enemy could simply retreat to safety, regroup and renew the battle at times and places of his own choosing. He retained the strategic initiative.

To jump from here to the conclusion that the unrestricted use of American power could have produced victory at acceptable costs raises some troubling questions, however. Could an unrestricted bombing campaign have forced North Vietnam to accept a settlement on our terms? Obviously, there is no way we can ever know, but there is reason to doubt that it would have. The surveys conducted after World War II raised some serious doubts about the effect of bombing on the morale of the civilian population of Germany and Japan, and the capacity of air power to cripple a pre-industrial society such as North Vietnam may have been even more limited. There is evidence to suggest that the North Vietnamese were prepared to resist no matter what the level of the bombing, even if they had to go underground. The United States could probably have destroyed the cities and industries of North Vietnam, but what then? Invasion of the sanctuaries and ground operations in North Vietnam might have made the strategy of attrition more workable, but they would also have enlarged the war at a time when the United States was already stretched thin. Each of these approaches would have greatly increased the costs of the war without resolving the central problem—the political viability of South Vietnam.

We must also consider the reasons why Johnson refused to expand the war. He feared that if the United States pushed North Vietnam to the brink of defeat, the Soviet Union and/or China would intervene, broadening the war to dangerous proportions, perhaps to a nuclear confrontation. Johnson may, of course, have overestimated the risks of outside intervention, but the pressures would certainly have been large and he would have been irresponsible to ignore the dangers. And even if the United States had been able militarily to subdue North Vietnam without provoking outside intervention, it would still have faced the onerous, expensive, and dangerous prospect of occupying a hostile nation along China's southern border.

Those who argue that the war was winnable also emphasize the importance of American public opinion in sealing our defeat. They shift blame from those who waged the war to those who opposed it, contending that an irresponsible media and a treacherous antiwar movement turned the nation against the war, forcing Johnson and later Nixon to curtail U.S. involvement just when victory was in grasp. As much mythology has developed around this issue as any other raised by the war, and we probably know as little about it as any. Studies of public opinion do indicate that despite an increasingly skeptical media and noisy protest in the streets, the war enjoyed broad, if unenthusiastic support until that point early in 1968 when it became apparent that the costs might exceed any possible gains—and, even then, Nixon was able to prolong it for four more years. Until the early 1970's, moreover, the antiwar movement was probably counterproductive in terms of its own goals, the majority of Americans finding the protestors more obnoxious than the war. Indeed, it seems likely that the antiwar protest in a perverse way may have strengthened support for the government. After 1969, public opinion and Congress did impose some constraints on the government, and the media probably contributed to this. But to pin the defeat on the media or the antiwar movement strikes me as a gross oversimplification.

The problem with all these explanations is that they are too ethnocentric. They reflect the persistence of what a British scholar has called the illusion of American omnipotence, the traditional American belief that the difficult we do tomorrow, the impossible may take awhile. When failure occurs, it must be *our* fault, and we find scapegoats in our own midst: the poor judgment of our leaders, the media, or the antiwar movement. The flaw in this approach is that it ignores the other side of the equation, in this case, the Vietnamese dimension. I would contend that the sources of our frustration and ultimate failure rest primarily, although certainly not exclusively, in the local circumstances of the war: the nature of the conflict itself, the weakness of our ally, the relative strength of our adversary.

The Vietnam War posed extremely difficult challenges for Americans. It was fought in a climate and on a terrain that were singularly inhospitable. Thick jungles, foreboding swamps and paddies, rugged mountains. Heat that could "kill a man, bake his brains, or wring the sweat from him until he died of exhaustion," Philip Caputo tells us in *Rumor of War*. "It was as if the sun and the land itself were in league with the Vietcong," Caputo adds, "wearing us down, driving us mad, killing us." Needless to say, those who had endured the land for centuries had a distinct advantage over outsiders, particularly when the latter came from a highly industrialized and urbanized environment.

It was a people's war, where the people rather than territory were the primary objective. But Americans as individuals and as a nation could never really bridge the vast cultural gap that separated them from all Vietnamese. Not knowing the language or the culture, they did not know what the people felt or even how to tell friend from foe. "Maybe the dinks got things mixed up," one of novelist Tim O'Brien's bewildered G.I.s commented in *Going After Cacciato* after a seemingly friendly farmer bowed and smiled and pointed the Americans into a minefield. "Maybe the gooks cry when they're happy and smile when they're sad." Recalling the emotionless response of a group of peasants when their homes were destroyed by an American company, Caputo notes that they did nothing "and I hated them for it. Their apparent indifference made me feel indifferent." The cultural gap produced cynicism and even hatred toward the people Americans were trying to help. It led to questioning of our goals and produced a great deal of moral confusion among those fighting the war and those at home.

Most important, perhaps, was the formless, yet lethal, nature of guerrilla warfare in Vietnam. It was a war without distinct battlelines or fixed objectives, where traditional concepts of victory and defeat were blurred. It was, Caputo writes, "a formless war against a formless enemy who evaporated into the morning jungle mists only to materialize in some unexpected place." This type of war was particularly difficult for Americans schooled in the conventional warfare of World War II and Korea to fight. And there was always the gnawing question, first raised by John Kennedy himself—how can we tell if we're winning? The only answer that could be devised was the notorious body count, as grim and corrupting as it was unreliable as an index of success. In time, the strategy of attrition and the body count came to represent for sensitive G.I.s and for those at home killing for the sake of killing. And the light at the end of the tunnel never glimmered. "Aimless, that's what it is," one of O'Brien's G.I.s laments, "a bunch of kids trying to pin the tail on the Asian donkey. But no . . . tail. No . . . donkey."

Far more important in explaining our failure is the uneven balance of forces we aligned ourselves with in Vietnam. With the passage of time, it becomes more and more apparent that in South Vietnam we attempted a truly formidable undertaking on the basis of a very weak foundation. The "country" to which we committed ourselves in 1954 lacked most of the essential ingredients for nationhood. Had we looked all over the world, in fact, we could hardly have found a less promising place for an experiment in nation-building. Southern Vietnam lacked a viable economy. The French had destroyed the traditional political order, and their departure left a gaping vacuum, no firmly established political institutions, no native elite capable of exercising effective political leadership. Southern Vietnam was rent by a multitude of conflicting ethnic and religious forces. It was, in the words of one scholar, a "political jungle of war lords, bandits, partisan troops, and secret societies." When viewed from this perspective, there were probably built-in limits to what the United States or any outside nation could have accomplished there.

For nearly 20 years, we struggled to establish a viable nation in the face of internal insurgency and external invasion, but the rapid collapse of South Vietnam after our withdrawal in 1973 suggests how little was really accomplished. We could never find leaders capable of mobilizing the disparate population of southern Vietnam. We launched a vast array of ambitious and expensive programs to promote sound and effective government, win the support of the people, and wage war against the Vietcong. When our client state was on the verge of collapse in 1965, we filled the vacuum by putting in our own military forces. But the more we did, the more we induced a state of dependency among those we were trying to help. Tragically,

right up to the fall of Saigon in 1975, the South Vietnamese elite expected us to return and save them from defeat. This is not to denigrate the leaders or people who sided with us or to make them the scapegoats for our failure. The point rather is that given the history of southern Vietnam and the conditions that prevailed there in 1954, the creation of a viable nation by an outside power may have been an impossible task.

IV

The second point central to understanding our failure is that we drastically underestimated the strength and determination of our adversary. I do not wish to imply here that the North Vietnamese and Vietcong were supermen. They made blunders. They paid an enormous price for their success. They have shown a far greater capacity for making war than for building a nation. In terms of the balance of forces in Vietnam, however, they had distinct advantages. They were tightly mobilized and regimented and fanatically committed to their goals. They were fighting on familiar soil, and they employed methods already perfected in the ten years' war against France. The Vietcong were close to the rural population of South Vietnam, adapted its ideology and tactics to traditional Vietnamese political culture, and used the American presence to exploit popular distrust of outsiders. North Vietnam skillfully employed the strategy of protracted war, perceiving that the Americans, like the French, could become impatient, and if they bled long enough they might tire of the war. "You will kill ten of our men, but we will kill one of yours," Ho once remarked, "and in the end it is you who will tire." The comment was made to a French general in 1946, but it could as easily have been said of the Second Indochina War.

Our fatal error, therefore, was to underestimate our adversary. We rather casually assumed that the Vietnamese, rational beings like ourselves, would know better than to stand up against the most powerful nation in the world. It would be like a filibuster in Congress, Lyndon Johnson speculated, enormous resistance at first, then a steady whittling away, then Ho Chi Minh hurrying to get it over with. Years later, Henry Kissinger confessed great surprise with the discovery that his North Vietnamese counterparts were "fanatics." Since our own goals were limited and from our standpoint more than reasonable, we found it hard to understand the total unyielding commitment of the enemy, his willingness to risk everything to achieve his objective.

The circumstances of the war in Vietnam thus posed a dilemma that we never resolved. To have achieved our goal of an independent non-Communist South Vietnam required means that were either morally repugnant to us, posed unacceptable risks, or were unlikely to work. Success would have required the physical annihilation of North Vietnam, but given our limited goals, this would have been distasteful and excessively costly, and it held out a serious threat of Soviet or Chinese intervention. The only other way was to establish a viable South Vietnam, but given the weak foundation we worked from and the cultural gap, not to mention the strength of the internal revolution, this was probably beyond our capability. To put it charitably, we may

very well have placed ourselves in a classic, no-win situation.

For reasons closely related to the problems we have discussed, I think it would also be wrong for us to attribute our recent woes exclusively to Vietnam. The war has affected us profoundly, to be sure, but our failure there was not so much the cause of our present plight as a symptom of our general decline from world preeminence, the result of broad historical forces beyond our control. Our great power in the years immediately after World War II was to a considerable degree an aberration, the result as much of the devastation wrought by the war in the rest of the world as of our own intrinsic strength. Inevitably, that power has declined, as the Soviet Union has matched us in military and nuclear hardware, as the industrialized nations have regained a competitive position, and as the new nations recently emerged from colonialism have gained in assertiveness. In a variety of different ways, Vietnam demonstrated the new limits to our power, and as much as we long nostalgically for the "good old days," we cannot reverse the forces of history.

As I stated at the onset, the current official view of Vietnam is being articulated at least in part to exorcise the presumed Vietnam syndrome as a first step toward a new global policy. The Reagan administration seems to favor a return to the days of global containment, relying on a massive military buildup and intervention in the world's trouble spot to check Soviet expansion and regain the position we have lost.

I believe that such an approach defies the experience of Vietnam and is both dangerous and ultimately futile. Soviet military power and aggressiveness pose a very real threat to us and may in many instances require a stern response. To assume that the Soviets are responsible for most of the crises that beset today's world, however, is to ignore as we did in Vietnam the local circumstances from which revolutions and regional conflicts derive and which may determine their outcome. To assume that these conflicts can best be dealt with through a form of containment can make bad situations worse. Reagan is probably right in saying that El Salvador will not become another Vietnam, but this may be a clever way of justifying actions that cannot otherwise be justified. The containment approach, in El Salvador, as elsewhere, can lead to unwise and possible counterproductive commitments to governments which are anti-Communist but also unpopular and unstable. To attempt to bolster such governments through military aid can prolong conflicts which might be ended earlier, inflict great harm on people we are presuming to help, and polarize still fluid situations, driving the insurgents into the arms of the Soviets or Cubans. In Central America, it will likely revive a latent, powerful anti-Americanism, the product of years of gunboat diplomacy.

To adapt to the new and more complex situation we face today requires at a minimum a greater tolerance for revolution, even though it may be leftist, greater patience and restraint, and a more subtle and sophisticated approach than was applied in Vietnam and is being applied in El Salvador. The first question we need to ask in judging crises in the Third World is to what extent they derive from local conditions and to what from Soviet initiative. Assuming that Soviet involvement is not decisive, as may be likely in most cases, we should work quietly and indirectly for a political settlement without making an irrevocable commitment to either side. Should Soviet involvement be the critical factor, we still need to ask whether Soviet success is likely, and if so whether over the long haul it will significantly alter the global balance of power. It may be that what appears a short-term success can turn out over the long term to be a source of weakness rather than strength. Assuming that a Soviet victory would endanger our security, we must still ask whether the local balance of forces is such that success on our part can be achieved with limited external assistance. If that is not enough, the dispatch of American forces is not likely to do the job either and could make things much worse. Rapid escalation, the "win" approach Reagan seems to think should have been tried in Vietnam may not be the solution either, since it may enlarge the conflict without providing any means to resolve it and might result in a protracted war which could lose support after the usual rally-round-the-flag phenomenon has run its course.

I therefore believe it is urgent for us to ask these questions and think in these terms. The world is more complex, confusing, and explosive than at any time in recent memory and will remain so for the forseeable future. Our power to manage events will probably continue to decline, and a military buildup of the most mammoth proportions will not change this. To those who insist that we must rid ourselves of the Vietnam syndrome and get about our business, I would respond that understanding of and perspective on the Vietnam experience is an essential basis for shaping a constructive and realistic foreign policy.

POSTSCRIPT

Could the United States Have Prevented the Fall of South Vietnam?

Was the Vietnam War immoral? Was it necessary? Could it have been won by the United States? Has the Vietnam War influenced our current foreign policy? In his article, Herring gives some pointed answers to these questions. He challenges the assumptions behind containment that guided the policies of every president from Truman through Johnson concerning Vietnam. This liberal criticism of the war in Vietnam is further documented in Herring's *America's Longest War,* 2d ed. (Wiley, 1986), which explores the major primary sources through the Johnson administration. PBS produced a 13-part television series on the war, which is available on videocassettes at many public and college libraries. Both Stanley Karnow's *Vietnam: A History* (Viking, 1983) and Stephen Cohen's collection of documents in *Vietnam: Anthology and Guide to a Television History* (Knopf, 1983), which are used as supplements to the televised series, have been heavily criticized for their antiwar bias by Norman Podhoretz, editor of *Commentary,* in "Vietnam: The Revised Standard Version" (April 1984).

Lewy disagrees with the liberal and radical critics of the war. One of the first historians to explore the Pentagon's military records about the Vietnam War, Lewy concludes that there was no genocidal campaign carried out by the air force or the army, as many (but not all) antiwar critics had claimed. Lewy also blames television for its "one-dimensional coverage of the conflict." Though critical of the liberal intelligentsia, Lewy is no mere apologist for the American military's version as to why the war was lost. Much of his book criticizes General Westmoreland's attempt to fight a conventional war of attrition against an unconventional enemy who insisted upon waging a guerrilla conflict.

Most conservative critics would agree with Lewy that the war could have been won, but they generally disagree with his negative assessment of the United States' military policy. Historian Gary Hess cogently summarizes several books with conservatives' criticisms, in "The Military Perspective on Strategy in Vietnam," *Diplomatic History* (1986).

In a brilliant review essay on the historiography of "Vietnam Reconsidered," *Diplomatic History* (Winter 1988), Robert A. Divine concludes that as historians "move beyond the early condemnation of a wicked policy to search for an understanding of how a great nation could go so wrong . . . Vietnam is likely to be seen more and more as a national tragedy."

ISSUE 16

Was Martin Luther King, Jr.'s Leadership Essential to the Success of the Civil Rights Movement?

YES: August Meier, from "On the Role of Martin Luther King," in August Meier and Elliott Rudwick, eds., *Along the Color Line: Explorations in the Black Experience* (University of Illinois Press, 1976)

NO: Clayborne Carson, from "Martin Luther King, Jr.: Charismatic Leadership in a Mass Struggle," *Journal of American History* (September 1987)

ISSUE SUMMARY

YES: Professor of history August Meier depicts King as a "conservative militant" whose ability to communicate black aspirations to whites and to serve as a bridge between the radical and conservative wings of the civil rights movement made him the critical link in the chain of nonviolent direct action campaigns of the 1960s.

NO: Associate professor of history Clayborne Carson concludes that the civil rights struggle would have followed a similar course of development even had King never lived because its successes depended upon mass activism, not the actions of a single leader.

On a steamy August day in 1963, Martin Luther King, Jr., mounted a podium constructed in front of the Lincoln Memorial in Washington, D.C., and, in the studied cadence of a preacher, delivered his famous "I Have a Dream" speech. For many Americans, black and white, King's speech represented the symbolic climax of the civil rights movement. The Civil Rights Act of 1964 and the Voting Rights Act of 1965 were merely denouement.

Actually, there was more that was symbolic at the March on Washington than King's electrifying oration. The call for this demonstration had been issued by A. Philip Randolph, a long-time civil rights activist, who had threatened in 1941 to stage a similar protest march to bring attention to the economic inequality suffered by African Americans. Randolph's presence at the head of the march reflected a realization of *his* dream. Moreover, several of the speakers that day paid homage to W. E. B. Du Bois, the godfather of the twentieth-century black protest movement in the United States. An embittered exile from the land of his birth, Du Bois had died the previous day (at the age of 95) in Ghana, West Africa. The presence of Randolph and Du Bois, in flesh and spirit, served as a reminder that the movement to extend full civil and political rights to black Americans on a basis of equality was not confined to the 1950s and 1960s. For decades, African Americans had endured an enforced second-class citizenship. But in the 1940s and 1950s, following constitutional victories spearheaded by the National Association for the Advancement of Colored People in the areas of housing, voting, and education, black Americans awakened to the possibilities for change in their status. These victories coincided with the rise of independent nations in Africa, led by black leaders such as Kwame Nkrumah, which encouraged pride in the African homeland among many black Americans. Finally, the nonviolent direct action movement, pioneered by interracial organizations such as the Congress of Racial Equality (CORE) and individuals like A. Philip Randolph, James Farmer, and Martin Luther King, Jr., issued a clarion call to blacks and their white supporters that full equality was around the corner.

So much has been said and written about Martin Luther King, Jr.'s role in the civil rights movement that it is virtually impossible to separate the image of King from the protests for desegregation and political and economic equality of the 1950s and 1960s. Is it, however, appropriate to focus attention solely on King's leadership? Does this not do a disservice to the many other leaders and organizations that contributed to the movement's success? What of the roles played by the rank-and-file participants who did not enjoy a leadership position in any of the civil rights organizations, but without whose support little progress would have been possible? The relationship between King and the movement is the focus of the following essays.

August Meier, writing in the wake of the passage of the Voting Rights Act of 1965, assesses King's role as essential to the effectiveness of the civil rights movement. While recognizing the importance played by organizations such as CORE and the Student Nonviolent Coordinating Committee (SNCC), Meier concludes that King best communicated the aspirations of black Americans to whites, and his willingness to compromise worked to keep channels of communication open and to make nonviolent direct action appear respectable.

Clayborne Carson is critical of the emergence of the mythical King who receives praise for civil rights successes at the expense of the black movement as a whole. While he accepts Meier's view of King as a skillful conciliator, Carson prefers to focus upon the valuable role played by local leaders and the mass activism of the Southern campaigns as essential to the successes of the movement.

YES   August Meier

ON THE ROLE OF MARTIN LUTHER KING

The phenomenon that is Martin Luther King consists of a number of striking paradoxes. The Nobel Prize winner is accepted by the outside world as *the* leader of the nonviolent direct action movement, but he is criticized by many activists within the movement. He is criticized for what appears, at times, as indecisiveness, and is more often denounced for a tendency to accept compromise. Yet in the eyes of most Americans, both black and white, he remains the symbol of militant direct action. So potent is this symbol of King as direct actionist that a new myth is arising about his historic role. The real credit for developing and projecting the techniques and philosophy of nonviolent direct action in the civil rights arena must be given to the Congress of Racial Equality [CORE], which was founded in 1942—more than a dozen years before the Montgomery bus boycott projected King into international fame. And the idea of mass action by Negroes themselves to secure redress of their grievances must, in large part, be ascribed to the vision of A. Philip Randolph, architect of the March on Washington Movement during World War II. Yet, as we were told in Montgomery on March 25, 1965, King and his followers now assert, apparently without serious contradiction, that a new type of civil rights strategy was born at Montgomery in 1955 under King's auspices.

In a movement in which respect is accorded in direct proportion to the number of times one has been arrested, King appears to keep the number of times he goes to jail to a minimum. In a movement in which successful leaders are those who share in the hardships of their followers, in the risks they take, in the beatings they receive, in the length of time they spend in jail, King tends to leave prison for other important engagements, rather than remaining there and suffering with his followers. In a movement in which leadership ordinarily devolves upon persons who mix democratically with their followers, King remains isolated and aloof. In a movement which prides itself on militancy and "no compromise" with racial discrimination or with the white "power structure," King maintains close relationships with, and appears to be influenced by, Democratic presidents and their emissaries,

From August Meier, "On the Role of Martin Luther King," in Meier and Rudwick, eds., *Along the Color Line: Explorations in the Black Experience* (University of Illinois Press, 1976). Copyright © 1976 by the University of Illinois Press. Reprinted by permission of the University of Illinois Press and the author. This article originally appeared in *New Politics*, vol. 4 (Winter 1965), pp. 1–8.

seems amenable to compromises considered by some half a loaf or less, and often appears willing to postpone or avoid a direct confrontation in the streets.

King's career has been characterized by failures that, in the larger sense, must be accounted triumphs. The buses in Montgomery were desegregated only after lengthy judicial proceedings conducted by the NAACP [National Association for the Advancement of Colored People] Legal Defense Fund secured a favorable decision from the U.S. Supreme Court. Nevertheless, the events in Montgomery were a triumph for direct action and gave this tactic a popularity unknown when identified solely with CORE. King's subsequent major campaigns—in Albany, Georgia; Danville, Virginia; Birmingham, Alabama; and St. Augustine, Florida— ended as failures or with only token accomplishments. But each of them, chiefly because of his presence, dramatically focused national and international attention on the plight of the southern Negro, thereby facilitating overall progress. In Birmingham in particular, demonstrations which fell short of their local goals were directly responsible for a major Federal Civil Rights Act. Essentially, this pattern of local failure and national victory was recently enacted at Selma, Alabama.

King is ideologically committed to disobeying unjust laws and court orders, in the Gandhian tradition, but generally he follows a policy of not disobeying federal court orders. In his recent Montgomery speech he expressed a crude, neo-Marxist interpretation of history, romanticizing the Populist movement as a genuine union of black and white common people, ascribing race prejudice to capitalists playing white workers against black. Yet, in practice, he is amenable to compromise with the white bourgeois political and economic establishment. More important, King enunciates a superficial and eclectic philosophy, and by virtue of it he has profoundly awakened the moral conscience of America.

In short, King can be described as a "conservative militant." In this combination of militancy with conservatism and caution, of righteousness with respectability, lies the secret of King's enormous success.

Certain important civil rights leaders have dismissed King's position as the product of publicity generated by the mass communications media. But this can be said of the successes of the civil rights nonviolent action movement generally. Without publicity it is hard to conceive that much progress would have been made. In fact, contrary to the official nonviolent direct action philosophy, demonstrations have secured their results not by changing the hearts of the oppressors through a display of nonviolent love, but through the national and international pressures generated by the publicity arising from mass arrests and incidents of violence. And no one has employed this strategy of securing publicity through mass arrests and precipitating violence from white hoodlums and law enforcement officers more than King himself. King abhors violence; as at Selma, for example, he constantly retreats from situations that might result in the deaths of his followers. But he is precisely most successful when, contrary to his deepest wishes, his demonstrations precipitate violence from southern whites against Negro and white demonstrators. We need only cite Birmingham and Selma to illustrate this point.

Publicity alone does not explain the durability of King's image, or why he remains, for the rank and file of whites and blacks alike, the symbol of the direct action movement, the nearest thing to a charismatic leader that the civil rights movement has ever had. At the heart of King's continuing influence and popularity are two facts. First, better than anyone else, he articulates the aspirations of Negroes who respond to the cadence of his addresses, his religious phraseology and manner of speaking, and the vision of his dream for them and for America. King has intuitively adopted the style of the old-fashioned Negro Baptist preacher and transformed it into a new art form; he has, indeed, restored oratory to its place among the arts. Second, he communicates Negro aspirations to white America more effectively than anyone else. His religious terminology and manipulation of the Christian symbols of love and nonresistance are partly responsible for his appeal among whites. To talk in terms of Christianity, love, and nonviolence is reassuring to the mentality of white America. At the same time, the very superficialities of his philosophy—that rich and eclectic amalgam of Jesus, Hegel, Gandhi, and others as outlined in his *Stride Toward Freedom*—make him appear intellectually profound to the superficially educated middle-class white American. Actually, if he were a truly profound religious thinker, like Tillich or Niebuhr, his influence would of necessity be limited to a select audience. But by uttering moral clichés, the Christian pieties, in a magnificent display of oratory, King becomes enormously effective.

If his success with Negroes is largely due to the style of his utterance, his success with whites is a much more complicated matter. For one thing, he unerringly knows how to exploit with maximum effectiveness their growing feeling of guilt. King, of course, is not unique in attaining fame and popularity among whites through playing upon their guilt feelings. James Baldwin is the most conspicuous example of a man who has achieved success with this formula. The incredible fascination which the Black Muslims have for white people, and the posthumous near-sanctification of Malcolm X by many naive whites (in addition to many Negroes whose motivations are, of course, very different), must in large part be attributed to the same source. But King goes beyond this. With intuitive but extraordinary skill he not only castigates whites for their sins but, in contrast to angry young writers like Baldwin, he explicitly states his belief in their salvation. Not only will direct action bring fulfillment of the "American Dream" to Negroes, but the Negroes' use of direct action will also help whites to live up to their Christian and democratic values; it will purify, cleanse, and heal the sickness in white society. Whites will benefit as well as Negroes. He has faith that the white man will redeem himself. Negroes must not hate whites, but love them. In this manner King first arouses the guilt feelings of whites, and then relieves them—though always leaving the lingering feeling in his white listeners that they should support his nonviolent crusade. Like a Greek tragedy, King's performance provides an extraordinary catharsis for the white listener.

King thus gives white men the feeling that he is their good friend, that he poses no threat to them. It is interesting to note that this was the same feeling that white men received from Booker T. Washington, the noted early twentieth century accommodator. Both men stressed their faith in the white man; both expressed the belief that the white man could be brought to accord Negroes their rights. Both stressed the importance of whites recognizing the rights of Negroes for the moral health and well-being of white society. Like King, Washington had an extraordinary following among whites. Like King, Washington symbolized for most whites the whole program of Negro advancement. While there are important similarities in the functioning of both men vis-à-vis the community, needless to say, in most respects, their philosophies are in disagreement.

It is not surprising, therefore, to find that King is the recipient of contributions from organizations and individuals who fail to eradicate evidence of prejudice in their own backyards. For example, certain liberal trade union leaders who are philosophically committed to full racial equality, who feel the need to identify their organizations with the cause of militant civil rights, although they are unable to defeat racist elements in their unions, contribute hundreds of thousands of dollars to King's Southern Christian Leadership Conference (SCLC). One might attribute this phenomenon to the fact that SCLC works in the South rather than the North, but this is true also for SNCC [Student Nonviolent Coordinating Committee], which does not benefit similarly from union treasuries. And the fact is that ever since the college students started their sit-ins in 1960, it is SNCC which has been the real spearhead of direct action in most of the South and has performed the lion's share of work in the local communities, while SCLC has received most of the publicity and most of the money. However, while King provides a verbal catharsis for whites, leaving them feeling purified and comfortable, SNCC's uncompromising militancy makes whites feel less comfortable and less beneficent.

The above is not to suggest that SNCC and SCLC are responsible for all, or nearly all, the direct action in the South. The NAACP has actively engaged in direct action, especially in Savannah under the leadership of W. W. Law, in South Carolina under I. DeQuincy Newman, and in Clarksdale, Mississippi, under Aaron Henry. The work of CORE—including most of the direct action in Louisiana, much of the nonviolent work in Florida and Mississippi, and the famous Freedom Ride of 1961—has been most important. In addition, one should note the work of SCLC affiliates, such as those in Lynchburg, Virginia, led by the Reverend Virgil Wood; in Birmingham, by the Reverend Fred Shuttlesworth; and in Savannah, by Hosea Williams.

(There are other reasons for SNCC's lesser popularity with whites. These are connected with the great changes that have occurred in SNCC since it was founded in 1960, changes reflected in the half-jocular epigram circulating in SNCC circles that the Student Nonviolent Coordinating Committee has now become the "Non-Student Violent Non-Coordinating Committee." The point is, however, that even when SNCC thrilled the nation in 1960-61 with the student sit-ins that swept the South, it did not enjoy the popularity and financial support accorded to King.)

King's very tendencies toward compromise and caution, his willingness to negotiate and bargain with White House emissaries, and his hesitancy to risk the precipitation of mass violence upon demonstrators further endear him to whites. He appears to them a "responsible" and "moderate" man. To militant activists, King's failure to march past the state police on that famous Tuesday morning outside Selma indicated either a lack of courage or a desire to advance himself by currying presidential favor. But King's shrinking from a possible bloodbath, his accession to the entreaties of the political establishment, his acceptance of face-saving compromise in this, as in other instances, are fundamental to the particular role he is playing and essential for achieving and sustaining his image as a leader of heroic moral stature in the eyes of white men. His caution and compromise keep open the channels of communication between the activists and the majority of the white community. In brief: King makes the nonviolent direct action movement respectable.

Of course, many, if not most, activists reject the notion that the movement should be made respectable. Yet American history shows that for any reform movement to succeed, it must attain respectability. It must attract moderates, even conservatives, to its ranks. The March on Washington made direct action respectable; Selma made it fashionable. More than any other force, it is Martin Luther King who impressed the civil rights revolution on the American conscience and is attracting that great middle body of American public opinion to its support. It is this revolution of conscience that will undoubtedly lead fairly soon to the elimination of all violations of Negroes' constitutional rights, thereby creating the conditions for the economic and social changes that are necessary if we are to achieve full racial equality. This is not to deny the dangers to the civil rights movement in becoming respectable. Respectability, for example, encourages the attempts of political machines to capture civil rights organizations. Respectability can also become an end in

itself, thereby dulling the cutting edge of its protest activities. Indeed, the history of the labor movement reveals how attaining respectability can produce loss of original purpose and character. These perils, however, do not contradict the importance of achieving respectability— even a degree of modishness—if racial equality is ever to be realized.

There is another side to the picture: King would be neither respected nor respectable if there were not more militant activists on his left, engaged in more radical forms of direct action. Without CORE and, especially, SNCC, King would appear "radical" and "irresponsible," rather than "moderate" and "respectable."

King occupies a position of strategic importance as the "vital center" within the civil rights movement. Though he has lieutenants who are far more militant and "radical" than he is, SCLC acts, in effect, as the most cautious, deliberate and "conservative" of the direct action groups because of King's leadership. This permits King and the SCLC to function— almost certainly unintentionally— not only as an organ of communication with the establishment and majority white public opinion, but as something of a bridge between the activist and more traditionalist or "conservative" civil rights groups as well. For example, it appears unlikely that the Urban League and NAACP, which supplied most of the funds,* would have participated in the 1963 March on Washington if King had not done so. Because King agreed to go along with SNCC and CORE, the NAACP found it mandatory to join if it was to

*Actually the March on Washington was financed largely through the philanthropist Stephen Currier, whose Taconic Foundation has also made possible the voter registration campaigns in the South in 1962-64.

maintain its image as a protest organization. King's identification with the March was also essential for securing the support of large numbers of white clergymen and their moderate followers. The March was the brain child of the civil rights movement's ablest strategist and tactician, Bayard Rustin, and the call was issued by A. Philip Randolph. But it would have been a minor episode in the history of the civil rights movement without King's support.

Yet curiously enough, despite his charisma and international reputation, King thus far has been more a symbol than a power in the civil rights movement. Indeed, his strength in the movement has been derived less from an organizational base than from his symbolic role. Seven or eight years ago, one might have expected King to achieve an organizationally dominant position in the civil rights movement, at least in its direct action wing. The fact is that in the period after the Montgomery bus boycott King developed no program and, it is generally agreed, revealed himself as an ineffective administrator who failed to capitalize upon his popularity among Negroes. In 1957 he founded SCLC to coordinate the work of direct action groups that had sprung up in southern cities. Composed of autonomous units, usually led by Baptist ministers, SCLC does not appear to have developed an overall sense of direction or a program of real breadth and scope. Although the leaders of SCLC affiliates became the race leaders in their communities—displacing the established local conservative leadership of teachers, old-line ministers, businessmen—it is hard for an observer (who admittedly has not been close to SCLC) to perceive exactly what SCLC did before the 1960's except to advance

the image and personality of King. King appeared not to direct but to float with the tide of militant direct action. For example, King did not supply the initiative for the bus boycott in Montgomery, but was pushed into the leadership by others, as he himself records in *Stride Toward Freedom*. Similarly, in the late 1950's and early 1960's, he appeared to let events shape his course. In the last two years this has changed, but until the Birmingham demonstrations of 1963 King epitomized conservative militancy.

SCLC under King's leadership called the Raleigh Conference of April, 1960, which gave birth to SNCC. Incredibly, within a year the SNCC youth had lost their faith in the man they now satirically call "De Lawd," and had struck out on their own independent path. By that time, the spring of 1961, King's power in the southern direct action movement had been further curtailed by CORE's stunning Freedom Ride to Alabama and Mississippi.

The limited extent of King's actual power in the civil rights movement was illustrated by the efforts made to invest King with the qualities of a messiah during the recent ceremonies at the state capitol in Montgomery. The Reverend Ralph Abernathy's constant iteration of the theme that King is "our Leader," the Moses of the race, chosen by God, and King's claim that he originated the non-violent direct action movement at Montgomery a decade ago, are all assertions that would have been superfluous if King's power in the movement was very substantial.

It is, of course, no easier today than it has been in the past few years to predict the course of the Negro protest movement, and it is always possible that the current state of affairs may change quite abruptly. It is conceivable that the ambitious program that SCLC is now projecting—both in southern voter registration and in northern urban direct action programs—may give it a position of commanding importance in civil rights. As a result of the recent demonstrations in Selma and Montgomery, King's prestige is now higher than ever. At the same time, the nature of CORE and NAACP direct action activities at the moment has created a programmatic vacuum which SCLC may be able to exploit. Given this convergence of circumstances, SCLC leaders may be able to establish an organizational base upon which to build a power commensurate with the symbolic position of their president.

It is indeed fortunate that King has not obtained a predominance of power in the movement commensurate with his prestige. For today, as in the past, a diversity of approaches is necessary. Needed in the movement are those who view the struggle chiefly as a conflict situation, in which the power of demonstrations, the power of Negroes, will force recognition of the race's humanity and citizenship rights, and the achievement of equality. Equally needed are those who see the movement's strategy to be chiefly one of capitalizing on the basic consensus of values in American society by awakening the conscience of the white man to the contradiction between his professions and the facts of discrimination. And just as necessary to the movement as both of these are those who operate skillfully, recognizing and yet exploiting the deeply held American belief that compromise among competing interest groups is the best *modus operandi* in public life.

King is unique in that he maintains a delicate balance among all three of these basic strategy assumptions. The tradi-

tional approaches of the Urban League (conciliation of the white businessmen) and of the NAACP (most preeminently appeals to the courts and appeals to the sense of fair play in the American public) basically attempted to exploit the consensus in American values. It would of course be a gross oversimplification to say that the Urban League and NAACP strategies are based simply on attempting to capitalize on the consensus of values, while SNCC and CORE act simply as if the situation were purely a conflict situation. Implicit in the actions of all civil rights organizations are both sets of assumptions—even where people are not conscious of the theoretical assumptions under which, in effect, they operate. The NAACP especially encompasses a broad spectrum of strategies and types of activities, ranging from time-tested court procedures to militant direct action. Sophisticated CORE activists know very well when a judicious compromise is necessary or valuable. But I hold that King is in the middle, acting in effect as if he were basing his strategy upon all three assumptions described above. He maintains a delicate balance between a purely moral appeal and a militant display of power. He talks of the power of the bodies of Negro demonstrators in the streets, but, unlike CORE and SNCC activists, he accepts compromises at times that consist of token improvements and calls them impressive victories. More than any of the other groups, King and SCLC can, up to this point at least, be described as exploiting all three tactical assumptions to an approximately equal degree. King's continued success, I suspect, will depend to a considerable degree upon the difficult feat of maintaining his position at the "vital center" of the civil rights movement.

Viewed from another angle King's failure to achieve a position of power on a level with his prestige is fortunate, because rivalries between personalities and organizations remain an essential ingredient of the dynamics of the movement and a precondition for its success as each current tries to outdo the others in effectiveness and in maintaining a good public image. Without this competitive stimulus, the civil rights revolution would slow down.

I have already noted that one of King's functions is to serve as a bridge between the militant and conservative wings of the movement. In addition, by gathering support for SCLC, he generates wider support for CORE and SNCC as well. The most striking example is the recent series of demonstrations in Selma, where SNCC had been operating for nearly two years with only moderate amounts of publicity before King chose that city as his own target. As usual, it was King's presence that focused world attention on Selma. In the course of subsequent events, the rift between King and SNCC assumed the proportions of a serious conflict. Yet people who otherwise would have been hesitant to support SNCC's efforts, even people who had become disillusioned with certain aspects of SNCC's policies during the Mississippi Summer Project of 1964, were drawn to demonstrate in Selma and Montgomery. Moreover, although King received the major share of credit for the demonstrations, it seems likely that in the controversy between King and SNCC the latter emerged with more power and influence in the civil rights movement than ever before. It is now possible that the administration will, in the future, regard SNCC as more of a force to be reckoned with than it has heretofore.

Major dailies like the *New York Times* and the *Washington Post*, basically sympathetic to civil rights and racial equality, though more gradualist than the activist organizations, have congratulated the nation upon its good fortune in having a "responsible and moderate" leader like King at the head of the nonviolent action movement (though they overestimate his power and underestimate the symbolic nature of his role). It would be more appropriate to congratulate the civil rights movement for *its* good fortune in having as its symbolic leader a man like King. The fact that he has more prestige than power; the fact that he not only criticizes whites but also explicitly believes in their redemption; his ability to arouse creative tension, combined with his inclination to shrink from carrying demonstrations to the point where major bloodshed might result; the intellectual simplicity of his philosophy; his tendency to compromise and exert caution, even his seeming indecisiveness on some occasions; the sparing use he makes of going to or staying in jail himself; his friendship with the man in the White House—all are essential to the role he plays, and invaluable for the success of the movement. It is fortunate, of course, that not all civil rights leaders are cut of the same cloth—that King is unique among them. Like Randolph, who functions very differently, King is really an institution. His most important function, I believe, is that of effectively communicating Negro aspirations to white people, of making nonviolent direct action respectable in the eyes of the white majority. In addition, he functions within the movement by occupying a vital center position between its conservative and radical wings, by symbolizing direct action and attracting people to participate in it without dominating either the civil rights movement or its activist wing. Viewed in this context, traits that many activists criticize in King actually function not as sources of weakness, but as the foundations of his strength.

NO

Clayborne Carson

MARTIN LUTHER KING, JR.: CHARISMATIC LEADERSHIP IN A MASS STRUGGLE

The legislation to establish Martin Luther King, Jr.'s birthday as a federal holiday provided official recognition of King's greatness, but it remains the responsibility of those of us who study and carry on King's work to define his historical significance. Rather than engaging in officially approved nostalgia, our remembrance of King should reflect the reality of his complex and multifaceted life. Biographers, theologians, political scientists, sociologists, social psychologists, and historians have given us a sizable literature of King's place in Afro-American protest tradition, his role in the modern black freedom struggle, and his eclectic ideas regarding nonviolent activism. Although King scholars may benefit from and may stimulate the popular interest in King generated by the national holiday, many will find themselves uneasy participants in annual observances to honor an innocuous, carefully cultivated image of King as a black heroic figure.

The King depicted in serious scholarly works is far too interesting to be encased in such a didactic legend. King was a controversial leader who challenged authority and who once applauded what he called "creative maladjusted nonconformity." He should not be transformed into a simplistic image designed to offend no one—a black counterpart to the static, heroic myths that have embalmed George Washington as the Father of His Country and Abraham Lincoln as the Great Emancipator.

One aspect of the emerging King myth has been the depiction of him in the mass media, not only as the preeminent leader of the civil rights movement, but also as the initiator and sole indispensible element in the southern black struggles of the 1950s and 1960s. As in other historical myths, a Great Man is seen as the decisive factor in the process of social change, and the unique qualities of a leader are used to explain major historical events. The King myth departs from historical reality because it attributes too much to King's exceptional qualities as a leader and too little to the impersonal,

From Clayborne Carson, "Martin Luther King, Jr.: Charismatic Leadership in a Mass Struggle," *Journal of American History*, vol. 74 (September 1987), pp. 448–454. Copyright © 1987 by the *Journal of American History*. Reprinted by permission.

large-scale social factors that made it possible for King to display his singular abilities on a national stage. Because the myth emphasizes the individual at the expense of the black movement, it not only exaggerates King's historical importance but also distorts his actual, considerable contribution to the movement.

A major example of this distortion has been the tendency to see King as a charismatic figure who single-handedly directed the course of the civil rights movement through the force of his oratory. The charismatic label, however, does not adequately define King's role in the southern black struggle. The term *charisma* has traditionally been used to describe the godlike, magical qualities possessed by certain leaders. Connotations of the term have changed, of course, over the years. In our more secular age, it has lost many of its religious connotations and now refers to a wide range of leadership styles that involve the capacity to inspire—usually through oratory—emotional bonds between leaders and followers. Arguing that King was not a charismatic leader, in the broadest sense of the term, becomes somewhat akin to arguing that he was not a Christian, but emphasis on King's charisma obscures other important aspects of his role in the black movement. To be sure, King's oratory was exceptional and many people saw King as a divinely inspired leader, but King did not receive and did not want the kind of unquestioning support that is often associated with charismatic leaders. Movement activists instead saw him as the most prominent among many outstanding movement strategists, tacticians, ideologues, and institutional leaders.

King undoubtedly recognized that charisma was one of many leadership qualities at his disposal, but he also recognized that charisma was not a sufficient basis for leadership in a modern political movement enlisting numerous self-reliant leaders. Moreover, he rejected aspects of the charismatic model that conflicted with his sense of his own limitations. Rather than exhibiting unwavering confidence in his power and wisdom, King was a leader full of self-doubts, keenly aware of his own limitations and human weaknesses. He was at times reluctant to take on the responsibilities suddenly and unexpectedly thrust upon him. During the Montgomery bus boycott, for example, when he worried about threats to his life and to the lives of his wife and child, he was overcome with fear rather than confident and secure in his leadership role. He was able to carry on only after acquiring an enduring understanding of his dependence on a personal God who promised never to leave him alone.

Moreover, emphasis on King's charisma conveys the misleading notion of a movement held together by spellbinding speeches and blind faith rather than by a complex blend of rational and emotional bonds. King's charisma did not place him above criticism. Indeed, he was never able to gain mass support for his notion of nonviolent struggle as a way of life, rather than simply a tactic. Instead of viewing himself as the embodiment of widely held Afro-American racial views, he willingly risked his popularity among blacks through his steadfast advocacy of nonviolent strategies to achieve radical social change.

He was a profound and provocative public speaker as well as an emotionally powerful one. Only those unfamiliar with the Afro-American clergy would assume that his oratorical skills were unique, but King set himself apart from other black preachers through his use of traditional black Christian idiom to advocate unconventional political ideas. Early in his life King became disillusioned with the unbridled emotionalism associated with his father's religious fundamentalism, and, as a thirteen year old, he questioned the bodily resurrection of Jesus in his Sunday school class. His subsequent search for an intellectually satisifying religious faith conflicted with the emphasis on emotional expressiveness that pervades evangelical religion. His preaching manner was rooted in the traditions of the black church, while his subject matter, which often reflected his wide-ranging philosophical interests, distinguished him from other preachers who relied on rhetorical devices that manipulated the emotions of the listeners. King used charisma as a tool for mobilizing black communities, but he always used it in the context of other forms of intellectual and political leadership suited to a movement containing many strong leaders.

Recently, scholars have begun to examine the black struggle as a locally based mass movement, rather than simply a reform movement led by national civil rights leaders. The new orientation in scholarship indicates that King's role was different from that suggested in King-centered biographies and journalistic accounts. King was certainly not the only significant leader of the civil rights movement, for sustained protest movements arose in many southern communities in which King had little or no direct involvement.

In Montgomery, for example, local black leaders such as E. D. Nixon, Rosa Parks, and Jo Ann Robinson started the bus boycott before King became the leader of the Montgomery Improvement Association. Thus, although King inspired blacks in Montgomery and black residents recognized that they were fortunate to have such a spokesperson, talented local leaders other than King played decisive roles in initiating and sustaining the boycott movement.

Similarly, the black students who initiated the 1960 lunch counter sit-ins admired King, but they did not wait for him to act before launching their own movement. The sit-in leaders who founded the Student Nonviolent Coordinating Committee (SNCC) became increasingly critical of King's leadership style, linking it to the feelings of dependency that often characterize the followers of charismatic leaders. The essence of SNCC's approach to community organizing was to instill in local residents the confidence that they could lead their own struggles. A SNCC organizer failed if local residents became dependent on his or her presence; as the organizers put it, their job was to work themselves out of a job. Though King influenced the struggles that took place in the Black Belt regions of Mississippi, Alabama, and Georgia, those movements were also guided by self-reliant local leaders who occasionally called on King's oratorical skills to galvanize black protestors at mass meetings while refusing to depend on his presence.

If King had never lived, the black struggle would have followed a course of development similar to the one it did. The Montgomery bus boycott would have occurred, because King did not initiate it. Black students probably would have rebelled—even without King as a role model—for they had sources of tactical and ideological inspiration besides King. Mass activism in southern cities and voting rights efforts in the deep

South were outgrowths of large-scale social and political forces, rather than simply consequences of the actions of a single leader. Though perhaps not as quickly and certainly not as peacefully nor with as universal a significance, the black movement would probably have achieved its major legislative victories without King's leadership, for the southern Jim Crow system was a regional anachronism, and the forces that undermined it were inexorable.

To what extent, then, did King's presence affect the movement? Answering that question requires us to look beyond the usual portrayal of the black struggle. Rather than seeing an amorphous mass of discontented blacks acting out strategies determined by a small group of leaders, we would recognize King as a major example of the local black leadership that emerged as black communities mobilized for sustained struggles. If not as dominant a figure as sometimes portrayed, the historical King was nevertheless a remarkable leader who acquired the respect and support of self-confident, grass-roots leaders, some of whom possessed charismatic qualities of their own. Directing attention to the other leaders who initiated and emerged from those struggles should not detract from our conception of King's historical significance; such movement-oriented research reveals King as a leader who stood out in a forest of tall trees.

King's major public speeches—particularly the "I Have a Dream" speech—have received much attention, but his exemplary qualities were also displayed in countless strategy sessions with other activists and in meetings with government officials. King's success as a leader was based on his intellectual and moral cogency and his skill as a conciliator among movement activists who refused to be simply King's "followers" or "lieutenants."

The success of the black movement required the mobilization of black communities as well as the transformation of attitudes in the surrounding society, and King's wide range of skills and attributes prepared him to meet the internal as well as the external demands of the movement. King understood the black world from a privileged position, having grown up in a stable family within a major black urban community; yet he also learned how to speak persuasively to the surrounding white world. Alone among the major civil rights leaders of his time, King could not only articulate black concerns to white audiences, but could also mobilize blacks through his day-to-day involvement in black community institutions and through his access to the regional institutional network of the black church. His advocacy of nonviolent activism gave the black movement invaluable positive press coverage, but his effectiveness as a protest leader derived mainly from his ability to mobilize black community resources.

Analyses of the southern movement that emphasize its nonrational aspects and expressive functions over its political character explain the black struggle as an emotional outburst by discontented blacks, rather than recognizing that the movement's strength and durability came from its mobilization of black community institutions, financial resources, and grass-roots leaders. The values of southern blacks were profoundly and permanently transformed not only by King, but also by involvement in sustained protest activity and community-organizing efforts, through thousands of mass meetings, workshops, citizenship classes, freedom schools, and informal discussions. Rather than merely accepting guidance from above, southern blacks were resocialized as a result of their movement experiences.

Although the literature of the black struggle has traditionally paid little attention to the intellectual content of black politics, movement activists of the 1960s made a profound, though often ignored, contribution to political thinking. King may have been born with rare potential, but his most significant leadership attributes were related to his immersion in, and contribution to, the intellectual ferment that has always been an essential part of Afro-American freedom struggles. Those who have written about King have too often assumed that his most important ideas were derived from outside the black struggle—from his academic training, his philosophical readings, or his acquaintance with Gandhian ideas. Scholars are only beginning to recognize the extent to which his attitudes and those of many other activists, white and black, were transformed through their involvement in a movement in which ideas disseminated from the bottom up as well as from the top down.

Although my assessment of King's role in the black struggles of his time reduces him to human scale, it also increases the possibility that others may recognize his qualities in themselves. Idolizing King lessens one's ability to exhibit some of his best attributes or, worse, encourages one to become a debunker, emphasizing King's flaws in order to lessen the inclination to exhibit his virtues. King himself undoubtedly feared that some who admired him would place too much faith in his ability to offer guidance and to overcome resistance, for he often publicly acknowledged his own limitations and

mortality. Near the end of his life, King expressed his certainty that black people would reach the Promised Land whether or not he was with them. His faith was based on an awareness of the qualities that he knew he shared with all people. When he suggested his own epitaph, he asked not to be remembered for his exceptional achievements—his Nobel Prize and other awards, his academic accomplishments; instead, he wanted to be remembered for giving his life to serve others, for trying to be right on the war question, for trying to feed the hungry and clothe the naked, for trying to love and serve humanity. "I want you to say that I tried to love and serve humanity." Those aspects of King's life did not require charisma or other superhuman abilities.

If King were alive today, he would doubtless encourage those who celebrate his life to recognize their responsibility to struggle as he did for a more just and peaceful world. He would prefer that the black movement be remembered not only as the scene of his own achievements, but also as a setting that brought out extraordinary qualities in many people. If he were to return, his oratory would be unsettling and intellectually challenging rather than remembered diction and cadences. He would probably be the unpopular social critic he was on the eve of the Poor People's Campaign rather than the object of national homage he became after his death. His basic message would be the same as it was when he was alive, for he did not bend with the changing political winds. He would talk of ending poverty and war and of building a just social order that would avoid the pitfalls of competitive capitalism and repressive communism. He would give scant comfort to those who condition their activism upon the appearance of another King, for he recognized the extent to which he was a product of the movement that called him to leadership.

The notion that appearances by Great Men (or Great Women) are necessary preconditions for the emergence of major movements for social change reflects not only a poor understanding of history, but also a pessimistic view of the possibilities for future social change. Waiting for the Messiah is a human weakness that is unlikely to be rewarded more than once in a millennium. Studies of King's life offer support for an alternative optimistic belief that ordinary people can collectively improve their lives. Such studies demonstrate the capacity of social movements to transform participants for the better and to create leaders worthy of their followers.

POSTSCRIPT

Was Martin Luther King, Jr.'s Leadership Essential to the Success of the Civil Rights Movement?

By 1966, despite the many successes associated with his direct action campaigns in the South, Martin Luther King, Jr.'s prominence had begun to decline. The victories had failed to produce a nation free from segregation and political intimidation. A "white backlash" had begun to block further gains, and growing black nationalist trends, reflected in the philosophy of Stokely Carmichael of SNCC, were producing a call for "Black Power." By the time of his assassination in April 1968, King's philosophy was being challenged by younger, more radical blacks who saw nonviolent direct action as an obsolete strategy.

The literature on King and the civil rights movement is extensive. August Meier, Elliott Rudwick, and Francis L. Broderick, eds., *Black Protest Thought in the Twentieth Century*, 2d ed. (Bobbs-Merrill, 1971), presents a collection of documents which places the activities of the 1950s and 1960s in a larger framework. The reflections of many of the participants of the movement are included in Howell Raines, *My Soul Is Rested: The Story of the Civil Rights Movement in the Deep South* (G. P. Putnam, 1977). Students should also consult Aldon D. Morris, *The Origins of the Civil Rights Movement: Black Communities Organizing for Change* (Free Press, 1984). Four invaluable studies of King are David L. Lewis, *King: A Critical Biography* (Praeger, 1970); Stephen B. Oates, *Let the Trumpet Sound: The Life of Martin Luther King, Jr.* (Harper & Row, 1982); David J. Garrow's Pulitzer Prize-winning *Bearing the Cross: Martin Luther King, Jr., and the Southern Christian Leadership Conference* (William Morrow, 1986); and Adam Fairclough, *To Redeem the Soul of America: The Southern Christian Leadership Conference and Martin Luther King, Jr.* (University of Georgia Press, 1987). For an understanding of two prominent civil rights organizations, see August Meier and Elliott Rudwick, *CORE: A Study in the Civil Rights Movement, 1942–1968* (Oxford University Press, 1973), and Clayborne Carson, *In Struggle: SNCC and the Black Awakening of the 1960s* (Harvard University Press, 1981). William H. Chafe, *Civilities and Civil Rights: Greensboro, North Carolina, and the Black Struggle for Freedom* (Oxford University Press, 1980), evaluates the impact of the movement on race relations in a single city. The black nationalist critique of King and the nonviolent direct action campaign is effectively presented in Malcolm X and Alex Haley, *The Autobiography of Malcolm X* (Grove Press, 1964), and Peter Goldman, *The Death and Life of Malcolm X* (Harper & Row, 1974). Finally, the texture of the civil rights movement is captured beautifully in the six-hour documentary "Eyes on the Prize."

ISSUE 17

Is the United States in a Period of Decline?

YES: Paul Kennedy, from *The Rise and Fall of the Great Powers: Economic Change and Military Conflict from 1500 to 2000* (Random House, 1987)

NO: Susan Strange, from "The Persistent Myth of Lost Hegemony," *International Organization* (Autumn 1987)

ISSUE SUMMARY

YES: Professor of history Paul Kennedy believes that the United States, like other great nations before it, has declined in power because of its excessive military commitments, its huge federal deficit, and its decreasing share of global production.

NO: Professor of internal relations Susan Strange maintains that the United States still possesses the structural power to reshape the global political economy through its military strength, financial clout, control over world knowledge, and production of goods and services.

On January 20, 1989, George Bush was inaugurated as the 41st president of the United States. Two hundred years ago another George took the oath of office as the new nation's first president. If the 55 men who wrote the Constitution at Philadelphia in 1787 woke up today, how would they perceive America? Would these men appreciate the nation's technological accomplishments and stature as the world's number one power? Or would they consider the United States as a country on the decline because it had departed from the values and hopes of the revolutionaries who established our republican government 200 years ago?

More than likely the Founding Fathers would be surprised to discover that the United States was still being governed under the oldest living constitution in the world. Even James Madison, the chief architect of the document, did not expect the government to last more than 20 years in its original form. The amendments that extended the vote to blacks and women would have horrified a group of men who believed that voters should be only white adult males who owned substantial amounts of property. The recent election campaign would also have surprised them. No doubt they would have approved of the debates between the major candidates, but the primary races and the conventions which the two major parties conducted would have been scorned by a generation which viewed political parties as factions divisive of the nation's best interests.

Certainly the Founding Fathers would be shocked by the size of the population and the diversity of its racial and ethnic groups. In 1790 there were only 3.9 million people in the United States; by 1990 the official population exceeded 240 million. Two hundred years ago the majority of blacks were slaves, whites were mainly Protestants from the British Isles, and Native Americans inhabited most of the land west of the original 13 states. Today the Indian population is virtually extinct; blacks were freed in 1865 and now constitute 12 percent of the population; and whites are no longer exclusively Protestants of English or Scottish descent. More often than not a middle-class white is an Irish-Catholic whose ancestor migrated to America during the potato famine in the mid-nineteenth century or a Jew whose grandfather fled from persecution in Russia to search for work and a better life.

There is little doubt that the Founding Fathers would be amazed at the technological achievements of succeeding generations. Think of how these men would have appreciated one air conditioning unit at Convention Hall in the summer of 1787. Wouldn't they marvel at the modern forms of transportation and communication—cars, planes, phones, and computers—which we take for granted today? At the same time wouldn't former president Thomas Jefferson have recoiled from the enormous military industrial complex which the world's most powerful nation has built to maintain its security? Wouldn't physicist Ben Franklin be horrified to learn that his simple electrical experiments with a kite and a key had led to developments which not only light up the world but could destroy it as well?

Has the United States entered a period of historical decline? In the following selections, Paul Kennedy compares contemporary America with seventeenth-century Spain, eighteenth-century France, and nineteenth-century China and England, and argues that the United States, like these other nations, has declined in power because of its excessive military commitments, its huge federal deficit, and its decreasing share of the world's production of goods and services. In opposition Susan Strange rejects the idea that the United States is declining in power, for it still possesses the structural power to reshape the global political economy through its military strength, financial clout, production capabilities, and control over world knowledge.

YES

Paul Kennedy

THE UNITED STATES: THE PROBLEM OF NUMBER ONE IN RELATIVE DECLINE

Although the United States is at present still in a class of its own economically and perhaps even militarily, it cannot avoid confronting the two great tests which challenge the *longevity* of every major power that occupies the "number one" position in world affairs: whether, in the military/strategic realm, it can preserve a reasonable balance between the nation's perceived defense requirements and the means it possesses to maintain those commitments; and whether, as an intimately related point, it can preserve the technological and economic bases of its power from relative erosion in the face of the ever-shifting patterns of global production. This test of American abilities will be the greater because it, like Imperial Spain around 1600 or the British Empire around 1900, is the inheritor of a vast array of strategical commitments which had been made decades earlier, when the nation's political, economic, and military capacity to influence world affairs seemed so much more assured. In consequence, the United States now runs the risk, so familiar to historians of the rise and fall of previous Great Powers, of what might roughly be called "imperial overstretch": that is to say, decision-makers in Washington must face the awkward and enduring fact that the sum total of the United States' global interests and obligations is nowadays far larger than the country's power to defend them all simultaneously. . . .

[T]he United States today has roughly the same massive array of military obligations across the globe as it had a quarter-century ago, when its shares of world GNP, manufacturing production, military spending, and armed forces personnel were so much larger than they are now. Even in 1985, forty years after its triumphs of the Second World War and over a decade after its pull-out from Vietnam, the United States had 520,000 members of its armed forces abroad (including 65,000 afloat). That total is, incidentally, substantially more than the overseas deployments in peacetime of the military and naval forces of the British Empire at the height of its power. Nevertheless, in the strongly expressed opinion of the Joint Chiefs of Staff, and of many civilian experts, it is simply not enough. Despite a near-trebling of the American defense budget since the late 1970s, there has occurred a "mere 5 percent increase in the numerical size of the armed forces on active duty." As the British and French military found in their time, a nation with extensive overseas obligations will always have a more difficult "manpower problem" than a state which keeps its armed forces solely for home defense; and a politically liberal and economically laissez-faire society—aware of the unpopularity of conscription—will have a greater problem than most.

Possibly this concern about the gap between American interests and capabilities in the world would be less acute had there not been so much doubt expressed—since at least the time of the Vietnam War—about the *efficiency* of the system itself. Since those doubts have been repeatedly aired in other studies, they will only be summarized here; this is not a further essay on the hot topic of "defense reform." One major area of contention, for example, has been the degree of interservice rivalry, which is of course common to most armed forces but seems more deeply entrenched in the American system—possibly because of the relatively modest powers of the chairman of the Joint Chiefs of Staff, possibly because so much more energy appears to be devoted to procurement as opposed to strategical and operational issues. In peacetime, this might merely be dismissed as an extreme example of "bureaucratic politics"; but in actual wartime opera-

tions—say in the emergency dispatch of the Rapid Deployment Joint Task Force, which contains elements from all four services—a lack of proper coordination could be fatal.

In the area of military procurement itself, allegations of "waste, fraud and abuse" have been commonplace. The various scandals over horrendously expensive, *under*performing weapons which have caught the public's attention in recent years have plausible explanations: the lack of proper competitive bidding and of market forces in the "military-industrial complex," and the tendency toward "gold-plated" weapon systems, not to mention the striving for large profits. It is difficult, however, to separate those deficiencies in the procurement process from what is clearly a more fundamental happening: the intensification of the impacts which new technological advances make upon the art of war. Given that it is in the high-technology field that the USSR usually appears most vulnerable—which suggests that American *quality* in weaponry can be employed to counter the superior Russian *quantity* of, say, tanks and aircraft—there is an obvious attraction in what Caspar Weinberger termed "competitive strategies" when ordering new armaments. Nevertheless, the fact that the Reagan administration in its first term spent over 75 percent more on new aircraft than the Carter regime but acquired only 9 percent more planes points to *the* appalling military-procurement problem of the late twentieth century: given the technologically driven tendency toward spending more and more money upon fewer and fewer weapon systems, would the United States and its allies really have enough sophisticated and highly expensive aircraft and tanks in reserve after the early stages of a ferociously fought conventional war? Does the U.S. Navy possess enough attack submarines, or frigates, if heavy losses were incurred in the early stages of a *third* Battle of the Atlantic? If not, the results would be grim; for it is clear that today's complex weaponry simply cannot be replaced in the short times which were achieved during the Second World War.

This dilemma is accentuated by two other elements in the complicated calculus of evolving an effective American defense policy. The first is the issue of budgetary constraints. Unless external circumstances became much more threatening, it would be a remarkable act of political persuasion to get national defense expenditures raised much above, say 7.5 percent of GNP—the more especially since the size of the federal deficit . . . points to the need to balance governmental spending as the first priority of state. But if there is a slowing-down or even a halt in the increase in defense spending, coinciding with the continuous upward spiral in weapons costs, then the problem facing the Pentagon will become much more acute.

The second factor is the sheer variety of military contingencies that a global superpower like the United States has to plan for—all of which, in their way place differing demands upon the armed forces and the weaponry they are likely to employ. This again is not without precedent in the history of the Great Powers; the British army was frequently placed under strain by having to plan to fight on the Northwest Frontier of India *or* in Belgium. But even that challenge pales beside the task facing today's "number one." If the critical issue for the United States is preserving a nuclear deterrent against the Soviet Union at *all* levels of escalation, then money will inevitably be poured into such weapons as the MX missile, the B-1 and "Stealth" bombers, Pershing IIs, cruise missiles, and Trident-bearing submarines. If a large-scale conventional war against the Warsaw Pact is the most probable scenario, then the funds presumably need to go in quite different directions: tactical aircraft, main battle tanks, large carriers, frigates, attack submarines and logistical services. If it is likely that the United States and the USSR will avoid a direct clash, but that both will become more active in the Third World, then the weapons mix changes again: small arms, helicopters, light carriers, an enhanced role for the U.S. Marine Corps become the chief items on the list. Already it is clear that a large part of the controversy over "defense reform" stems from differing assumptions about the *type* of war the United States might be called upon to fight. But what if those in authority make the wrong assumption? . . .

The final question about the proper relationship of "means and ends" in the defense of American global interests relates to the economic challenges bearing down upon the country, which, because they are so various, threaten to place immense strains upon decision-making in national policy. The extraordinary breadth and complexity of the American economy makes it difficult to summarize what is happening to all parts of it—especially in a period when it is sending out such contradictory signals. . . .

The first of these is the country's relative industrial decline, as measured against world production, not only in older manufactures such as textiles, iron and steel, shipbuilding, and basic chemicals, but also—although it is far less easy to judge the final outcome of this level of industrial-technological combat—in global shares of robotics, aerospace, automobiles, machine tools, and computers. Both of these pose immense problems: in traditional and basic manufacturing, the gap in wage scales between the United States and newly industrializing countries is probably such that no "efficiency measures" will close it; but to lose out in the competition in future technologies, if that indeed should occur, would be even more disastrous. In late 1986, for example, a congressional study reported that the U.S. trade surplus in high-technology goods had plunged from $27 billion in 1980 to a mere $4 billion in 1985, and was swiftly heading into a deficit.

The second, and in many ways less expected, sector of decline is agriculture. Only a decade ago, experts in that subject were predicting a frightening global imbalance between feeding requirements and farming output. But such a scenario of famine and disaster stimulated two powerful responses. The first was a massive investment into American farming from the 1970's onward, fueled by the prospect of ever-larger overseas food sales; the second was the enormous (western-world-funded) investigation into scientific means of increasing Third World crop outputs, which has been so successful as to turn growing numbers of such countries into food *exporters*, and thus competitors of the United States. These two trends are separate from, but have coincided with, the transformation of the EEC into a major producer of agricultural surpluses, because of its price-support system. In consequence, experts now refer to a "world awash in food," which in turn leads to sharp declines in agricultural prices and in American food exports—and drives many farmers out of business.

It is not surprising, therefore, that these economic problems have led to a surge in protectionist sentiment throughout many sectors of the American economy, and among businessmen, unions, farmers, and their congressmen. As with the "tariff reform" agitation in Edwardian Britain, the advocates of increased protection complain of unfair foreign practices, of "dumping" below-cost manufactures on the American market, and of enormous subsidies to foreign farmers—which, they maintain, can only be answered by U.S. administrations abandoning their laissez-faire policy on trade and instituting tough countermeasures. Many of those individual complaints (e.g., of Japan shipping below-cost silicon chips to the American market) have been valid. More broadly, however, the surge in protectionist sentiment is also a reflection of the erosion of the previously unchallenged U.S. manufacturing supremacy. Like mid-Victorian Britons, Americans after 1945 favored free trade and open competition, not just because they held that global commerce and prosperity would be boosted in the process, but also because they knew that they were most likely to benefit from the abandonment of protectionism. Forty years later, with that confidence ebbing, there is a predictable shift of opinion in favor of protecting the domestic market and the domestic producer. And, just as in that earlier British case, defenders of the existing system point out that enhanced tariffs might not only make domestic products *less* competitive internationally, but that there also could be various external repercussions—a global tariff war, blows against American exports, the undermining of the currencies of certain newly industrializing countries, and a return to the economic crisis of the 1930s.

Along with these difficulties affecting American manufacturing and agriculture there are unprecedented turbulences in the nation's finances. The uncompetitiveness of U.S. industrial products abroad and the declining sales of agricultural exports have together produced staggering deficits in visible trade—$160 billion in the twelve months to May 1986—but what is more alarming is that such a gap can no longer be covered by American earnings on "invisibles," which is the traditional recourse of a mature economy (e.g. Great Britain before 1914). On the contrary, the only way the United States can pay its way in the world is by importing ever-larger sums of capital, which has transformed it from being the world's largest creditor to the world's largest debtor nation *in the space of a few years.*

Compounding this problem—in the view of many critics, *causing* this problem—have been the budgetary policies of the U.S. government itself. Even in the 1960s, there was a tendency for Washington to rely upon deficit finance, rather than additional taxes, to pay for the increasing cost of defense and social programs. But the decisions taken by the Reagan administration in the early 1980s —i.e., large-scale increases in defense expenditures, plus considerable decreases in taxation, but *without* significant reductions in federal spending elsewhere— have produced extraordinary rises in the deficit, and consequently in the national debt, as shown in Table 1.

The continuation of such trends, alarmed voices have pointed out, would push the U.S. national debt to around $13 *trillion* by the year 2000 (fourteen times that of 1980), and the interest payments

Table 1

U.S. Federal Deficit, Debt, and Interest, 1980–1985
(billions of dollars)

	Deficit	Debt	Interest on Debt
1980	59.6	914.3	52.5
1983	195.4	1,381.9	87.8
1985	202.8	1,823.1	129.0

on such debt to $1.5 *trillion* (twenty-nine times that of 1980). In fact, a lowering of interest rates could bring down those estimates, but the overall trend is still very unhealthy. Even if federal deficits could be reduced to a "mere" $100 billion annually, the compounding of national debt and interest payments by the early twenty-first century will still cause quite unprecedented totals of money to be diverted in that direction. Historically, the only other example which comes to mind of a Great Power so increasing its indebtedness in *peacetime* is France in the 1780s, where the fiscal crisis contributed to the domestic political crisis. . . .

[G]iven the worldwide array of military liabilities which the United States has assumed since 1945, its capacity to carry those burdens is obviously less than it was several decades ago, when its share of global manufacturing and GNP was much larger, its agriculture was not in crisis, its balance of payments was far healthier, the government budget was also in balance, and it was not so heavily in debt to the rest of the world. In that larger sense, there is something in the analogy which is made by certain political scientists between the United States' position today and that of previous "declining hegemons."

Here again, it is instructive to note the uncanny similarities between the growing mood of anxiety among thoughtful circles in the United States today and that which pervaded all political parties in Edwardian Britain and led to what has been termed the "national efficiency" movement: that is, a broad-based debate within the nation's decision-making, business, and educational elites over the various measures which could reverse what was seen to be a growing uncompetitiveness as compared with other advanced societies. In terms of commercial expertise, levels of training and education, efficiency of production, standards of income and (among the less well-off) of living, health, and housing, the "number one" power of 1900 seemed to be losing its position, with dire implications for the country's long-term *strategic* position; hence the fact that the calls for "renewal" and "reorganization" came at least as much from the Right as from the Left. Such campaigns usually do lead to reforms, here and there; but their very existence is, ironically, a confirmation of decline, in that such an agitation simply would not have been necessary a few decades earlier, when the nation's lead was unquestioned. A strong man, the writer G. K. Chesterton sardonically observed, does not worry about his bodily efficiency; only when he weakens does he begin to talk about health. In the same way, when a Great Power is strong and unchallenged, it will be much less likely to debate its capacity to meet its obligations than when it is relatively weaker. . . .

A quite different problem, but one equally important for the sustaining of a proper grand strategy, concerns the impact of slow economic growth upon the American social/political consensus. To a degree which amazes most Europeans, the United States in the twentieth century has managed to avoid ostensible "class" politics. This is due, one imagines, to the facts that so many of its immigrants were fleeing from socially rigid circumstances elsewhere; that the sheer size of the country allowed those who were disillusioned with their economic position to "escape" to the West, and simultaneously made the organization of labor much more difficult than in, say, France or Britain; and that those same geographical dimensions, and the entrepreneurial opportunities within them, encouraged the development of a largely unreconstructed form of laissez-faire capitalism which has dominated the political culture of the nation (despite occasional counterattacks from the left). In consequence, the "earnings gap" between rich and poor in the United States is significantly larger than in any other advanced industrial society; and, by the same token, state expenditures upon social services form a lower share of GNP than in comparable countries (except Japan, which appears to have a much stronger family-based form of support for the poor and the aged).

This lack of "class" politics despite the obvious socioeconomic disparities has obviously been helped by the fact that the United States' overall growth since the 1930s offered the prospect of individual betterment to a majority of the population; and by the more disturbing fact that the poorest *one-third* of American society has not been "mobilized" to become regular voters. But given the differentiated birthrate between the white ethnic groups on the one hand and the black and Hispanic groups on the other—not to mention the changing flow of immigrants into the United States, and given also the economic metamorphosis which is leading to the loss of millions of relatively high-earning jobs in manufacturing, and the creation of millions of poorly paid jobs in services, it may be unwise to assume that the prevailing norms of the American political economy (low governmental expenditures, low taxes on the rich) would be maintained if the nation entered a period of sustained economic difficulty caused by a plunging dollar and slow growth. What this also suggests is that an American polity which responds to external challenges by increasing defense expenditures, and reacts to the budgetary crisis by slashing the existing social expenditures, may run the risk of provoking an eventual political backlash. . . .

This brings us, inevitably, to the delicate relationship between slow economic growth and high defense spending. The debate upon "the economics of defense spending" is a highly controversial one, and—bearing in mind the size and variety of the American economy, the stimulus which can come from large government contracts, and the technical spin-offs from weapons research—the evidence does not point simply in one direction. But what is significant for our purposes is the comparative dimension. Even if (as is often pointed out) defense expenditures formed 10 percent of GNP under Eisenhower and 9 percent under Kennedy, the United States' relative share of global production and wealth was at that time around *twice* what it is today; and, more particularly, the American economy was not then facing the challenges to either its traditional or its high-technology manufactures. Moreover, if the United States at present continues to devote 7 percent or more of its GNP to defense spending while its major

economic rivals, especially Japan, allocate a far smaller proportion, then *ipso facto* the latter have potentially more funds "free" for civilian investment; if the United States continues to invest a massive amount of its R&D activities into military-related production while the Japanese and West Germans concentrate upon commerical R&D; and if the Pentagon's spending drains off the majority of the country's scientists and engineers from the design and production of goods for the world market while similar personnel in other countries are primarily engaged in bringing out better products for the civilian consumer, then it seems inevitable that the American share of world manufacturing will steadily decline, and also likely that its economic growth rates will be slower than in those countries dedicated to the marketplace and less eager to channel resources into defense.

It is almost superfluous to say that these tendencies place the United States on the horns of a most acute dilemma over the longer term. Simply because it is *the* global superpower, with far more extensive military commitments than a regional Power like Japan or West Germany, it requires much larger defense forces—in just the same way as imperial Spain felt it needed a far larger army than its contemporaries and Victorian Britain insisted upon a much bigger navy than any other country. Furthermore, since the USSR is seen to be the major military threat to American interests across the globe and is clearly devoting a far greater proportion of *its* GNP to defense, American decision-makers are inevitably worried about "losing" the arms race with Russia. Yet the more sensible among these decision-makers can also perceive that the burden of armaments is debilitating the Soviet economy; and that if the two superpowers continue to allocate ever-larger shares of their national wealth into the unproductive field of armaments, the critical question might soon be: "Whose economy will decline *fastest*, relative to such expanding states as Japan, China, etc.?" A low investment in armaments may, for a globally overstretched Power like the United States, leave it feeling vulnerable everywhere; but a very heavy investment in armaments, while bringing greater security in the short term, may so erode the commercial competitiveness of the American economy that the nation will be *less* secure in the long term.

Here, too, the historical precedents are not encouraging. For it has been a common dilemma facing previous "number-one" countries that even as their relative economic strength is ebbing, the growing foreign challenges to their position have compelled them to allocate more and more of their resources into the military sector, which in turn squeezes out productive investment and, over time, leads to the downward spiral of slower growth, heavier taxes, deepening domestic splits over spending priorities, and a weakening capacity to bear the burdens of defense. If this, indeed, is the pattern of history, one is tempted to paraphrase Shaw's deadly serious quip and say: "Rome fell; Babylon fell; Scarsdale's turn will come."

In the largest sense of all, therefore, the only answer to the question increasingly debated by the public of whether the United States can preserve its existing position is "no"—for it simply has not been given to any one society to remain *permanently* ahead of all the others, because that would imply a freezing of the differentiated pattern of

growth rates, technological advance, and military developments which has existed since time immemorial. On the other hand, this reference to historical precedents does *not* imply that the United States is destined to shrink to the relative obscurity of former leading Powers such as Spain or the Netherlands, or to disintegrate like the Roman and Austro-Hungarian empires; it is simply too large to do the former, and presumably too homogeneous to do the latter. Even the British analogy, much favored in the current political-science literature, is not a good one if it ignores the differences in *scale*. This can be put another way: the geographical size, population, and natural resources of the British Isles would suggest that it ought to possess roughly 3 or 4 percent of the world's wealth and power, *all other things being equal*; but it is precisely because all other things are *never* equal that a peculiar set of historical and technological circumstances permitted the British Isles to expand to possess, say, 25 percent of the world's wealth and power in its prime; and since those favorable circumstances have disappeared, all that it has been doing is returning down to its more "natural" size. In the same way, it may be argued that the geographical extent, population, and natural resources of the United States suggest that it ought to possess perhaps 16 or 18 percent of the world's wealth and power, but because of historical and technical circumstances favorable to it, that share rose to 40 percent or more by 1945; and what we are witnessing at the moment is the early decades of the ebbing away from that extraordinarily high figure to a more "natural" share. That decline is being masked by the country's enormous military capabilities at present, and also by its success in "internationalizing" American capitalism and culture. Yet even when it declines to occupy its "natural" share of the world's wealth and power, a long time into the future, the United States will still be a very significant Power in a multipolar world, simply because of its size.

The task facing American statesmen over the next decades, therefore, is to recognize that broad trends are under way, and that there is a need to "manage" affairs so that the *relative* erosion of the United States' position takes place slowly and smoothly, and is not accelerated by policies which bring merely short-term advantage but longer-term disadvantage. This involves, from the president's office downward, an appreciation that technological and therefore socioeconomic change is occurring in the world faster than ever before; that the international community is much more politically and culturally diverse than has been assumed, and is defiant of simplistic remedies offered either by Washington or Moscow to its problems; that the economic and productive power balances are no longer as favorably tilted in the United States' direction as in 1945; and that, even in the military realm, there are signs of a certain redistribution of the balances, away from a bipolar to more of a multipolar system, in which the conglomeration of American economic-cum-military strength is likely to remain larger than that possessed by any one of the others individually, but will not be as disproportionate as in the decades which immediately followed the Second World War. This, in itself, is not a bad thing if one recalls Kissinger's observations about the disadvantages of carrying out policies in what is always seen to be a bipolar world . . .; and it may seem still less of a bad thing when it is recognized how much more Russia may be affected by the changing dynamics of world power. In all of the discussions about the erosion of American leadership, it needs to be repeated again and again that the decline referred to is relative not absolute, and is therefore perfectly natural; and that the only serious threat to the real interests of the United States can come from a failure to adjust sensibly to the newer world order.

NO

Susan Strange

THE PERSISTENT MYTH
OF LOST HEGEMONY

In its extreme form, the myth that the United States today is just a little old country much like any other and has, in some sudden and miraculous way, lost its hegemonic power may seem more plausible than do some of these other myths. But when it is subjected to close and searching scrutiny, it is just as far from truth. And unless cool and rational analysis undermines its power to move minds and shape attitudes, it can be every bit as dangerous. In living memory, the optimism of the United States gave Americans and others a vision of a new, better and attainable future for the world; today, the myth of lost hegemony is apt to induce in everybody only pessimism, despair, and the conviction that, in these inauspicious circumstances, the only thing to do is to ignore everyone else and look after your own individual or national interests. Thus, some of the same American contributors to *International Organization* who are personally persuaded of the benefits of more international cooperation and conflict resolution, may paradoxically be contributing to a *less* cooperative environment by subscribing to and perpetuating the myth of lost American power. . . .

Contrary to conventional American wisdom, I shall argue that my critique of hegemonic stability theory leads to five quite important concluding propositions. These are:

• The great game of states has changed over the last quarter-century in a very fundamental way, for reasons that are primarily economic, not primarily political.

• In this new great game of states, structural power decides outcomes (both positive and negative) much more than relational power does, and the United States' structural power has, on balance, increased.

• There has always been an inherent conflict in U.S. foreign policy between its goals of liberalism for the pursuit of its commercial and financial interests and the exigencies of realism in the pursuit of political and military national interests. Now, in a world depression, perceptions of U.S. national interests are more apt to be perceived in terms of the short run than of the long, so that

From Susan Strange, "The Persistent Myth of Lost Hegemony," *International Organization*, vol. 41, no. 4 (Autumn 1987). Copyright © 1987 by the World Peace Foundation and the Massachusetts Institute of Technology. Reprinted by permission of The MIT Press, Cambridge, MA, and the World Peace Foundation.

"realism," "unilateralism," or "domesticism" in U.S. policy is now much more evident than liberal internationalism.

• The use of hegemonic structural power in ways that are destructive of international order and cooperation has been an important cause of world economic instability and continuing crisis.

• A necessary condition, therefore, for greater stability and cooperation lie within the United States, rather than in the institutions and mechanisms of international cooperation. . . .

FOUR ASPECTS OF STRUCTURAL POWER

Structural power is the power to choose and to shape the structures of the global political economy within which other states, their political institutions, their economic enterprises, and (not least) their professional people have to operate. This means more than the power to set the agenda of discussion or to design (in American phraseology) the international "regime" of rules and customs.

Structural power is to be found, not in a single structure, but rather in four separate but interrelated structures. They are like the four sides of a pyramid. Each is held up and supported by the other three. These four structures are not peculiar to the global political economy or world system. The sources of superior structural power are the same in very small human groups, like the family, or a remote and isolated village community, as they are in the world at large. In each of these, structural power lies:

• with the person or group able to exercise control over—that is, to threaten or to defend, to deny or to increase—other people's security from violence;

• with those able to control the system of production of goods and services;

• with those able to determine the structure of finance and credit through which (in all but the most primitive economies) it is possible to acquire purchasing power without having either to work or to trade it;

• with those who have most influence over knowledge, whether it is technical knowledge, religious knowledge, or leadership in ideas, and who control or influence the acquisition, communication, and storage of knowledge and information.

This breakdown of the components of structural power is only common sense. But it is often obscured by theoretical discussions about the nature of the state or of power that are either far too abstract or far too narrow. Structural power has four aspects, each reinforcing or detracting from the other three. In the international political economy, all four are important, and the state which is dominant in most aspects of structural power is the most powerful.

Take, first, power in the security structure. So long as the possibility of violent conflict threatens personal security, the state which offers protection against that threat exercises power—and does so even though the same defense force that gives protection may itself be something of a threat to security. Today, as in the past three decades, the United States controls the only force of intercontinental missiles carrying nuclear warheads that are any sort of a match for the corresponding force controlled from Moscow. Soviet power in the security structure was once inferior, and is now roughly equal. But among the other countries involved in the NATO alliance, the

Table 1

Nuclear forces: United States and NATO/Europe

	United States	NATO excluding US
Missiles		
ICBM	1,010	—
Intermediate	278	18
Tactical	144	171
Aircraft		
Long range	199	—
Medium range	55	—
Land-based strike	1,182	1,236
Carrier-based strike	666	38
Nuclear submarines	85	16
Total defense budgets (1984)	$237 billion	$40 billion

Source: International Institute for Strategic Studies, *The Military Balance*, 1986–87, pp. 200–212.

United States is still pre-eminent, as Table 1 shows.

Not only are America's NATO [North Atlantic Treaty Organization] allies so much weaker in nuclear weapons that they are dependent on U.S. protection, their dependence is increased by their inferiority to the Soviet Union and its Warsaw Pact allies in conventional weapons, especially on land and in the air. It need hardly be added that Japan is a negligible force in terms of armaments; it is inferior even to South Korea. And it is this fundamental asymmetry in the security structure of the non-communist world that is often and easily overlooked in contemporary discussion of international economic issues. Always in the background, there is the contrast between the provision of security by the United States defense forces and the dependence of its partners upon them. The preponderant power of the United States in the security structure operates on land, at sea, in the air, and (most markedly) in space. There is no comparison between such a universal basic force and the very limited naval preponderance which was the main backing to British economic power in the earlier period of supposed hegemony.

Almost as important is the continued domination by the United States of the world's production structure. Who decides who shall produce what, how and with what reward, has always been almost as fundamental a question in political economy as who decides what defense shall be offered against security threats. Some American analysts' choice of indicators has misled them into thinking that their country is suffering economic decline. It is not the share of industrial manufactured products made in the United States nor the share of U.S. exports of manufactures to world markets that counts. We should look instead at the proportion of total world production of goods and services produced: a) in the United States, and b) by enterprises ultimately headquartered in the United States and responsible to the gov-

Table 2

Percentage of total output produced in United States

	1970	1980	1985 (est.)	1990 (est.)
Manufacturing	37.7	36.8	36.4	36.9
High tech	4.1	5.7	7.1	8.5
Capital goods	4.0	4.0	3.2	3.3
Consumer durables	4.8	4.4	4.8	4.6
Consumer nondurables	9.4	8.8	8.2	7.6
Basic goods	8.4	7.4	6.6	6.4
Services	48.1	51.5	52.2	52.1
All others	14.3	11.7	11.4	10.9

Source: Data Resources, Inc., *Business Week*, 14 January 1985.

ernment in Washington. We should note which corporations lead, rather than the percentage of world output produced in the United States, or the share of world exports produced in the United States. For example, of the largest corporations producing computers, the top six are American, as are twelve of the top twenty. Between them, they produce 62.3 percent of total world production and have over 50 percent of the world turnover. IBM alone dominated the market with 35.6 percent of world turnover in 1983, though it is now an open question whether some of the market will go to smaller competitors. The significance of this dominance is underlined by estimates that the present world demand for computers (estimated at $200 billion) will *quadruple* by 1991. It is the same story with integrated circuits. Texas Instruments and IBM are the leading world producers, even ahead of the Japanese. In telecommunications, too, AT&T and ITT are the top two companies in terms of sales. Both are sustained by the great size of the homogeneous domestic market—an asset the Americans are inclined to forget but one of which Europeans are acutely aware. Dr. W. Dekker, presi-

dent of Phillips Corporation, recently warned European governments that if they could not combine to provide a comparably uniform home base, European companies like Phillips, Siemens, Nixdorf, Bell, ICL, Ericsson, and Olivetti would be unable to survive and certainly could not stay based in Europe. "If Europe does not unite, industrial innovation will pass Europe by," he concluded.

Broken down into categories, we see from Table 2 that, while the U.S. shares of basic products (including steel, chemicals, paper) and consumer goods have declined between 1970 and 1980, the U.S. share of high technology products is actually larger. And, it is estimated that this share will more than double the 1970 level by 1990. Similarly, American service industries will hold their share—50 per cent or more—of the whole world market.

In the oil business, which remains the lifeblood of the world's industries and transport system, the seven American major oil companies dominate the top ten, together outnumbering and overpowering by far even the largest European and Japanese and OPEC [Organization of the Petroleum Exporting Countries] enterprises. In the aircraft business, the big names are still American—Lockheed, Boeing, and McDonnell Douglas. Six of the top nine companies, including the two largest, are American. Although there are big Swiss and British names in pharmaceuticals, the corporations with the biggest research budgets are American; and three of the largest five companies are American. Among the big industrial conglomerates, hedging their bets across a variety of sectors, it is again the Americans who lead.

In short, a perusal of any list of the top 100, 500, or 1,000 corporations producing for a world market will quickly bear out the contention that the decision-making power over the world's production structure still lies, not in Europe or Japan, but in the United States. Of the leading 300 enterprises in the world, 142 are U.S.-based.

One reason for this dominance over production is that the United States provided the first large mass market for manufactured consumer goods. The laws and policies of U.S. governments therefore shaped the corporations that first exploited that market. They then discovered the managerial techniques for controlling international networks of foreign subsidiaries. The mode of operations and the *mores* of today's business world were first made in America; developments in the United States still influence it more than developments anywhere else.

The third leg of American structural power is almost as important. America has the ability to control the supply and availability of credit denominated in dollars, and thus to exert predominant influence for good or ill over the creation of credit in the world's monetary system. In this respect, the conventional indicators are all turned upside down. How much gold and foreign exchange the U.S. government holds compared to Germany or Japan is beside the point when the United States is the only government capable of creating dollar assets that are accepted and saleable worldwide. In some sense, a financial system largely operating in dollars has no need of reserves. In most countries, whether the balance-of-payments is in surplus or deficit indicates the strength or weakness of its financial position. With the United States, the exact converse can be true. Indeed, to run a persistent deficit for a quarter of a century with impunity indicates not American weakness, but rather American power in the system. To decide one August morning that dollars can no longer be converted into gold was a progression from exorbitant privilege to super-exorbitant privilege; the U.S. government was exercising the unconstrained right to print money that others could not (save at unacceptable cost) refuse to accept in payment. And in the period 1973-1983, when the dollar-deutschmark exchange rate became even more volatile, the power to decide whether or when central banks should intervene to check market trends rested solely with the United States. West Germany alone was powerless. The asymmetry was quite striking, just as it was later in the 1980s for the dollar-yen exchange rate.

The significance of the dollar's predominance has also been well illustrated by the experience of Third World and Eastern European debt in the 1980s. American banks were foremost in lending to Latin America and were bailed out; German banks were foremost in lending to Poland and were not. The great majority of foreign bank loans were denominated in dollars. When first Mexico, then Brazil, Argentina, and the rest were unable to service their debt, the United States possessed two weapons more powerful than those of any other government: it could make advances in dollars to meet an emergency; and it could twist the arms of the largest and most influential banks in the system to follow its example with renewed medium-term credit. The evidence of American domination of the world's financial system is plentiful enough.

Not only were banks in the United States responsible for the lion's share of total bank assets in the industrial world but, more important, something like three-quarters of all these assets were denominated in dollars. The ability of the United States to move this market is unequalled. By its unilateral decision, the International Banking Facilities (IBF) legislation of 1981, which allowed U.S. banks the same freedom to conduct "offshore" transactions from home, practically halted the expansion of Eurodollar assets in U.S. bank branches abroad. These assets had grown in 1980 by $126 billion. In 1982, the growth was a mere $20 billion. A 1975 decision to deregulate markets (by allowing stockbrokers to compete in their charges) made comparable changes in policy irresistible for Britain, as for Japan.

Finally, implicit in much of the evidence already cited, America continued to dominate the world's knowledge structure. Knowledge is power, and whoever is able to develop or acquire a kind of knowledge that is sought by others, and whoever can control the channels by which it is communicated and the access to stores of knowledge, is able to dominate. In past times, priests and sages often exercised such dominance over kings and generals. The jealousy with which priesthoods guarded

their knowledge and restricted access to it has been a common feature of all great religions. Today, the knowledge most sought after by those who pursue power or wealth, military or corporate leadership, is technology—the technology of new materials as well as new processes, new products, and new systems of collecting, storing, and retrieving information and new systems of communication. Overall, the United States still leads in the advanced technology sectors—including those at the developing stage, such as artificial intelligence (space, ecology, ocean mining, and biotechnology) and the fast-growing new technologies of microcomputers, microelectronics, telecommunication, robots and factory automation, and data processing. The major flows of data still go to data banks in the United States.

Three factors have combined to give the United States this leadership in knowledge. One is the large home market operating under uniform (or nearly uniform) laws and regulations in standards and performance criteria. The Japanese have this, too, but the Europeans do not. As a result, U.S. companies can more easily specialize, while European corporations of comparable size are tempted to diversify, but in so doing often spread their R&D [research and development] too thin. Where Europe had a 15 percent share of the world market in semiconductors as recently as 1977, today it has less than 8 percent. A recent Office of Technology Assessment report to Congress on prospects in biotechnology concluded that the old world of Europe "will be outspent by the new, outplanned by the rising sun (of Japan), and fragmented by national rivalry." The same is true of almost all high technology sectors in which United States and

Japanese shares have increased while Europe's have declined. The telecommunications field, dominated by procurement by national monopolies (usually state-owned), is a classic example of the political disunity's fatal consequences on economic performance.

The second factor is the stimulus, support and headstart a large defense budget offers. It is true that IBM gained its lead in computers by developing the marketing techniques necessary to find large numbers of commercial buyers. But the first boost came in 1954 from the U.S. defense program, which financed 60 percent of IBM's R&D. Similarly, the first international circuits were built in 1962 and 1963 almost exclusively for defense and the space program. Even as late as 1968, 37 percent of U.S. production was absorbed by the National Aeronautics and Space Administration and the Department of Defense. Orders from the government carried much less risk and provided an invaluable beachhead for the conquest of commercial markets.

The third factor is the great size, wealth, and adaptability of American universities. In Europe's political history, the university has been the traditional bastion of political dissidence and opposition. This situation has sometimes produced an arm's length attitude to both government and business, so that European universities have often been slower than their American counterparts to seize the opportunities offered by both to expand research. Gerd Junne of Amsterdam University has found that in biotechnology, as in some pharmaceutical fields, the European multinationals spent more in American universities than in the ones at home in Europe. According to Junne: "In biotechnology, more than in other new technology, European managers have located much of their research in America or pay American researchers to do research for them."

One further factor really relates more to the dominance of the United States over access to the largest and most innovative capital markets, both at home in the United States and abroad in the so-called Euromarkets. They are able to finance new development rather more easily than even the Swiss or Japanese corporations. IBM left its competitors behind when it spent $5 billion developing the third generation of computers. New, small enterprises in Silicon Valley find it easier to find venture capital in the United States than they would in Europe.

All in all, therefore, there is little question about the combined structural power the United States derives from the security structure, the production structure, the credit (or financial) structure, and the knowledge structure. Neither Europe nor Japan can equal the Americans' performance across all four structures. Since each of them interacts with the other three, and the European and Japanese are so far behind militarily, it seems likely that America will enjoy the power to act as hegemon for some time to come. How the power is used is a different question.

THE ALTERNATIVE EXPLANATION

Once American predominance in structural power is conceded, we can look for other explanations of international economic disorder and the proliferation—despite all the summit conferences—of unsolved issues like that of Third World debt, volatile and unpredictable exchange rates and commodity prices, the precariousness of international banks, the multiplication of protectionist trade measures, and continued conflict over trade in agriculture and services.

A far more plausible explanation for the erosion of so-called international regimes than the decline in American hegemonic power lies within the American political system rather than in the role of the United States in the international system. Stability in these regimes requires, above all, some consistency on the part of the leading participant. The United States is ill-suited to sustaining this consistency in policymaking, partly by reason of its constitutional provisions, and partly thanks to the coalition-building practiced by its dominant political parties. The hallowed doctrine of the separation of powers has been an excellent safeguard against the abuse of executive power. But it has tended to make policymakers in Washington ever mindful of the capacity of powerful lobbies and interest groups operating upon or within Congress to distort, frustrate, or even reverse strategies adopted by the White House towards the outside world.

Take, for example, Henry Kissinger's post-OPEC strategy to strengthen the hands of the oil-consuming countries against the organized power of the oil producers. The International Energy Agency was set up with much fanfare and endowed with an elaborate institutional structure. But all its efforts (save the expansion of oil stockpiles, which would doubtless have taken place anyway) were rendered practically ineffective by the ability of the Nixon and Carter administrations, in the face of Congressional opposition, to raise the domestic price of energy high enough and fast enough to affect the short-term impact of demand on supply.

Again, the disruptive strategy of introducing the voluntary export restriction into the conduct of international trade relations has been most responsible for the decline of a multilateral, non-discriminatory regime based on the GATT [General Agreement on Tariffs and Trade] rulebook. And this, too, was the direct result of pressure from the Congress on successive administrations.

By all accounts, too, the Reagan administration surprised even its own delegations to the United Nations Conference on the Law of the Sea when, at the very last moment, it decided to reject the draft negotiated text which had consumed so much time and diplomatic effort. This, at least, could not be attributed to the need to placate the Congress so much as to reassessment of United States' interest in the prospects for exploiting new technology for deep-sea mining.

Cafruny's study of shipping comes to a similar conclusion, even while it notes that technical change and the shifting imperatives of the market exacerbate existing conflicts among domestic interests. Policy, he says, has become ever more incoherent, "ranging from ruthless anti-trust enforcement to protectionism." (The quotation is from a British trade minister.) Most industry analysts, Cafruny says, "refer to domestic politics to explain policy incoherence; indeed, most European and American officials and shipowners reject the proposition that America has a 'shipping policy.' " In the same way, the complaint that American trade policy is often contradictory, the left hand playing a protectionist card while the right hand bangs down a free trading trump, is met by the revealing assertion that America neither has nor seeks to have an "industrial policy." Americans may believe this, but no one else does. European companies, especially in high technology industries, are acutely aware of the advantages that U.S. corporations have enjoyed as a result of fat defense contracts. Government procurement for advanced technology and government protection for older industrial sectors is not irrational, although in the long run it may not be the best strategy for safeguarding national economic interests.

Besides the inconsistency of American trade policy across sectors, there is the tendency—as in monetary policy—to suddenly reverse the entire policy direction. Here, we must note that the American political system has far less built-in resistance to such political U-turns. No American president has to consider the risk of revolt in the parliamentary party and the consequent prospect of unwelcome early elections. As political scientists have observed, the very certainties of the American system may even encourage a certain cyclical repetition of policy shifts—for instance, to relieve unemployment at one stage or to check inflation at another. In Washington, there are few if any permanent senior bureaucrats, as there are in London, Paris, Bonn, or Tokyo, so firmly ensconced in positions of considerable blocking power that they provide a deterrent counterweight to political whims and fancies.

From outside the United States, it seems fairly clear to non-Americans why this sort of explanation is not very palatable to American academics—and even less so to American policymakers. It is not easy for either to admit that the conduct of American policy towards the rest of the world has been inconsistent, fickle, and unpredictable, and that United States administrations have often acted in flat contradiction to their own rhetoric. While pronouncing the virtues of liberalism for all in trade and investment, they have practiced partiality towards their own and protection and discrimination against successful newcomers like Japan or Taiwan. While preaching the ideals of internationalism and multilateral decision-making, they have never hesitated, as Patrick Sewell has written, to spring unilateralist surprises on America's friends as well as on its opponents. Nor have they felt any inhibitions about indulging in sudden ventures in bilateralism—with Israel, Mexico, or Canada, for example. They have done so because there is—and always has been—an inherent and unresolved conflict between the two sets of ideas that have influenced American policymakers ever since the end of World War II—between the liberalism preached by neoclassical economists and by internationalist political scientists and the realism practiced by the U.S. Departments of State and Defense.

The conflict has been between the realism necessary to any great power, which leads to unilateralist power politics, and the liberalism necessary to a great economy dependent on world markets, which leads to internationalism (whenever realism and domestic politics permit). Charles Krauthammer has remarked on this inherent conflict, but its implications are unlikely to gain ready acceptance in American intellectual circles. As K. Holsti observed and documented recently, the trend to parochialism in the American literature on world politics has actually been increasing. Books or articles in foreign languages are almost never read or cited. Only a few non-American writers, even in English, are regularly assigned to students in U.S. universities. American awareness of how others see the failure of international cooperation in relation to the continuing power of the United States is actually less now than it might have been a generation ago. This may be because the rising generation are native-born Americans, while many of the older American academics were born and educated in Europe; they occasionally returned on visits, and most read at least two European languages. These old men—there were few women—are now passing from the scene.

It is much easier for Americans to assert with Keohane, Fred Bergsten, and others that the decline of American power means that collective goals require collective collaboration and that, if this is elusive, there is nothing more the United States can do. Their arguments tend to overlook the fact that collective action is still possible but *only* when the United States takes the lead—when, in short, it still chooses to act as leader. The recent history of exchange rate stabilization, after the Plaza accord of September 1985 and after the Group of Seven meeting in Paris in February 1987, easily demonstrates this conclusion. We can also see it in the field of policies on ocean pollution or whaling. After Bhopal, the United States is likely to lead the world in setting standards of corporate liability for chemical accidents. Its leadership was vital to the rescheduling of Mexican and Brazilian debt. The United States initiated—and forced others to follow—action against financial fraud and insider dealing. These examples may be too few and far between, but they are enough to reject the myth of America's lost hegemony.

That is why I think it legitimate to talk of the "myth" of lost hegemony.

POSTSCRIPT

Is the United States in a Period of Decline?

Kennedy gives this argument a historical dimension that social scientists have often made during the past 15 years. He compares the decline in America's power with similar problems experienced by other countries in past eras. Kennedy bolsters his argument around two major premises. First, that America has declined in its relative share of the world's production of old-fashioned manufactured goods such as iron and textiles, new-styled knowledge equipment in the computer and scientific fields, and in agricultural production. Second, Kennedy believes that America's problem has been compounded by overextended military commitments which have produced swollen military expenditures and an astronomical and constantly growing national budget deficit.

Professor Strange challenges Kennedy's view. She argues that it is misleading to measure the relative power of a nation's share of global production. "In this new great game of states," she argues, "structural power decides outcomes (both positive and negative) much more than relational power does, and the United States' structural power has, on balance, increased."

Kennedy's *The Rise and Fall of the Great Powers* received an enormous amount of publicity and was favorably reviewed in major newspapers and weekly magazines. But scholars were generally more critical. Owen Harris, in "The Rise of American Decline," *Commentary* (May 1988), and W. W. Rostow, in "Beware Historians Bearing False Analogies," *Foreign Affairs* (Spring 1988), both reinforce Professor Strange's point that huge defense spending does not necessarily deplete a nation's economic strength.

In *The Present Age: Progress and Anarchy in Modern America* (Harper & Row, 1988), conservative sociologist Robert Nisbet finds the United States to be "a deeply flawed giant; not yet moribund but ill—quieted, shambling and spastic of limb, often aberrant of mind." For a conservative critique of Nisbet, see "Robert Nisbet's America," by Mary Tedeschi Eberstadt, *Commentary* (August 1988).

Joseph S. Nye, Jr., one of Kennedy's many critics, argues that the decline theories are based upon arbitrary schematizations and an imprecise usage of such terms as balance of power and hegemony, in *Bound to Lead: The Changing Nature of American Power* (Basic Books, 1990). Nye's thesis is similar to that of Alfred D. Chandler, Jr., (see Issue 2) when he argues that only the United States possesses such great resources of land, population, scientific discovery, technology, and military power. Also worthy of perusal are the essays by John Lukacs on "America's True Power," *American Heritage* (March 1989), and "The Stirring of History: A New World Arises from the Ruin of Empire," *Harper's Magazine* (August 1990).

CONTRIBUTORS
TO THIS VOLUME

EDITORS

JAMES M. SORELLE, a native Texan, received a Bachelor of Arts (1972) and a Master of Arts (1974) degree from the University of Houston and a Ph.D. from Kent State University (1980). He has taught at Ball State University and currently is an assistant professor of history at Baylor University. In addition to introductory courses in Western civilization and American history, he teaches upper-level sections in African American, urban, and late nineteenth- and twentieth-century United States history. His scholarly articles have appeared in the *Houston Review, Southwestern Historical Quarterly,* and a forthcoming anthology, *Black Dixie: Essays in Afro-Texan History in Houston.* He also has contributed entries to *The Handbook of Texas.*

LARRY MADARAS was born in Bayonne, New Jersey, in 1937. He attended Xavier High School in New York City and received his Bachelor's degree from Holy Cross College in 1959, an M.A. from New York University in 1961, and a Ph.D. from New York University in 1964. He has taught at Spring Hill College, the University of South Alabama, and the University of Maryland at College Park. He is currently teaching history and political science full-time at Howard Community College in Columbia, Maryland. He has been a Fulbright Fellow and has held two fellowships from the National Endowment for the Humanities. He is the author of dozens of journal articles and book reveiws.

STAFF

Marguerite L. Egan   Program Manager
Brenda S. Filley   Production Manager
Whit Vye   Designer
Libra Ann Cusack   Typesetting Supervisor
Juliana Arbo   Typesetter
David Brackley   Copy Editor
David Dean   Administrative Assistant
Diane Barker   Editorial Assistant
David Filley   Graphics

AUTHORS

RICHARD M. ABRAMS is a professor of history at the University of California, Berkeley. He is the author of *The Burdens of Progress* (Scott, Foresman, 1978).

STEPHEN E. AMBROSE is the Alumni Distinguished Professor of History at the University of New Orleans and the author of the diplomatic history text *The Rise to Globalism* (Penguin Books, 1985).

LOIS W. BANNER is a professor of history at the University of Southern California. She is the author of *Elizabeth Cady Stanton: A Radical for Women's Rights* (Little, Brown, 1980).

JOHN BODNAR is an associate dean of the faculties, an associate professor of history, and the director of the Oral History Research Center at Indiana University at Bloomington.

McGEORGE BUNDY is a professor of history at New York University. He was president of the Ford Foundation and head of the National Security Council under Presidents John F. Kennedy and Lyndon B. Johnson.

CLAYBORNE CARSON is an associate professor of history at Stanford University and a senior editor of the Martin Luther King, Jr., Papers Project at Stanford University's Martin Luther King, Jr., Center for Nonviolent Social Change.

ALFRED D. CHANDLER, JR., is the Straus Professor of Business History at Harvard Business School. He is the author of the Pulitzer Prize-winning *The Visible Hand: The Managerial Revolution in American Business* (Harvard University Press, 1977).

CARL N. DEGLER is a professor of history at Stanford University and a Pulitzer Prize-winning author.

W. E. B. DU BOIS (1868–1963), considered to be the most prominent black intellectual in the twentieth century, was a founding member of the National Association for the Advancement of Colored People and the first African American to receive a Ph.D. from Harvard University.

LEON FINK is an associate professor of history at the University of North Carolina at Chapel Hill.

ERIC FONER is a professor of history at Columbia University and has recently published the major synthesis of *Reconstruction: America's Unfinished Revolution, 1863–1867* (Harper & Row, 1988).

The late **ERNEST S. GRIFFITH** was a professor of political science and political economy at American University and served as Director of the Legislative Reference Service at the Library of Congress.

OSCAR HANDLIN is the Carl M. Loeb Professor of History at Harvard University and a Pulitzer Prize-winning historian. He is coauthor, with Lilian Handlin, of *Liberty in Expansion* (Harper & Row, 1989).

LOUIS R. HARLAN is a professor of history at the University of Maryland and the chief editor of *The Booker T. Washington Papers* (University of Illinois Press, 1984).

DAVID HEALY is a professor of history at the University of Wisconsin-Milwaukee and the author of several books and articles on U. S. relations in the Caribbean.

GEORGE C. HERRING is a professor of history and chair of the Department of History at Kentucky University. He is the author of *America's Longest War: The United States and Vietnam* (Random House, 1979).

RICHARD HOFSTADTER (1916–1970) was a professor of history at Columbia University and is considered to be among the best American historians of the post–World War II generation. His books *The American Political Tradition and the Men Who Made It* (Alfred A. Knopf, 1948) and *The Age of Reform: From Bryan to F.D.R.* (Alfred A. Knopf, 1955) are considered classics.

GEORGE F. KENNAN is a professor emeritus in the School of Historical Studies at the Institute for Advanced Study at Princeton, where he has been teaching since 1950. A member of the first American delegation to the U.S.S.R. in 1933, Kennan is a prolific author with more than 20 books to his credit.

PAUL KENNEDY is the J. Richardson Dilworth Professor of History at Yale University and the author of *The Realities Behind Diplomacy: Background Influences on British External Policy, 1865–1980* (Allen Unwin, 1983).

WALTER LaFEBER is a professor of history at Cornell University and the author of several major books concerning Central America.

WILLIAM E. LEUCHTENBURG is the William Rand Kennan Professor of History at the University of North Carolina at Chapel Hill and a contributing editor of *American Heritage* magazine.

GUENTER LEWY is a professor emeritus of political science at the University of Massachusetts-Amherst and the author of *America in Vietnam* (Oxford University Press, 1978).

ARTHUR S. LINK is a professor of history at Princeton University. He is a coeditor of the Woodrow Wilson papers and the author of the definitive multivolume biography of President Wilson.

RICHARD L. McCORMICK is a professor of history at Rutgers-The State University in New Brunswick, New Jersey, and the author of *The*

Party Period and Public Policy: American Politics from the Age of Jackson to the Progressive Era (Oxford University Press, 1986).

AUGUST MEIER is a professor of history at Kent State University and coauthor, with Elliott Rudwick, of a text on black history, *From Plantation to Ghetto* (Hill & Wang, 1976).

NORMAN POLLACK is a professor of history at Wayne State University and the author of *The Just Polity: Populism, Law, and Human Welfare* (University of Illinois Press, 1987).

ARTHUR M. SCHLESINGER, JR., is the Albert Schweitzer Professor of the Humanities at the City University of New York and the author of prize-winning books on Presidents Andrew Jackson, Franklin Roosevelt, and John F. Kennedy.

ANNE FIROR SCOTT is the W. K. Boyd Professor of History at Duke University and the author of numerous books and articles on women's history, including *Making the Invisible Woman Visible* (University of Illinois Press, 1984).

MARTIN J. SHERWIN is the Walter S. Dickson Professor of History at Tufts University and the director of the Nuclear Age History and Humanities Center. He is the author of the prize-winning *A World Destroyed: The Atomic Bomb and the Grand Alliance* (Random House, 1977).

The late **N. V. SIVACHEV** was the director of the Department of Modern and Contemporary History in the School of History at Moscow State University from 1977 until his death in 1983. He spent time in the United States studying at Columbia University.

SUSAN STRANGE is a professor of international relations at the London School of Economics. She is the author of *Casino Capitalism* (Basil Blackwell, 1986).

JON C. TEAFORD is a professor of history at Purdue University and the author of *The Twentieth Century American City: Problem, Promise, and Reality* (The Johns Hopkins University Press, 1986).

JOHN TIPPLE is a professor of history at California State University, Los Angeles.

D. F. TRASK is the chief historian of the U.S. Army Center of Military History and the author of *Victory Without Peace: American Foreign Relations in the Twentieth Century*.

C. VANN WOODWARD, considered by many of his contemporaries to be the greatest living American historian, is Sterling Professor Emeritus of History at Yale University.

INDEX